THE CREATIVE INTELLIGENCE MODEL

Building Innovative Skills

SECOND EDITION

NORMA CARR-RUFFINO

**Professor of Management
San Francisco State University**

Pearson
Custom
Publishing

Please visit our website at www.pearsoncustom.com

ISBN 0–536–62566–2

BA 992908

PEARSON CUSTOM PUBLISHING
75 Arlington Street, Suite 300, Boston, MA 02116
A Pearson Education Company

To Fredo
Who's always there

And to Andrea, Bubba, Elisha, Lauren,
Meghan, Natalie, and Steven
The Millennium Generation

Table of Contents

How This Book Can Change Your Life

This book can change every aspect of your life, opening it up to greater adventure, surprise, excitement, delight, achievement, and deep satisfaction. If you're ready and willing to recognize and work with the many facets of your Creative Intelligence and to develop its amazing potential, you will become more creative in your business or professional life, as well as your personal life. You'll do this not only by learning about recent research regarding your three brains and seven major intelligences, but also by recognizing how you use them as you go about your daily life.

You'll begin to recognize and experience each intelligence as it operates in your own life and to sense the role it plays in your ability to be creative. You'll learn how to boost the power of each intelligence and to apply each one to the problems and opportunities you encounter at work and at home. You'll begin to sense how your brains integrate all of these intelligences in ways that enhance your ability to live in the world more creativity—how you tap that integrated intelligence that I call Creative Intelligence. You'll use Self-Awareness Opportunities to explore all of your intelligences. And you'll use each intelligence in applying a myriad of Creative Techniques to real-world Case Studies.

Maybe you're already working on your innovative skills but find that the materials available, while helpful, are really scattered bits and pieces of the puzzle. The Creative Intelligence Model is the first comprehensive framework that enables you to pull all the ideas and techniques together. With this model, you'll have a framework for stashing all the ideas and information you'll ever encounter on the topic of creativity. You'll be able to see how all the bits and pieces fit together into a wholistic creativity model. And you'll see the role each plays in your personal Creativity Profile.

Innovative Skills You Will Learn:

1. *How to use a personal Creativity Profile,* based on the Creative Intelligence Model, an instrument for evaluating the progress you make in developing each of your intelligences—the entire picture of your innovative skills.

2. *How to use your Creative Intelligence, made up of your 3 minds and 7 intelligences,* to creatively tackle challenges, opportunities, and problems and to achieve innovative results and outcomes.

3. *How to recognize opportunities and solve problems,* working through each step to successful resolution in more creative ways.

4. *How to use a wide range of problem-solving techniques* that are based on your seven intelligences.

5. *How to overcome personal barriers* to developing and utilizing your creative intelligence.

6. *How to negotiate creatively with others,* using creative collaboration, win-win strategies, and conflict resolution

7. *How to develop creative futures,* by understanding paradigm shifts, recognizing phases in the high-tech life cycle, and creating future scenarios.

Chapter 1
Creative Intelligence:
A Comprehensive Model

Groom your curiosity like a high-spirited horse,
and ride across the sun-struck hills every day. Diane Ackerman

What is the most crucial career skill you can offer to the business community today? To answer that question, think about what companies and nations must do to survive and thrive in the fast-paced global marketplace. Experts in the new web-linked global economy are continually formulating new rules for successful business ventures and careers.

The New Rules

Don Tapscott [1999] gives these top-five rules for success in the Net Economy.

Rule 1: Matter (as in material things). It matters less.

Rule 2: Space. Distance has vanished. The world is your customer—and your competitor.

Rule 3. Time. It's collapsing. Instant interactivity is critical and is creating accelerated change.

Rule 4: People. The crown jewels in the world of work are people with creative intelligence. Brain power can't be measured, but it's the prime factor driving the Net Economy. More than ever in history, huge value is being leveraged from smart ideas, and the winning technology and business models they create. So the people who can deliver them are becoming invaluable, and methods of employing and managing them are being transformed.

Rule 5: Growth. It's accelerated by the network.

The New Hot Skills

In a recent poll of Fortune 1000 executives, 90 percent said their firms are doing more than ever to encourage employee creativity and innovation. They're looking for people with new ideas to help them survive and thrive in the networked global marketplace [Half 1999].

What Leaders Are Saying

Author Thomas L. Friedman (1999) says that those companies (and countries) that are the most creative, open-minded, tolerant, and diverse will be the leaders.

T.J. Rodgers, founder of Cypress Semiconductor, says the winners and losers will be differentiated by brainpower. It takes 2 percent of Americans to feed us all, and 5 percent to make all the stuff we need. All other business activity will center on service and on information technology, and in that world, humans and their brains are what count. But how can you make the best use of your brain?

Alan Greenspan says that companies and countries get richer by getting lighter and smarter. We know that companies (and countries and people) get lighter by substituting ideas, knowledge, and information technologies for heavy stuff, such as machinery, cable, vacuum tubes, and tape. But how do they get smarter?

Robert Shapiro, Monsanto chairman, says that your only sustainable advantages are the way you learn and the way you manage and exchange information—as a company (and as a country, and as a person)

Bill Gates says that at Microsoft they know only one thing: In four years, every product they make will be obsolete. The only question is whether Microsoft will create the new products that make the current ones obsolete—or whether their competitors will. This process is called creative destruction, and today managers must learn how to facilitate this creative destruction. And *Charles Schwab* says that "On the Internet, business either innovates or vegetates."

In fact, futurist Rolf Jensen [1999] predicts whole new job categories in a future marketplace for buying and selling new dreams that fulfill people's heartfelt desires. His dream jobs include: Director of Mind & Mood, Vice President of Cool, Chief Imagination Officer, Director of Intellectual Capital, Visualizer, Assistant Storyteller, Chief Enacter, and Court Jester.

As you can see, today's global marketplace endlessly demands the imaginative, the new, the experimental, the faster, the better, and the cheaper. The high level of market competition in that world puts a premium on creative intelligence and innovative skills—the kind you'll learn to develop by working through this book.

Pulling Together Bits & Pieces: Creative Intelligence Model

Most people believe they are not creative—and that artists, inventors, and geniuses are creative because they were born with a special gift. A few people believe that you can learn to be more creative, and they buy books, take various types of classes, and do exercises designed to boost creativity. The results are rather haphazard and nebulous for most. Why?

> *No comprehensive model for developing personal creativity has been available*

When I look around my office at the dozens of books and many files full of articles on creativity and innovation, I realize that each of them offers only a bit, a segment—some large, some tiny—of the creativity field. Most of us have been like the mouse trying to figure out what the elephant was all about, by checking out part of a toenail or a neck hair. We need a picture of the elephant with a description of its major parts and how they work together as a unified whole. The Creative Intelligence Model offers that holistic map. Once you understand it and practice it—as you will in this book—any and every creativity theory, idea, strategy, or technique that you know or will ever learn can be plugged into this model. Anything you do that leads to creativity, anything you hear about creativity, will fit somewhere in this framework.

Now when you need creative ideas, you'll have the whole array of creative sources to choose from. You'll understand the types of contributions that each intelligence can make to the creative process, how you can boost each intelligence, the range of creative techniques that are based on each intelligence, and ways of applying those techniques.

What Is Creativity?

We know business needs creativity, but exactly what is this hot skill? Creativity is the *ability* to bring something into being, to originate, to give rise to, to bring about, to produce. When you're being creative you're seeing things in new ways, putting things together in new ways, making things work in new ways, expressing thoughts and feelings in new ways, or imagining new things. Some words often associated with creativity are *originate, conceive, give birth to, author, formulate, invent* . Other words are *derive, devise, forge, make, form, produce, cause, start, begin, initiate, flow.*

Infotech overturns the conventional wisdom that "knowledge is power." It's really creativity, amplified, that creates that power. Technology creates a powerful amplifier for creativity. We've never before had access to such oceans of information. Creativity is the key to turning that knowledge into something of value, moving from the most basic knowledge level to the higher-value levels, as follows:

1. Facts, information, data

2. Insight, making your own connections, the "a-ha" experience

3. Ideas, relationships among interconnected insights that you can act on

4. Ideas that customers or stakeholders see as valuable

Using all your intelligences creatively enables you to move knowledge to higher levels. In this way you and your organization can generate knowledge that leads to the discovery and exploitation of new business opportunities

Any time you get involved in the process of recognizing and resolving problem-opportunity situations and moving to higher levels of knowledge, you'll find contradictions, unknowns, and puzzles. This causes you to feel tension and stress that you'll want to relieve, and creativity is the only way. Creative intelligence enables you to recognize conflicts that need resolution, gaps that need filling, hidden connections that need to be made, and the inter-relationships that lie within the sea of information that comes your way.

A measure of creative intelligence is the ability to make new and different connections between things. One form of increased resources for creativity is greater availability of diverse input that infotech provides. Infotech makes it easier for you to bring together previously disconnected data, designs, ideas, and research findings. This increases the chances that you will see new connections among them and in turn generate new insights and ideas. People from different specialties, perspectives, and interests are more likely to come in contact, via infotech, and to clash. But infotech also provides more ways to work through these clashes and to develop new knowledge in useful directions

What Is Innovation?

We know that Microsoft and other organizations must have constant innovation, but how is that different from creativity—or is it? Innovation is the *act* of beginning something new, introducing something different, a change, or a new creation. So you could *be* creative—have the ability to bring something into being—but never take the *action* needed to innovate. Some words and phrases often associated with innovation are *change, novelty, modernization, modification, new idea, new way, new method.*

Where Do Creative Ideas Come From?

Do you still believe that just a few people are blessed with creative ideas, and the rest of us just copy them or use them? Studies show that creative ideas come from all persons who work with an open mind, use creative processes, try out new viewpoints, ideas, or methods, and find their own sources of motivation, which drive them to get up every day and do the work. And now you'll have the Creative Intelligence Model to accelerate the process. Still, creative ideas are not likely to zap you from the sky unless you're doing the work of looking at problems and opportunities with a commitment to finding solutions and profitable ideas. That's what you will do in every chapter of this book.

How Can Creative Intelligence Help You?

People who are open, flexible, rapid learners, and most important, creative and innovative, hold a major trump card in the job market. But how about creativity in the rest of your life? Research indicates that the group identified as "cultural creatives" are breaking out of traditional molds [Ray 1997]. They're each creating their own lifestyle, one that gives them a sense of fulfilling their unique potential—what they're in this world to learn and what they came to contribute. They're creating lives that are not only fun and exciting but lives that have value and meaning for them. Creative people are better able to

- create more exciting and fulfilling relationships and personal lives
- develop new products, services, methods, and ventures
- recognize and solve tough problems
- sense future trends
- identify and visualize emerging opportunities
- build collaborative personal relationships
- resolve conflicts
- negotiate win-win deals and agreements

How can you become one of these people? By just using the Creative Intelligence Model and following the steps we'll cover here—step by step. You are born with amazing creative potential. This book contains the map and the steps for developing that potential.

Why Don't We Use Our Creative Potential?
Cultural Myths and Personal Blocks

We use only about 10% of our brain capacity. Scientists have been telling us this for years, but they haven't told us how to use the other 90%. Most people assume that using all their brain capacity means doing things to boost their I.Q.s, their rational intelligence. But recent scientific information points to at least seven identifiable intelligences, not just the rational intelligence that I.Q. tests primarily measure. Still academia, business, and Western culture generally honor and develop only rational intelligence—although you must develop all your intelligences in order to boost your Creative Intelligence.

Children are born with a great deal of creativity, and therefore with the traits that produce creativity—curiosity, spontaneity, flexibility, and fearlessness in taking risks in order to learn and gain new skills. Most children are willing to embark on new escapades, to try out new ideas. They're born with a sense of enchantment with the world around them, and they frequently feel awe, wonder, and "magic moments." This is the state in which creativity occurs. Children tend to naturally feel forgiveness and gratitude, which feed the openness to the world that in turns enhances creativity. Without intending to, our culture often smashes children's creativity and many of the traits that produce it—with the myths they pass on about what's valuable. Parents do it with toddlers, teachers do it with young students, and bosses do it with employees. Here are some typical myths our culture has created around intelligence, myths that reflect traditional mainstream values.

Myth 1: Only rational intelligence is pure and reliable.

By the time we become adults, most of us have gained many inhibitions and blocks to using all our intelligences. We've learned to rely mainly on our rational intelligence—and we credit our successes to it. We've probably lost much of our curiosity. We may have become arrogant, thinking we know more than we do. We may have closed ourselves off to new ideas, especially if they're too "far out," and we're almost certainly afraid to risk the chance of failure that goes along with trying something new and different.

Myth 2: Dreams don't count.

It's fairly certain that the great geniuses and inventors throughout history have used more of their brain capacity than ordinary persons use. Einstein used his basic intelligence to dream the theory of relativity, and often spoke of the necessity of using intuition to make new breakthroughs. Elias Howe dreamed the process that led to the first sewing machine, and the list goes on.

Myth 3: Feelings are suspect.

Emotions, and even true feelings, are sentimental, suspect, and polluted by personal subjectivity.

Myth 4: Expressing feelings causes problems and signals weakness.

Some typical adages we often hear in our culture include: Don't cry. Stiff upper lip. Don't get mad. Be nice. Don't be afraid. Buck up.

Myth 5: Imagination is chaotic and unruly.

Related cultural sayings include: *It's just your imagination. It's only in your head.* These are ways of denying or negating the visualization power of your sensory intelligence.

Myth 6: Stories are child's play.

Imaginative storytelling, even future scenarios, are pointless and personal.

Myth 7: Intuition is irrational and unreliable.

Some related cultural beliefs about intuition, which many of us buy into, include: *It's airy-fairy. It's touchy-feeling. It's woo-woo. It's wacky. Be realistic. Be rational. Be objective.*

Five Fundamental Types of Blocks to Creativity

You pick up your basic beliefs from many elements of your culture—your family, school, church, government, and the media are key cultural elements. Certain beliefs and actions are conducive to creativity, while others create blocks. To make the most of your Creative Intelligence, you must recognize and overcome self-limiting beliefs or actions. Here are few to watch out for.

Perceptual Blocks

Blocks based on the way you perceive your environment include

- accepting as facts information that's really assumption
- recognizing you have a problem without identifying the root cause
- ignoring information that gives clues to the underlying (root) problem
- focusing on only a part of the problem, or focusing on solutions rather than defining the problem
- assuming you can apply what works in one case to another
- information overload
- failure to use all your senses and intelligences
- seeing situations as problems and ignoring the opportunities they can offer

Emotional Blocks

Certain emotions and their related attitudes and actions can interfere with your freedom to explore and manipulate ideas, your ability to conceptualize (create ideas, theories) fluently and flexibly, and your ability to communicate ideas to others in persuasive ways. These emotional blocks include

- fear of failure
- fear of making a mistake
- fear of risk-taking
- impatience—inability to tolerate ambiguity (uncertainty) and chaos

- snap judgments—being too quick to judge people and new ideas
- tenseness—inability to relax, incubate ideas, sleep on it
- distrust, suspicion, lack of openness, closed mind

Rational-Logical Blocks

Rational-logical blocks stem from misuse or over-reliance on left-brain logic. Here are some common blocks.

- Not choosing the right mental approaches
- Being unwilling to use new solution approaches, which limits generation of alternatives. Using only techniques that worked before
- Reluctance to use intuitive techniques
- Inability to abandon an unworkable approach and try something new

Cultural Blocks

Most cultural blocks are based on embracing typical do's and dont's, taboos, and stereotypes, while clinging to your need for the safety of the known out of fear of the unknown. These beliefs often create blocks to creativity:

- Fantasizing and reflecting are a waste of time
- Logic and reason are all that matter
- Intuition and personal judgments are too fuzzy and changeable to be worth much
- Any problem can be solved by scientific thinking and enough money
- It's not good to be too inquisitive (curiosity killed the cat).
- Problem solving is serious business—so humor and having fun are to be avoided.

Environmental Blocks

Corporate cultures often contain creativity blocks. You may not be able to change these, but you can recognize them and perhaps move on to a more nurturing environment.

- Few goals or rewards for creativity
- A rigid, mechanistic, authoritarian company structure
- Autocratic managers who value only their own ideas
- No training for creativity
- Little or no support for creativity
- Few if any creative successes to build upon
- Punishing mistakes and failures and ignoring willingness to risk and to learn from mistakes

Overcoming Creativity Blocks

You can learn to make quantum leaps in your thinking. The strong analytic skills that rational intelligence provides you, and that have been so effective in the past, are not enough for today's demands for innovation. The sequential, cause-and-effect type of change of the past called for having a vision, developing a plan, and reaping the harvest. But change now is better seen as energy and forces, which we understand through the instinct of our basic intelligence, the feelings of our emotional intelligence, and the insights of our higher-level intuitive, associative, and sensory intelligences. It's a world of subtle rhythms and mysterious forces rather than one of certainty, control, and clear rules. It can be mysterious and challenging, but the rewards for innovating can be huge.

Creativity-Oriented Environments

Creativity is as natural a function of the mind as breathing or digestion are natural functions of the body. But new ways of thinking may seem risky to you, and putting forth new ideas risks rejection of those ideas. Such risk invariably arouses in most people some distrust, anxiety, even downright fear. To manage the risk of being creative, you need faith in yourself and your work environment. When you look for a job, look for an employer that provides a trustworthy environment, one that's

- Safe, casual, liberating
- Not so small as to be limiting
- Not so big as to kill intimacy
- Creature comfortable, but stimulating
- Not too open, not too closed
- Able to provide some areas free from distractions and intrusions
- Able to provide time targets when needed, but able to be flexible when necessary

If you are self-employed, see if you can create this type of environment for yourself.

A Creativity-Boosting Process

In this book, you will work on all the internal creativity blocks, one by one, as you learn more about each of your major intelligences. In the chapters that follow, you will learn about each of your intelligences—its essence, its power, what myths and self-limiting beliefs may block you from using it, how it works, how you experience it, and how to use it to boost your creativity. You will practice specific creative techniques that tap each intelligence, and you will apply them to business problem-opportunities. You will also complete some self-awareness activities for assessing your current use of each intelligence so you can determine where you want to do further skill building.

You will be working with the following powerful skills, becoming more aware of them, building them, and weaving them into a prime personal resource: your creative intelligence.

1. Dreams and instincts of your basic intelligence; pattern intelligence's recognition of habits and behavior patterns, ability to focus, and selectivity; and parameter intelligence's boundary setting and boundary recognition.

2. Drive and persistence of your motivational intelligence

3. People skills of your emotional intelligence, which include the involvement, passion, and caring of your affectional intelligence

4. Connections and interconnections of your associative intelligence

5. Imagining, fantasies, and enchantments of your sensory intelligence

6. Insights and instant knowing of your intuitive intelligence

7. Planning, sequencing, and cause-effect connections of your rational intelligence

To begin, let's take a look at your brain—well, actually human brains in general. All your life you've probably heard it said that we only use about 10 percent of our brain capacity, or potential intelligence. You've probably wondered: "Why don't we use more of it?" You may have thought, "Gee, I'd like to use more of my potential, but how do I go about it?"

Creative Intelligence: Using All Your Brain

Elaine DeBeauport has categorized the full range of human intelligence by mapping out ten types of intelligence, based on her review of the latest brain research findings. Her book *The Three Faces of Mind* [1996] won a Hoover Award for its contribution to the field. You actually have three brains, the neocortex connected with your thinking processes, the limbic brain connected with your emotional processes and the basic pattern-parameter brain connected with your instinctual and routine behavior. Table 1.1 explains briefly the seven types of intelligence that stem from your three brains. Figure 1.1 is a symbolic picture of these brains, and Figure 1.2 shows the Creative Intelligence Model of how the seven intelligences fit together and can be boosted to achieve greater creativity.

Table 1.1 Seven Intelligences and What They're About

7 Intelligences	*What They're About: Associated Words*
Basic >**Patterns** >**Parameters**	reptile brain, brain stem, survival, attraction, repulsion perseverance, living in the present moment, dream state programming, repetition, habits, imitation, deception territory, boundaries, limits
Emotional	mammalian brain ,limbic brain, people skills, feelings love, empathy, compassion, caring, joy, elation, anger influencing, open to influence
Motivational	desire, wants, goal, drives, life purpose limbic brain, mammalian brain
Associative	right brain, neocortex, similarities, comparisons relationship to, connection with, analogies, similes, metaphors
Sensory (spatial)	right-brain, neocortex, image, imagination, fantasy, visual musical, tones, chords, dancing, movement, motion athletics, smelling, tasting
Rational	left-brain, neocortex logical, sequential, intellectual step-by-step mathematical, scientific, I.Q., SAT, GMAT
Intuitive	right-brain, neocortex, inner knowing, esp, psi between the lines, wholistic, global connection, spiritual inner connections, beyond time-space

Figure 1.1 Symbolic Picture of the Three Brains

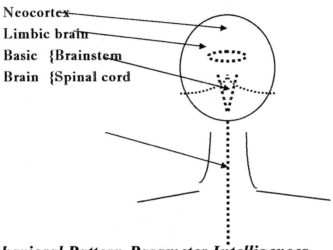

From back of head

Neocortex

Limbic brain

Basic {Brainstem

Brain {Spinal cord

Behavioral Pattern-Parameter Intelligences of the Basic Brain (Doing)

The basic brain consists of your brain stem and spinal cord. It's sometimes called the reptilian brain because it's been in the evolutionary chain the longest of the three brains, and reptiles have this type of brain. DeBeauport [1996] found that three major intelligences stem from this brain: basic, pattern, and parameter intelligence, which we will combine for discussion purposes. These intelligences are crucial for removing personal blocks to creativity; for example, rigid habit patterns, limits or boundaries you place on yourself, and denial of dreams. But in general, basic pattern-parameter intelligences are less directly connected to creativity than the other intelligences.

Basic pattern-parameter intelligence focuses on what you instinctively move toward and move away from—those people, situations, and things you tend to seek out and embrace, or those that you avoid. These movements become your habits, routines, and little rituals, and developing this intelligence requires that you recognize your habit patterns and those of others. Most of these patterns are deeply ingrained in your culture and family. They're based on what you were taught and what you decided about life. Some patterns are necessary and helpful in your current life. Other patterns form barriers to creativity and innovation and tend to sabotage your efforts to develop new skills and to change your life.

Parameter intelligence refers to limits or boundaries. Your basic-brain movements, toward things and away from things, all take place within specific boundaries and limits—your own, those of others, those of organizations. They're related to your territory, your comfort zone, and to the concept of paradigms and paradigm shifts—rules and boundaries for succeeding in a particular situation or paradigm and moving beyond these limits to create new paradigms. You boost your parameter intelligence by recognizing unnecessary and limiting boundaries, rules, and paradigms—your own and others.

Start using your associative intelligence now by reviewing Table 1.1. Study the words in the column opposite each type of intelligence. These words relate powerfully to what each intelligence is all about. If you can understand how these words relate to each intelligence, you'll begin to recognize which intelligence you're using at any particular time. By raising your awareness of when you're functioning from emotional intelligence or sensory intelligence, you can begin to beef up each intelligence and eventually put them all to work toward boosting your creativity.

Figure 1.2 Creative Intelligence Model

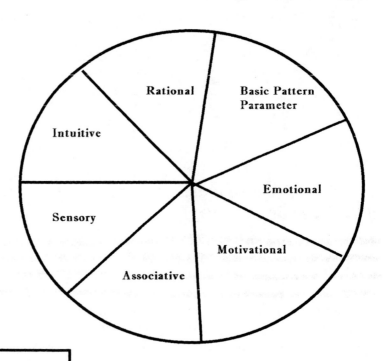

Creative Intelligence = 7 Intelligences

Boosting Each Intelligence

1. Identifying your own myths and blocks
2. Recognizing this intelligence at work
3. Boosting this intelligence
4. Learning creative techniques based on it
5. Applying creative techniques to situations

Note: The pie and its segments are a theoretical model, and the proportions are approximate and symbolic since the exact proportion that each intelligence plays in creativity cannot be pinpointed

Emotional Intelligences of the Limbic Brain (Feeling)

All mammals have a limbic brain. It's sometimes called the middle brain because it lies under the neocortex and above the brain stem. A major function is producing the emotions we need in order to conceive and nurture our young and to relate together in groups in order to raise them.

Emotional intelligence is your awareness, expression, and management of your emotions, of your feelings and moods It allows you to tune into the feelings and moods of other people and therefore is the key to developing your people skills, which are built upon empathy and compassion. Affectional intelligence is seen as a part of emotional intelligence for our purpose of boosting and working with the various intelligence. Affectional intelligence comes into play when you are affected by people, things, or situations and when you affect or influence them.

Motivational intelligence tunes into what turns you on in life, what you want or desire, what you feel passionately about. It's built upon self-awareness—knowing what you like to do and are good at, seeing how this ties in with your purpose in life, why you're here, and finding your niche in the workplace where you can achieve this purpose or life mission. It's the drive to fully develop and express yourself creatively.

Mental Intelligences of the Neocortex (Thinking)

Your neocortex is made of up two distinct halves, often called the left brain and the right brain. Rational intelligence is a function of your left brain and your right brain is the seat of three intelligences: associative, sensory, and intuitive.

Rational Intelligence is seated in the left neocortex. It's sometimes called left-brain thinking. You use it to study how the parts of things work and fit together into a whole, with a special focus on the parts. You use it when you focus on step-by-step reasoning, cause-and-effect logic, and how things occur over time. This is virtually the only intelligence that has traditionally been respected and nurtured in Western academia, science, and business. That part of the brain, perhaps 10 percent, that most educated adults use most often is the rational left-brain.

The right neocortex, where you do "right-brain thinking," provides you with three major types of intelligence. This type of thinking is simultaneous, spatial, associative, whole-to-parts with more focus on the whole, and timeless.

Associative Intelligence is what you use when you focus on relationships between things, how things are alike or different.

Sensory Intelligence occurs when you use your senses—when you see, hear, smell, taste, and feel your body moving kinesthetically in space. It's related to visualizing things, drawing them, expressing them musically, dancing, doing sports, cooking creatively, etc.

Intuitive intelligence is your higher-level inner knowing. It bypasses or aids the step-by-step, sequential-time, cause-effect ways of learning and goes directly to more wholistic, timeless experiences. In a sense all life over all time may be felt as having a wholeness and a connection that is timeless. We're learning more about how we are all energetically connected and how we can naturally tune in to other persons, their feelings, and life situations.

Now that creativity in the workplace is such a hot skill, moving beyond rational intelligence is becoming respectable. While it will always be essential, rational intelligence is only a small slice of the intelligence pie, as shown in Figure 1.2.

Creative Intelligence = Seven Intelligences

Your creative intelligence is the result of using all your seven intelligences at the appropriate times and in the best combinations and interactions. Creative intelligence involves a synergistic process of calling upon all your intelligences in a way that results in a brilliance greater than the sum of the parts. This is sometimes called the "flow" factor.

The "Flow" Factor

When you have creative ideas and use them to initiate innovations, you inevitably tap several or all of your intelligences. This creative intelligence has undergone a great deal of research and is called the "flow factor" by University of Chicago professor Mihaly Csikszentmihadlyi [1990]. His research indicates that when you're in the creative state of "flow, these things are going on:

You have clear goals. This means you must know how to see clearly what needs to be done and know how to set clear, on-target goals

Your activity becomes the goal. The work becomes an end in itself because it has deep meaning for you. This means you have learned what truly motivates you, have some sense of your deeper purpose in life, and are able to find work that helps you achieve that purpose.

You forget time. Time flies by as you become caught up in the work—time is just an extended present in which you're making meaning.

You're focused on what you're doing. You've learned how to focus your consciousness so that the level of awareness you need to do the job merges with your actions

You screen out distractions. This means you can sustain a single-minded focus so you're aware only of what's relevant here and now. It's a matter of intense concentration

The challenges you face are well balanced with your skills. This means you know how to seek out appropriate challenges, have gained some problem solving skills and have developed the confidence you need to take on new problems.

No self-consciousness, no need to protect ego. Strangely enough, research indicates that your Real Self or Higher Self expands when you're in the flow state. This means you're not involved in negative ego concerns, and you're able to tap into all three levels of consciousness—conscious, subconscious, and superconscious.

No worry of failure. You're too involved to be concerned with failure; it's not an issue.

You get immediate feedback. You know how to get information about you're how your work is judged, and you're able to accept constructive criticism

Flow produces positive emotional experiences, and people are three time more likely to report that such positive experiences occur at work than at leisure [Csikszentmihadlyi 1990]. One way to increase the percentage of time you experience flow in your work, therefore, is to boost your motivational intelligence. That's because this intelligence is all about discovering what really lights your fire—and basing your goals on that. Your work then holds meaning and value for you.

How All Your Intelligences Work Together

In your daily life, your three brains, with their various types of intelligence, work together to help you protect yourself and to learn, grow, and create. You rarely use *only* your basic intelligence of moving toward and moving away from something, or *just* your pattern intelligence of following old imprinted habits. Usually these basic experiences are accompanied by some type of emotion, ranging from very mild to intense. And these emotions fuel your motivation to take action. They also help you to remember and to learn because the more emotional the experience, the more vivid it is in your memory. And when you have a vision of something new that you want to create or achieve, it's probably based on some similar pattern or type of thing that you have already experienced. You associate this old experience with a new vision that goes beyond the old parameters and pattern. Often you tap your intuition for inspiration about what to create next in your life and for guidance in how to respond to life's challenges and opportunities. Intuitive messages may come to you through your dreams via the basic brain, through your feelings via the emotional brain, and through your senses, associations, and thoughts via the neocortex.

You learn, or gain intelligence, through all three brains. For example, using your basic brain you learn primarily by trial-and-error experiences and by imitating role models. Using your emotional brain, you learn through your feeling responses to various experiences. They provide a charge that motivates you toward or away from such experiences. Using your neocortex, you learn by analyzing, planning, and evaluating in a rational way. You learn by associating one thing to another—comparing, contrasting, and studying relationships. You learn through your senses— seeing, hearing, smelling, tasting, and touching things in the physical world. You also learn by tuning into messages from your intuition—which puts together all the other learning and brings in information from the interconnected Web of Life at all three levels of consciousness.

In today's job marketplace, you boost your value by boosting your ability to use all your intelligences to respond creatively to today's rapidly changing problems and opportunities. Many of these problem-opportunities are taken on by teams of people. Therefore, learning how to function creatively within a team, how to lead team innovation, and how to apply creative group techniques are crucial skills that you will learn in this book. Learning how to sell your own creative ideas to the team and others, and how to sell the team's ideas to others, are all part of the Creative Negotiation chapter.

Using your creative intelligence to create an optimal future is perhaps the most important way you can use your new skills. You'll do this in the Creative Futures chapter. You need all your intelligences to recognize paradigm problems and opportunities and to take the lead in creating paradigm shifts and responding to them. Learning how to create a range of future scenarios can help you prepare for the future, and better yet, create the one you want.

Your Personal Creative Intelligence

This book is about boosting your personal creative intelligence. You'll do this by learning about the many intelligences you have to draw upon, becoming aware of how each type functions and what it feels like, and boosting each intelligence. Then you'll pull them all together to resolve problem-opportunity situations, to create and sell new ideas, and to weave stories of the future that enable you to create it the way you want—or at least be better prepared to deal with it. Let's begin by exploring how personal traits are in fact work traits that can boost or sabotage your creativity. You'll look at some typical blocks to creativity and ways to overcome them.

Your Personal Traits Are Your Work Traits

In completing this book, your main goal is to boost your level of creativity and in turn improve your skills in 1) envisioning workplace opportunities and how to profit from them, and 2) solving workplace problems that arise.

But remember, the workplace is a microcosm of the world at large. No one suddenly "becomes a business or professional person" upon commencing a workday or entering an office. Everything that happens in your work life is a reflection of what's happening in your private life; for example:

- How you use your relationship skills in the workplace is how you use them in family and personal situations.

- How your relate to your boss is how you relate to parent figures and other authority figures.

- How you relate to people who report to you is how you relate to younger brothers and sisters and their friends, to pets and other animals, and to all situations where you have more power than others.

- How you solve problems in your work life is how you solve them in the rest of your life.

- How you perceive the workplace or marketplace is how you perceive the world in general.

- The level of positive well being you bring to your job is the level of positive well being you bring to the rest of your life—it affects your own health and can affect the health of others who are susceptible to your influence.

- The level of intuitive awareness you bring to work situations is the level of intuitive awareness you bring to the rest of your life.

- The level of creativity you bring to workplace problems and opportunities is the level of creativity you bring to your private life.

Using Creativity in Problem-Opportunity Situations

You can use your creative intelligence in every aspect of your life where you encounter problems that need solving and opportunities to contribute something to the world and to your own growth.

The Problem-Opportunity Viewpoint

Do you think primarily in terms of problems you must solve? Or do you focus primarily on opportunities for getting ahead? How about both? Creative people tend to see problems as opportunities to create something new or better. They also realize that opportunities can contain inherent problems that must be addressed if a project is to be successful.

- *Opportunities* signal a chance to initiate something new that leads to a better life or to a new source of business profits.

- *Problems* signal a need for you to make a current situation work more effectively by getting to the root of a problem, exploring many alternate solutions, and selecting the best solution for your purpose.

Both opportunities and problems may be hidden from your awareness. So learning to recognize them is a valuable skill. Although problems are often noticeable because they may be in your face and may bug you, making sure you don't settle for solving superficial problems is important. Learning to ask key "why" questions to get at deeper "root" problems is also a valuable skill.

You will be using many creative techniques to resolve problem-opportunity situations. Realize that a particular creative technique may be highly effective for working on one stage of the problem-solving process and not particularly effective for another stage. Problem-opportunity stages are usually thought of as a rational process, but creativity can occur at every step of the process. You can greatly boost your results by using Creative Intelligence, the integration of all your intelligences.

Six Problem-Opportunity Stages—Related Intelligences

The problem-opportunity process can be seen as six major stages. At most of these stages, you'll begin by exploring and generating ideas and follow by analyzing and evaluating the ideas and selecting the best ones.

When you explore and generate ideas, you need an open, free, imaginative approach that uses your right-brain intelligences. These intelligences include your intuition, your ability to associate or connect things, and your five senses, especially your ability to imagine and visualize something new. You allow your emotional intelligences to come into play in the exploratory process. You break out of your basic brain's old patterns and limiting parameters to move toward new possibilities. When you're exploring, let your rational left-brain rest because evaluating in order to organize and plan tends to kill the idea-generating process. Evaluation just throws a wet blanket on your idea factory.

When you've generated enough ideas, then you use your rational intelligence to review them, organize them, evaluate them, and decide on which ones to use to take you to the next stage of the process. Than you test your final decision for its emotional and intuitive validity.

Stage 1. Analyze the Environment

Key Question: What are the ongoing opportunities, threats, comparisons with competitors, and other environmental issues?

You'll begin by exploring the environment and generating ideas about how the environment is affecting your situation and how the situation in turn is affecting the environment, using all your intelligences except the rational. When you've generated enough ideas about what's going on in the environment, then use the rational process of reviewing, organizing, evaluating, and selecting the ideas to take you to the next stage of the process.

Stage 2. Recognize Problems and Opportunities

Key Questions: What problems need solving? What opportunities need attention? Here again, you'll begin by exploring and generating ideas about where the problems and opportunities lie, followed by the rational process.

Stage 3. Identify Root Problems, Opportunities, and Assumptions

Key Questions: What is the underlying or root problem that we need to address? What hidden assumptions do we have that may be faulty? What opportunities are we overlooking?

Again, begin with exploring and generating ideas about which of the issues you explored in Stage 2 are actually problems or opportunities that need further exploration—as well as possible assumptions that are faulty. Follow with reviewing, organizing, evaluating, and deciding which ideas to take to the next stage.

Stage 4. Generate Alternatives

Key Question: How many creative ideas, solutions, or plans can we come up with that address this problem or opportunity? Process: First rational-creative, then purely creative. Organize all the information and ideas to get a handle on them. Then explore the information, make random associations, and remain open to emotional, sensory, and intuitive input in order to generate ideas.

Stage 5. Choose from Alternatives

Key Question: Which plan has the best chance of bringing us the most success in this situation? Process: Rational. This stage is all about evaluating and deciding—it's primarily rational, but your final decision must "feel" right; use your emotional and intuitive intelligence to evaluate it.

Stage 6. Sell, Implement, Evaluate Results, Followup

Key questions:

- What can we do to get the people we need behind this plan?
- What do we need to do to make it work?

- How can we get the best results from this plan?

- What feedback mechanisms do we need to set up in order to evaluate how well the plan is doing? Do we have a good Plan B or C if Plan A doesn't work out as we expect?

- What can we do to minimize the risk factor and to boost the success factor?

  All four steps in Stage 6 require exploring and generating ideas:

1. Selling the action plan—explore ideas for selling the plan, generate ideas and select the best ones.

2. Implementing the plan—explore ideas for carrying out the plan, generate ideas for how to do it and select the best ones.

3. Evaluating the results of the plan—explore ideas for the kinds of feedback you need to best evaluate how well the plan is working. Gather the evidence. Using this feedback, evaluate the overall plan and each of its aspects.

4. Following up to improve the plan—based on the evaluation of plan results, explore ideas for solving any newly discovered problems and taking advantage of newly discovered opportunities, generate new ideas for modifying the plan, and select the best ones.

Creativity Showcase

Some innovative solutions to current problems—for your information and inspiration—and as food for thought.

Gas-Engine Automobiles--Problems

During the 20th century, gasoline-engine automobile had these problematic impacts in the United States:

- Combusted 8 million barrels of oil a day, 450 gallons per person a year.

- Emitted one-fourth of U.S. greenhouse gases, threatening global climatic stability and agriculture.

- Created in all metropolitan areas noise and air pollution that affects people's sleep, concentration, and intelligence.

- Made the air in some cities so toxic that the very old, very young, and certain others cannot go outdoors on smoggy days.

- Through air pollution caused dramatic increases in asthma, emphysema, heart disease, and bronchial infections.

- Injured 250 million people, and killed more Americans than have died in all the wars in the country's history.

- Killed a million wild animals per week, plus tens of thousands of domestic pets.

- Created 7 billion pounds of unrecycled scrap and waste every year.

- Paved over for streets and highways an area equal to all the farmland in Ohio, Indiana, and Pennsylvania, requiring $200 million per day to keep them operable.

- Reshaped the layout and design of communities, making it necessary to own and operate an automobile in order to participate.

- Made the United States depending on foreign oil at a cost of $60 billion a year.

- Required large U.S. military expenditures to be ready to defend our oil interests in the Middle East.

Innovative Solutions

To solve a few of these problems, such as gasoline dependency and environmental pollution, we could explore at least four major design features that create problems in today's cars.

1. Cars are made of steel and are very heavy. The average car is about 20 times heavier than the driver, and most of us feel safer in a heavy car. However, some researchers claim that lighter cars could also be safer cars. They suggest a concept similar to packing delicate glass to be shipped: "people cushioned in foam, surrounded by a superstrong nutshell, wrapped in bubblepack."

2. Cars not only carry more weight than necessary, they carry engines that are about ten times larger than average driving requires. These engines actually need only one-sixth of their available power in order to cruise on the highway and several times less in the city.

3. Cars don't move through the surrounding air very efficiently.

4. Cars don't use their fuel efficiently. On average they use only 20 percent of their fuel to actually turn the wheels. Of the resulting force, 95 percent moves car and only 5 percent moves the driver. Five percent of 20 percent is one percent—the proportion of gasoline that is actually used to get the driver from one place to another. Plenty of room for improvement here!

What are some ways to solve those problems? Designers are coming up with new aerodynamic designs and materials. In addition, they have produced concept cars of several types including:

- Electric cars powered by batteries that must be recharged. No practical replacement for the gasoline-engine car has emerged in this category.

- Fuel-cell cars. The wheels are driven by electricity that is generated within fuel cells that combine air with hydrogen in a chemical process, with the only waste by-product being clean water. These are solid-state, no-moving-parts, no-combustion devices. The process is silent, efficient, and reliable. These cars are expected to be the wave of the future, but none are commercially available yet. Perfecting the chemical process for mass use is an ongoing challenge.

- Hybrid-electric drive cars. The wheels are turned by an electric motor. The electricity is produced onboard from fuel, as needed—either gasoline or an alternative fuel such as methane made from plant materials. Honda's 2000 Insight was the first hybrid sold in the United States, followed by the 2001 Toyota Prius. It became available to Japanese buyers in 1997. Honda's two-door coupe claims 70 miles per gallon, while Toyota's four-door Prius gets 50. Both are priced at about $20,000.

A major advantage of electric-powered engines: 90 percent or more of the electricity is used to move the car along. Early hybrid cars are getting about 50 miles per gallon and reduce 90 percent of the toxic emissions in the process. Ultralight hybrid-drive cars could get 80 to 200 miles per gallon, a 600 to 800 mile range between re-fuelings, and zero emissions.

All major auto manufacturers have either hybrid or fuel-cell cars, or both types, on their drawing boards and test tracks. Eventually the new designs should greatly reduce four major costs in today's auto industry:

1. Time it takes to turn a conceptual design into a new car for sale
2. Investment required for producing a car
3. Space and time needed for assembling the car
4. Number of parts in the auto body

Some experts estimate that hypercars could decrease each of these high-cost aspects by up to tenfold. Hypercars will certainly increase our *resource productivity*, allowing us to get the same amount of utility from a product or process, while using less material and energy.

Food for Thought

1. How can cars be made even more fuel-efficient, design efficient, and environmentally friendly?

2. How will a paradigm shift such as this affect the huge segment of our economy that's related to gasoline-engine cars? (In 1999 five of the seven largest U.S. industrial firms produced either cars or their fuel) And how can we creatively ease the transition?

3. What will happen to the infrastructure of the current auto industry? Oil companies? Steel mills? Service stations? Auto mechanics? If you were a decision maker in such an industry or business, what creative solutions could you generate to deal with this paradigm shift?

Self-Awareness Opportunities

SAO 1.1 What's Your Creativity Quotient?

Purpose: Self-assessment of your current level of creativity.

Instructions: To the left of each of the following 49 statements, place either the letter a, b, or c.

a=agree; b=in-between or don't know; c=disagree

1. Whenever I solve a problem, I'm sure that I'm following the correct procedure. *a*

2. It would be a waste of time to ask questions if I had no hope of getting answers. *c*

3. I concentrate harder on what interests me than most people do. *b*

4. I feel that a logical step-by-step method is best for solving problems. *a*

5. In groups I sometimes state opinions that seem to turn some people off. *b*

6. I spend a great deal of time thinking about what other people think of me. *b*

7. It's more important to do what I believe is right than to try to win others' approval. *c*

8. People who seem uncertain about things lose my respect. *b*

9. More than other people, I need to have things interesting and exciting. *c*

10. I know how to keep my inner impulses in check. *c*

11. I'm able to stick with difficult problems over extended periods of time. *c*

12. On occasion I get overly enthusiastic. *a*

13. I often get my best ideas when I'm doing nothing in particular. *a*

14. I rely on intuitive hunches and the feeling of "rightness" or "wrongness" when I move toward the solution of a problem. *a*

15. When problem solving, I work faster when analyzing the problem and slower then putting together the information I've gathered. *a*

16. I sometimes get a kick out of breaking rules and doing things I'm not supposed to do. *c*

17. I like hobbies that involve collecting things. *c*

18. Daydreaming has provided the impetus for many of my more important projects. *c*

19. I like people who are objective and rational. *c*

20. If I had to choose, I would rather be a physician than an explorer. *c*

21. I can get along more easily with people if they belong to about the same social and business or professional class as I do. *c*

22. I have a high degree of artistic sensitivity. *c*

23. I'm driven to achieve high status and power in life. *b*

24. I like people who are most sure of their conclusions. *a*

25. Inspiration has nothing to do with the successful solution of problems. *c*

26. When I'm in an argument, my greatest pleasure would be for the person who disagrees with me to become a friend, even at the price of sacrificing my point of view. *a*

27. I'm more interested in coming up with new ideas than trying to sell them to others. *b*

28. I would enjoy spending an entire day alone, just thinking and hanging out. *c*

29. I tend to avoid situations in which I might feel inferior. c
30. In evaluating information, the source is more important to me than the content. c
31. I resent things being uncertain and unpredictable. b
32. I like people who follow the rule, "Business before pleasure." c
33. Self-respect is much more important than the respect of others. a
34. I feel that people who strive for perfection are unwise. c
35. I prefer to work with others in a team effort to doing it by myself. a
36. I like work in which I must influence others. b
37. Many problems in life cannot be resolved in terms of right or wrong solutions. a
38. It's important for me to have a place for everything and everything in its place. a
39. Writers who use strange and unusual words merely want to show off. c
40. I'm different, and I don't mind being different. c
41. I don't necessarily play by the rules. c
42. I have trouble being accurate, punctual, and proper. c
43. I'm sensitive to the art and beauty in more than art and beauty. c
44. I see things where others do not. c
45. I think about new things but usually don't take action on them till others do. -2 a
46. I'm content with the average or normal. -2 a
47. I know when to let go and how to do it. a
48. I have faith in my vision, my craft, and the creative process. c
49. I'm able to concentrate and to focus energy on a single goal. a
50. The 10 words that best describe me are: (circle 10 of the following)

absent-minded	factual	polished	persevering
acquisitive	fashionable	practical	persuasive
alert	flexible	predictable	poised
cautious	formal	quick	retiring
clear-thinking	forward-looking	realistic	self-confident
courageous	good-natured	resourceful	self-demanding
curious	habit-bound	restless	sociable
dedicated	helpful	modest	stern
determined	impulsive	observant	tactful
dynamic	independent	open-minded	thorough
efficient	informal	organized	understanding
egotistical	inhibited	original	unemotional
energetic	innovative	perceptive	well-liked
enthusiastic	involved		

Before you score your responses, examine the ways that your personal beliefs, traits, and habits are related to the seven types of intelligence that make up your Creative Intelligence. Your scores are related to these types of intelligence.

Typical Creative Traits—by Type of Intelligence

Your Creative Intelligence at work depends upon certain personal qualities. Research on what makes people creative indicates that certain learned beliefs and habits are usually present. Here the tendencies are categorized according to the type of intelligence each draws upon—and each item in the Creativity Quotient self-assessment is related to one or more of these types of intelligence.

Basic Pattern-Parameter Intelligence

- You've learned to overcome obstacles and keep going; you don't give up
- You've learned to keep going through many rejections, learning from each one.
- You have a strong urge to go beyond established limits, to break rules, make up new rules. This means you understand paradigms and paradigm shifts. You know that in order to take a creative lead in solving problems within a paradigm, you must see outside the current boundaries and rules and create new ones that work.
- You question conventional wisdom. You frequently ask why.

Emotional Intelligence

- You're passionately curious and inquisitive
- You have a passion for the new. You've become fascinated with new combinations, new forms, new ways
- You have enough confidence and love of adventure to risk looking foolish—for the work.
- You've learned to view life's "successes and failures" as learning experiences, rather than issues of ego and self-worth.
- You can see lessons where others might see failures

Motivational Intelligence

- You've found a sense of your purpose in life and then have found work that has meaning for you and ties into your life purpose. This enables you to feel a passion for the work and to get lost in it .
- You're able to get into the "flow."
- You're motivated by goals, task focused
- You're energetic, productive
- As you become more creative, you become more consumed by your work
- You like some alone-time to pursue your passions.

Rational Intelligence

- You've learned to generate a large number of new ideas
- You're comfortable with not knowing, while you gather information and work through learning processes.

Associative Intelligence

- You've learned to see relationships in new ways
- You use the power of metaphors, analogies, and other ways of learning-through-association.

Sensory Intelligence

- You've learned to think in images, visualizations.
- You often think in terms of tones, or chords, of musical harmony.
- You often rely on taste, smell, or your kinesthetic sense to achieve what you want or to create something new.
- You've learned to see things in new ways, so you can often see things others miss

Intuitive Intelligence

- You're open to intuition, fantasy, imagination, feelings, new ideas, artistic expression

Scoring: To compute your Creativity score, circle and add up the values assigned to each item. The values are as follows:

A agree	B between	C disagree	Type of Intelligence This Statement Relates to
1. ⓪	1	2	Basic Parameter; Rational
2. 0	1	②	Basic Pattern
3. 3	①	0	Motivational
4. (-1)	0	3	Emotional; Rational
5. 2	①	0	Basic Parameter
6. -1	⓪	3	Basic Parameter; Motivational
7. 3	0	(-1)	Basic Parameter
8. 0	①	2	Emotional
9. 3	0	(-1)	Association; Emotional
10. 1	0	③	Emotional; Basic Parameter
11. 4	1	⓪	Basic
12. ③	0	-1	Motivational
13. ②	1	0	Intuitive
14. ④	0	-2	Intuitive
15. (-1)	0	2	Intuitive; Associative
16. 2	1	⓪	Basic Parameter
17. 0	1	②	Associative
18. 3	0	(-1)	Sensory—Visual
19. 0	1	②	Associative
20. 0	1	②	Motivational
21. 0	1	②	Associative

22.	3	0	-1	Sensory
23.	0	1	2	Motivational
24.	-1	0	2	Associative
25.	0	1	3	Emotional
26.	-1	0	2	Emotional; Basic Parameter
27.	2	1	0	Associative
28.	2	0	-1	Motivational
29.	0	1	2	Emotional
30.	-2	0	3	Associative
31.	0	1	2	Associative
32.	0	1	2	Sensory
33.	3	0	-1	Emotional
34.	-1	0	2	Emotional
35.	0	1	2	Motivational
36.	1	2	3	Motivational
37.	2	1	0	Basic Parameter
38.	0	1	2	Basic Parameter
39.	-1	0	2	Associative
40.	2	0	2	Basic Parameter; Emotional
41.	2	0	2	Basic Parameter
42.	2	0	2	Basic Parameter
43.	2	1	2	Sensory
44.	2	1	2	Sensory
45.	-1	0	2	Motivational
46.	-1	0	2	Associative; Motivational
47.	2	1	0	Intuitive
48.	2	0	2	Intuitive
49.	3	0	-1	Motivational

50. The following words have values of 2:

Adventurous, bold, courageous dedicated dynamic energetic flexible independent innovative involved observant passionate, perceptive resourceful self-demanding

The following words have values of 1

alert determined forward-looking humorous informal open-minded patient playful restless self-confident thorough

The rest of the words have values of 0.

Add up all the above values. Compare your scores to the following:

100 to 142 = exceptionally creative

70 to 99 = very creative

50 to 69 = above average

40 to 49 = average

20 to 39 = below average

below 20 = not creative—yet!

57 pts

Followup: Review your response and score on each item.

Note which intelligences your positive scores are related to. These are traits, beliefs, and practices you can build your creative intelligence upon—focus on these and expand the time and effort you devote to these.

Note which intelligences your negative scores are related to. Make a list of beliefs, attitudes, and habits you want to change in order to boost your creativity.

No matter where you are now, you can develop these intelligences that make up Creative Intelligence by engaging in the processes presented in this book. What you learn here is merely the beginning—the planting of the seeds of creativity. It's up to you to continue the developmental process throughout your career—and throughout your life.

SAO 1.2 What Problems & Opportunities Do You Face?

Purpose: To identify problems and opportunities in your personal life, work life, school life. These are not the questions you will necessarily end up with—they're just thinking triggers.

Self-Starter Questions:

What would you like to have or to accomplish?

What work-related idea would you like to work on?

What work-related relationship would you like to improve?

What would you like to do better?

What do you wish you had more time to do?

What more would you like to get out of your job?

What are your unfulfilled goals?

What excites you in your work? What angers you?

What misunderstandings do you have at work? What have you complained about?

What changes for the worse do you see in the attitudes of others?

What would you like to get others to do?

What changes would you like to introduce?

What takes too long? What's wasted? What's too complicated?

Where are the bottlenecks? In what ways are you inefficient?

What wears you out? What in your job (or home, or school) turns you off?

What would you like to organize better?

In what ways could you make more money at work?

Typical business challenges:

What new product (or service) is most likely to replace our current product or service?

What creative suggestions can I make about new product (or service or process) ideas?

How can I cut costs and increase production?

How can we better differentiate our product from all others?

What new product (service, process) is needed? What extension is a current product's market?

How can I sell 20 percent more?

What new selling techniques can I create?

Can I reduce the cost of current selling techniques?

How can I become indispensable to my company—in a positive sense?

How can we better handle customer complaints?

How can we improve the role that service plays in sales of our products?

How can we improve our advertising?

How can we encourage everyone in our organization to actively look for better ways?

What procedures could we begin that would reduce unnecessary paperwork?

What rewards would be more meaningful to employees?

How can we become more customer-oriented?

How do we need to change our corporate image? How can we do that?

How can we outperform the competition?

Which of our products or services can we turn into the leading product or service in the industry? How?

Case Studies

Cases are great opportunities to apply to workplace situations what you learn about creative intelligence. They give you chances to build your Creative Intelligence—along with your problem-solving skills. Most of the chapters that follow include a number of creative techniques that you can try out on the chapter cases. For all these cases, ask yourself the following questions.

1. What problems do I see?

2. How can I probe beneath the surface to get at root problems?

3. What opportunities (hidden or obvious) can I find to take initiative, cut costs, and/or make money?

4. What creative alternatives can I generate?

5. As a consultant, what should I recommend as the best viewpoints and actions?

6. To answer these questions, what creative techniques can I experiment with to respond to this case? After completing the case analysis, ask: Which creative techniques produced the best results?

The Kid Fun case is a true story that demonstrates the personal qualities that trigger creativity and the fact that creativity comes naturally to us as children and needs to be encouraged by parents if we are to retain it. Although you have not yet learned about specific creative techniques, try your hand at coming up with creative ideas in response to the case questions.

Case 1.1 Kid Fun

Stevie Ruiz is 13 years old. His company Kid Fun is only two years old. Stevie is president of the company, which is owned in equal fourths by Stevie, his mom **Donna**, his dad Alfredo, and **Luis Martinez**, the CEO. The company makes toys, which are invented by Stevie and his mom Donna.

Kid Fun's initial product Water Talkie was Stevie's idea. Stevie hopes to help other children realize that the goal of becoming a successful inventor-entrepreneur is as exciting as becoming a rock singer or a basketball star—and probably more attainable. He supports such organizations as

- Winners' League Foundation, which has a pilot program to bridge the gap between science fairs and the marketplace.

- National Gallery for America's Young Inventors, sponsored by the Partnership for America's Future, which aims to bring kids' ideas into production.

- BizWorld, started by Silicon Valley venture capitalist Tim Draper to teach kids how business works. BizWorld goes into third grade classrooms with kits that guide kids in money-making projects, so they end up actually understanding profit and loss statements.

Ever since he was a baby, Stevie has demonstrated a persistent curiosity. He's always been fascinated by how things work, taking apart intricate items such as clocks and radios, with his parent's blessing! That same sense of wonder propels his budding business career. His parents have created an environment where he can freely express his ideas, and this has given him great confidence in his creative ability.

The idea for Water Talkie came to Stevie on a family vacation in the Bahamas when he was 10 years old. He went snorkeling for the first time, with his dad. Stevie got very excited over the underwater sights and he wanted to chat with his dad about them, but how can you chat with your face in the water? Back at the beachside café, he started thinking about making a contraption that would allow underwater talk. He began drawing ideas on drink coasters. His dad says, "You want to encourage that kind of creativity." On the airplane going home his grandmother gave him a notepad and pencils. His drawings began to look like a megaphone. Stevie pinpointed the major problem: "How am I going to keep the water out?" At home, he began searching the Internet for information. He decided to find two soccer cones, cut off the tips, and replace them with snorkel mouthpieces. He used a toilet-bowl screw to clamp the cone opening, changing it from a round shape to an oval.

The family enlisted Luis Martinez as a partner on the project because of his business

expertise and connections. Stevie designed a mouthpiece for the toy, and Luis brought in a dental engineer, who combined it with a blow valve and a tube taken off a snorkel. The result was a product that allows users to talk with underwater partners who are less than 15 yards away. Stevie took $267 of his own savings and worked with his partners to develop packaging for the toy.

Stevie's mom Donna had some previous success in marketing inexpensive novelties. She had developed "The Formula" for making money, which she describes this way: You start with an inexpensive product idea, something that costs under $2 to make and retails for around $10. You put dynamic packaging with that. You sell in very high volume. Finally—and this is the step that most people don't follow—you go out to get a large order that will cover your costs before you do anything about manufacturing the product. Also, it's critical not to depend on the retailers' ability to sell the product. You must make the right agreement when you take the order from the retailer: "You buy it, you own it; we don't buy back product that you can't sell." It's very important that inventors do that, so the retailer is motivated to find ways to generate sales of the product—not just stick it on the shelf and see what happens.

According to The Formula, it was time to get a big Water Talkie order. Stevie wrote a letter to the head of Toys R Us and followed up with a phone call. The CEO asked Stevie to come to the home office to show him the product. After a 2-hour presentation, Stevie and his mom got an on-the-spot order for 50,000 units. They are off to a great start.

- What potential problems and/or opportunities do you think Kid Fun faces now?

- What kinds of products should Kid Fun develop next? In general? Can you think of some specific toys that Kid Fun should consider?

- What specific recommendations would you make as a consultant to Kid Fun?

References

Csikszentmihadlyi, Mihaly. *Flow: The Psychology of Optimal Experience*. New York: Harper and Row, 1990.

DeBeauport, Elaine. *The Three Faces of Mind*. Wheaton, IL: Quest Books, 1996.

Friedman, Thomas L. *The Lexus and the Olive Tree*. New York: Farrar Straus Giroux, 1999.

Half, Robert. See "Tomorrow in Brief," *The Futurist*, Aug-Sep 1999, 3. See also Robert Half International, www.rhii.com.

Hawken, Paul, Amory Lovins, and L. Hunter Lovins. Natural Capitalism: Creating the Next Industrial Revolution. Boston: Little, Brown, 1999.

Ray, Paul. "Three Subcultures and Their Values," *American Demographics*, February 1997, 30-33.

Jensen, Rolf. *The Dream Society: How the Coming Shift from Information to Imagination Will Transform Your Business*. New York: McGraw-Hill, 1999. Rolf Jensen is director of the Copenhagen Institute for Futures Study in Denmark.

Nadler, Gerald and Shozo Hibino. *Breakthrough Thinking*. Rocklin Ca: Prima Publishing, 1994.

Tapscott, Don. Creating Value in the Network Economy, Cambridge, MA: Harvard Business School Press, 1999.

Tapscott, Don. Growing-Up Digital: The Rise of the Net Generation. New York: McGraw-Hill, 1999.

Tapscott, Don. Blueprint to the Digital Economy: Converting Digital Promise into Reality. New York: McGraw-Hill, 1998.

Chapter 2
Basic Pattern-Parameter Intelligence

We may realize freedom, but when it comes to our habits, we are completely enslaved.

Sogyal Rinpoche

Your oldest brain consists of your brain stem and nervous system. It's often called the reptilian brain because all reptiles have this type of brain. We'll call it the basic brain. It's the brain you use when you set up repetitive patterns, which allow you to successfully cope with the overwhelming stimuli you receive every second. It's also the brain you use when you establish and recognize boundaries, or parameters. And these patterns and boundaries can either block your creativity or enhance it. The basic brain is closely associated with your dream state, which can be a powerful source of creative breakthroughs for you. It seems to function at the lowest-frequency, densest vibrational level, that of your physical energy body. Some say it's centered in your base-of-spine (root) chakra, related to survival, safety, security, family, community, vitality, and joy of living.

Words to associate with this intelligence include: *survival, attraction, repulsion, repetition, imitation, deception, habit patterns, territory, boundaries, limits, perseverance, living in the present moment, dream state, physical energy body, base-of-spine chakra, red, tone do or C, reptilian brain, brain stem.*

Myths & Realities

Western culture has discounted the power of basic pattern-parameter intelligence in many ways—from beliefs that dreams aren't important to myths about intelligence being "set in concrete" from birth and therefore people don't change and can't change.

Myth 1: Dreams don't count

Most people in our culture report either that they don't dream or that they rarely dream. In fact everyone dreams every night. And if you were to be awakened just as you started to dream each night, depriving you of this dream time, after just a few nights you would have psychotic episodes (go nuts), according to research at the sleep institute at Stanford University.

Many native tribes throughout the world, such as those in North America and Australia, consider the dream time just as real, or even more close to reality, than waking time. They honor their dreams, verbalize them to each other, and ponder their messages and meanings. Western culture generally ignores dreams or dismisses them as meaningless fantasy, perhaps caused by indigestion ("You mean you ate pickles and salami before bedtime? No wonder you had nightmares!").

Myth 2: Your level of intelligence depends on your genes; you either have it or you don't.

The myth is that either you're born with intelligence, creativity, genius—or you're not. It's all a matter of the genes you inherit. Scientists are discovering that this is far from true. Only about 34 percent of your intelligence is based on your genes (nature), and the other 66 percent is based on your inner and outer environments (nurture). So how you express yourself biologically depends on both nature and nurture, according to Dr. Bernie Devlin and his co-workers [1997].

You *can* boost your intelligence throughout your life by creating a nurturing inner environment of constructive beliefs, thoughts, feelings, and choices. You can also create a nurturing outer environment by surrounding yourself with constructive people and situations. You have great power to create your own intelligence, and your own life.

Myth 3: The genes and traits you're born with are what you keep throughout your life.

The myth is that you're born with a fixed set of genes that never change. If you came up a little short when they passed around the smart genes, you're out of luck for life, the story goes. The reality is that you can and do change your genetic makeup according to what you believe, think, feel, and do in life—as well as the external environment you were born into and the ones you choose as you move through life.

Leading-edge research in cell biology indicates that "environmental signals" are primarily responsible for selecting the genes that you (and all organisms) express. Your genes alone do not control your fate. Rather your inner and outer environment exerts significant control over your genes. This began when you were a fetus in your mother's womb and continues throughout your life. Your inner and outer environments profoundly affect your physical development, your behavioral characteristics, and your level of intelligence [Cairns 1998].

Myth 4: People can't really change their basic nature and habits.

It is true that your basic personality is in place by age 5 or 6 and you may change very little after that stage of life. It's also true that if your parents, teachers, psychologists, or other authorities try to get you to change, they may find the task impossible. And it's true that if you try to change a basic habit pattern through will power alone, you may conclude that it's impossible. However, psychologists have found powerful ways to get at critical incidents that led to the formation of a belief, a decision, and a habit pattern and to return in memory to that incident and re-experience it in new ways that lead to new habit patterns.

The reality is that if you really want to change your habit patterns and go beyond your current limitations, you can do so. You'll be motivated to find the techniques you need—and many good ones are available these days. If you really believe that personal growth is an ongoing lifetime adventure that's tied to your reason for being here, you *will* change, and bit by bit you'll become a different person. Who would you be if you could be the "ideal you"? Would you be a more creative you? A more compassionate you? A more attractive you? It's all up to you.

How Basic Intelligence Works

Basic intelligence involves moving toward what attracts you and moving away from what repels you. Pattern intelligence involves developing routines that help you to survive and to handle the complexity of your environment. Parameter intelligence is about establishing a territory that fits in with your survival and growth needs as well as setting limits on your own behavior and that of the people you interact with. With the purpose in mind of boosting your creative potential, we will combine these three types of intelligence and call them basic pattern-parameter intelligence.

Basic Intelligence

Everything around you is alive and impacting you with its vibrations Basic intelligence is your way of coping with this deeply pulsing level of life, sometimes moving toward things that attract you for your growth, sometimes moving away from things to protect yourself, as shown in Figure 2.1. Survival is a biological imperative of all organisms, and basic intelligence is survival intelligence.

Figure 2.1 Basic Brain: Moving Toward and Away From

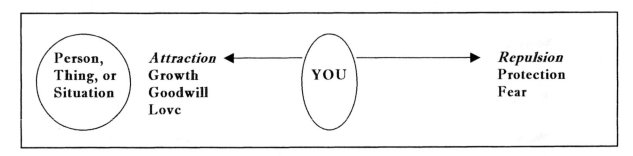

At any one moment, you can either move forward toward attraction, growth, love/expansion or backward toward repulsion, protection, fear/contraction.

Your survival imperative is to use your energy to either grow or to protect yourself. You cannot move in two opposing directions at once. You cannot go forward and backward at the same time. You cannot expend your available energy on protection without taking energy away from your growth process.

Within your basic brain you sort about 100 million impulses each second, deflecting what you perceive as trivial, and letting in what you perceive as vital. At night when you enter into the deep relaxation of sleep, you allow in more information, which appears as vivid images, verbal messages, symbols, and metaphors in your dreams. And in waking moments, still more information that has been processed through the intuitive mind may show up as a sudden realization or unexpected awareness.

Your basic reptile brain is concerned primarily with your territory, home, boundaries, your social groups, and social status and hierarchy within groups. Stemming from this may be acts that indicate possession and the emotions of possessiveness, insecurity, and fear, based primarily on not getting and keeping that territory you view as "mine" or losing part of that territory. Basic reptile behavior involves the following types of action.

1. *Imitating others*—to learn about your physical world and your culture

2. *Deceiving others*—for survival, avoidance, manipulation. Deception in adults can range from an accepted way to play the game, feint in sport or finesse in cards, to the criminal deceptions of the con artist.

3. *Setting parameters*—establishing your territory, where it's safe to go, where you need to go. Setting boundaries and limits for all aspects of your life. Establishing paradigms, models of how life works with rules for success within that model.

4. *Imprinting habits*—these habits become automatic, forming a moving-toward or moving-away-from response to a particular stimulus. Your mind tends to attach to key scenarios in your

1. *Imitating others*—to learn about your physical world and your culture
2. *Deceiving others*—for survival, avoidance, manipulation. Deception in adults can range from an accepted way to play the game, feint in sport or finesse in cards, to the criminal deceptions of the con artist.
3. *Setting parameters*—establishing your territory, where it's safe to go, where you need to go. Setting boundaries and limits for all aspects of your life. Establishing paradigms, models of how life works with rules for success within that model.
4. *Imprinting habits*—these habits become automatic, forming a moving-toward or moving-away-from response to a particular stimulus. Your mind tends to attach to key scenarios in your childhood (to imprint), which ever after influence your behavior in the form of subconscious habit patterns, unless you consciously change the attachment.
5. *Establishing routines and subroutines*—patterns that organize a complex environment, from your morning coffee, to your favorite chair, to your routine for getting to work, various work routines and habits, to your sleep habits and everything in between.
6. *Repeating actions*—in order to recognize similarities, to decide when to continue, when to stop, when to change.
7. *Reenacting*—returning to the scene of a "crime," reenacting familiar scenarios (same song, 55th verse)

Through repetition and reenactment, you become addicted to your routines. You repeat your routines over and over because they make you feel secure, give you an orderly, peaceful life. This is handy for continuing behavior that works, but creates growth blocks when the behavior is either too limiting or actually harmful.

With basic pattern-parameter intelligence you order, arrange, and organize energies and vibrations into routines you can trust, that you can count on to work for you. Through a more aware, advanced pattern-parameter intelligence, you can become conscious of your boundaries and routines and see which ones serve you and which ones sabotage you. You can try out alternate routines and expanded boundaries that can boost your growth and your creativity.

Pattern Intelligence

While the function of your neocortex or forebrain is to organize incoming signals into images, thoughts, and intuitive knowing, and the function of your limbic brain is organize the energy of those signals into emotions, the function of your basic brain is to organize them into patterns.

Brain:	Organizes Incoming Signals Into:
Basic	patterns
Limbic	emotions
Neocortex	thoughts, images, intuition

How does pattern intelligence work?

Ever since you came into the world, you have been developing patterns of behavior. As a child nearly all your waking moments were spent in learning what works in the physical world and what doesn't. Your sleeping moments were spent integrating that learning. Your parent figures and others in your family, community, society, and the culture at large influenced you to decide what works and what doesn't, what is right and what isn't. They were responsible for socializing you (some would say programming you).

You have accumulated a unique set of patterns of believing, thinking, feeling, deciding, and acting. These patterns, or programs, are essential, for they free you from constantly re-making routine decisions, from "reinventing the wheel," so you have time to learn and do new things.

Your patterns also imprison you when they cause you to stay in a rut when you would benefit by venturing out and trying new things. Old patterns can block your efforts to become more creative, especially when you are unaware of your ingrained habits and limited ways of perceiving, thinking, and acting. About 99 percent of your life is run by past learning, most of it at the subconscious level. It has become automatic behavior unless you deliberately pay special attention to it.

Your patterns filter all the information that comes your way—filter it through your worldview, made up of your habitual beliefs, attitudes, thoughts, emotions, and action choices. At any one moment, about 4 billion bits of data are available for your attention, but you are conscious of only about 2,000 bits. This means that you are conscious of only about one bit of data out of every two million bits that come your way.

What is pattern intelligence all about?

It's about recognizing your patterns, breaking old limiting patterns, forming new ones. When you feel stressed, you tend to return to your old patterns of behavior. Instead of viewing this as a failure to maintain new behavior, realize that this return is actually occurring at a new, higher level of awareness

Parameter Intelligence

What is a Parameter? A boundary, limit, or frontier. *What is its purpose?* To guide energy into repetitive patterns so you can go on automatic to conserve energy for higher purposes, to provide stability, safety, and security. Culture, the society, teaches us acceptable parameters in these categories:

- Values (the most important beliefs to hold)
- Religion (where we're from, why we're here, where we're going)
- Routines and rituals in day-to-day work life, home life, community life
- Stories, myths, legends—about heroes, heroines, role models, villains
- How to use time and space
- How to communicate
- Professions—how to make a contribution, earn a living

Parameters are related to paradigms, covered in detail in a later chapter. *What is a paradigm?* It is 1) a set of rules that 2) establishes or defines the boundaries of a model and 3) tells you how to behave inside the boundaries in order to succeed. Creativity often involves creating a new model or new parts of a model, such as new rules or new boundaries. We call this a paradigm shift.

Source of Your Survival Imperative: Spirit, Cell, Gene

How do these patterns and parameters really work? And how can you become aware of them and change the ones that block your creativity? Let's get down to the real basics—the cellular level and even the genetic level.

Every cell in your body has a major priority—to survive—and

survival perception and actions are focused on either protection or growth,

but never both at the same time.

When you're busy defending and protecting yourself, you cannot grow! Only when you have some minimal sense of security and confidence can you grow.

While your genes hold the original blueprint that produced your body, and the template for reproducing replacement cells and parts, the cell nucleus containing your genes is *not* the brain of the cell. The cell's membrane is its brain. This membrane receives signals from other body cells and from your external environment. It processes those signals and sends out its own signals, based on your thinking-feeling belief system. Your cells also produce and send throughout your body molecules of emotion, based upon your perceptions of reality, which in turn are strongly influenced by your belief system. And all this interaction actually changes the content of your genes and therefore your cells and your physical body.

From Spiritual Body to Physical Body

Many philosophical and religious disciplines, ancient and modern, have speculated that we have seven energy bodies, beginning with pure spirit, which vibrates at the fastest, highest, lightest frequency of all. Each succeeding energy body vibrates at a slower frequency of beats, stepping down to lower-tone, slower, heavier beats.

All seven bodies occupy the same space. Often these bodies are pictured with the physical body at the core, but since they occupy the same space, how about visualizing them with your spirit at the core, as in Figure 2.2? Are you likely to be more in touch with your lighter, higher-frequency bodies if you think of them as within rather than "out there"?

Table 2.1 displays a theory of energy relationships adapted from theosophic, shamanic, Eastern, and other ancient traditions—which are now being explored anew in light of revelations from quantum physics, such as morphic fields (Sheldrake). Only the physical body has been measurable in the past, but scientists are beginning to find ways to measure certain aspects of the etheric and astral bodies. Still, most of the information about the energy bodies and energy centers (chakras) is "theoretical," rather than factual, in the rational, scientific sense.

Spirit Body

Pure spirit is that part of you that comes from the Source of the universe. We are all connected to the whole at the spirit level, so the highest form of Intuitive Intelligence comes through the spirit body. This highest energy level of the seven energy centers in the shamanic tradition is the called the crown chakra. The more aware you become of your Spirit Body, the more open you are to the information that's available from that frequency level, the more intuitive you will be.

Soul Body

In some traditions, the Soul Body is the part of you that returns to the physical world in life after life, learning lessons and working out personal-growth issues in each life until you are finished with physical-life lessons and are ready to continue your growth on higher-frequency planes. If this is true, then at the soul level you are constantly applying lessons from your various life experiences as

Figure 2.2 Theory of Seven Energy Bodies

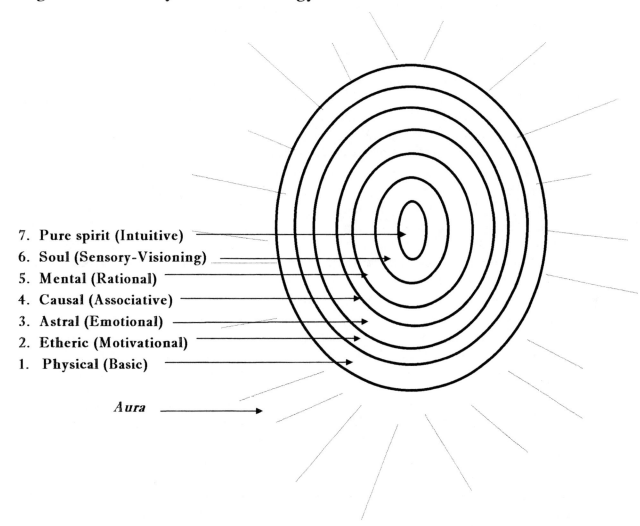

7. Pure spirit (Intuitive)
6. Soul (Sensory-Visioning)
5. Mental (Rational)
4. Causal (Associative)
3. Astral (Emotional)
2. Etheric (Motivational)
1. Physical (Basic)

Aura

Table 2.1 Theory of Energy Relationships:

Intelligence Type	Energy Body	Chakra	Color	Tone	Function
7 Intuitive	Spirit	Crown	Red-violet	ti, B	Being, connecting to spirit
6 Sensory	Soul	Brow	Blue-violet	la, A	Visioning, insight, imagination
5 Rational	Mental	Throat	Blue	so, G	Thinking, expressing thoughts, communicating, personal will
4 Associative	Causal	Heart	Green	fa, F	Linking higher-lower vibrations, centering personal growth, unconditional love
3 Emotional	Astral	Stomach	Yellow	mi, E	Feeling, emotions as sensors, control, personal power
2 Motivational	Etheric	Abdomen	Orange	re, D	Body blueprint, life purpose, sorting out, choosing, sexuality, creativity
1 Basic	Physical	Spine	Red	do, C	Survival, safety, security, territory, family, community, vitality, joy of living

part of your ongoing growth cycle. The all-seeing "third eye," or sixth chakra may be equated with your Sensory-visioning Intelligence, which involves seeing beyond the time-space limitations of the physical realm.

Some scientists are saying that "life," or animation, is the result of protein movements translated as "behavior." It is initiated by signals from outside the cell and ultimately outside the organism. Put another way, your genes cannot control their own activity; they cannot turn themselves on or off, they're not "self-emergent." They must be activated by a signal from the environment outside the cell. Your physical body also does not ultimately turn itself on or off. Some sort of signal from the external environment must do that. Where could this signal come from? Some biochemists say that it must be your "spirit self" that sends the signal to begin life and end it [Lipton 1998].

So, where is your Real Self? Since the "life" that moves your cells comes from outside the organism, it must be your "spirit self" that sends electromagnetic signals to your cells, to your physical body. This must mean that the Real You is immortal. When your cells die, when your body dies, the "real you, spirit you, electromagnetic you in the external environment" is still there [Lipton 1991]. And according to the emerging theory of living systems, your mind is not a thing but a process—a process of knowing that is integral to the process of life itself. This process operates through a specific structure, the brain.

Traditionally, people in Western society have thought of the brain and the mind as one, but now we see the mind as process and the brain as a structure the mind uses. The concepts of soul and spirit originally referred to the force of life and the activity of consciousness, expressed in the metaphor "breath of life." [Capra 1996]. Many scientists are returning to that concept.

Mental Body

This is the realm of thought energy, creativity, and invention, where we formulate what is possible for us to create in our lives. The mental realm may be tied more closely to your Rational Intelligence than to the other intelligences—in its most creative aspects, that is. And the chakra it relates most closely to may be the Throat chakra, tied to thinking and expressing thoughts, to your will, and to communicating. Strong ideas and mental energy patterns create mental thoughtforms.

Thought Fields can be either self-enhancing or self-sabotaging. Disruptive thought loops within the mental body have a profound effect on the emotional field of the astral body and the chakras of the etheric body. The pattern may be:

> *Self-sabotaging thoughts→Negative thought loops in the mental energy field→*
> *Contracting feeling loops in the astral emotional field→*
> *Blockage in the etheric chakras and meridians→Symptoms in the physical body*

Causal Body

In the causal body we formulate the causes and effects of what we are creating in our lives. This could be closely related to your Associative Intelligence and the fourth chakra, the heart chakra. This is where you blend and meld together the energies of higher vibration and density with the lower energies. This ability to relate and associate all things is your personal anchor, especially powerful when you develop the compassion and unconditional love inherent in this center.

Some traditions believe that the causal body retains a record of your past lives, and so it carries the memories and energetic recording of both growth experiences and traumatic events that your soul has experienced on its learning path. Your soul maintains the same causal body from lifetime to lifetime, allowing you to continue your growth. At the same time, if you don't resolve traumas and conflicts during your current life, they'll be carried over into your next lifetime. It's said that when you can view a situation from the higher spiritual level of the causal plane, it's like climbing a hill and looking down on the events unfolding below. You can see the true cause-effect relationships of what's happening, which are impossible to see when you're down in the valley amidst the activity.

When you're seeing at this level, you're seeing through the eyes of your Higher Self, which sees the total pattern of your life from the causal-plane level. Time and space don't operate in the same ways on this plane. If you learn something about symbolic language and apply it to everyday events in your life, you begin to intuit a pattern to seemingly random events. From the causal plane, you can see how events that seem accidental or coincidental may contain hidden messages from your Higher Self. As you become more aware of these synchronicities, they tend to happen more often.

Astral Body

The astral body is the realm of emotional energy. Here you formulate what's probable for you to create in your life, and you test the possibility of creating something new. Your astral body is closely related to your Emotional Intelligence in that it contributes certain types of energy information to the physical body. It is said to be quite mobile and can move about independent of the physical body. Part of your consciousness can move into your astral body at times and probably does so frequently during your dream state. Many people who have been in the near-death state have reported that their primary consciousness left their physical bodies, hovered about the death scene, and watched and heard all that went on below.

The astral body is said to be magnetic in nature and its energy is strongly influenced by your thinking and feeling states. It creates patterns of magnetic attraction in your thoughts and in the emotional-energy patterns of your energy fields. So you tend to "magnetically attract" more of the same emotional energy to yourself. Strong thoughts and emotions are said to create a kind of energy structure sometimes called "thoughtforms" that hang out in your aura. They attract people of like mind or people who recognize an energy they want to play with.

Molecules of Emotion. Candace Pert (1997) is the scientist best known for identifying the molecules of emotion. When she focuses on the measurable, physical aspects of emotions, perhaps she's really looking at the following:

$$interface\ of\ mental \rightarrow astral \rightarrow etheric \rightarrow physical$$

Here is the theory that is evolving from Pert's work: Thought energy rouses certain emotions, which in turn affect the meridians and chakras of the etheric body. This activates an electro-chemical cascade with effects throughout the physical body.

If you were to take a magneto-encephalogram, as opposed to an electro-encephalogram, it would read the magnetic vibrations, your brain activity that extends outside your head. Your thoughts and feelings are electromagnetic energy and they affect the electromagnetic field within you and around you.

When you create a frequency of fear, that electromagnetic frequency attunes to the fear-related aggressive frequency of other beings—or their defensive fear-related feelings or any other fear-based feeling. On the other hand, when your thoughts and feelings create a frequency of love or goodwill, it attunes to the love-based frequency of others and resonates with people who are feeling love, kindness, empathy, compassion, and similar emotions. This in turn affects your physical body. Your electromagnetic field constantly alters your DNA, RNA, blood vessels and cells, muscle firing, hormone release, etc. [Lipton 1992]

When you experience a perception, and consequently have a thought that triggers an emotion, your body creates molecules of emotion from atoms within your blood stream. These molecules then travel through your blood stream and attach to certain cells in your body. Emotions are either growth-enhancing (expansive) or protection-related (contracting). They can't be both at the same time.

Scientists are finding that those people who, most of the time, create an inner environment that signals self-respect and love of life in all its forms are the healthiest, and there the best survivors, of all [Pert 1997]. So an important part of the new scientific vision is that the survival imperative is shifting from the harsh, competitive "survival of the fittest" vision to the kinder, cooperative "survival of the most loving" vision.

Emotions, Blocks, and Creativity This concept is important for your personal growth and well being—for breaking through blocks to creativity and boosting your creative intelligence. Remember, your survival imperative and related biological behavior is either growth-promoting or protection-related. The energy investment that you need to support protection responses comes at the expense of your personal growth. When you *perceive* your inner and outer environment to be supportive, the signals you send to the cells throughout your body are expansive, love-based signals. Those signals encourage the selection of growth-related genetic programs. When you perceive your environment to be threatening or otherwise something to avoid, you will relay fear-based signals that pull resources from growth-related behaviors, in order to create protection-related behaviors.

Remember also, you are not defined by your genes at the moment of conception. Your environmental experiences play an essential role in shaping your characteristics. Your attitudes and emotions have a fundamental impact on your development, beginning with your mother's attitudes and emotions when you lived in her womb. This process continues throughout your life with your own beliefs, attitudes, thoughts, feelings, and decisions about life, and your resulting action choices, which lead to experiences that in turn affect your thinking, feeling, etc.

Etheric Body

The etheric body is the one most closely tied to the physical body. It's the interface between your physical body and emotional-astral body. It may be most closely tied to your Motivational Intelligence, which deals with taking actions that help you to achieve your life purpose—the action blueprint you want your life to take. It may be centered in the Abdominal chakra that also deals with sorting out, choosing, letting go, sexuality, and creativity.

The etheric body is sometimes called an "invisible" duplicate of the physical body. It's the body blueprint that your cells originally followed to create the physical you, and that they still follow to repair and maintain your physical body. While each cell's DNA determines the form and function of that cell, how do the millions of cells get direction for coming together and forming the physical body as a whole? Some scientists believe that the etheric body serves as the growth template for the physical body. Some verification of this can be observed by tearing a piece out of a whole leaf. Kirlian photography will then show the whole leaf with the torn-out area looking like a misty, ghostly part of the leaf.

Your etheric body is the realm of energy meridians of ancient Chinese medical practices, such as acupressure and acupuncture. It's also the realm of the non-physical energy chakra system within the physical body, which is used in ancient Hindu medical practices and in many ancient shamanic traditions.

Chakras are energy vortexes or centers within the etheric body—seven major chakras and several minor ones. Meridians are the energy pathways throughout the etheric body, all within the physical body. Acupressure sites are related to junctions of the meridian pathways. There are more than 360 acupressure points that some doctors and healers work with. The emotional energy work you will do, using SAO 3.9, focuses on 15 of those sites that have proven to be related to specific emotions and physical conditions.

Physical Body

The physical body houses the personality that we bring into the dense physical realm. We must have a personality and a physical body in order to join the physical field of play. As a physical being, this is your most basic body, most closely aligned with your Basic Intelligence and with your base-of-spine chakra, center of survival, safety, territory, family, community, vitality, joy of living.

We've always been able to measure the physical body because we perceive it with all our physical senses. We can measure and weigh our body and its organs. As science progressed, we learned how to identify and measure the body's cells and the molecules and atoms they're made of. Now quantum physics can identify and measure the contents of atoms, getting deep into the electro-magnetic properties of the wave/particles that make up our physical body and physical world. In the following section, we'll review some concepts that are changing our perception of who we are and how our world works.

New Ways of Viewing Physical Reality

Some of the New Physics is not very new, having evolved in the late nineteenth and early twentieth centuries, but few people have truly integrated these findings into their everyday way of thinking about their the physical plane. Table 2.2 gives an overview of some differences.

Polarity of the Physical Body

The physical body is made up of electromagnetic energy. It has both a top-to-bottom (north-south) polarity, or direction of electrical energy flow, and a side-to-side (east-west) polarity.

Table 2.2 Old and New Physics

Old Physics	New Physics
Based on physics of Isaac Newton	Based on physics of Einstein and quantum mechanics
Views the human body as a bio-machine	Views the body as a dynamic energy system
Sees the brain as a bio-computer	Sees Mind and Spirit as the true source of consciousness
Views consciousness as a byproduct of the brain's electrical activity	
Medicine tries to "fix" abnormal body mechanisms with drugs and surgery	Alternative healing works with various forms of energy, and frequencies of energy.

Quantum (Subatomic) World

Energy fields contain information and affect the physical world. The effects can be seen and measured—in wave or particle form. Whether energy is seen as waves or particles is affected by the expectations of the observer.

We know that beliefs are electromagnetic energy. So is your body, primarily. Your cells—therefore you—are nearly all empty space. Most of us think of our bodies as solid and dense, but 99.999 percent of each cell is empty space. The rest is mostly liquid, watery. Your cells of course consist of many "crystalline-lattice" molecules, which in turn are made up of many atoms. Each atom of your body contains the same ratio of matter to space as you'll find in our solar system—meaning your body is nearly all space! It just seems dense because tiny particles within each atom spin around the area fast enough to seem solid, like a spinning fan or propeller seems solid—

especially if you try to stick you hand between the blades! This concept has many implications. For example, electromagnetic energy—such as sounds, music, and people's thoughts and feelings—vibrates through your spatial body and makes a significant impact, whether you're aware of the impact or not. Instead of focusing on your body's apparent density, try focusing on its 99.999 percent space.

Holographic Body, Holographic Universe

Holograms are the 3-D, laser-generated "pictures" that can be viewed from all angles, as if they were 3-D objects. Karl Pribram saw how the physical basis of holograms corresponded with the mathematical basis, Fourier mathematics. Pribram was probably the first scientist to show, in the 1960s, the connection between holograms and consciousness. His research on about 2,000 monkeys allowed him to make the connection. In them, he had observed interference patterns between memory and incoming visual information, a process similar to that of holography. Other experiments have shown that such responses in human beings can be duplicated by using Fourier mathematics, which is the basis of holographic images.

If the brain puts together the internal memory frequencies with new external experiential frequencies, who is interpreting the resulting holograms? This is a new angle on the old question, Who experiences our experiences? Primbram responded, "Maybe the world is a hologram!"

David Bohm, student of Albert Einstein and one of the 20th century's foremost theoretical physicists, is the author of a standard text on quantum mechanics, used in universities world-wide. Just as Pribram began seeing the world as a hologram, Bohm's papers were actually describing nature as a hologram, a holographic universe.

Split-brain (left-cortex, right-cortex) research and the three-part-brain findings established that all humans have an inner creative resource with great breadth and depth. You have a scientific basis for believing in your own experience of seeing things in a new, creative way.

Assume the world is a hologram, which means your perceptions form your world. Your thoughts, in the form of holograms, have a major impact on what you actually experience as the world. What exists inside you is what is manifested as the entire world. Assume the universe is holographic. It seems concrete—fixed, dense, "real," the same to all rational, sane humans, right? Wrong. This is an illusion that you create by your own mental construction. The fact that most of us see the same stuff "out there" means that we have deep consensus reality agreements about what's "out there" in physical reality. People who move ahead of consensus reality, and people who opt out of consensus reality, can see quite different things "out there." In the truest sense, it's all "in here," inside your own mind.

In a holographic world, each individual is one fragment of the whole. Any piece of a holographic image can project the entire 3-D system. That means the entire universe is within each of us. Bohn says, "Mind and matter are two parallel streams of development arising from a common ground beyond both." He says there is an implicate order (an enfolded order?) and there is an infinite sea of energy, and this unfolds to form space, time, and matter. He speaks also of an "underlying realm of infinite dimensionality" (the quality of having measurable physical dimensions). The godlike implicate realm projects itself into the four-dimensional world that we know (time plus space—height, breadth, depth).

Consensus Reality and Morphogenic Fields

Biologist Rupert Sheldrake takes the ideas of physics into the biological and psychological realms. We all tune into morphic resonance—the communication of thoughts across space and time through morphogenic fields. He says people are like television sets that pick up invisible information from a non-local source. Our function is to tune in to the vibrations that are always available. This field was referred to by psychologist Carl Jung as the collective unconscious and in recent times by various psychologists as a superconscious field. All humans have access to this field and tap into it, but most are not aware of it. Some bring it into conscious awareness, and we often call this Intuitive Intelligence, or extrasensory perception (esp), clairvoyance, psychic awareness, and similar terms.

Sheldrake observed that in rat experiments, the later-generation rats were finding the solution to the maze almost ten times faster than the first generation had. He concluded that later-generation rats were picking up information in the morphogenic fields, which are invisible pattern-making structures in nature. This means that cultures that are not even in contact can convey ideas to each other, contributing to a global human consensus reality. It also means that you can tap into human information throughout the world and through all the ages by attuning to their thought frequencies.

Cell "Brain" and Cell Pattern-Keeper

If the cell had a "brain," which cell part would it be? Most people would say the nucleus because it holds the genes, the DNA strands of life. But the DNA in the nucleus of the cell holds the templates, the patterns, to make the "spare parts" and "new parts" needed to repair and maintain the physical body. The "brain" of a cell is its membrane (think *mem-brain*) because that is the cell part that interacts with the environment, taking in information and sending out information. Receptors in the cell membrane take in molecules of emotion and other information from the environment of the cell, the physical body, and the external environment. The cell processes the information and emits responses (information) through the cell membrane into that environment.

Cell receptors are made aware of their environment by signals they receive. Cell effectors create physical responses to the signals. Perception is defined as awareness of the environment through physical sensation. A cell receptor-effecter could be called a "unit of perception." See Figure 2.3, which is a symbolic representation of certain cell functions. Since the cell membrane is the cell part most closely involved with perception and therefore consciousness, it is most analogous to the "brain."

Figure 2.3 Symbolic Representation of Certain Cell Functions

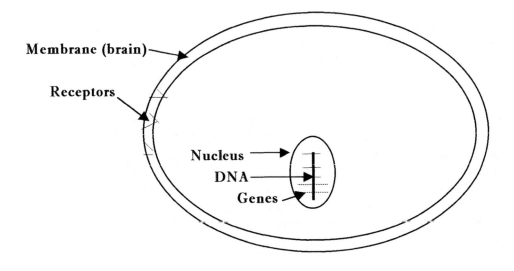

Membrane (brain)

Receptors

Nucleus

DNA

Genes

Genes That Change   Mutator genes can modify other genes to better respond to the environment-through an *intention* to change. If a cell perceives a stressful environment but doesn't have a gene program, a behavior, to deal effectively with that particular stress, the cell can rewrite the existing gene program in order to deal with the stressful condition. These DNA changes are adaptive mutations that enable the cell to specifically alter its genes. Such mutations depend on your perception of your environment. If you perceive a stress that is actually not there, your misperception can actually change your genes unnecessarily to accommodate your false belief.

In other words, your response to your perceived environment can change your genes, but perception is not necessarily reality. Less than 10 percent of cancer cases are due to hereditary factors in the genes. Change your belief about the environment and you change your vulnerability to cancer. In this way you control your genes. Beliefs run your health because they create your reality. Your beliefs either harm or enhance your well being. You're probably not even aware of most of your harmful beliefs because you long ago stored them in your subconscious mind.

Cellular Intelligence. You have an inner environment made up of everything within your body. You also have an external environment made up of everything outside your body. In that inner environment, your basic intelligence is closely associated with your brain stem and nervous system. But every cell in your body also has basic intelligence. Each of your cells continually learns about its environment and interacts with that environment—and with your inner body environment, and with your perception of your external environment.

Each cell exchanges information through its membrane, its "skin," which functions as its brain. And your body as a whole continually exchanges information with your external environment through that major organ called your skin. So the brain of each cell is its membrane, its "skin," and electromagnetic signals from the environment are picked up by cell receptors in the membrane, just as all information is. Signals come into the cell as information, as input, they are processed, and they are channeled out of the cell as feedback, output [Lipton 1998].

Therefore, your environment—inner and outer—and even more importantly, how you perceive your environment—directly controls the activity of your genes. Energies, via their vibrations or resonances, impact the way these molecules of emotion communicate with the cells throughout your body.

Your cells "read" their environment, evaluate that information, and then select a behavioral program to maintain their survival. Receptors respond to both energy signals and molecular (matter) signals. Pulsed electromagnetic fields regulate virtually every cell function, including the creation of the DNA, RNA, proteins and cell division. This is another way of explaining that what goes on in your body is controlled by energy forces that include beliefs, attitudes, thoughts, feelings, and decisions.

Mainstream Psychology Cognitive therapy of mainstream psychology is based on evidence that your beliefs—which form your attitudes, which in term impact your thoughts, which trigger your feelings—all create the conditions within your body, as well as how you perceive and interact with your external world, as shown in Figure 2.4. If you change one of your key beliefs, or if you change any link in the chain, you change your behavior and your experience of the world. If you change your behavior and observe what happens, you may change a life decision or a belief about the world and therefore your experience of the world. If a psychologist intervenes to help you change any link in the chain, your experience of the world will change.

Figure 2.4 Your Mind: Raw Materials—and Tools for Changing

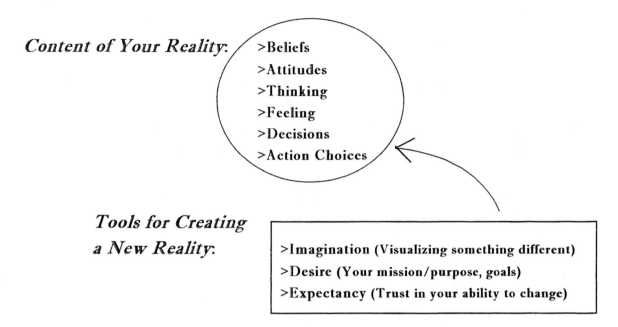

The change process involves 1) relaxing in order to tap into all seven energy bodies and the morphic field of superconscious, 2) visualizing a multisensory image of something new and different, along with the feeling tones within the human relationships involved in that new image, and 3) letting go of the need to make the change happen, retaining the intention to go for it, and trusting the universe to bring the change about in a way and time that is best for you and for the world at large.

How You Create Your Reality

To create something new, your conscious mind goes through a three-phased creation cycle as displayed in Figure 2.5.

1. *Be.* As pure *Be-ing, Spirit*, you become inspired to create. You have many ideas or concepts, you choose one to focus on, and you develop a plan that you envision in your mind as reality.

2. **Do.** You are now motivated to *do* things that bring the idea into form, and you take action. Your body moves toward carrying out your action plan.

3. *Have.* Now you *have* the results, your body experiences it in your physical life, and you *feel* emotions connected with the results. As you experience your creation as completed, you now have a resource for creating similar experiences or things, and you also learn what not to do or how to do it more elegantly. The creation begins to disappear from your focus, to dissolve. Your main attention goes back to pure be-ing, Spirit, so you can focus on inspiration for the next round of creation.

Figure 2.5 The Creation Process: Be-Do-Have

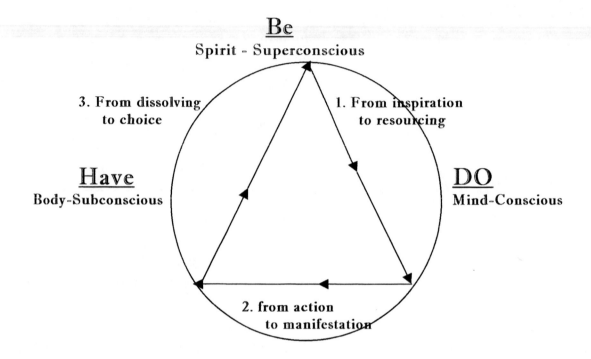

Seeing the way you create from this be-do-have perspective can help you to become aware of the different forms of consciousness you're able to access. First is the superconscious mind from which you came and to which you will return, and which constantly inspirits your physical life. Next is your personal conscious mind that you're aware of in your daily waking state. Last is your subconscious mind, which holds in memory storage every aspect of all your experiences from this physical lifetime. These experiences are so profuse that you cannot hold them all in your conscious mind, where you need to focus on current growth and protection concerns.

Be-ing, Spirit = superconscious mind. Your life purpose (and therefore the source of your motivational intelligence) lies here. Collective consciousness is also here—the collective wisdom of humanity, the planet, of all consciousness. You can get in touch with this information. Here lies the Web of Life, the reason that quantum physicists say "the mere flap of a butterfly wing in China is felt around the world."

Mind = conscious mind, action, doing. This is the function of awareness that focuses, categorizes, selects, and registers impressions, makes associations, determines meaning, carries out ideas. Mind is personal will, combining thought with desire to create action.

Body = subconscious mind, physical form, having. Action brings about results, an outcome of ideas, something we can see, touch, or experience. Once we have completed the creation, the process for creating similar things or situations is repeated and tends to become an automatic habit pattern. The process and the sensory experience are stored in the subconscious.

How You Experience Your Basic Brain

The four main ways your basic brain speaks to you are 1) through your physical body, 2) through your behavior patterns, 3) through your ability to see yourself—your limits and territory—in relation to your environment, and 4) through your dreams.

Through Your Physical Body

Your body is a web of life within the universal Web of Life. Realize that your spirit self is energy that has vibrated into atoms, particles, neutrons, protons, cells, clusters of cells that we call patterns, and later, patterns that we call the structure of the human body-brain-being. Accept your body-brain-being and love yourself, all of you. Ask your body: Are you expanding or contracting? Yes or no? Trust your first response. Validate your body's messages.

Through Your Behavior

Go into neutral, without needing to vote on whether your behavior is good or bad. Observe your behavior—actions, patterns, rhythms, routines—and accept it. Value your actions as much as thoughts, feelings, imagination.

Through Self-Awareness

Become more conscious of how you already create your reality. First, look at your life within your environment. Take responsibility for what you like and don't like. Ask, "How am I creating this? What am I initiating here, moving toward, what am I allowing, and what am I avoiding?" Ask your body, "What do you need now—to feel safe, to rise to challenges and opportunities?"

Through Your Dreams

You tap all levels of consciousness through your dreams—subconscious, conscious, and superconscious—all brain-wave levels, and the universe.

The most precious gift of your basic brain is that it can allow you to neutrally observe yourself living your life. The secret to using that gift is to become conscious of the entire range of energy that you experience, from the slowest and densest to the fastest and airiest. And then to practice moving toward nurturing conditions and away from harmful patterns, parameters, and situations. Keep your mind attuned to your constantly shifting energy patterns. Remember, you are constantly changing, whether you're conscious of it or not, and you're even changing your DNA, constantly. So live your life as a dynamic being rather than as a fixed personality

Be in the present moment as much of the time as possible. Pretend you're doing whatever it is you're doing as if for the first time—because in a very real way it is the first time that the you of the moment—different from all previous you's—has done this particular thing in this particular context or environment.

Through Body Signals

Creativity thrives on vibrant health, so recognize early warning signals of the need to change your habits, to express your emotions, to process fear-based feelings, to release them, etc. If you don't listen to these "early-on" subtle messages, your body will "up" the signal until you either change your habits or die. Here's the typical "ramping-up" process.

1. Instinctual urges—subtle vibration—resonances, moving toward or away from, restlessness, pressures

2. Nervousness—a stronger vibration—the jitters. Ask yourself, "Is it anxiety or excitement?"

3. Sensory information—louder message—sensations such as hot, itchy, cold, etc.

4. Emotions, contracting—frustration, resentment, anger, sadness

5. Physical tension, stress, addictive behavior

6. Physical pain

7. Illness or disease

8. Drama, shock, trauma—accidents, divorce, crime, violence (you're either a victim or a perpetrator), etc.

9. Depression, paralysis, unconsciousness, insanity

10. Death and rebirth—you didn't listen, so you must start over

As you can see, the body signals get denser and more intense. Your subconscious or superconscious mind is trying to get the attention of your conscious mind, telling it that you need to pay attention to patterns going on at a more subtle level. Be open and aware of these anxiety signals. The moment you notice one, stop and ask your body, *What is the message?* Don't wait for a crisis to intervene and force change.

Look for those habit patterns that run you but don't nurture you. Don't condemn them. Instead accept, observe, and own them, so you can change them. Condemned patterns usually don't get owned but instead go underground where you can't find them.

Remember, you can have much more personal freedom than you know. You are free to be conscious of resonances or dissonances with various persons and situations, to become aware of whether they're on same wave length as you or not, whether you resonate with them or not. You're free to move toward nurturing behavior, to select nurturing role models, and to imitate nurturing behavior. You're free to stop and to move away from harmful behavior, to substitute nurturing behavior. You're free to find new forms of expressing yourself.

How to Boost Your Creativity through Basic Intelligence

You can boost your creativity through your basic pattern-parameter intelligence in so many ways. In doing so, you will learn how to access the energy of your basic brain, decide which patterns to keep and which to change, tap into all three levels of consciousness to master meditation and dream states, master pattern-change processes, use them for interrupting old patterns and making new pattern connections, understand what to expect and how your emotions tie you to old patterns, how to boost your energy level, and how to increase your options.

Booster 1. Learn How to Access Basic Brain Energy

To get in touch with your basic brain, try the following techniques.

1. *Rhythms*. Enter into the rhythms of what's happening. Slow down the speed of your breathing, thinking and other body functions. Focus on rhythm, action, movement. Notice them while doing ordinary physical routines, such as walking, dressing, working out. Notice how you're moving easily, attending to the action within a defined space and time, without much distraction of thoughts or feelings Sometimes the rhythm, action, movement is more intense as when you're in sync while dancing, swimming, or playing ball.

2. *Instinctual movement*. Notice how people seem to instinctively move toward or away from people, places, ideas, colors, feelings, things, events. Notice how you do this.

3. *Observation*. Go into neutral emotionally, step outside yourself, observe yourself and your behavior as if it did not really belong to you. See it in the context of all that's around you. Look for patterns, limits, and boundaries. See how your behavior serves you, or not.

4. *Dreams*. Pay attention to your dreams for information from your basic brain, your subconscious and superconscious minds.

5. *Addictive Patterns*. Notice your addictions, your patterns or habits that you feel compelled to do. Which ones are constructive? Which are neutral? Which ones a form of self-sabotage?

6. *Withdrawal Patterns*. Have you withdrawn or distanced yourself from beliefs, thoughts, feelings, decisions, and actions that are beneficial to you? That's how people develop antisocial, addictive, and even criminal habit patterns. When you withdraw again and again, until you are no longer aware of your avoidance, it becomes an automatic habit. Neither reward nor punishment seems to have much success in changing antisocial behavior unless it takes into consideration this basic brain patterning and conditioning and deals with changing the habit patterns at their root origins.

Booster 2. Decide Which Patterns to Keep and to Change

Observing your habit patterns and parameters sounds easier to do than it actually is. But this is some of the most important personal growth work you'll ever do, and it will pay off by removing some major blocks to higher-level creativity. The self-awareness opportunities at the end of this chapter will help you do this work.

Revisit the Scene of Key Life Decisions

Get in touch with problem patterns, one at a time. Meditate to find connections between the pattern and critical incidents from your past. Re-visit the old scenario to see it in new ways and to make new decisions in order to change the old habit pattern. Get in touch with the needs, wants, and feelings you had at that time, whether it was last year or, more likely, when you were a child. As an adult, give your former self what you needed at that time—the nurturing, support, love, whatever the need. Now let the former you make a new conclusion and decision about the situation. Let these new beliefs, thoughts, feelings, and decisions serve as the basis for new habit patterns.

To break up ineffective habit patterns, become aware of your beliefs that led to this behavior. What new beliefs will you adopt to replace the old? Repeat your affirmations of new beliefs. Develop some new patterns, new rituals, that focus your mind and re-establish new beliefs. Ritual is made up of belief, conscious thought, and perhaps some art or music to vividly symbolize the belief. Find ways to consciously act-out your new habit patterns. Remember, repetition creates new habit patterns.

Break Out of Limiting Boundaries

To begin with, learn to accept, without the need to explain or defend, the fact that you and others are territorial. Learn to respect rather than invade others' territories and to understand that you have territorial rights also. The expansive emotions of humor, curiosity, openness, and flexibility can be very helpful here.

Set some reasonable limits and boundaries for expending your energy. This means that the signals you send out and the ones you let in make sense. It means you focus your energy and attention on those things that are most important for your growth and survival. Otherwise you'll scatter yourself all over the map and won't be able to achieve much of anything.

Two major problems you can create for yourself are:

- believing parameters last forever
- ignoring the fact that life's rhythms keep changing

You're most likely to try to hold onto old parameters—including home territory, relationships, friends, jobs, etc. when you experience a sudden loss of parameters. Pay special attention to parameter behavior at these times:

- end of a relationship (or major relationship shift, or fear of such a change)
- end of a job
- change of home

Do you try to defend your parameters by controlling people and situations? This is an old paradigm that is not successful or satisfying in the long run. All you can really control is yourself—your own beliefs, attitudes, decisions, and action choices. Try this new paradigm:

1. Understand life as a dynamic rather than static process—feel it, act it, as a dynamic process.

2. Evaluate your current parameters

3. Stay flexible, loose, moving toward and away from.

4. Change parameters, create new parameters, when energy drops—shift to what you want, like., love—shift to what represents a new, high-energy experience.

5. Wear your reality lightly—don't let it weigh too heavily. Review your values, beliefs, habits, roles—how do they need to shift? Remember, we're all here to learn! We don't have to do it right the first time.

6. Act out your basic intelligence—moving toward new growth and away from old limitations.

Booster 3. Tap Into All Levels of Consciousness

You are constantly accessing three levels of consciousness: the conscious, subconscious, and superconscious. You're aware of course of those times when you're in the conscious mind state. You can easily bring information from your subconscious and superconscious minds into your awareness by learning some very simple meditation and dream-recall skills.

First, be aware that when your brain activity is measured, the resulting electro-encephalogram, reveals that you access four major brain states.

Beta state occurs at 13 to 25 cycles per second. This is the rational, active state.

Alpha state occurs at 8 to 12 cycles per second. This is the drifting, hypnogogic state you experience just before and after sleep. In this state your intuition is high, your connection to the subconscious and superconscious mind is strong. This is a good time to focus on goals, problems, and questions that you want answered. Closing your eyes encourages the formation of the alpha state.

Theta state occurs at 5 to 7 cycles per second. This is the deep meditation state. Your intuition is very high. This is a good time to be open to information, messages, answers, and inspiration from your subconscious and superconscious mind.

Delta state is 1 to 4 cycles per second. This is the state of deep or full sleep. Dreams occur during this state and your intuition is very high.

To take advantage of these brain states and to access information from your subconscious and superconscious mind, you need to develop some skills. To reach the meditative state, you need to deeply relax. To tap information and create new realities, you need to visualize situations and results. To bring them into your every day life, you must let go of fearful needs and shift to relaxed desires. To gain information from the dream state, you must learn to program your dreams and to interpret them.

Be in the Present Moment

Learning to focus on the present moment—and to totally be in the here and now—is a powerful way to aid the relaxation process and to turn off mind chatter. Chatter is often associated with guilt, resentment, and worry. Remember, when you're feeling guilty or resentful, you're really living in the past. When you're worrying, you're living in the future. Action in the here and now is the only way to influence events. The key is to focus on the present moment and determine what, if anything, you need to do. If you need help with this, repeat the relaxation process in SAO 2.1 for "getting in the here and now." It's designed to bring you into the present moment by helping you focus on the sensations your body is experiencing now. Practice it frequently when you're not under stress, and you'll soon be able to use it quickly, even in stressful situations.

Master Relaxation Processes

The goal of relaxation processes is to cut through tension and mind chatter to reach a deeply relaxed state. As with all the techniques and processes for commanding your inner resources, these may take some time to master in the beginning. With practice, however, you'll be able to use your skills even in the midst of stressful situations, and you'll be able to go into deeper states of relaxation more quickly.

Achieve the Alpha State Advantage

The ultimate goal is to be able to move into a state of relaxation so deep that you're producing alpha brain waves. Although biofeedback mechanisms are available for helping you develop this ability quickly, you can learn well enough without them. Research indicates that closing you eyes helps to achieve this relaxed state that lets you communicate more effectively with your subconscious. You can give it new messages, even messages that override key decisions about life that you made long ago—viewpoints that no longer serve you. You can enlist the aid of your subconscious in reaching your goals and solving problems—so that your verbal and nonverbal actions are well integrated and your entire being is moving toward achieving what you decide you want in life.

You get double payoffs, therefore, for learning to relax deeply. The relaxation alone is an immediate antidote to stress. It enhances your sense of well-being, your health, and potentially your longevity. In addition, when you combine it with visualization—that is, mental imagery—it helps you create the life you want. But more about that later.

Set the Stage

Four conditions are helpful for mastering these relaxation processes.

- A quiet, calm place as free from distraction as possible
- A comfortable body position
- A mental focusing device to help you shut off your mind chatter (internal dialogue) and go deep within yourself
- A passive attitude that lets you merely observe distracting thoughts, let them go, and bring your mind back gently to your focusing device Keep in mind that you can't *make* relaxation occur; you can only *let* it occur.

Once you've found a quiet place, experiment with comfortable positions. (A favorite of many is sitting in a comfortable but firm chair with back perfectly straight, legs and arms uncrossed, feet flat on the floor, and arms resting on the thighs.) Then experiment with the processes included in SAO 2.2, Deep Relaxation to find the ones that work best for you.

Visualize the Results You Want

Once you're in a deeply relaxed state, you can talk to your subconscious and tell it what you want. Your subconscious is amazingly competent at moving you toward the results you request—if you'll only relax and let it do its work. It tunes in better to pictures and feelings, however, than to words. That's why visualizing results and getting in touch with the feelings you want to experience along with those results is so powerful.

How to Visualize

What if you have difficulty *making pictures* when you close your eyes? Don't worry. Everyone differs to some extent in the way they visualize. If you see no picture at all, you're still thinking of it in your *mind's eye*, and that's adequate. It may help to think of what it might be like if you *could* see the picture you're thinking about. Think in terms of *allowing* pictures rather than making them.

When to Visualize

When should you practice your visualization skills? Shortly before going to sleep each night is a time preferred by many people because it's a quiet time when they're ready to relax fully. To make the most of your personal power, practice deep relaxation and visualization at some time every day so that it becomes a deeply ingrained habit—a way of life that you can put to use almost automatically. If you do this, you'll soon discover that you can use these skills—quickly, with your eyes wide open, and with no one the wiser—any time you're dealing with potentially stressful situations. You'll be able to stay centered or to regain your composure quickly even if you're taken by surprise.

The processes described in SAO 2.3, Visualization, are designed to enlist the aid of your subconscious in handling specific types of situations. You can adapt them to any kind of situation; just remember that important final step, letting go.

Learn To Let Go

Have you ever observed someone sabotaging herself because she was trying too hard? You probably thought, *Why doesn't she relax a little?* Can you think of a time when you probably sabotaged yourself by trying too hard or caring too much? Why do people do this? Usually it happens because they're too strongly attached to having the situation turn out just the way they want. They cling—perhaps desperately—to the idea or picture of certain end results. Therefore, they create a tension-producing need to achieve those results, often accompanied by fear that they won't.

Think preferences, not needs

Think of some situations in which you achieved the results you wanted—times when you moved relatively effortlessly toward your goal. Think of top athletes who have done that. Top achievement is usually a result of *relaxed concentration*. You fully intend to achieve certain results, and your mind and body are focused on the process of doing so. You *desire* and *prefer* those results, but you don't desperately *need* them, and you're not focused on fear connected with failure to achieve the results.

Prevent Self-Sabotage

You prevent the self-sabotage caused by tension-producing needs when you add a letting-go step to the visualization process you use for goal-setting. SAO 2.4, Letting Go of Needs, offers several techniques for this final step of the personal power process.   Remember, when you let go of your goal, you retain a clear picture of having it, but you release the needs and fears related to not having it.   This process frees you to work toward your goal in a relaxed, confident way, which in turn makes it easier to gain the cooperation and support of others.   But you must truly become comfortable with the idea of *not* achieving your goal.   If letting go is accompanied by sadness, regret, or unwillingness, you need to work on your fear of failure.

Allow Abundance

You can also adopt a viewpoint that there is abundance in the world.   When you let go of your goal pictures, you *put them out into the universe.*   The view that there is abundance in the universe implies that everything that happens eventually works toward your benefit.   Therefore, if you give a goal situation your best shot, you're confident of achieving it.   If it doesn't turn out the way you pictured, then your deep inner self had the wisdom to know that those results were not best for you at this time.   That's the time to ask, *What lesson can I learn*

Use Your Dream Time

Psychoanalyst Carl Jung was the first respected leader to give dreams an importance similar to that given by aboriginal tribes. Jung wrote of dreams as images that can convey important messages from the subconscious mind, messages the conscious mind may not want to recognize.   The messages therefore often appear as symbols, metaphors, and archetypes that have universal meanings among human beings.

You can even use your sleep time to move you toward your goals.   For years we've heard managers say, before making an important or difficult decision, *Let me sleep on it and get back to you tomorrow*—and for very good reason. Research studies increasingly point to the importance of sleeping, and especially dreaming, to our mental health and ability to function well during waking hours. Your subconscious mind is very powerful, and the superconscious mind is infinite. You can draw on these resources almost effortlessly by using the dream state to help you solve problems, resolve conflicts, and come up with new ideas.

Problem-Solve and Create

You can program your dreams to help you solve problems and get creative ideas. A powerful technique is to focus on a problem, question, or concern as you drift off to sleep, confident that your dreams will bring an answer.   Another approach is to visualize the results you want to create just before you fall asleep.   Other techniques include writing down brief notes about your dreams upon waking, or during the day as you recall them, and interpreting your dreams. See SAO 2.5 and 2.6.

Expand Personal Awareness

Once you become accustomed to using your sleep and dream time, consider taking it a step further into pure research.   Jungian analysts believe that your dreams can provide symbolic information about what's going on in your life at the subconscious level—and bring you helpful information through your superconscious mind from the interconnected Web of Life.   You can expand your awareness and see relationships, events, and problems from a broader perspective by tapping into your dream world. You are the best interpreter of your own dreams and at a deep level, you already know the meaning of universal symbols.   But to re-learn their meanings, see Betty Bethards' *The Dream Book: Symbols for Self-Understanding,* a small, simple book that I have found to be the most helpful.

To sum up, follow these suggestions for using your dream time to boost your creativity:

- Trust your own experience

- Open up to your dreams. Be willing to be gullible, vulnerable, a believer, at least for a while. Take a "what if???" approach.

- Break up your patterns, your habits, in order to open up to new ideas and to create newness in your life.

- Program your dreams—to solve problems, get new ideas, have new experiences, create what you want.

- Play with symbols to interpret your dreams. Your subconscious and superconscious minds love pictures and symbols, so your intuition often brings messages in symbolic form.

- Connect dream-time and wake-time. Become aware of how your dreams may be anticipating what's going on in your wake-time life—or how they're responding to it.

Call on Your Subconscious and Superconscious Minds

Your greatest resource of inner power is your superconscious mind. Keep in mind that concept as you work to boost your basic pattern-parameter intelligence through waking meditations and night-time dream work.

Work with your spirit self, the superconscious

Your spirit self, that surrounds your physical body, sends signals that have specific resonances. Through your spirit self you can work with future energies, Higher-Self energies, and universal (all-that-is) energies.

Work with symbols

Both your Superconscious and Subconscious Minds tend to speak in symbolic language. If your learn to pay attention to symbols that come up in your life, you can start to "hear" messages through these powerful sources. Refer to good dream books and other books on symbolism to raise your awareness. Use your knowledge of symbolic language to analyze the hidden meanings behind the events of your everyday life—as well as to interpret your dreams. See recommended books in the References section of this chapter.

Work with your negative ego

Your negative ego is the part of you that judges whether people are better-than or worse-than you are—or some ideal you hold. It's that part that's over-concerned with how people judge you as better-than or worse-than. When you give your power to your negative ego, it uses manipulation and games to try to control people and events. You're usually not conscious that you've given your power away, because you established these patterns early in life and then forgot about them. But you can gradually become aware and your whole self can take back that power.

Work with presence, empowerment

Become aware of old, now-ineffective habit patterns that live in your subconscious mind. Revisit your past, if necessary, to re-experience critical situations that led you to make key decisions about life, perceive these experiences anew, make new decisions, and create new habit patterns. Retrieve your visions and dreams from the past, keeping the lessons you learned, the gifts and treasures. Risk moving forward to connect with the Web of Life, with an ever-changing now that becomes the future. Let's anticipate boosting your emotional intelligence: see how often you can let go of emotions that focus your attention negatively on the past (resentment, revenge, guilt) or the future (worry) and spend more of your time fully present in each moment of NOW.

Work on your inner environment

Focus on beliefs and thoughts that you can experience as true, beautiful—that trigger expansive, love-based emotions, especially trust, respect, enchantment, peace, wonder, compassion, inspiration, intrigue for the unknown. Cherish your heart-felt desires and passions as creative generating energies. Begin with yourself—love for yourself, self-trust, self-respect—and then expand those emotions to the world in general and to the people in your life. If you feel threatened by people or situations in the world, do a reality check about the real dangers. Then ask yourself how you can protect yourself. Keep in mind this purpose in all your meditations and goals: "with harm to none and for the highest good for all."

Booster 4. Use Pattern-Change Processes

You can pick and choose from many change processes to become aware of your basic pattern-parameter actions, identifying those that are helpful and those that block your creative potential.

Identify Types of Behavior Patterns

Think in terms of the types of patterns you follow. Certainly people follow their own relationship and work patterns. You can extend this awareness to your work organization, looking at profit or productivity patterns.

Relationship Patterns

Notice your relationship patterns. When you want to connect with new acquaintances, or deepen current connections to a person, consider these actions that include observing their patterns, imitating them, learning from them, searching for deeper patterns of meaning, and appreciating their patterns.

- Observe other persons' patterns to discover their key rhythms
- Begin to move in their rhythms, imitating
- Identify yourself with the other person
- Keep their rhythms when you're with them
- Travel with them, accompany them as they go about their activities
- Quiet your rational and emotional brains, letting your basic pattern-parameter brain lead the way.

If it's a personal relationship, ask yourself, does this relationship (the other person) expand my life or contract it? If it's a work relationship, keep in mind that building authentic work relationships, inner person to inner person, is essential for team creativity.

Work Patterns

Notice your work patterns. Gently guide yourself, seduce yourself, into the rhythm of the work you need to do.

Productivity-Profit Patterns

Start noticing the patterns of work and relationship in your organization. How are they productive or non-productive? Research indicates that people who learn to recognize profit patterns are better able to anticipate new sources of profit before they develop. This means they're more likely to come up with creative ideas for capturing "tomorrow's profit zones" [Slywotzky 1999]

Use Pattern Intervention Processes

You can find many processes for breaking old habit patterns that undermine your creativity and success, processes for establishing new patterns. For example, you can revisit old scenarios. What happened last year is still alive in your memory. So is what happened when you were three years old. That child is still a vital part of you, and you can nurture that child now as an adult. In your mind you can revisit childhood events and perceive them through new eyes. When you do, you'll find it easy to change the decisions and beliefs you established back then. You can do that in "now time." Another process is to notice how certain behaviors link together into a pattern. You can then change just one little behavior that's a key link in the chain. This can break up the behavior pattern, leaving space for creating a better one. Still another process involves connecting with role models who can inspire and teach you, . See SAOs 2.7 through 2.10.

Forming ingrained habit patterns does not happen in one cycle. Behavior chains linked together are repeated numerous times before they become automatic patterns that function near or at the subconscious level. It stands to reason that you may not change some of your most ingrained habits after one cycle of new behavior. Such change often involves one step forward and two steps back, and hopefully progresses to two steps forward, one step back. Remember, just being able to recognize that you've "done it again" is great progress! And the steps backward can offer you a new perspective if you choose. They can help you to remember the old behavior more vividly and to see how far you've really come—and where you're heading. The steps back can give you the momentum you need for the next step forward.

The poem that follows, adapted from a poem by Nyoshui Khenpo [1992] expresses the process poignantly.

Cycle 1:	**Cycle 3:**
I walk down the street.	*I walk down the same street.*
There's a deep hole in the sidewalk	*There's a deep hole in the sidewalk.*
I fall in.	*I see it's there.*
I'm lost . . I'm hopeless.	*I still fall in . . . it's a habit.*
It isn't my fault.	*My eyes are open.*
It takes forever to find a way out.	*I know where I am.*
Cycle 2:	*It's my fault.*
I walk down the same street.	*I get out immediately.*
There's a deep hole in the sidewalk.	**Cycle 4:**
I pretend I don't see it.	*I walk down the same street.*
I fall in again.	*There is a deep hole in the sidewalk*
I can't believe I'm in the same place	*I walk around it.*
But it isn't my fault.	**Cycle 5:**
It takes a long time to get out.	*I walk down another street.*

The change process forms a personal growth spiral, shown in Figure 2.6. The important thing to remember: Don't be discouraged when you find yourself in the midst of an old habit pattern, or when you realize, "I've done it again!" Personal growth toward freedom and creativity is more like a spiral than a straight line of change. Each time you cycle back into the old type of behavior, it's always at a higher level of awareness—following the growth spiral.

Figure 2.6   Personal Growth Spiral—Awakening Consciousness
(*Note*: Start below.)

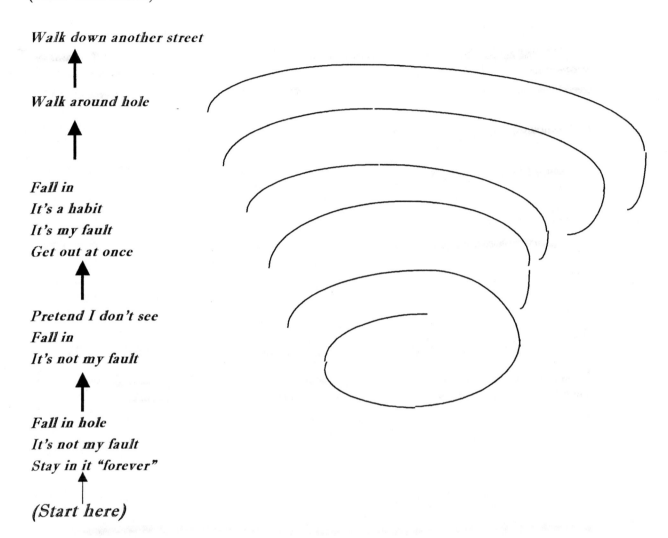

Walk down another street

Walk around hole

Fall in
It's a habit
It's my fault
Get out at once

Pretend I don't see
Fall in
It's not my fault

Fall in hole
It's not my fault
Stay in it "forever"

(Start here)

Booster 5. Understand Emotional Ties to Your Habits

Some major emotional ties that keep people stuck in their ineffective habits include worry, guilt, resentment, and revenge.

Worry

Worry is negatively living in the future. On the other hand, suppose you're intelligently concerned about probable future threats and you follow up immediately with reasonable action to prevent threatening events from occurring or to minimize their impact. This is a positive way to create an optimal future. Worry is actually socially accepted addiction. People tend to nod approvingly when you express worry. You may conclude: *"If I worry about you, that means I care about you. . . . If I worry about events, that means I care about them."*

Actually worry tends to create anxiety stress in the now. Instead of getting stuck in worry, ask, *"What can I do about it NOW?"* Then Do it! Ask, *"What can I not prevent?"* Or, *"What is too far-fetched for me to spend energy trying to prevent it?"* Then let go of worry. Trust in the universe to work toward the highest good. The only reason to go to a worst-case scenario is to face your fear dragons and realize that you can survive the worst that could reasonably happen. Then let it go. Have the intention to create best-case scenarios and realize you have the strength to live through the worst.

Guilt, Resentment, Revenge

These emotions involve negatively living in the past and creating stress in the now. Instead of getting stuck in guilt, resentment, or revenge, ask, *"What can I learn from these past events NOW?"* Get it! Then ask, *How can I forgive myself* (guilt) *and others* (resentment) *for these past events?"* Here are some constructive thoughts::

- *Remember, we're all growing.* Even though we do things that hurt, we're all doing the best we can, given our stage of growth.

- *Don't take it personally.* The hurtful things we do are connected with our life scripts, our stage of personal growth, our habit patterns, parameters, fears, and other limitations. When someone hurts you, don't take it personally. That person would have reacted the same way toward anyone who represented to them what you did at that point in time.

- *Forgive—yourself and others.* Feel gratitude for the experience. Let go of guilt, resentment, or revenge. Forgive *not* necessarily because the other person deserves it—but because you do. When you feel forgiveness and gratitude, you give yourself a great gift—a lightness, a freedom that opens up your heart and mind to let in new ideas and experiences. You boost your creative potential!

Booster 6. Use Basic Intelligence to Boost Your Energy Level

When your body signals stress—when you experience pain, illness, boredom, fatigue, accidents—it's time to use your basic pattern-parameter intelligence. Ask yourself some questions:

- *What are the major routines of my day and night?*
- *How are they creating this body signal?*
- *What patterns or beliefs are keeping me in my stressful routines?*
- *How can I move away from these routines, patterns, beliefs?*
- *What new ones could I try?*

You have two basic choices about how to break out of old patterns and become more creative:

1. *Growth by Crisis*—ignoring messages or signals from the subconscious and superconscious.
2. *Growth by Design*—allowing information and messages from the subconscious and superconscious into your consciousness.

Booster 7. Keep Your Options Open

Are you limiting your creative options by thinking about decisions in either/or terms? Do you tend to think "Either I have to put up with the boss's nasty comments or I have to quit"? This gives you only two possible options. Open up your options by thinking also in both/and terms. "I can both work with a boss who makes nasty comments and maintain my self-respect while limiting the boss's behavior by doing x, y, and z." Some decisions should be limited to two either/or options, but in most situations there are actually dozens, if not hundreds or even thousands of small variations in the many responses you could make or initiatives you could take. In some cases the best decision may involve "either this, or that or that or that or that, etc. In other cases it may involve "both this, and that, and that, and that, and that. . . or some combination of all these." So don't "think the world apart" into this *or* that when it's this *and* that, an interconnected web.

Creativity Showcase
Using Pattern Intelligence
for Creative Solutions and Ideas

Some innovative solutions to current problems—for your information and inspiration—and as food for thought.

Problem—Consumer Behavior Data

Sometimes a set of business problems has so many variables that you can't get a handle on them. "There are many self-organizing forces out there in consumer behavior, but you need the right tool set, and the right mindset, to find them," says Colin Crook, board member of CASA (Center for Adaptive Systems Applications, a division of PriceWaterhouseCoopers). The right complex adaptive model enables marketing people to conduct serious strategic and tactical analysis (WSJ 1999).

Innovative Solution

Complexity theory explains how order (pattern) springs from disorder. Under the right conditions, large systems that appear chaotic will, by themselves, organize into well-ordered states. In nature we see bees organize into hives and air currents organize into thunderstorms. In business we see business finance schemes organize themselves into stock markets and computer users organize themselves into the Internet. We see this process in many kinds of complex adaptive systems.

Studying these self-organizing processes and patterns often calls for the same kind of complex mathematics, nonlinear dynamics, used in nuclear weapons research. In 1999 CASA had 40 nuclear mathematicians and social scientists working as corporate consultants to study the complex systems of business. They created a program to simulate the buying actions of 200,000 actual Americans, calling the sample a "focus group of 200,000." Using this program, corporate clients can tweak the parameters of a marketing campaign and watch the consumers cluster into buying patterns. A complex adaptive system evolves before their eyes on the computer screen. Citicorp staff, for example, uses the software to

- Take thousands of credit histories, find patterns, and create new formulas for scoring credit card applicants and spotting frauds.

- Take the customer-service records of millions of incoming phone calls to Citicorp's call center, uncovering patterns that help the center improve its response times and still reduce required work hours (and thus salary expense).

- Provide simulation software to help employees increase their intuition and expertise in responding to economic developments.

CASA plans to connect corporate clients directly to CASA's computers. Then these clients can use CASA's programs to transmit their data and to model their problems the moment they occur. They can adapt their responses almost instantly.

Creative Techniques Using Basic Intelligence

You now have a number of methods to help you boost your basic pattern-parameter intelligence. At the same time you can begin working with some specific creative techniques that rely primarily on this type of intelligence. Use these to work on the real-life business cases that follow.

CT 2.1 Environmental Patterns and Trends

Look for early signs of opportunities and threats that are approaching. Pick a few topic areas that have special impact on your career or business. Follow them on the internet and other news sources. Read what the forecasters are saying; for example John Naisbett and Faith Popcorn. How can you use this information to move into a new opportunity area? To take action to ward off or sidestep a threatening development?

CT 2.2 New Parameters

How can you expand the parameters of your career or business? Conduct regular opportunity searches into areas that are unrelated to your career or business. How can you apply your knowledge or expertise in another business area? Read about trends in other areas. Even literature in such areas as science fiction and romance can give you ideas. Be open and make connections.

CT 2.3 If It Doesn't Work, Follow It

This technique uses your basic intelligence of moving toward or away from something. If a project takes an unexpected turn and seems to be not working out, instead of fixing it, what if you were to follow it? Can you find a use for the idea that doesn't work? Would it work in some other situation? For some other purpose? For some other project? (For example: post-it notes uses weak glue that wasn't strong enough for the original purpose of the research)

CT 2.4 Reverse Your Assumptions

To recognize the parameters you are subconsciously setting that could in turn limit new ideas about the situation, try listing all your assumptions about the situation, then reversing them.

Suppose your assumptions include: we don't have enough money for really big changes, we need to get this project finished as quickly as possible, and our competitor has more resources than we do. Try reversing those assumptions: we have access to enough money for some really big changes, we have some leeway for our deadline date, and we have more resources than our competitor. What new possibilities does the reversal suggest? New pathways, doors to new ideas?

This process may also help you come up with new ideas for addressing the situation.

CT 2.5 Look for Patterns

Go over all the available information. Look for patterns, boundaries, relationships. Draw a diagram that shows these patterns or relationships. Seeing the data visually helps trigger your pattern and parameter intelligence, leading to a deeper understanding and creative ideas.

CT 2.6 Fishbone Pattern Diagram

The main purpose of the fishbone diagram is to generate a list of possible causes of a problem that you organize in a fishbone pattern in order to see patterns and relationships.

At the center left edge of a sheet of paper, write a brief phrase that describes the problem and encircle it. This is the head of the fish. Draw a straight line, representing the fish backbone, from the head to the right edge of the paper. This line is the backbone of the fish. Next, draw straight lines that are angled off from either side of the backbone. These are the vertebrae or fishbones that you'll use to organize problem causes.

Put the simplest, most obvious causes first, near the head of the fish by writing them beside a fishbone, encircling them, and attaching them to the fishbone with a straight line. Try to put causes that are similar or closely related along the same fishbone. Consider putting causes that pull against each other on opposite sides of the backbone. Keep brainstorming causes, putting the most subtle and complex ones near the tail. When you feel you've listed all possible causes, study the diagram for relationships. You may want to re-do the diagram to show a different pattern of relationships. Use your imagination to find unique ways to arrange the list of causes. Ask such questions as:

- Have all parts of the problem been explored and all possible causes listed?
- What are the relationships between causes?
- What is the relative importance of these causes?
- Will solving simple causes and issues first help us to handle the more complex ones?

CT 2.7 Why-Why Pattern Diagram

Write the problem statement on the center left side of a sheet of paper and encircle it. Ask why this problem is occurring and list the causes under the problem statement, beginning at the top of the page, encircling each one, and moving down the page in column form. For each cause, ask "why is this occurring?" and list each reason to the right of the cause, encircling it and connecting by a straight line to the cause. If you need to delve further into any of the reasons why, again ask "why is this occurring?" and write the answers to the right of the reason, encircling and connecting.

CT 2.8 Mind Mapping

Write the problem or opportunity statement in the center of a sheet of paper and encircle it. Brainstorm ideas about how to solve the problem or explore the opportunity. Write your major ideas on lines drawn outward from the main statement like highways from a city.

As you think of new aspects that relate to a major idea, write them on (minor) road lines drawn outward from the (major) highway line. You can go into further detail by brainstorming ideas for each new aspect and writing it on street lines connected to a road line.

Use your imagination to highlight relationships by using colored pens, highlighting, circling certain ideas, starring them, etc.

Study your mind map, looking for associations, relationships, and new ideas.

Case Studies—Applying the Creative Techniques

In working on these cases, you may use creative techniques from any of the chapters. However, the creative techniques described in this chapter may be especially appropriate. Keep these self-questions in mind.

1. What problems do I see?
2. How can I probe beneath the surface to get at root problems?
3. What opportunities (hidden or obvious) can I find to take initiative, cut costs, and/or make money?
4. What creative alternatives can I generate?
5. As a consultant, what should I recommend as the best viewpoints and actions?

6. To answer these questions, what creative techniques *discussed in this chapter* can I experiment with to respond to this case? After completing the case analysis, ask: Which creative techniques produced the best results?

Case 2.1 Fast Print

Fast Print Inc. has 12 stores in a large metropolitan area. **Renee Carter**, CEO, inherited the company from her father nearly 5 years ago. About 90 percent of the revenues come from printing jobs. These are done primarily for privately-owned corporations, such as banks, retail stores, sports teams, but also for some nonprofit organizations. Fast Print produces presentation folders, business cards, pamphlets, brochures, posters, newsletters, coupons, tickets, and similar printed matter that these organizations need. Most of the large printing jobs come from repeat customers.

The other ten percent of Fast Print's revenues come from their copy service. About half their copying jobs are for law firms, and the other half are jobs are for commercial or retail businesses.

Fast Print relies on getting their new customers through referrals and word of mouth. They have only two salespersons. One salesperson, **Jeff**, has been with the company for thirty years and has a very large client base. He keeps track of clients with help from an assistant in a computer database. He does not acquire new clients, but keeps track of current ones only.

Jennifer, the other salesperson, has been with the company about five years. She doesn't have a large client base. She networks her current clients to obtain new clients and referrals. She keeps track of her customers in a Rolodex.

Both salespersons regularly call their clients to see if they are satisfied with their orders and if they need anything else printed or copied. The individual store managers call the customers when their orders are ready. The customers usually have their orders delivered.

One of Fast Print's biggest problems right now is competition for printing and copying jobs. In many instances, owners of office buildings are installing in-house printing and copying stores for use by all the businesses in their building. These businesses find that such in-house print shops are closer and more convenient, and often less costly. Similarly, many schools and universities have installed their own in-house print and copy centers. They do many print and copy jobs, large and small, and so represent a significant market segment.

Copy competitors are a problem for Fast Print, also. Kinko's is their greatest competitor for copying jobs because they have more locations and most of their stores are open 24 hours a day. Many of them are located near universities. Kinko's and other, smaller copy shops have taken away about twenty percent of Fast Print's copying jobs in the past year.

Another competing factor is that more small businesses and home office owners are buying their own copiers. New technology allows cheaper, more reliable copy machines.

Today sales reps Jennifer and Jeff are meeting with CEO Renee Carter and her executive team to discuss all these problems and to generate some creative solutions. They will address these types of questions.

- What are the surface problems and the root problems that Fast Print is facing?
- What opportunities are they overlooking?
- How can Fast Print expand its market share and revenues?
- Which CTs discussed in this chapter did you use in solving this case problem?
- Which CTs were most helpful and what ideas did they spark or inspire?

 Root Problem - why

Case 2.2 Synex Corp - Growing Pains

Jim Perez is CEO of Synex Corp., a three-year-old distributor of data telecommunications equipment. When Jim hired his startup team of employees, he was happy to take on just about anyone who would take the leap of faith with him—relatives, friends, almost anyone who would answer a help-wanted ad.

Brian was one of Jim's first hires. He impressed Jim with an enthusiastic handwritten response to a newspaper ad. When the man showed up for a 7 a.m. interview, Jim hired him on the spot. "Brian was great for the first year or so. Oh, he had some problem working with women, and his lunch hour was a main priority, but when the company was small, none of that mattered," says Jim. But when business began booming, Brian could no longer avoid women coworkers, and his sacred lunch hour began interfering with customer demands. Meanwhile Brian seemed to think he had earned the right to keep all the little privileges he had become used to. Jim says, "Brian felt he didn't have to change, but as we grew, his habits got in the way."

Jim hired **Amy** as the part-time bookkeeper, who was 20 years old and inexperienced but working on her accounting degree. She installed QuickBooks, which worked fine, but now Synex is running $6.5 million through the company and the accounting system seems to bog down at times.

Jim hired his sister **Wanda** as the first purchasing agent. She's two years older than Jim and very protective of him and his business. She has her fingers in every pie in the company, getting involved in all the projects she can, even though they're not in her job description. **Larry Rafferty**, Jim's partner, reports that many of the newer employees have been complaining about her meddling in their projects—though of course they don't feel free to say anything to Jim about the problem.

Larry approached Jim a few months ago about the need to integrate clear systems and procedures into the company's day-to-day management so that everyone's "on the same page, marching to the same drumbeat." Larry and Jim created a management protocol and stressed that everyone should follow this new way of doing things. Wanda has been very resistant to such a move. She likes things the way they are.

- What are the surface problems and the root problems that Synex is facing?
- What opportunities are they overlooking?
- What should Jim do next?
- Which CTs discussed in this chapter did you use in solving this case problem?
- Which CTs were most helpful and what ideas did they spark or inspire?

Self-Awareness Opportunities

SAO 2.1 Be-Here-Now Consciousness

Purpose: To bring yourself fully into the present moment as an aid to letting go of concerns about the past and the future, to prepare yourself for deep relaxation.

Variation 1—Focusing on the Five Senses

Step 1: Breathing. Take a few deep breaths.

Step 2: Seeing. Become internally aware of what you see around you. Look at it in detail as if you've never seen it before. Pretend you just arrived from another planet. Notice colors, patterns, textures.

Step 3: Hearing. If the situation permits, close your eyes. What do you hear? Notice every little sound, identify it, describe it mentally.

Step 4: Touching. Now focus on your sense of touch—the feel of your clothes against your skin, the air on your skin, the floor under your feet, the chair under your seat if you're sitting. Describe the sensations to yourself.

Step 5: Smelling and tasting. If there are noticeable odors around you or tastes in your mouth, become aware of them; identify and describe them.

Did you notice that your focus moved away from your mind and its internal chatter about the past or future and into your body and what it was sensing in the present moment? Here's an alternate technique that may work for you.

Variation 2—Progressive Muscle Relaxation

In this process, you bring your attention into the present moment by focusing on your body, and you also begin the relaxation process. You will alternately tense and then relax all the muscle groups in your body beginning with the toes and moving upward.

Tense up the toes of your right foot, hold it, then quickly release them all at once. Notice the resulting feeling of relaxation in those muscles. Continue up your right leg, tensing and relaxing the calf muscles and the thigh muscles. Then do the left leg; next, progress up through the various muscle groups in the trunk of your body, then the right and left arms, and finally the neck and head. Pay special attention to the muscles of the jaw line and between the eyes; both are places where we tend to retain tension. Then let any tensions that's left rise up through an imaginary opening in the crown of your head.

SAO 2.2 Deep Relaxation

Purpose: To experiment with various methods of deep relaxation.

Deep relaxation begins with deep breathing. The goal is to slow down your breathing pattern. So start with one of the breathing processes. Then move into one of the focusing devices. If you have trouble moving out of a focus on mind chatter and into a passive attitude, do a process for getting in the here and now.

Deep breathing—Variation 1. Breathe in through your nostrils, counting slowly as you do so; hold the breath, starting your counting over again; breathe out through your mouth, lips slightly parted, again counting. The actual process: Breathe in 1-2-3-4-5; Hold it 1-2-3-4-5; Breathe out 1-2-3-4-5. Each time you repeat the process, extend the time you take to breathe in, hold it, and breathe out, counting to 6, then to 7, etc. See how long you can extend it.

Deep breathing—Variation 2. Visualize yourself stepping into the top of an escalator. As you breathe slowly in and out, watch yourself descending on the escalator into a deeper and deeper state of relaxation and count: 10-9-8-7-6-5-4-3-2-1.

Deep breathing—Variation 3. Close your eyes, take a deep breath, and enjoy the pleasure of feeling yourself breathe. As you breathe in, say quietly to yourself, *I am.* As you breathe out, say to yourself *relaxed.* Or say, *I am...calm and serene* or *I am...one.*

Deep breathing—Variation 4. Focus all your attention at the tip of your nostrils. Quietly *watch* in your mind's eye the breath flowing in and out past the tip of the nostril. Count from 1 through 10 each time you breathe in and each time you breathe out. Continue counting from 1 through 10 each time you breathe in and out until you're completely relaxed.

Focusing device—Candle flame. Place a lighted candle about a foot in front of you and focus all your attention on the flame. As thoughts float by, notice them, let them go, and gently bring your attention back to the flame. This form of relaxed concentration can help you notice how your thoughts and senses keep grabbing at your awareness. The goal is to free your awareness from its identification with thoughts. We cling to our senses and thoughts because we're so attached to them. While focusing on the candle flame, you start becoming aware of that clinging and attachment and the process of letting go.

Focusing device 2—Centering. Focus all your consciousness into the center of your head. Visualize a point of light about a foot in front of your eyes. Now focus all your attention on the point of light.

Focusing device 3—Grounding. Visualize the center of the earth as a very dense place of rock or metal. Focus all your attention on the center of the earth, and picture a huge iron bar there. Next bring your attention to your spinal cord. Visualize a large cable or cord running from the base of your spine all the way to the center of the earth. Picture a big hook on the other end of the cord; now hook it into the bar at the center of the earth. Feel a slight pull toward the center of the earth and a slight heaviness of the body.

Focusing device 4—Your peaceful place. Think of a place where you usually feel especially serene, relaxed, and happy, such as the beach, the forest, a meadow, or the lake. Picture yourself there. Re-experience in your mind's eye all the sights, sounds, smells, and tastes you experience there. Focus on your sense of touch, too—the sun, water, and air on your skin, the sand, earth or grass under your feet. Bring in as much vivid detail as you can. Get in touch with the positive feelings you experience there—your sense of well-being, confidence, serenity.

SAO 2.3 Visualization

Purpose: To practice envisioning what your want to create in your life.

Step 1: Focus on the here and now and move into a deeply relaxed state by using any combination of processes from SAO 2.

Step 2: Select the visualization that applies to your situation from the ones listed here (or adapt one of them to fit your situation).

Step 3: Use one of the letting-go processes from SAO 4.

Basic Visualization

1. *Create a clear, concise, consistent picture.* In your mind's eye, develop a clear, concise picture of the desired outcome you want, the end result, the state of being, especially the feeling tone within you and flowing between you and others, in this state of having what you want. Don't get into *how* the result will come about, but stay focused on the end result you want.

2. *Charge it with passion.* Allow your passion, your strong desire, to charge that picture with energy.

3. *Become the essence of that picture.* What one word best describes the picture for you? Is it success, abundance, joy, love, peace, elegance, competence, connectedness? *Become* that quality as you focus on your mind's-eye picture.

4. *Persist until it materializes.* Bring up the picture as often as possible, each time seeing the same clear picture—not fuzzy, vague, or changing—each time charging it with passion and desire, and each time freely letting it go. The more attention and focus you give it, the greater the likelihood of success.

Visualization variation 1—Problem resolution.

Relax deeply. Get in touch with your problem situation. If thinking of it or picturing it causes you to feel anxious, focus again on a relaxation technique. Repeat until you're able to picture your problem situation without feeling anxious.

What do you want the end results of this situation to be? How do you want it to be resolved? Picture that happening—in vivid detail, bringing all your senses into play: colors, patterns, textures you see; sounds you hear; and things you touch, smell, and taste. Picture your interactions with the other person(s) involved, focusing on your specific feelings and feelings flowing between you and others; for example, understanding, acceptance, warmth, good will. Focus on the pictures and feelings until you feel quite comfortable and secure with them. Now use a letting-go technique to release them.

Visualization variation 2—Goal achievement.

Follow the process described in variation 1, but instead of focusing on a problem situation, focus on a goal you want to achieve. Picture yourself actually achieving the goal. Include all the people involved in helping you reach the goal; focus on the positive feelings flowing between you and them. Now let go.

Visualization variation 3—Evaluating goals.

You can carry the process used in variation 2 a step further to help you evaluate possible goals. (For example, if you're not sure whether getting a master's degree should be merely one alternate activity for achieving a career goal or a goal in itself, picture yourself having achieved the career goal without the master's degree.) Picture all the consequences of having achieved the goal. How do you feel about each? Is anything missing? What? Would a different goal have led to better results?

Visualization variation 4—Handling stage fright.

Use this process to overcome the *jitters* that accompany any type of presentation you must make before a group. For best results, practice the visualization several times before your presentation. Just before going to sleep the night before the presentation is an especially good time to visualize positive results. Follow the process described in variation 1, but instead of picturing a problem situation, picture yourself making a successful presentation. See yourself focusing on the major thrust of your message and getting it across in a clear, dynamic, persuasive way. See your audience understanding and accepting it. Get in touch with your positive feelings and theirs. Now let go.

SAO 2.4 Letting Go of Needs

Purpose: To experiment with processes for letting go of the need to cling to the results you want, to put your purpose out into the universe, trusting that all will work to your benefit.

Step 1: Move into a state of deep relaxation (SAO 2).

Step 2: Visualize the end results you want (SAO 3).

Step 3: Let go of your pictures of end results by one of the following methods (or devise your own method for putting your goals out into the universe):

Variation 1—Hot air balloon

Picture a beautifully colored hot air balloon with a lovely passenger basket. It's tied to the ground with velvet ropes. Put the picture of your end results into the basket—and the feelings related to the picture. Untie the ropes and watch the balloon float away, up into the sky and away toward the horizon. As it floats out of sight, repeat to yourself, *Let go, let go.*

Variation 2—Space capsule

Follow the process described in Variation 1, substituting a sleek space capsule for the hot air balloon. Picture all the latest technology and equipment for controlling the capsule; put your end results inside the capsule; lock it; watch it blast off and disappear into space.

Variation 3—Bottle at sea.

Follow the process described in Variation 1, substituting a large glass bottle for the hot air balloon. Put your end results inside; place the cork in the bottle top; throw the bottle into the ocean. Watch the tide carry it out to sea; see it disappear toward the horizon.

SAO 2.5 Programming Your Dreams

Purpose: To set up your dreamtime so it will provide you with valuable information for creative projects, new ideas, and problem-solving.

Preliminaries: It's best not to set an alarm but merely tell yourself what time you intend to awaken. Try this on weekends first when you don't feel pressure to be somewhere at a specific time. Learn to instruct your subconscious and to trust this ability.

Keep a pen and note paper beside your bed so you can jot down a few notes about the night's dreams before arising. Dreamtime is wispy and dreams disappear all too easily in the hard light of day.

Step 1: Before you go to sleep, think about a problem you want to resolve, an opportunity you want to tap into, or a question you want to find an answer to. Formulate your desire into a brief question, such as "Should I go to work for ABC Co. or XYZ Co.?" Or "What opportunities am I overlooking?" or "What should I do next?" Hold this question in your mind as you drift off to sleep.

Step 2: When you awaken, lie still, drift, and allow dream memories to come in. Don't reach for your notepad too soon. When a wispy memory comes in, follow it. Allow it to develop as fully as possible. Then jot down the key elements of your dream. Pay special attention to the overall feeling tone of the dream. If you had to define the tone, what would you say? Scary? Romantic? Nurturing? After you've completed your notes, give the dream a title and date it.

SAO 2.6 Interpreting Your Dreams

This process is adapted from one developed by Elaine DeBeauport. You can use your rational and intuitive intelligences to interpret dream messages from your basic brain.

Write your dream on lined paper, skipping every other line. Go back and underline key words and images that stand out as important, that have emotional punch. ("I was speeding along in my car and I was fighting with my best friend.")

Above these underlined words or images, write the characteristics, qualities, or traits that each one represents to you. (For the image "my car," the key trait might be "rugged, speedy, or beat-up." For the image "best friend," it might be "gentle, weird, honest, or serious.")

Write the symbolic story of the dream above the original story, using the phrase "the energy of (trait) within me" when you come to key words or images. (So a line might be, "I was speeding along in "the energy of ruggedness within me," and I was fighting with "the energy of weirdness within me.")

SAO 2.7 Reliving Old Scenarios: Pattern Intervention

Purpose: To break up old habit patterns and to create new ones.

Step 1. Pick a Pattern. What aspect of your life is not working the way you would like? Why? What habit pattern could you be trapped in that contributes to your life not working?

Step 2. Find a Source. What critical incident in your past might be related to this pattern? Take a few moments to do some deep breathing, deep relaxation, and meditation. Focus on the desire to get in touch with the pattern and its source. Allow old pictures and thoughts to come up

Step 3 Relive the Scenario. When you hit on a possible incident, go back in your mind to this old scenario. Who is there? What's their relationship to you? What are you doing? What are they doing? How do you feel?

Shift away from your focus on what your mother, father, or other key person did or did not do in this scenario. Instead, focus on what you probably concluded under those conditions. What did this former you (this child?) probably decide? What did this child deeply need or want in this scenario? Love? Attention? Support? Understanding? Information? Truth?

Step 4. Nurture Your Child. Now, as an adult, you give that child, the former you, what the child needed and wanted. Do it, with as much emotion and drama as possible—make it real and memorable.

Step 5. Re-decide. Now let this child make a new conclusion and decision about the situation. Let these new beliefs, thoughts, feelings, and decisions serve as the basis for your new habit patterns.

Step 6. Make a New Habit. Think of a one-liner that passionately expresses your new belief or decision about life. Plan some new activities or rituals that will focus your mind and re-establish this new belief. What are some ways you plan to act-out your new belief? How will you make sure that you repeat the new behavior often enough to make it a new pattern?

SAO 2.8 Breaking a Link: Pattern Intervention

Purpose: To break up old habit patterns by working with one link in the behavior chain.

The breaking-a-link process includes these steps:

1. What are your major behavior patterns—for better or worse? Identify as many as you can and list them.

2. Which habit patterns are self-empowering? Mark them as ones you want to keep.

3. Which habit patterns are self-sabotaging? Mark them as ones you want to change.

1. Take the first habit pattern that you want to change. Notice how it causes you react to a particular type of situation. List the links in your chain of reaction. ("I see a stranger. I mentally clam up. I try to avoid contact or to get away as soon as possible," etc.)

2. Decide where you want to intervene—at which step, breaking which link?

3. Imagine two or three possible substitute actions, then choose one.

4. Mentally see your old reaction in exaggeration or write about it; then see or write the word STOP when you reach the "breaking link."

5. Remember to practice this new reaction every time you encounter a situation that triggers the old habit pattern. In this way you replace the old link with a new "breaking link."

6. Reward yourself in some small way, in order to support the new link.

SAO 2.9 Reversing the Negative Energy of Self-Sabotaging Thoughts

Purpose: Breaking up old thought patterns in preparation for establishing new ones.

Note. About 80% of the people who seek help with personal problems, when tested, show signs of negative electromagnetic energy flows. You can correct specific emotional states by working with the acupressure points in the etheric energy body to break up old programs and patterns. But first, take a few minutes to work through the following processes for rebalancing general body energy and for rebalancing psychological thought energy within your body. [Adapted from the work of Peter Lambrou and George Pratt, psychologist at Scripps Institute, La Jolla CA]. (Total time—10 to 15 minutes)

Rebalancing General Body Energy

Purpose: To realign the body's electrical polarity (positive-negative electrical energy flow). Do this process before you do the Psychological Thought Energy process.

1. Seated, cross your left ankle over your right ankle (vice versa if more comfortable).

2. Extend both arms straight out in front of you.

3. Cross your right arm over your left arm (vice versa if more comfortable).

4. Rotate the palms of your hands so that they are facing; interlock your fingers

5. Rotate your interlocked hands down toward your stomach

6. Continue rotating inward so that you bring your hands up close to your chest, under your chin. Now you have crossed the center line of your body with your hands, arms, and legs.

7. *Focus on your breathing*: Inhale through your nose while touching tip of tongue to roof of mouth. Exhale through your mouth, resting tongue on floor of mouth.

8. *Focus your thoughts on the concept of balance. Picture in your mind an image that represents balance*.

9. Breathe in this manner for about 2 minutes, holding the "balance image" as consistently as possible.

Rebalancing Psychological Thought Energy

Purpose: To reverse negative electrical energy flows resulting from self-sabotaging thoughts. The electromagnetic energy of though is believed to be the causal agent of emotional disturbance. If you verbalize a statement (thought) at least 3 times, you cannot avoid creating a thought field associated with that statement. The following 12 themes cover virtually all the subconscious self-sabotaging themes. Each thought begins with the positive thought, "I deeply and completely accept myself," followed by a statement of a self-sabotaging theme.

1. All Limiting Patterns

I *deeply and completely accept myself—even with all my problems and limitations*.

Repeat 3 times as you **rub chest spot** with a counter-clockwise circular motion of your first 2 (index and middle) fingertips. Rub firmly and quickly. Find the "sensitive spot" by first locating the indentation between your collar bones, at the center of your body. Bring your fingers down about 3 inches and then to one side about 3 inches until you sense the "sensitive spot" in the chest area, above the heart and below the collar bone.

2. Unsafe Future for Self

I *deeply and completely accept myself—even if it isn't safe for me to get over this problem*.

Repeat 3 times as you **rub the chest spot**.

3. Unsafe Future for Others

I *deeply and completely accept myself—even if it isn't safe for others if I get over this problem*.

Repeat 3 times as you **rub the chest spot**.

4. "I-Can't" Beliefs

I *deeply and completely accept myself—even if it isn't possible for me to get over this problem*.

Repeat 3 times as you **rub the chest spot**

5. Lack of Self-Permission

I *deeply and completely accept myself—even if I will not allow myself to get over this problem*.

Repeat 3 times as you **rub the chest spot**

6. Lack of Will Power

I *deeply and completely accept myself—even if I won't do what's necessary to get over this problem*. Repeat 3 times as you **rub the chest spot.**

7. No Benefit for Self

"I deeply and completely accept myself—*even if getting over this problem will not be good for me*." Repeat 3 times as you **rub the chest spot.**

8. No Benefit for Others

"I deeply and completely accept myself—*even getting over this problem will not be good for others*." Repeat 3 times as you **rub the chest spot.**

9. "Special" Problem or Blockage

"I deeply and completely accept myself—*even if I have a unique block to getting over my problems*." Repeat 3 times as you **rub the chest spot.**

10. Holding onto Problems Now

I *deeply and completely accept myself—even if I want to keep this problem.*

Repeat 3 times as you **rub the chest spot.**

11. Holding On to Problems in the Future

I *deeply and completely accept myself—even if I will continue to have this problem.*

Repeat 3 times as you **tap under your nose**, center line, above your upper lip. Tapping technique: for most spots, such as under the nose, use index and middle (first 2) fingertips. Tap firmly a dozen or so time, whatever feels "right."

12. Not-Deserving Beliefs

I *deeply and completely accept myself—even if I don't deserve to get over this problem*.

Repeat 3 times as **tap under your lower lip**, center line, above your chin

SAO 2.10 Reprogramming Self-Sabotaging Beliefs

Purpose: To focus your attention on beliefs in general and to get in touch with your own self-empowering or self-sabotaging beliefs and to reprogram the negative energy of self-sabotaging beliefs by working with the related acupressure points.

Most people are very vague about what their beliefs are. That's because we formed most of them at a young age, based on the beliefs of our culture, our family members, and our friends—and reinforced by our experiences, as we perceived them and interpreted them.

Self-Empowering Beliefs Checklist

Self-Image Beliefs

1. I like myself
2. I'm a good person
3. I have personal value and worth
4. I deserve good things in life
5. I deserve to be loved
6. I have a good mind
7. I have a good body
8. I want to be creative
9. I want to create a fulfilling life
10. I love myself
11. I deserve to feel safe
12. I deserve to be creative
13. I deserve to create a fulfilling life

Relationship Beliefs

1. I can trust men
2. I can trust women
3. I can release all unnecessary personal baggage
4. I can create and keep healthy personal boundaries and limits
5. I deserve a healthy, loving, mutually satisfying relationship
6. I can easily see the good in others
7. I can give love
8. I can receive love
9. I can attract the right person for a loving relationship
10. I can attract the right people to enrich my life

Prosperity Beliefs

1. It is okay to be wealthy
2. It is okay for me to be wealthy
3. I can easily attract abundance, money
4. Abundance and money are attracted to me
5. I have a healthy relationship with abundance
6. Abundance has a healthy relationship with me
7. I am a money magnet
8. I am an abundance magnet

Self-Confidence Beliefs

1. I'm unlimited
2. I'm intelligent
3. I'm creative
4. I can learn to do most anything and do it well; I learn quickly and easily
5. I have some good talents, skills, and abilities
6. I can fit in under any and all circumstances, if I want to
7. People like to be around me
8. I'm an attractive person
9. I run my life well
10. I can ask the right people for help when I need it
11. I have the resources to solve my own problems and I use them
12. I can be in charge of my own security
13. I can do nurturing and empowering activities for myself
14. I'm an unlimited being who can do anything I set my mind to

Step 1. Self-Empowering Beliefs

To start your wheels turning about your own beliefs, check out the self-empowering beliefs listed here. Put a check mark beside those beliefs that are a part of your belief system.

Step 2. Power Boosts

Review the beliefs that you checked. How do these beliefs empower you? Think of recent instances where these beliefs have boosted your personal power.

Step 3. Self-Sabotaging Beliefs—Power Drains

Review the beliefs that are unchecked—those that you have not adopted. Do you have an opposing belief? Maybe it's one of the Typical Self-Sabotaging Beliefs. For example, if you do not believe "it's okay to be wealthy," what do you believe about you and wealth? That power or money corrupt? How does that belief empower or sabotage you? Can you think of a recent instance when your belief has worked against you? Are you ready to change this belief? Repeat this process for each of the unchecked beliefs.

Typical Self-Sabotaging Beliefs

• I'm not good enough • I'm not capable enough • I'm not lovable/likeable enough • I don't deserve success • It's crucial that everyone like me. • If someone doesn't like me, I must be worthless • I must work and struggle to survive	• Power corrupts • Money corrupts • I must always try my hardest. • I must always be doing something "useful." • I should never have to feel bad • I should never make anyone feel bad • Life is worthless without a partner to share it

Step 4: Reprogram Self-Sabotaging Beliefs

Pick an emotion you want to work on, using the list below, and note the body area you'll rub.

Emotion Body Area to Rub	Emotion Body Area to Rub
Struggle - top of head at crown	*Emotional trauma* - chin
Payoffs - eyebrow by nose	*Guilt and shame* - collar bone points
Anger - eyebrow by temple	*Lack of forgiveness* (resentment, revenge) - under arms
Fear - under eye	*Negative physical results* - wrist
Sadness - under nose	*Remaining reasons* - other wrist

Release the deep roots and causes for emotional blocks by making the following simple physical motions and deeply intending the verbal affirmations, inserting the emotion you're working on and the body area it connects to:

Gently rub your ----(body area for the emotion you selected)-------------- as you say:

I am gently, completely, permanently eliminating all the ---(emotion)---in all the roots and the deepest causes of anything that keeps me from owning all these self-empowering beliefs.

Take a deep breath, and as you release it, say:

I am now releasing all of the --------(emotion)--------.

Stop rubbing, hold the pose with your hand on the point, sit still until you feel a shift.
Wait at least 10 seconds before moving to the next release.

SAO 2.11 What is Your Personal Growth Phase?

Purpose: To gain self-understanding about your focus for personal growth at this time in your life.

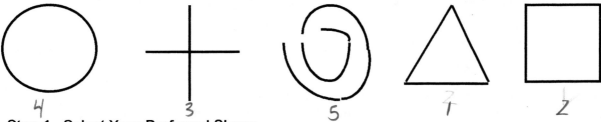

Step 1. Select Your Preferred Shape

Which of the five figures above do you like best? Next best? Number them 1 through 5 in order of preference, with 1 as your favorite figure.

Step 2. Interpret Your Preferences

1 = Where you think you are, the part of the creative process that is now most attractive to you. Your idea of the future and your source of inspiration. However, this symbol represents where you think you are, where you would like to be, not necessarily where your greatest strengths are.

2 = Your strengths, your inherent gifts and innate talents.

3 = Where you are, where your current growth process is centered, the true task you are engaged in now, though you may be overlooking it, holding it in your subconscious mind.

4 = Your motivation, which represents past challenges and situations that have motivated you to change, to do things differently. It may describe a situation you have resolved or moved beyond.

5 = Old, unfinished business, a process you have outgrown or one you resist or dislike. It indicates areas of boredom, patterns of denial, or a part of you that you still disown. You will need to reclaim this process and integrate it later.

Other Ranking Implications. Look carefully at your relative rankings. The figures you ranked as 1 and 5—and conflicts between meanings of the two—reveal clues to your internal struggle. The figure you ranked 3 symbolizes your middle ground, perhaps the key to integrating the conflicting figures, and the clue to your well-being. This represents the skill or quality you need in order to mediate between the past and the present.

Step 3. Interpret the Symbols

Now that you've ranked the symbols, here are the interpretations of each one and what your particular ranking of it means regarding your personal growth journey.

Circle = Wholeness, Unity

- Aspiring to independence and individuation.
- Need most - space, room to find yourself, develop own identity.
- Fear most - entrapment, being caught in a situation that will restrict, restrain you.

1 = desire to be independent, self-sufficient, has your attention, is source of inspiration now

2 = the heroic journey is now effortless for you; your strengths are self-reliance, resourcefulness

3 = individuation is occurring at your core, once you go into process, your creativity flows into all areas of life

4 = a past heroic journey motivated you to become responsible and self-reliant, caused you to move to your present core work in 3.

5 = you may be resisting or denying the process of individuation and have no interest in exploring the heroic journey.

Equi-distant Cross = Relationship

- Coupling, synthesizing, integrating, balancing process.
- Need to connect—to creative project, group, person, self
- Integration and balanced connection

1 = You believe relationship is most important in your life now.

2 = Your strength is in people skills; relationships come easy; achieving balance is natural

3 = The relationship process is occurring deep within; once you go into it, your creativity will be fully available to you.

4 = A past shared journey inspired you to focus on relationships, stimulated you to begin your core work in 3.

5 = You're resisting the need to connect, integrate, balance, or you're not interested in it now.

Spiral = Growth, Evolution, Change

- Process of coming to the same point again and again but at a different level, seeing things in a new light, resulting in a new perspective on things.
- Strong need for variety and change
- Dread of the routine,
- You can easily multitask
- You're creative, ingenious,
- You're good at initiating and following up on projects, but may have difficulty completing them.
- Challenge: to grow at different levels of awareness, to handle change creatively, with integrity.

1 = You believe the growth process is most important for you. You want the flexibility to change.

2 = You handle change easily; flexibility and multitasking are your strengths.

3 = You're deeply into the change process. Honor changes occurring within. Trust the change process and great energy will come into all life areas.

4 = Past challenges to make changes prepared you for breakthrough work in 3.

5 = You're unlikely to show interest in the change process

Triangle = Goals, Dream, Visions

- Self-discovery, revelation
- Intense focus on identifying, pursuing a goal
- Innate gift of vision, a need to follow your dreams
- Worst fear: no dreams to pursue
- Perseverance despite obstacles and delays
- Pitfall: being so focused on the future that you neglect the present

1 = Envisioning process is most significant now; you desire to manifest certain goals, dreams.

2 = You're a visionary; you can create goals and attain them.

3 = The envisioning process is central to your current development. When you go deep into the process, your full powers are accessible. Now is the time to actualize your goals and dreams.

4 = Achieving past visions and goals inspired you to move in the direction of your core work in

5 = You're resisting the process of honoring your dreams, setting goals, and don't desire this now.

Square = Stability

- Solidity, security
- Strong needs: consistency, accountability, completion
- Process: building a foundation
- Strong need for consistency, accountability, completion
- Fear: not accomplishing, wasting efforts
- Value: results, integrity, authenticity, responsibility

1 = Your focus, or source of inspiration, is stability and authenticity. Your chief value is to align your actions with your words.

2 = Your strengths: responsibility, authenticity, full commitment when you give your word, reliability

3 = The process of stability is now occurring at your core, is crucial for you to stabilize, carry out creative projects. You need things to be tangible, productive. You must express your authenticity now. Go fully into the process and untapped creativity is yours.

4 = Past situations calling for responsibility, stability, consistency prepared, motivated you to do the core work in 3.

5 = You may be denying the stability process. The need to be consistent, congruent is not a focus for you now.

SAO 2.12 Finding Power in Your Personal Paradox

Purpose: To understand how your weaknesses are just the other side of the coin of your strengths.

Note: This process is adapted from a process developed by Jerry Fletcher [1997].

Step 1. Find your core personal paradox

- Randomly list your major personal traits, both those you consider a strength and those you consider a weakness—try to list 20 or 30 traits.

- Review the list, placing a plus or minus sign by each to denote strength or weakness.

- Find pairs of traits that are opposites, self-canceling, paradoxical, strength-weakness.

- Work with these pairs for a while until you identify one pair that represents a central conflict that you repeatedly struggle with.

Examples*: do-nothing achiever, ambitious slowpoke, hesitant risk-taker, ruthless helper, spontaneous planner, careless planner, passionate robot, iron butterfly, gentle warrior, velvet jackhammer, cutthroat pussycat, creative imitator, vague analyst, meticulous tolerator, silken sergeant, compulsive free spirit*

Important: Instead of denying, avoiding and rationalizing your weak side, admit it, embrace it, and be willing to work with it in order to discover its constructive aspects.

Step 2. Discover the many facets of your core personal paradox

- Place your core pair of traits in the middle of a blank sheet of paper

- Focusing on the *strength*, list above it other, related traits that are positive expressions of that core strength, becoming more positive as you move upward.

- List below that *strength* other, related traits that are negative expressions of that core trait, becoming more negative as you move downward.

- Focusing on the *weakness*, list above it other, related traits that are positive expressions of that core trait, becoming more positive as you move upward.

- List below that *weakness* other, related traits that are negative expressions of that core trait, becoming more negative as you move downward.

Important: Stick with expressions of the core trait, so that you have a vertical range of expressions of that same trait, from its most positive to its most negative expression.

Examples:

charismatic	enabler	real	visionary	trustworthy	peacemaker
doer	strong	natural	pilot	credible	gentle
lively	take charge	pristine	initiative	genuine	careful
intense	fearless	untouched	instigator	honorable	moderate
passionate	powerful	pragmatic	influencer	principled	nonthreat
enthusiastic	do-er	candid	guide	respectable	careful
enterprising	active	direct	committed	sincere	neutral
Energetic	**Steamroller**	**Crude**	**Leader**	**Honest**	**Wimp**
overwhelming	self-absorbed	thoughtless	self-important	tells all	passive
tiring	domineering	insensitive	weighty	self-	ineffectual
insensitive	oblivious	uncaring	superior	righteous	fearful
steamroller	detached	rough	dominating	better-than	weak
frantic	threatening	gross	frightening	inflexible	coward
				obsessive	

- Discover your *Self-Empowering Strength-Weakness Pair*, the most positive pair of traits that your core pair could lead to.

- Discover your *Self-Sabotage Strength-Weakness Pair*, the most negative pair of traits that your core pair could lead to.

Examples, using above Core Paradoxes:

Core Strength-Weakness	Self-Empowering Pair	Self-Sabotage Pair
Energetic Steamroller	Charismatic Enabler	Frantic Threatener
Crude Leader	Real Visionary	Gross Frightener
Honest Wimp	Trustworthy Peacemaker	Obsessive Coward
Other Examples:		
Do-nothing Achiever	Breakthrough Mapmaker	Carping Workaholic
Self-doubting Overachiever	Prepared Genius	Hopeless Drudge
Conventional Extrovert	Reliable Communicator	Shortsighted Windbag
Driven Indifferent	Focused Pressure-Resister	Obsessive Slob

Step 3. Define a problem situation, apply your Strength-Weakness Pair

- Think of all your options or choices for responding to this situation.

- Describe how this situation affects you—emotionally, psychologically, and practically

- Evaluate your past responses and efforts to deal with this situation. How do these responses reflect your core strength-weakness pair? Have they been primarily from the negative, bottom self-sabotage pairs of traits?

- How could you use your positive, self-empowering pairs of traits—from the top half of your chart—in responding to this problem?

- Write a goal statement with a time target. *I'm going to find a way to . . .* and list the objective outcomes you would like, in terms of what the solution must include but leaving room for various ways the solution might be reached.

- Add a *from. . . to . . .* statement to indicate how the situation will change. For example: *"I'm going to find a way to move from being ignored by my contact to our developing a productive relationship,"* and *"from my getting no attention or action from my contact to our working together for our mutual success and profit."*

Does this goal statement incorporate your Self-Empowering Strength-Weakness Pair of traits? List action steps you can take, what you can do to act out this positive combination of your strength-weakness traits. How can these two conflicting traits work together to empower you to achieve your goal?

- Think of other situations that are creating tension and conflict in your life. Repeat Step 3.
  Suggestions:

- Brainstorm with another person.

- First work on the *weakness* trait of your Core Strength-Weakness Pair, choosing actions to raise it into balance with the strength.

- Look at both core traits, even the weakness in its more positive expressions, moving up toward the Self-Empowering Strength-Weakness Pair.

- Work on embracing both traits, keeping in mind that both traits in your Self-Empowering Strength-Weakness Pair work together to produce more power than the strength can produce by itself.

Notice how you tend to express Self-Empowering pairs of traits in tandem, but swing erratically from side to side when you express the Self-Sabotage pairs of traits.

SAO 2.13 Identifying a Problem Within Your Organization

Purpose: To apply the concepts learned in this chapter to an actual case you have encountered.

1. If you have a job in the workplace, or own your own business, imagine the ideal situation for continuously creating highly effective products, services, or processes that fulfill the mission and goals of your organization and that motivate and satisfy employees to contribute in creative, supportive ways. What would it look like? What kinds of experiences would employees, customers, suppliers, and other stakeholders have?

   If you're a student at a college or university, imagine the ideal situation for student learning, for success, and for career preparation. What would it look like? What kinds of experiences would students have?

2. Comparing the ideal to the existing situation, what are the major differences?

3. Why do you think these differences exist? What problems or opportunities do the differences suggest to you?

4. Now write a one- to two-page case study about this issue. Follow the Guidelines for Writing a Case Study.

Guidelines for Writing a Case Study

Step 1. Gather case information

Your sources can be interviews or your own experience, depending on the assignment. Look for realistic, valid situations and incidents that indicate 1) a problem that needs creative solutions or 2) untapped opportunities that need ideas and actions to create something new or different.

If appropriate, reassure interviewees that real names will not be used in the case. Interview questions that often lead to good case studies are those that ask for success stories, war stories, horror stories, etc.—and those that ask about the differences between current reality and an ideal situation.

Step 2. Write the case problem

Gather and write enough details of the situation to give readers a clear and realistic picture of what the people in the case must deal with. Remember, that the readers are not familiar with any of the characters or facts in the situation, so you must provide this information. For human relations aspects, give information about personalities, quirks, traits, skills, etc. of key persons. When finances enter the picture, spell out necessary details. Give enough information for readers to make an intelligent assessment of the situation.

On the other hand, don't inadvertently state what you think the problems obviously are. It's the reader's job to dig into the case and ferret out the problems and overlooked opportunities. For example, it's inappropriate to state that "Ray is jealous of Susan." Instead, you must tell the reader what Ray says and does in this regard, and let the readers come to their own conclusions. In this way, your case should contain clues to the problems or potential problems that the manager and/or organization need to address. Don't spell out the problems. A common student error is to give some analysis, and even solution, within the case, leaving little work for the reader to do.

In order to make the case realistic, you want to give readers just the information they would have if they were bystanders in this situation—hearing what people way, watching what they do, reading memos, etc. What makes a case realistic is that it's like being on the job and trying to figure out what's really going on and what to do about it.

At the end of the case, ask one or more specific case questions. These are "bottom-line" questions that will guide you and your readers in analyzing the case and developing creative ideas for resolution. These questions might ask what are the key issues, surface problems, root problems, and overlooked opportunities. You might ask what key figures should do. "What actions do you recommend?" "What should ABC Co. do next?" The questions should help readers to focus their attention on the important issues and desired outcomes.

Step 3: Write the Case Key

In a separate section entitled "Case Key" write your analysis of the case—your answers to your own case questions. Tell how you reached your conclusions and recommendations—reveal your thinking process—the how and the why. State which Creative Techniques you used to solve this case, which ones you found most helpful, and why. Relate the case analysis to the relevant chapters in the textbook.

Step 4: Make Copies

If this case is to be analyzed by a class or a work team, make enough copies for everyone. This version should NOT include the Case Key and should be single spaced to save paper. If the case is a project for course credit, turn in 2 copies in double-space format, and include the Case Key.

References

Cairns, J., Overbaugh, J. and Hiller. 1998,"The Origin of Mutants," *Nature* 335, 142-145.

Capra, Fritjof. *The Web of Life*. New York: Anchor Books, 1996.

De Beauport, Elaine. *The Three Faces of Mind*. Wheaton, IL: Quest Books, 1996.

Devlin, B., M. Daniels, and K. Roeder,   "The Heritability of IQ," Nature 333, 1997, 468-471.

Dunne, J.W. *An Experiment with Time* (on dreams). London: Faber and Faber, 1958.

Fletcher, Jerry and Kelle Olwyler. *Paradoxical thinking : how to profit from your contradictions*. San Francisco, CA : Berrett-Koehler Publishers, 1997.

Ingis, B. *Natural and Supernatural* (on dreams). London: Hodder and Stoughton, 1977.

Khenpo, Nyoshui. from *The Tibetan Book of Living and Dying* by Sogyal Rinpoche, edited by Patrick Gaffney and Andrew Harvey. San Francisco, CA : HarperSan Francisco, 1992.

Lambrou, Peter and George Pratt. *Instant Emotional Healing: Acupressure for the Emotions*. New York: Broadway Books, 2000.

Lipton, Bruce H. "Nature, Nurture and the Power of Love," *Journal of Prenatal and Perinatal Psychology and Health*, 13(1), Fall 1998.

Lipton, B.H., Bensch, K.G., and Karasek, M. "Histamine-modulated Transdifferentiation of Dermal Microvascular Endothelial Cells. *Experimental Cell Research*, 279-291, 1992.

Lipton, B.H., Bensch, K.G., and Karasek, M. Microvessel Endothelial Cell Transdifferentiation: Phenotypic Characterization. *Differentiation* 46, 117-133, 1991.

Oschman, James L. *Energy Medicine: The Scientific Basis*. New York: Churchill Livingstone, (Harcourt), 2000.

Pert, Candace. *Molecules of Emotion : Why You Feel the Way You Feel*. NY : Scribner, 1997.

Radin, D. *The Conscious Universe*. San Francisco: Harper, 1997.

Sheldrake, Rupert. *A New Science of Life: The Hypothesis of Formative Causation*, 2d ed. London: Blond and Briggs, 1985.

Sheldrake, Rupert, *Presence of the Past: Morphic Resonance and Habits of Nature*, 1988.

Sheldrake, R., T. McKanna and R. Abraham *The Evolutionary Mind. Santa Cruz*: Trialogue Press, 1998.

Slywotzky et al. *Profit Patterns*. New York: Mercer Management Consulting, 1999.

WSJ. Petzinger, Thomas. "The Front Lines," *Wall Street Journal*, March 12, 1999, B-1.

Books about the Language of Symbols:

Andrews, Ted. *Animal Speak: A Comprehensive Dictionary of Animal, Bird, & Reptile Symbol*ism. St. Paul, MN, 1997.

Bethards, Betty. *The Dream Book: Symbols for Self-Understanding*. Rockport, MA: Element, 1995.

Fontana, David. *The Secret Language of Symbols*. San Francisco: Chronicle Books, 1994.

Meadows, Kenneth. *Rune Power. The Secret Knowledge of the Wise Ones.* Boston: Element Books, 1996.

Tresidder, Jack. *Dictionary of Symbols.* San Francisco: Chronicle Books, 1998.

Chapter 3
Emotional Intelligence
Powers of the Heart

Love as though you've never been hurt. Anonymous

Emotional intelligence is your ability to understand and manage your own feelings—and to understand the feelings of people around you. It's emotional awareness, the ability to know which emotions you're feeling and why. It's realizing the links between what you feel and what you think, do, and say. Managing your emotions doesn't mean denying "negative" feelings or suppressing them. That doesn't work anyway. But you can assess your beliefs, which affect your attitudes, which affect your thoughts. You can begin to notice how one thought triggers another, and how certain types of thinking invariably lead to specific feelings. You can learn to break up self-sabotaging thought trains by focusing on different, equally true thoughts. Thoughts trigger feelings. Change your thinking and you change the feelings you experience.

This intelligence may be naturally related to your astral (or emotional) energy body, which is turn is associated by some with your stomach (solar plexus) chakra that deals with emotions as sensors, boundaries, control, and personal power—as well as the range of emotions in general.

Words to associate with emotional intelligence are: *influencing, being open, feelings, empathy, compassion, people skills, elation, anger, frustration, astral energy body, stomach chakra, yellow, tone mi or E, limbic-mammalian brain.*

Emotional Skills

Emotional intelligence focuses on awareness, expression, and management of your emotions, on your feelings and moods It's tuning into the feelings and moods of other people and therefore is the key to developing your people skills, which are built upon empathy and compassion. Affectional intelligence is one aspect of emotional functioning that focuses on opening your heart, allowing yourself to be affected by people or things, and learning to affect or influence other people, situations, or things. To summarize, here are the key skills you develop when you increase your emotional intelligence:

1. *Self-awareness*—becoming aware of and in touch with your own feelings and emotions

2. *Emotional management*—being able to manage all your emotions and moods without denying or suppressing them.

3. *Empathy for others*—being able to read others' emotions accurately, to put yourself in their place, and to feel compassion toward them

4. *Relationship skills*—being able to build and maintain positive relationships with others

Effect on Creative Intelligence

Emotional intelligence directly boosts your creative intelligence in many ways. First, we know that intuitive messages often come to people through their feelings—such messages often have a feeling component. Therefore, when you're in touch with your feelings, know which emotions you're feeling and why, and are able to link your emotions to what's going on in your life, you boost your intuitive intelligence.

We also know that creativity is tied to certain characteristics, including such emotions as curiosity, playfulness, excitement, and enchantment. You can learn to trigger these types of emotion by assessing and shifting your beliefs, attitudes, and thought processes in ways that support or block such emotions.

Another element of creativity is being able to put yourself inside another person's head, to feel empathy and compassion for others. In fact, author Daniel Goleman [1996] cites this as a key indicator of emotional intelligence. It leads to a better understanding of other people, to sensing their feelings and perspectives and taking an active interest in their concerns. This emotional ability gives you access to valuable information others have to offer.

Your emotional intelligence is associated with your limbic brain, which is located primarily in your skull under your neocortex. It's sometimes called the mammalian brain because this type of brain is common to mammals. On the other hand, in *Molecules of Emotion* researcher Candace Pert [1997] states that she can no longer make a strong distinction between the brain and the body. Virtually every cell of the body is involved in emotional intelligence, with some organs more central than others.

Myths & Realities

Myths about emotions are numerous. They include notions that feelings are too personal and subjective to have any validity in business, science, or academia; that feelings can be categorized as either good or bad; and that women are too emotional and men are relatively unemotional.

Myth 1. Feelings are too subjective be trusted.

Feelings are too subjective, sentimental, polluted by the personal and therefore impure to be trusted. The culture discounts emotional expression and therefore emotional intelligence. Society generally has urged us to suppress our emotions, especially "troublesome ones." We have even classified them into good feelings and bad feelings.

The American culture, especially the sciences and nearly all of academia, has traditionally relied on rational intelligence. Facts that experts in a field can agree upon are considered the content of reality. Situations and things that can be observed and measured are considered "pure," not polluted by personal thinking and feeling. Mainstream American culture has traditionally believed that reality and power reside in the external world of objects and events, and in the sciences that study that world. The inner world of the heart has been viewed as romantic fantasy, escape from the harsh realities of the world, and not a power source for dealing with the real world. The "self" has been seen more as a danger to be suppressed, an obstacle to objectivity to be overcome, than a potential to be fulfilled.

The reality is that research strongly indicates that every rational thought and action is colored by personal emotions [Capra 1996]. Emotional intelligence involves recognizing the important roles that emotions play in our lives and using emotional power to create a better life

If you want to become fully conscious, you must remember that your mouth is linked to your emotional brain. What you say is always colored by your emotions. You can never speak objectively unless you're merely recording verified data. Otherwise, everything you say is emotional or subjective. Your voice tone and quality carry your real emotional message. Emotion is mixed in with the mental message.

You cannot see objectively either. Visual impulses must pass through your emotional brain. Remember, the brain is an energy system, and emotions are vibratory states in continuous flux. They are not descriptions of a fixed reality.

Myth 2. Emotions are either positive or negative, good or bad.

It's true that normal people would prefer to feel ecstasy rather than terror. However, emotional intelligence is based on being willing to experience any and all emotions that come up, to receive the information that those emotions can offer, and to be willing to release them once the event that triggered them is over. When you negatively label emotions, such as sadness or anger, you frighten yourself away from experiencing them. You deny them, suppress them, rationalize them and don't get the information and the lessons they can offer. Suppressed emotions don't "go away," but store themselves in your cells to simmer, fester, and pop out uncontrollably later. But to fully feel these emotions until you grasp what they want to tell you is always a positive, life-giving experience. In fact, it may be urgently necessary.

You need to gain for your feelings the freedom you now grant your thoughts. To be healthy, you must celebrate all your emotions as positive, constructive forces in your life. You must feel your emotions fully without necessarily acting them out. You need the same inner space for practicing your feeling ability that you have for practicing your thinking ability.

Myth 3. Men and women experience emotions differently.

We stereotype emotional women as moody and emotional men as weak. We discount people who hug "too much, cry too easily," or in other ways are "too emotional." On the other hand, we admire people who are thoughtful and rarely call anyone "too thoughtful."

It's true that men and women have some physical differences that involve emotions. Jo Durden-Smith, author of *Sex and the Brain* [1993], says, *Scientists have found more connecting nerve fibers between the two hemispheres in women's brains than in men's.*" She says this could be why women are often better at skills that involve both hemispheres, such as reading, which requires the ability to translate visual symbols (right brain) into language (left brain). This may also explain why men have more difficulty talking (left brain) about their emotions (right brain), and why women have greater peripheral awareness and pay more attention to detail. Studies done in business settings reveal that men and women are equally efficient at recalling the verbal content of a conversation, but women are much better at remembering the person's physical appearance and the features of the room they were in. Women also recall more emotional information and personal impressions then men. Durden-Smith notes that men tend to say that emotional information is irrelevant, but this is usually not so; for example, "*If a client seems unhappy, an astute businessperson ought to find out why.*" All these skills are believed to contribute to intuitive insights, and the ability to connect rational and emotional information in itself plays a key role.

On the other hand, studies indicate that most male-female emotional differences are actually cultural stereotypes; for example, the belief that women are more emotional in general than men. Some studies indicate that boy infants are actually more emotional than girl infants, but that begins to change quickly. Parent figures communicate their beliefs and taboos about boys being strong, brave, and courageous, not showing fear or sadness, and not crying. By the time boys start to school, their emotional profile has dramatically changed [Pollack 1998].

How Emotional Intelligence Works

Can you use your emotions consciously and skillfully to cope with life? Emotions contain information, just as certainly as a thought, image, or action does. You can *read* the information of your feelings instead of just experiencing them or trying to avoid them. Emotional intelligence is a process of learning how to go into your feelings, learn from them, express them in appropriate ways, and shift out of them. Emotional intelligence enables you to live the truth of your entire mind-body system rather than only the selective process of your rational mind.

To experience emotional growth, you must be willing to do the following: Feel continuously and consciously, talking about feelings when it fits. Express your feelings in many ways. Listen to others talk about their feelings without needing to take responsibility for what they feel. Keep allowing more emotional range as you grow—expressing more intimate feelings, having more freedom to feel and to express, enjoying more expansive feelings.

Emotions Can Spark Your Creative Intelligence

True intelligence is all about functioning effectively in the world. This requires skills and awarenesses in building relationship, connectedness, and community. It calls into play feelings, intuition, and imagination. Objectivity is only one aspect of intelligence—whether it's applied to science, business, academia, or personal life. To be truly intelligent, you must respect otherness, which in turn is based on love, intimacy, and co-creation of reality. It's all about relationships—connectedness.

When you speak from your creative intelligence, you speak from your curiosity or hope, your empathy or passion, not from your fear (of being wrong, not good enough, rejected, lonely, cut off). You speak to the creative intelligence of the other, especially to the heart. Give in to your yearning for connectedness to others, to the Web of Life. Turn inward into the spiral of growth. Remember the be-do-have creation cycle. You can *have* fear without *being* fear. What you can *be* is someone yearning for connectedness, someone willing to take action anyway, and you can speak of fear from that place of *being*.

Emotional-Affectional Intelligence: Influencing

Affectional intelligence is the aspect of emotional intelligence that helps you to enter into your emotions. It's all about influencing and being influenced. You can use your higher intelligences, such as rational or intuitive, to select what you *wish* to be affected by. In this way you consciously use the affectional process.

You are often deeply affected by what you can do and by what you believe you cannot do. The expansive emotions that come with "*I can*" include elation, enthusiasm, joy, and satisfaction. The contracting emotions that come with "*I can't*" include sadness and anger. Emotional intelligence is the process that enables you to live both the highs and the lows of all your emotions in a constructive way.

By realizing that you can *choose* how to perceive the world and respond to it—choose how you'll allow it to affect you, to change you—you create your own reality, your own world. Your interactions with your environment are cognitive interactions, so the process of living itself is a process of cognition. "*To live is to know*." This new view of cognition (knowing, thought) involves the entire process of life—including perception, emotion, and behavior. What we perceive is conditioned largely by our conceptual framework and our cultural background.

Each organism does not bring forth *the* world but *a* world, one that's always dependent on the organism's structure. Since organisms within a species have similar structures, they bring forth similar worlds. Humans share an abstract world of language and thought, and through this we bring forth a consensus reality. There *is* a material world, but it does not have any predetermined features. Things exist, but they're dependent on the process of cognition. We each make our own map of the material world "out there," and the mapmaking itself brings forth the features of the territory.

Your capacity to be affected by people and situations is a conscious choice, and to be deeply affected can lead you into the motivational feelings of wanting and desire, as well as all the emotions, from sadness and anger to joy and love. Affection is the result of being affected and can lead you into the full range of feelings.

You must be selective in what you allow to affect you deeply, or you'll be in continuous crisis. You can also select the times for letting yourself be deeply affected by the difficult emotions. Your rational and intuitive ability to select wisely is crucial.

Do you close the door on affection, love, and passion because you've had bitter experiences when you opened it in the past? You rational mind may be saying, "never again, no way, it's not worth it." Do you need to learn *how* to be affected? How to love, with all its implications?

Affection obviously impacts your sexual relationships. Studies indicate that you cannot easily repress your sexuality without also limiting and repressing your capacity to feel—and your capacity to create. Conversely, if you limit your capacity to feel, you also limit your capacity to be sexual. In fact when you restrict, inhibit, or contract your feelings, you affect all the organs of your body. Sexuality is more than just biological; it's also emotional and physical and sets off a tremendous energy that can dominate all your intelligences.

Emotional Intelligence Brings Unique Information

Emotions carry information that emerges from your inner life—as well as your external world. It brings you information that may be unavailable in any other form. Are you listening to these emotions or suppressing them? If you suppress them, you lose the signals of your reactions to the world, very important information!

Repression of emotional information over time can lead to internal violence (illness) as well as violence (mental or physical) toward others. If you ignore your emotions, that emotional energy runs free at the subconscious level to sabotage your projects. You refuse to feel your frustration and to find out what's really going on. You may find yourself saying, "I'm not interested any more," or "I don't feel like it." The information is within you. Your reactions are already registered, and they provoke emotions in order not to be ignored. Emotions exist as internal signals of your reaction to a situation in the world. They provide a personal text that is different from your physical or mental reactions to a situation.

Expansive feelings, as they deepen, yield warmth and energy in your body. Both expansive and contracting feelings can give you reams of information, insights, images, thoughts, and deep clues to your actions, patterns, and routines. If you can go into the feelings and open up to their messages, you can begin to notice your deepest patterns of behavior, learn from them, and become aware of wider aspects of yourself. Fully feeling your feelings gives you the freedom to develop empathy for yourself and others. You can feel into all the emotions of life itself. Emotional intelligence shows you how to be involved in all your emotions. Don't judge emotions before feeling them. Respectfully travel through all information that presents itself to you.

Emotional Intelligence Frees You to Express Yourself

You have many options for expressing yourself, and for responding to other people's emotional expression, as pointed out in the section on options. The main point here is to allow yourself and others the freedom to feel the full range of emotions, though not necessarily to act them out in hurtful ways.

Sadness and Tears

When you experience sadness, ask yourself, "why am I sad?" Pay attention by entering and holding with this feeling until you grasp the information. It may seem negative, but it becomes positive when you treat it as information.

If sadness includes the desire to cry, let yourself cry. If you're in a business culture where emotional expression is taboo, make some excuse to get away briefly so you can have a good cry. When a friend needs to cry, encourage him or her to do so. Teaching yourself or others *not* to cry is teaching contraction, restriction, and stress buildup. Crying is the natural expression of the heart, and tears are a language of the emotional brain. Honor them as a sign of human sensitivity. See them as a sign of emotional intelligence, not weakness. Tears are a normal reaction when you're deeply touched, whether by sadness or by beauty, joy, appreciation, love, or many other emotional tones. They are an emotional and physical release from tension and stress.

Sadness may be related to grief, which is one of the deepest feelings you need to work with. Once you've processed it, you'll have a greater capacity for feeling the compassion you need in order to build deep relationships. Compassion expresses the power of love—as well as that utterly vulnerable, endlessly touching inner child that you need to work with.

Anger

When you experience anger, remember that it too has a positive side. It can rouse you from boredom or complacency. It can make you aware of what really matters to you—what you fear losing or not getting—so much so that you get really riled

When you're struggling between "I can" and "I can't," you often feel frustration or anger. You can deny this feeling and shove it down inside until you become sick, or you can turn it outward into shouting or physical action. Those are the extremes but there are many other options, as discussed later. Remember, all the feelings that begin as troubling, contracting experiences can evolve into constructive, expansive experiences once they're processed. For example,

- Rage may become the energy to start a creative new project or a new organization.

- Fear may develop into the courage that helps fight complacency, dullness, or prejudice—first within yourself and then in your team or organization.

You may become more aware of when you and others are angry by recognizing some of the ways people express anger, which include:

Rational mode: arguing, jumping to conclusions, rationalizing, justifying, disapproving backed up with a long list of reasons.

Intuitive mode: becoming disoriented and chaotic, using absolutes ("you always . . I never"), expressing incomplete thoughts, generalizing ("people usually . . "), evading.

Internal mode: resentment, sadness, silence, withdrawal, depression, internal explosions, susceptibility, physical symptoms, illness

Physical mode: becoming physically unbalanced, banging into things, having accidents, intensifying such habits as smoking, drinking, repetitive speech, either turning to groups or gangs or turning away to isolation.

Dealing with another person's anger can be stressful. Keep in mind that you do not have to take responsibility for that anger. The person has many options for viewing each situation and responding to it and that is his or her responsibility. If you believe you have been unfair or hurtful, that's your responsibility to correct and work out. If not, keep in mind that the person would be angry with anyone who represented what you do in this moment—it's not about you personally. You may want to express exactly what you can and can't do, focusing more on the can-do, perhaps repeating this in various ways until the person calms down.

Emotional Intelligence Prevents Violence

Your feelings provide a safeguard for runaway thoughts or actions of the other brain systems. One of your deepest resources is the sensing, reflecting, humanizing capacity of your emotional brain, which reflects to you the human dimensions of life. Feeling allows you to access this information. It helps you to see how you ignore yourself, hurt yourself, disrespect yourself, and this self-awareness helps you to see how you do that with others.

If you constantly block your feelings, you'll eventually experience numbness, boredom, a tendency to blame others for your boredom, and finally withdrawal. Before people become violent, they go through an emotional process of not respecting the other person, moving away, categorizing the other, judging, refusing to be affected by the other. If you want to avoid becoming emotionally or physically violent with others, you must be able to access all the contracting feelings connected to this withdrawal process. You need this awareness to motivate yourself to change it to an expansive process that begins with self-respect and respect for the other.

Consciously decide to allow yourself to be affected—perhaps first by a warm gesture, a beautiful flower, a little bird, a glowing rainbow or magnificent sunset, a lyrical melody. Move on to being affected by a friend's heartache, then a community crisis, and even a major national problem. Allow yourself to fully feel your feelings. Learn to read them for information about what's going on with you moment by moment. As you develop empathy for yourself and respect for the you that has a wide range of experiences, thoughts, and feelings, gradually you no longer need to avoid your feelings.

Emotional Intelligence Can Heal Old Wounds

Emotions remain in the long-term memory and in the subconscious for as long as you live. Any time you want, you have the freedom to access and work with emotions you experienced in the past. Perhaps you made decisions in childhood, based on certain emotions, decisions that block or limit you in your current life. For example, you may transfer old fear to current situations. When you're confronted in daily life with people, ideas, or situations that you fear, you tend to avoid them, which in turn blocks your energy. These people, ideas, and situations are part of the constant flow of energy around you—a part that you block off. You use huge amounts of energy just to keep holding onto your lack of awareness. It takes great energy to refuse to feel or be affected, to refuse to confront the person, idea, or situation. You can get your energy back by facing things now and becoming aware of what you are refusing to let affect you.

How can you regain the energy you blocked off in the past? Ask yourself, "Where did I leave my energy? When in the past was I unwilling to be affected by a person, idea, or event?" When you want to recall a situation from your past in order to live it again emotionally, visualize the situation, make it larger in your mind, let it surround you, and allow yourself to be affected. Find the situation you avoided, relive it in your mind, and discover what you need in order to cope with it directly. You can look again at those decisions, give your child-self what it needs to experience different emotions, and reach new decisions about life. Get whatever new information arises from the experience. What new, better decision does it suggest now?

You can keep changing earlier life decisions until you achieve the quality of life you want. The goal is to be willing to face any and every thing you have ever experienced—to face anything you've been avoiding that therefore is blocking your energy flow—to face all the important issues, eventually, as you're ready and able to deal with each problematic experience. But you don't want to do it all at once, of course. Take it step by step.

Emotional Intelligence Sparks Creativity

Creativity occurs when you're experiencing expansive emotions. You literally expand the space within and around you, opening up and allowing new thoughts and emotions to come in. Your emotional brain provides you with constant signals. If you pay attention to them, you'll figure out how to create more of the life you want—and to do it more imaginatively. You'll open up to more possibilities and probabilities. If you don't pay attention to emotional signals, however, they will increase their effect on your body until they get your attention—until they make you really tired or in pain or ill. Why don't you always pay attention to the little glimmers and flashes of emotional signals? Why would you choose to ignore your feelings?

Do you have difficulty admitting that you feel sadness, anger, depression? That's not unusual because in our culture, people often react poorly when you express these emotions. Therefore, many people try to deny them and ignore them. But when you restrict your feelings, you restrict the organs of your body, which over time leads to weakness, to stress. When you are stressed, you're contracted and unwilling or unable to expand. Your organs remain in a contracted condition that later becomes a constricted condition. They don't have permission to slow down, to contract into sadness or frustration or anger. They're stuck in contraction, stuck in stress.

As situations in your life become tougher, it becomes more difficult to repress emotions. When you finally burst out in anger and hostility, you're out of control. Anger becomes like a shock wave to your system.

But remember, feelings are the exercise of the organs, just as walking is exercise for the muscles. Practice feeling consciously every day. Relive the great emotions of confidence and love—wonder, awe, gratitude, and forgiveness. Meditate and notice any contracting feelings, such as sadness or anger, that come up. Be willing to process them, using the processes discussed later in this chapter.

When you experience fear, tension, or anxiety, you restrict and contract your breathing. When you experience love and joy, you relax and expand your breathing. If you want to live the full range of emotions, pay attention to your breathing. Learn to breath fully and deeply. This helps you to relax, the first step to achieving a meditative state. Boosting your emotional intelligence in all these ways enables you to spend more time in expansive emotions, which open you up to new, creative ideas.

The Mind-Body Nature of Emotions

Thinking and feeling, and knowing, take place throughout your body, in every organ and cell. Scientists now know that your heart has many brain cells that are in turn connected to your head brain. Candace Pert [1997], says, "White blood cells are bits of the brain floating around in the body. This means that knowing is a phenomenon that expands throughout the body. So is feeling"

Molecules of Emotion

Cellular knowing and feeling operate through an intricate chemical network of *peptides*, a network that integrates your mental, emotional, and biological activities. Peptides are the biochemical (physical) form of emotions. Most peptides, if not all, alter emotional states and behavior. Each peptide may evoke a unique emotional "tone" or vibration. The group of about sixty peptides may constitute a universal biochemical language of emotions.

The limbic system of your brain is highly enriched with peptides, but it's not the only part of the body where peptide receptors are concentrated. The entire intestine is lined with peptide receptors and may explain "gut feelings," experiencing your emotions in your gut. All sensory perceptions, all thoughts, and all bodily functions involve peptides. The nodal points of the central nervous system, which connect the sensory organs with the brain, are rich in peptide receptors that filter and prioritize sensory perceptions. All your perceptions and thoughts are therefore colored by emotions.

Endorphins and other chemicals are found in the brain, immune system, endocrine system, and throughout the body. These molecules are released from one place, diffuse all over the body, and tickle the receptors on the surface of every cell in your body. These neuro-peptides, brain chemicals, and their receptors on your cell surfaces are the molecules of emotion. These brain chemicals can be described by locating their effect on a scale between quietness and excitement. It is a two-way communication system between various body systems.

If you're depressed and you refuse to shift to "I-can" thinking and other active, self-empowering thought patterns, you're depriving your brain and body of natural excitants. If you're continually frustrated and refuse to focus on thought patterns that calm you, you're depriving your body of the quiescent state that natural chemicals like endorphins provide.

You don't need artificial mood-altering drugs when you know how to enter into emotional states, how to make use of them without harming yourself or others, and then how to shift out of them. You can become skilled in releasing the natural chemicals you need and want. Emotional intelligence allows you to reclaim your power by experiencing all of your emotions in order to access your natural brain chemicals, to govern, protect, and exercise the organs of your body, and to receive information for creating the life you want.

Creative Intelligence of the Heart Brain

Scientists are finding that when people use certain exercises for imagining their feelings within their hearts, they're able to break out of old emotional patterns faster and more directly than when they use traditional mind or brain imagery. The heart is a storehouse of emotional memories and energy patterns that make us who we are as individuals. In fact, the five small waves that make up your electrical heart signal create a unique energy pattern as personal as your fingerprint. Research conducted by the Institute of HeartMath and reported in the *American Journal of Cardiology* indicates that your heart plays a large, independent role in drafting your emotional blueprints. Your heart's electrical signals shape the way your brain thinks about certain kinds of events, and your heart itself may be able to "remember" emotional experiences.

That's because your heart has its own brain—a network of neurons identical to many of the kinds of neurons and neural networks that your brain has. Your heart brain and head brain are connected by the "vagus nerve" made up of thousands of nerve fibers that continually flash messages between your heart and head brains. You don't think and remember only in your head. Memories are now seen as patterns of energy that groups of neurons can store in various parts of your body.

Creative Intelligence of the Heart

Your heart has a unique way of making its memories and ideas felt: it's your body's largest rhythmic generator, sending electromagnetic signals up to 5,000 times stronger than those from your head. That strong signal, combined with the surges of blood your heart sends throughout your circulatory system, can either harmonize or overpower and disrupt the weaker rhythms and currents sent by your brain and other organs. Your changing heart rhythms affect your brain's ability to process information, including

- problem solving

- decision making

- creativity

- feelings

Your heart rhythm is the product of two types of hormones produced by your nervous system—adrenaline that revs you up and tranquilizers that relax you. Your heart also makes its own unique "balance hormone" that makes you feel serene and peaceful.

When your body and mind are relaxed, your heart beats in an easy, consistent (coherent) rhythm. Over time, those relaxed heart pulses "entrain" the weaker brain and body signals so they throb in sync with the heartbeat. *This is the "flow state" of creative intelligence.*

Stress (even positive stress excitement) disrupts the flow state. It causes the heart to beat in erratic rhythms, which in turn causes bioelectric "incoherence." The heart beats fitfully, making synchronization among the body's organs and systems impossible. Prolonged incoherence leads to

- decreased brain functioning, including creativity, empathy, and rational thought

- heart disease, impaired immunity, rapid aging, cancer, destruction of brain cells, early death

Unmanaged tension underlies up to 90 percent of all visits to doctor's offices. We adapt to unmanaged stress all too easily. It becomes a subconscious process, but we pay a price.

Stress Damage Reversal

A powerful way to prevent or reverse this stress-damage process is to use emotional intelligence. Adopt beliefs, attitudes, decisions, and thought patterns that trigger the expansive emotions—especially the feelings of *forgiveness, appreciation, gratitude, and love.*

Prolonged and frequent experience of these love-based emotions reverses the stress-damage process and establishes bioelectrical coherence. The brain's electrical activity is brought into entrainment with heart rhythms. As you experience expansive feelings, the changed information flow from the heart to the brain can modify brain function.

A peaceful heart helps you think more clearly and creatively. When you focus on the image of love and appreciation in your heart center, you increase the likelihood that all kinds of body cells become synchronized around your heart's electrical signal. You gain power—creative, emotional, physical, and spiritual power. Heart-centered techniques can help you find within yourself new feelings of peace, empathy, and intuition that in turn result in greater personal creativity and productivity. See the Self-Awareness Opportunity, Heartfelt Stress Reduction.

Heart signals impact your affectional intelligence—how you affect others and how they affect you. That's because your heart signal can entrain other persons' electrical brain patterns and alter their moods, making them more tranquil or tense. And their heart signals can have the same effect on you.

When two people meet, who will have the most impact? That depends on which of you is the most aware and focused. If you're feeling "higher" than your friend, and you're also more focused than he is, he'll become more expansive during the meeting. On the other hand, if he's feeling "lower" than you, and he's also more focused than you are, then you'll become more contracting during the meeting. The impact may be fairly equal—where you're feeling a little more expansive than he, and the two of you have about the same degree of focus. When this happens, you leave the meeting feeling a little less "up," and he leaves feeling a little less "down."

Heart signals probably impact your basic intelligence as well. For example, when you take an instant dislike to someone, it's probably due at least in part to clashing heart rhythms. And love may be literally a matter of two hearts beating in harmony.

How to Boost Your Emotional Intelligence

The steps to emotional intelligence are simple but often difficult in practice. And practice is exactly what you need to boost this intelligence, which is so important for breaking through creative blocks and for opening up to intuitive messages about creative projects.

1. Recognize that emotions have a physiological basis within your brain and every cell of your body, as discussed in the previous section.

2. Give emotions equal status with rational thoughts, visual images, and intuition

3. Move beyond gender stereotypes about women being "too emotional" and "real men" not being emotional.

4. Stop, slow down, feel your feelings—do feeling meditations. Your feelings are states of consciousness. Learn to stay in your inner world without interference. Learning to feel is learning to travel in your inner world.

5. Process your emotions, especially those that you tend to avoid or suppress.

6. Feel and express your emotions when you want to, how you want to—realizing your many options for viewing events, thinking about them, and expressing your feelings about them.

Booster 1. Overcome Gender Stereotypes

Gender stereotypes can block both women and men from fully developing their emotional intelligence. The stereotypes center on beliefs that men are not, or should not, be very emotional and that women are more emotional, and that's okay as long as they don't try to become leaders of organizations.

Beliefs about raising boys and girls lead to some emotional problems for men. For example, girls typically get payoffs of sympathy or approval when they cry, show fear, express sadness or other tender feelings, show sympathy for others, and nurture others. Boys usually get disapproval or even punishment for such behavior. In our culture, little boys are trained to be *real men* from an early age through such messages as

- *Big boys don't cry.*
- *Big boys are brave and strong.*
- *Keep a stiff upper lip.*
- *Don't be a chicken.*

Little boys are usually reprimanded or belittled when they cry, show sadness, or express fear. The result is that men often repress and deny most of their emotions and eventually become numb to them. But most boys usually receive approval, admiration, or at least acceptance when they express dominance and anger in actions ranging from assertion to aggression. Such *masculine* expressions of emotion by girls, however, usually meet with disapproval or rejection.

Recognize Male-Female Emotional Patterns

These different socialization patterns set the stage for adult behavior. As they've grown up, most women have stayed in touch with their feelings and have developed the ability to express their emotions. However, they tend to be significantly less assertive than men. In contrast, most men have a healthy dose of assertiveness and some have an unhealthy dose of aggressiveness. But most men in general are significantly less aware of their feelings. They're therefore less able to verbalize them and act on them.

In the male-dominated business world, therefore, it is generally acceptable to express anger or aggression within certain limits. However, a display of tears or fear signals you can't handle the game; that is, you can't handle real responsibility on the line where key decisions are made and where the real power is wielded. It's especially important to manage fear because some political game players can sniff out the nonverbal signs of fear like bloodhounds, and they'll quickly move in for the kill if it suits their purposes. Others will simply assume that you're too weak to handle a leadership role. Obviously, women are at a real disadvantage here. They can be blocked professionally by these stereotypes:

- *Women are too emotional to be leaders. They go to pieces in a crisis*

  (overlooking the fact that nearly all mothers get their children through the numerous crises growing up entails without *going to pieces*.)

- *You can't afford to put someone in top management who might burst into tears in the crunch.*

- *Women are just too flighty to handle a high-level leadership role.*

- *Women don't roll with the punches like men do.*

- *A man can keep problems in perspective better than a woman.*

Manage the Differences

As a matter of fact, women *do* report being in positive moods and in negative moods about twice as often as men, according to author Ed Diener's research [1991], which would indicate that women experience feelings more intensely. However, it does not follow that women are helpless victims of their feelings or must somehow act out all their feelings. Nor does it follow that men cannot begin to get in touch with the full range of their feelings and experience them more intensely. Remember, infant boys actually exhibit more emotion than infant girls.

Openness to feelings is essential to openness to intuitive information. Therefore, women are known to be more emotional and more intuitive than men, on average. Both of these states are normally governed by the right-brain, while rational thought and action are governed by the left-brain. Language, or verbal ability, is a rational, left-brain activity in which women excel, however. Women are obviously not lacking in left-brain abilities, but because their traditional roles centered on nurturing others, they focused almost exclusively on the language area, neglecting the strategic, tactical, mechanical and mathematical areas.

In recent decades, careers using both right-brain and left-brain abilities have opened up to women. Many women have acquired the business and professional skills to move into these fields—and many have excelled in them.

Integrate Emotional and Rational Intelligences

Emotionally intelligent people on average appear to experience deeper, richer, and more expressive emotional lives, according to author Daniel Goleman's research [1995]. The traits of playfulness, sensuality, and spontaneity correlate with higher intuitive ability. In addition, it's significantly easier to develop rational abilities and intellectual intelligence than to develop emotional intelligence and intuition. To live up to your potential, honor and respect all your abilities—especially your emotional intelligence. Learn to express it appropriately in business and professional settings. Help others to understand and respect this type of intelligence.

Booster 2. Recognize Contracting and Expansive Feelings

A powerful concept that can help you manage your emotions is the classification of emotions generally into two basic types:

1. the stressful, contracting emotions that are considered fear-based

2. the self-empowering, expansive emotions that are considered love-based

We all intuitively understand the terms "contracting" and "expanding" because we experience them daily in our emotional life. Our language reinforces this concept with such contracting terms as *uptight, little black cloud, don't be so heavy, play the heavy, got the blues.* And such expansive terms as *sunny, walking on air, being on Cloud 9, lighten up.*

Your feelings continually expand or contract your heart. Are you able to feel your emotions, allow the expansive ones, and guide them in a continuous process through the inevitable contractions on to the expansions? You cannot stay in any one state all the time. What goes up must come down and vice versa. But you can learn to ride the waves and avoid being stuck or drowned. Live the contracting emotional energies as well as the expansive ones, and learn that they can inform and enrich your life.

Figure 3.1 is a symbolic picture of how we look and feel when we're experiencing these two types of emotions. Table 3.1 for a verbal picture of typical emotions in each category

Figure 3.1 Contracting and Expansive Feelings

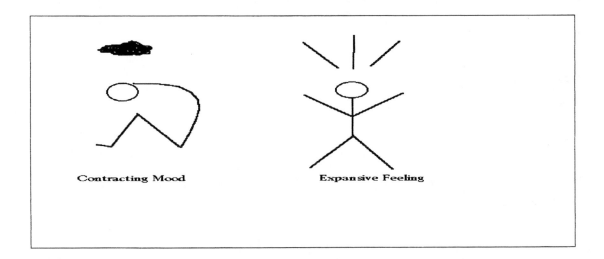

Contracting Mood   Expansive Feeling

Identify Your Contracting Feelings

Think about the feelings you associate with the stress in your life. Which emotions come to mind? Many people mention anger, embarrassment, resentment, frustration—feelings listed as contracting emotions in the Map of Emotions. When you experience these stressful emotions, how do you respond? Do you focus within on stressful thoughts (of the type that preceded the stressful emotion?). Do you clam up, close up, even withdraw? These feelings are low-energy states that act as energy drains and cause people to avoid you—or to be attracted to you for the wrong reasons

The Map of Emotions shows the milder forms of contracting emotions at the top of each column, moving toward generally more intense feelings at the bottom. Key bottom-line contracting emotions are highlighted at the bottom of each column. The underlying, bottom-line emotion is fear, the realm of your negative ego. But how fear be related to anger or rage? You'll work with such questions later as you bring root fears out of the shadows. For now, consider the research finding that anger, and in fact all the contracting emotions, involve some type of fear—fear of losing something you value or fear of not getting something you want

Figure 3.1 Map of Emotions

Expansive Emotions	*compassion* forgiveness empathy commitment devotion affection caring appreciation respect acceptance admiration infatuation tolerance connection self-acceptance	*passion* enthusiasm excitement eagerness desire optimism mindfulness openness honesty sincerity determination perseverance yearning nostalgia self-confidence	*wonder* awe bliss beauty gratitude imagination curiosity mirth, fun playfulness interest amusement innocence surprise thoughtfulness self-awareness	*LOVE* joy ecstasy happiness enjoyment peace serenity certainty hope calmness satisfaction solitude comfort relief self-love
Contracting Emotions, Moods	annoyance impatience blame resentment frustration hostility stubbornness anger rage hatred powerlessness bitterness regret sadness guilt *shame*	ego-pride judgment dislike pity (other) disgust contempt revulsion condemnation arrogance defensiveness doubt worry anxiety resignation exhaustion *depression*	somberness envy jealousy hatred hurt withdrawal shock loss despair humiliation paranoia hopelessness apathy victim, martyr rejection *loneliness*	distraction mischievousness confusion caution vulnerability embarrassment shyness self-pity suffering remorse victim dread desperation hysteria terror *FEAR*

Your tendency will probably be to judge the contracting emotions as bad or negative and the expansive ones as good or positive. Avoid that tendency, simply because it leads to denying your contracting emotions. Clearly, you normally enjoy the expansive emotions the most—and they are the typical creativity triggers—but you get valuable information from the entire range of emotions. That's how you learn and become more intelligent. And obviously, you sometimes need to experience fear, anger, and similar emotions in order to avoid disaster. Likewise, when you've suffered a significant loss, you need to feel the pain and sadness that goes with that. You need to go through a normal grief process. The more open you are to experiencing the contracting emotions that want to come up, the more quickly you'll be able to move fully into them, through them, and out the other side.

Once you become aware of contracting feelings, you're in a position to process them, so you can use that emotional energy to achieve what you want to create in your life. You may get some ideas for identifying or labeling your feelings by studying the Map of Emotions. Your goals are:

- to process contracting, low-energy, stressful feelings before they settle in and build into a mood
- if a mood does gain hold, to process the feelings it contains
- to allow yourself to spend as much time as possible in the self-empowering, high-energy *expansive* feelings.

Some people say they fear evil, which is difficult to deal with because it's such a vague, nebulous force. Evil is lack of respect for others and the acting-out of that disrespect. The more blatant and extreme the lack of respect, the greater the evil. It is always connected to a lack of self-respect. Let's make it personal. Wherever you harbor a pocket of self-hate, you'll express it as hatred for others. Self-hate is basically a lack of self-respect and is often expressed as lack of respect for others, who serve as a sort of scapegoat for you. Despising them makes you feel better, superior. This is negative ego in action. The cure is to root out your pockets of self-hate so you can build respect for yourself as a human being. The process helps you to feel empathy and compassion for others in the place of dislike or disgust or hatred. The process can lead to feelings of acceptance and ultimately unconditional love.

When you don't process contracting emotions, they don't go away. Instead they build up within your mind and body. If you hide them away securely enough, they'll stay hidden until they express themselves as illness. If you're lucky, they'll first express themselves as an outburst or a mood. As you know, moods can last hours, days, even years. You walk around with your little dark cloud hovering over you and all around you. Your cloud may take the form of self-pity, guilt, blame, resentment, anxiety, or some other dominant contracting emotion. How can this be lucky? If you become aware of your mood, you have the choice of getting at the root emotions and processing them before illness sets in.

Identify Your Expansive Feelings

In the Map of Emotions the expansive emotions at the bottom of each column represent the beginning stages of personal expansion, and usually begin with some type of self-love. They move upward toward the more intensely expansive feelings, with the key expansive emotions highlighted at the top of each column. The root emotion here is goodwill and love, the realm of your higher self.

What happens when you process and release those contracting emotions and moods you experience? You free yourself to move into one or more of the *expansive feelings*. Think about what happens when you feel curiosity, excitement, admiration, empathy, love, happiness, or joy— any of the expansive emotions identified in the Map of Emotions. For all of us these emotions are an *up*, a *high*, and lead to reaching out to others, sharing and interacting with others in an upbeat way. They're high-energy states that act as energy boosts and therefore attract people to you—for the right reasons.

Expansive emotions feel light and airy, causing you to reach up and out toward life and toward other people. You experience a lot of space within the expansive emotions and therefore more possibilities. You're more willing to take chances, to do something new and challenging because you're focusing on the bright side of people and situations.

Consider "I Can-I Can't" Viewpoints—Power Versus Blockage

When you don't get what you want, do you focus on the "I can't?" Do you react *passively*, from a sense of powerlessness, leading to sadness or boredom? Or do you respond *aggressively*, leading to feelings frustration, resentment, and anger? In general women in our culture feel more permission to feel sad—or most any other emotion except anger.

On the other hand, men have permission to feel anger—and not much else. Do you give yourself permission to feel only anger? If so, you may have learned to channel *all* your feelings into the feeling of anger. Frustration, resentment, and anger can easily go into the extreme of hatred, which is a combined mental-emotional state, or into violence, which is a physical-emotional state.

When you can focus on the "I can" aspect of a situation, even when you don't get what you want, you tend to move through the sadness or anger more quickly. You can move on to thoughts that allow you to feel good or excited about life. When that happens, peptides fill your cell receptors, allowing little chance for viruses to enter the cells. When you focus on "I can," you take back your power. Here's a self-empowering goal: to live most of the time in the expansive, love-of-life side of the emotional map *and* to learn what to do when you fall into the contracting emotions.

Booster 3. Feel Your Feelings

Many people, especially men, have learned to control their feelings by suppressing them and pretending they don't exist. This practice creates a number of negative side-effects. Here's an overview of how you can process your feelings in a healthy way.

All the feelings have their purpose. Be willing to feel the whole range of feelings. That's what makes you a complete human being. Take emotions out of the either-or framework of negative and positive. Frame them as notes on a scale—with tonality, depth, volume, intensity, counterpoint, atonality, dissonance, and resonance. Which emotions feel thicker, slower, lower? Which are thinner, faster, higher? You can begin to recognize when you need to calm yourself and when you need to increase your excitement level.

Suppressed feelings don't go away. They tend to build up inside until they reach the *explosive stage*. You tend to forget the incident that triggered the feeling and the fact that you suppressed the feeling. Therefore, your outbursts of anger, self-pity, fear, and so forth come as a surprise to you, and they're out of your control.

Suppressed feelings can cause illness. Feelings that simmer and fester within you continue to create stress long after the stressful situation has passed. You then become vulnerable to stress-related illnesses, especially ulcers, high blood pressure, heart disease, cancer, migraine headaches, allergies, and asthma.

Suppressed feelings block personal growth. If you deny your feelings as a way of coping with life, you'll become more and more out of touch with yourself—how you really feel about things, the way you really are, the true effects of people and events on your life, all the facets of the ways you really respond to those people and events.

Such denial will inhibit your personal growth and development as a creative, autonomous person. It will numb you so you can't feel your heart's desire. As a result, you'll find it more and more difficult to be clear about your values and therefore your goals and to evaluate situations and opportunities in light of those goals. This leads to such problems as tunnel vision, workaholism, and burnout. Therefore, you want to be able to feel your feelings.

When you're in touch with your emotions—able to feel your fear, anger, and sadness as well as your excitement, compassion, and joy—you have a major advantage. For one thing, in order to process an emotion, you must be aware of it and able to feel it. For another, in order to empathize with another person's emotional state, you must be able to feel what they're feeling. People who repress and deny their feelings over the years become numb and have difficulty feeling anything, including what others are feeling.

Emotional intelligence boosts your creativity and gives you a leading edge in the workplace. Business cultures traditionally haven't allowed much space to acknowledge emotions. Most business cultures don't embrace the belief that experiencing and expressing emotions can be beneficial. Nor do they have the tools or methods to access and acknowledge emotional expression. Yet emotions are always with us, always in play. So the business leader who knows how to help individuals and teams channel their emotional power has an obvious edge. The first step in gaining emotional intelligence is to become aware of the key stressors in your life and the feelings those stressors trigger within you. The SAO called "What Feelings Do Your Stressors Trigger?" will get you started.

Booster 4. *Process Contracting Feelings*

Dealing with stressful, painful emotions takes courage. But the investment pays off in mental health and powerful personal growth. Author Greg Braden [1994] says it well: *You always have the ability to see beyond the pain, into what the pain is saying to you. Your life is a gift through which you may come to see yourself from many viewpoints, and know yourself as all possibilities.* Here's a basic overview of how to process emotions so that you can fully experience them and release them. In the sections that follow, you'll see how to work with emotions that are especially problematic, such as surface emotions that cover up deeper feelings, emotions that cluster and hang around as moods, and persistent anger or rage.

Step 1: *Identify the specific feeling*

Become aware of the emotion you're experiencing. Label the feeling as specifically as possible. Be sure you use a word that indicates something you *feel* and not merely a rational thought or character trait. For example, use *self-confident* or *certain* rather than *ready to make a move* or *decisive*.

Step 2: *Locate the emotion in your body*

If it's an emotion, locate it in your body by identifying where you feel some tension, some tightness, some pain, some upset, something different, something that doesn't feel normal.

Step 3: *Get at root emotions*

Ask, *Why do I feel (anger, sadness, etc.). So what? What difference does that make? Why do I care about that? So what will happen if. . . .* Keep asking these kinds of questions until you feel a shift, a sense that you've reached the bottom line, the root emotion that's stressful for you. (More about this step later. If you're processing an emotion now, you may want to skip to the section on root emotions, then return to Step 4 below.)

Step 4: *Fully experience all emotions that come up*

Allow the feeling to be there in your body; fully experience it being there.   Be willing to feel the emotion with intensity. Be in the present moment with it, paying attention, with intent to fully feel it, fully believing that you can move on out of the emotion when it's processed. The crucial attitude is your willingness to feel the feeling, to let it get more intense, if it needs to, to move deeper into another emotion, a root emotion—or to get less intense. Be willing for it to change locations in your body—or to move anywhere on the emotional map that it wants to go. In order to get at root emotions and then to release them, you may need to use some SAOs, such as "Worst-Case Scenario" and "Put It in Perspective."

Step 5: *Heal the emotion and the negative belief*

By using some simple acupressure techniques, along with some ways of thinking about your situation, you can actually heal the pain and damage of contracting emotions. And you do it at the etheric-body level, which is much more powerful and lasting than working at the physical-body level. The TAT (Tapas Acupressure Technique) method is very simple and powerful, as described in SAO 3.7. If you need further work, try Reversing Self-Sabotaging Thoughts, SAO 3.8, Emotional Acupressure, SAO 3.9, and Clearing Out Contracting Energy, SAO 3.11.

Step 6: *Release the emotion*

If you're willing to feel the emotion, and any related emotions that want to surface, you will eventually be able to release the feeling or allow it to be lifted. Let it go. Allow it to be lifted.

You may have trouble letting go of certain emotions. Some people say that in those sticky cases, it helps if they picture themselves surrendering to the flow of the universe and ask the universe to lift the emotion. Others say they call on their Higher Self to lift the emotion. Still others call on some higher power. Look to your belief system and find the greater power that can help you. The important aspect is to realize that you don't have to lift the emotion all by yourself. All you have to do is be *willing* for it to be lifted. Are you willing for it to be lifted? Can you believe you can get back to neutral?

Step 7: *Review your options*

You have many options about how to view a situation or to think about it. You also have many options about what actions to take when you experience an emotional response to a situation.

Options for Viewing a Situation. A dozen people will probably view a single situation in a dozen somewhat different ways. This means you have many options about how to view any particular situation.

Anger Example: Your boss is angry. If you can see the threatened little boy thrashing around behind his angry outburst, you feel more empathy than anxiety. Your empathetic response is more likely to meet the needs of the *little boy's* anxiety underneath his anger. You're more likely to see a number of options for responding to the event.

Judgment Example: A friend betrays a confidence. What options do you have for perceiving this event, what ways of thinking about it? What will you say to yourself? Here are a few options you can try—to see what effect they have.

- *She's not a true friend, and she doesn't really care about me, and I'm devastated.*
- *Just wait. I won't get mad—I'll get even.*
- *She was feeling needy when she did that.*
- *She probably meant well*
- *It's about her problems—it's not about me personally.*
- *I can handle this.*
- *This won't really matter to me in the long run.*

Envy Example: You feel a stab of envy upon learning that a co-worker got a promotion to a job you'd love to have. Your knee-jerk reaction is to put her down and accuse the boss of being unfair. Ask yourself, *Are these envious thoughts working as a barrier to my creativity and achievement? Are they draining my energy away, giving it to this situation? Are they setting up an "I-can't" dynamic? Do they reflect a fear that I'm not good enough? That I couldn't really get that kind of job—ever?* You can choose from a wide array of options for viewing the situation; for example:

- *What's it like to be in her place? How does she feel?*

- *What did she do to qualify for that promotion? What are the steps?*

- *I admire her ability to get that promotion.*

- *That promotion is worth putting time and energy into.*

- *What can I do to get that type of job?*

These types of thoughts can serve as a remedy for envious thoughts because they lead to an "I-can" dynamic. Notice that these thoughts trigger empathy and admiration. Here you are mentally identifying with success instead of rejecting it.

Thinking triggers emotions. Think about a recent situation that triggered an upsetting emotion for you. What other ways could you have chosen to perceive the situation? What emotions might have come up in each of these ways? As you practice different ways of thinking about an event, you'll notice that very different types of thinking patterns lead to very different emotions.   By choosing a specific thinking pattern, you can choose a different emotional response.

Options for Expressing Emotions. You also have many options about what to do in response to a situation and in response to your emotions. In the situation just mentioned, what are some actions you could have taken? What would be the likely outcome of each type of action? More about options later, including acting-out options.

A major advantage of processing your contracting emotions as they occur is that you can avoid denying the emotion and getting stuck in "bad moods." Another power is that you can process your emotions internally. You don't need to share the process, though it usually helps to share your feelings with a trusted confidante. Processing is very active, but you can do it within. Doing so will allow you to build and maintain a professional image and make better business decisions. Keep in mind these two tips:

- Process contracting emotions *before* you make a business decision or take action.

- Try to make decisions and take action when you're experiencing expansive emotions.

Booster 5. Bring Root Fears Out of the Shadows

Some emotions play around near the surface of your consciousness, while others are rooted much deeper in your being and even at levels below consciousness. Processing an emotion, such as anger, can help you to become aware of deeper-level emotions. When you get in touch with root fears, bring them out of the shadowy subconscious into the light of conscious awareness, examine them, and fully experience them, then you are more likely to be able to release them. When you move into and through all the emotions brought up by an event and then release them, you move into a lighter space, a space rooted in love-goodwill.   Root fears typically express themselves in all-too-common life problems, as shown in Table 3.2.

You can begin the process of bringing root fears out of the closet by asking yourself such questions as:

- *Why am I angry?*
- *What am I afraid of?*
- *What do I fear will happen?*

When you get some answers, you then may need to ask:

- *What difference will that make?*
- *Why do I care about that?*
- *So, what would happen then?*

Table 3.2 Typical Root Fears

Root Fears: ——————————▶	How these fears express:
Not being good enough ——————▶	**Self-worth issues**
Not lovable enough	Can't reach expectations for relationships
Not capable enough	Can't fully receive
Not deserving	
Abandonment ——————————▶	**Driving away relationships**
Rejection	or always being left in relationships
Separation	
Loneliness	
Fear of living fully ——————————▶	**Inability to love or to express love**
Fear of surrendering to the flow of life	Need to control people and situations
Not trusting the process of life—based	
on fear of rejection and abandonment	

The answers may be something like:
- *I won't get enough attention.*
- *I won't have any power.*
- *People will think . . . .*

Underneath your anger or sadness or anxiety, you'll probably find you're concerned about not getting something you want or losing something you have. As Table 3.2 indicates, you'll probably uncover a root fear that says one or more of the following.
- *I don't really deserve . . . .*
- *They'll think I'm not good enough.*
- *They'll find out I'm not really good enough.*
- *I'm not lovable or likable enough.*
- *I'm not capable enough.*

As you continue the process of asking why, you may come to the next root fear:
- *I'll be rejected, abandoned, separated, and alone.*

This is the fear that you'll be without those human connections so crucial to your well-being. It's the bottom-line fear. You may then say to yourself, *Okay, so I don't want to feel rejected and lonely. Then why don't I reach out to others and connect?* This question may bring you to another root fear, the fear of living fully, of surrendering to the flow of life, of trusting yourself and the universe. It's rooted in the bottom-line fear that if you trust, reach out, live fully, you'll be rejected—either now or later when you become deeply attached—and you'll be abandoned.

The way these root fears express themselves in your life is truly ironic, for when you're holding them, they seem to attract to you the very results you most fear. When you harbor the fear that you're not good enough, people often can't see who you really are, so it's hard to create authentic relationships. And it's very difficult for you to fully receive from others when you harbor the feeling that you don't deserve, which in turn blocks productive or loving relationships.

When you're caught in the root fear of rejection and abandonment, you tend to drive away those who could have mutually supportive relationships with you, so you create being bypassed or left in relationships. You may drive people away by being needy and controlling because you fear losing the relationship—choking the relationship by holding on too tight. You may drive people away because you express your fear as defensiveness, often interpreting people's actions as slighting you. You may drive people away because you're afraid of giving more than you might get. This often results in the decision, *I'll drop him before he drops me.*

When you're caught up in such fears, and people reach out to you in loving ways, you can't fully receive because you feel you don't deserve or you doubt their sincerity. When you fear giving yourself to the process of living life fully, you can't trust life, so you need to control people and situations. It's very difficult to fully feel and express love and goodwill when you're caught up in control issues.

The reason we call these emotions the contracting emotions is that when we experience them, we also experience a withdrawal from others—back into ourselves. This intensifies the feeling of isolation and separation—the most stressful of feelings. In contrast, when we process and let go of these feelings, we're able to reach out, move outside our shell, to trust and to expand. We rise up into the more expansive emotional realms.

Booster 6. Lift Your Moods

Sometimes several contracting emotions cluster together and hang around to become moods. Once you've worked at getting at root emotions, try the follow suggestions for lifting a mood:

- Learn what a mood is and how moods develop.
- Try out the belief that you can have feelings without your feelings having you
- Follow specific mood-lifting steps
- Let contracting emotions serve as a learning tool instead of making them wrong

What Is a Mood?

When you don't process contracting emotions, you hold them in your body and in the space around you as a mood. Moods may include such ongoing emotions as irritation, blame, guilt, and self-pity. You know people who stay in long-term moods that make them perpetually irritable, overly sensitive, or defensive. Those who are frequently moody, we call *difficult people* because such moods cause them to act in aggressive, passive aggressive, or passive ways.

A mood is usually not felt in a specific part of the body but is generalized in the body. A mood is like an aura you carry with you. In reality, you're choosing to be there in a mood, so it will last as long as you want. (If you suspect that you're subject to manic-depressive mood swings, you may be unable to manage your moods on your own, but help is available from professionals.) One of the motivations for being in a contracting mood is the need to deny certain emotions.

How Do Moods Develop?

When you deal with a contracting emotion by denying it (*I'm not angry*) or repressing it (*I simply won't feel angry any more*), you hold onto it. Just as you feel your emotions in a specific part of your body, you also subconsciously store them in a specific part of your body when you don't release them. Denial and repression can become such a habit pattern that they become automatic, below the level of consciousness. You're no longer aware that you're stuffing your anger. You may also hold onto an emotion through conscious choice (*I have every right to be angry, and I'm not going to forgive or forget*) based on self-justification or self-righteousness.

Have Feelings Instead of Feelings Having You

Remember, you are not your emotions—unless you repress them and therefore store them in your body. Emotions are energies that you experience, and although they create molecules that communicate to cells in various parts of your body, if you allow yourself to experience them and process them, they dissipate. This is one reason to watch your language when you talk about feelings. When you say "I *am* afraid" what are you telling yourself? Say instead, "I *feel* afraid." Take back your power and take charge of your emotions. Habits become like ruts or paths. A similar event tends to trigger a particular emotional habit pattern, and you find yourself being caught up without conscious awareness of how you're allowing yourself to be victimized by your own emotional reactions—and your way of thinking about them and speaking of them. Take charge of the situation by letting yourself fully experience whatever emotion comes up, knowing that you can work with the emotion.

Follow Specific Mood-Lifting Steps

How do you lift a mood? Try these steps.

1. Become aware of your moods. Listen to the people who care about you when they give you feedback about your moods.

2. Realize that only you can create a mood and only you can process the emotions beneath the mood. Take full responsibility for your feelings.

3. Be willing to process old, stuffed emotions and to get at root emotions.

4. Once you're able to release contracting, stressful emotions, what's left is your natural state of being—expansive feelings. Allow them, encourage them, groove on them, and think of them as your old friends.

5. Realize that both types of emotions are normal and human. When you do this, you no longer need to label your feelings as good or bad, right or wrong.

Let Contracting Feelings Be a Learning Tool

You'll no doubt continue to create situations that bring up stressful emotions from time to time. We do this to learn more about ourselves and others—to test relationships, our own limits and capacities, and in general to continue our personal growth and development.

Most of us don't go around consciously creating stressful situations for ourselves, but stress still happens. It happens even to those who have made great strides toward becoming self-aware, taking responsibility, developing satisfying relationships, and creating their own success. The point: Don't become discouraged if you're not always able to create "the perfect life" or to always feel high. That higher part of you knows the lessons you need to learn and the path of growth you need to follow.

The key to creating the life you want is to understand your emotional life and to take conscious control of it by dealing constructively with all your feelings as they come up—remembering that often your growth path is unclear and you must feel your way through to learn those lessons you need to master.

Booster 7. Channel Anger to Resolve Conflict

We've mentioned that our culture condones anger expressed by men under certain circumstances, such as when people have lied to them, betrayed them, or falsely accused them. Women are permitted to cry and express hurt and upset in such situations, but business women can rarely show anger without paying a price. As one woman said, "Looking back, every time I lost my temper, I lost."

Most people see anger as an antisocial force, something to be avoided. We don't know what to do with it except hold it back or pretend it's not there. Therefore, most of us waste a great deal of energy by holding anger inside. Repressing anger doesn't make it go away. The repressed anger may make us feel irritable or depressed. In turn we may develop various types of anger-related illnesses. The anger may burst out in an uncontrolled manner at unexpected times, resulting in shouting, cursing, threats, even violence. Anger itself does not cause these problems. Our inability to process and express anger properly is the root problem.

We assume we get angry because someone did something to us. Actually we decide when to get angry based on our beliefs and the resulting perceptions of ourselves, others, and the world. Our anger tends to be especially volatile when we believe that the other person's attitude or action belittles us or lowers our self-esteem. This touches on our root fear of *not good enough*.

People nearly always get angry with other people, not inanimate objects. We most often get angry with people we love or like. People we don't like are the least likely targets of our anger because we tend to ignore or avoid them.

If we learn to manage our anger constructively, it becomes a valuable aspect of cooperative conflict in our relationships. It can help us to confront our problems, rather than denying or burying them. It can help us define our position in relation to the issues, the conflict, or the problem that triggers the anger. It can serve as a guide to where we stand and how we feel about situations and relationships. It can help us to understand ourselves. Anger is a feeling to feel, express, move through, and get over with, not to repress or hang onto. Repressing it over the years is linked to the development of cancer.

Follow the Anger Trail

Anger can alert you to problem situations and relationships that need attention and to what's really going on within you.

Dealing With Conflict. Anger's specific value in dealing with conflict includes

- helping you to identify hidden problems that can then be dealt with and resolved to strengthen a relationship

- getting the other person's attention and motivating him or her to deal with the conflict

- transforming internal anxiety or frustration into external conflict, moving you to action, and increasing your sense of power to influence situations

- building your confidence in speaking out and challenging others

- releasing frustration

Building Relationships. Anger's specific value in building cooperative relationships includes

- signaling the value you place on another person, and perhaps your dependence or interdependence

- deepening your awareness and knowledge of others in your life and as a result you learn more about their values and commitments

- allowing you to signal that you want to work out problems and improve the relationship, including how you work together to get things done

Learning About Yourself. Anger's specific value in helping you to learn more about yourself includes

- motivating you to analyze the source of your anger and as a result learn more about yourself, your values, and your commitments

- motivating you to take vigorous action to deal with problems, achieve your goals, and build your skills

When you don't express anger, others are often not clear if the problems are important to you and therefore whether they merit attention. They may not understand the depth of your concern.

Manage Anger Constructively

Five steps to managing anger constructively are 1) taking a cooperative stance, 2) stating your position, 3) finding out the other persons' position, 4) working out a resolution, and 5) making the conflict a learning situation. The process is based on giving assertive feedback about how someone's behavior affects you.

Step 1. Establish your personal stance.

- Express commitment to the relationship; express positive feelings toward the other as a person even though you're angry about certain behavior.

- Use anger to get at the root of the problem and to strengthen the relationship, not to express self-righteousness and moral superiority, which often serves as a reason to hold onto the anger.

- Avoid saying things you don't mean or doing things you'd never do under normal circumstances; an old adage can work here: *take some deep breaths and count to 10.*

- Avoid triggering anger in the other person with belittling remarks or actions. Express yourself with I-messages about your own feelings, rather than judging and blaming the other as a person.

Step 2. State your position.

- Describe your feelings, using the energy that anger generates to express yourself but not judging or belittling the other person.

- Make your expression cathartic; let it release the energy and don't repress it.

- Specifically identify the exact behavior that bothers you; knowing exactly the action that angered you helps the other person feel less threatened; seeing your feedback as an attack on an action rather than on their personality and self-esteem is a relief.

- Take responsibility for your anger; remember that no one can make you feel anything without your permission.

- Allow your nonverbal actions to be natural and therefore in alignment with your verbal expression of anger.

Step 3. Question and understand the other person's viewpoint.

- Don't assume you know what the other person was or is thinking and feeling; ask questions.

- Be aware of the other person's feelings, such as defensiveness and anxiety, in the face of your anger.

- Ask the other person how she or he feels about your expression of anger.

Step 4. Ask for a resolution to the problem and reach agreement.

- Ask what the other person proposes as a resolution.

- Express what you need from a resolution.

- Explore alternative resolutions and find the one that best meets both your needs and that you both can live with.

Step 5. Make it a learning process.

- Be sure the solution resolves the anger-producing situation.

- Put the anger behind you; let it go; anger is a feeling to move fully into and fully out of, not to hang onto.

- Celebrate together your success in expressing and responding to anger and in resolving the problem.

- What skills did you both improve upon by successfully dealing with anger?

Booster 8.   Decide How to Express Feelings—Choices, Choices

You've figured out by now that you can't directly control your emotions and trying to do so leads to denying and repressing them. What you can control are the choices you make for how to think about people and situations and how to act in response to them. You can control your choice to process those contracting emotions that do occur. When you process your emotions, you take conscious control of your emotional state. Sometimes emotions feel like a wild horse with you as the rider. You're tossed around, jerked about, powerless and helpless, at the mercy of the horse. Learning to process emotions is like learning to ride the horse, going with its movements but in charge of the situation.

Other emotions feel like a whirlpool, sucking you in, pulling you down. When you begin processing the emotions, you can quit fighting, take charge, go down to the depths where the whirlpool ends, then move to one side with a powerful, releasing kick so that you can rise up to calmer waters. After you process an emotion, you feel more free to review all the options and choices you have for viewing situations and acting on them.

If feelings overpower you on the job, remember you always have the choice of temporarily shifting out of that emotion by using your other brain systems. You can shift to other realities that involve thinking, imagining, sensing or doing, which will move you out of emotional trauma for a time. For example, the sensory appeal of beautiful art or music are powerful. Shifting your attention to something beautiful to look at or listen to may be the fastest way to change your mood. You can always come back to the emotional experience and process it You can access each of the three brain systems in a way that's fairly independent of the others, although the three usually work in tandem. To feel is a choice, a freedom, a decision to enter the range of feelings, as clearly as when you choose to watch a film or take a walk.

Even when you revert to old victim thought patterns—which we all do from time to time—and contracting emotions flood in, you still have options for expressing and processing the feelings. You can choose what you say to yourself, what you learn from the experience, whether you interpret the event as a personal attack, how you interpret someone's criticism of you, and how you express contracting emotions.

Thought Options: There Are Many Ways I Can Think About This

Feelings become toxic only when you step out of your power and allow yourself to become victimized by them. You can take your power back by recognizing the many options you have for choosing a belief, attitude, worldview or thought that starts a positive thought-train. Learn which thoughts start a chain of thoughts that take you into an expansive emotion (from neutral to joy) rather than a contracting emotion (from irritation to terror). You have the power to choose how you want to perceive a crisis, an insult, or any other event and therefore what emotions may come up as a result of your perception.

Your perceptions are formed by your thoughts, or more specifically a thought that logically leads to another thought that in turn logically leads to another—and on and on. We can call this a *thought train*. For example, your roommate growls at you as you enter the kitchen.

- You think *Oh, no, she's in a bad mood this morning and she's going to take it out on me.*

- Then you think, *She's done this several times lately.*

- Next you think, *I'm getting sick and tired of her moods and being dumped on.*
  What kind of feelings does this thought-train arouse? What type of action does it lead to?
  On the other hand, you can choose to think:
- *She's having a difficult morning.*
- Then you can think, *It has nothing to do with me.*
- Next, you're likely to think, *I'm having a good morning.*
- This may lead to the thought, *Maybe that will have a positive effect on her, but she's free to feel any way she wants to feel.*

Compare the feelings that this thought-train arouses—and the likely actions—with the previous thought-train.

Figure 3.2. Thought-Trains: One Thought Leads to Another

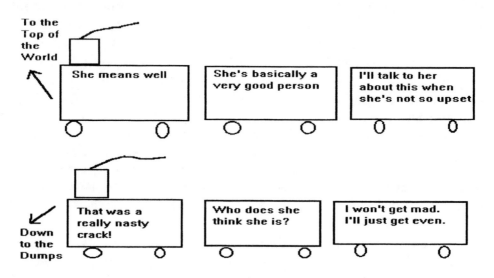

When you take charge of the situation, you have available to you the emotional energy you're holding within your body. You can let this *stuck energy* start flowing. You can use it to fuel expansive thought-trains. Pay attention to your thought-trains. Notice that when you hop onto a thought about the bright side of the picture, the good that's there, and what you want to create in the situation, you board a thought-train that can take you up through the expansive emotions. You can even go the *top of the world* emotionally speaking to the heights of awe, wonder, passion, goodwill, love. But when you hop onto a thought about what's wrong, how awful someone is, or what you fear will happen, the thought-train takes you down into the contracting emotions, even *down to the dumps*, as symbolized in Figure 3.2. Instead of focusing on what you're against or don't like, you can shift to the reverse—what you're FOR, what you do like and want.

If a stressful emotion keeps coming up, by all means process it. After that, remember you can become aware of fear-based thoughts moment by moment and break your old contracting thought-train patterns. Try this: as you inhale, pretend you're breathing in love/goodwill through your heart. As you exhale, breathe out blame, judgment, anger, all the contracting emotions. Picture yourself emptying out the old and filling up with love/goodwill. Next, allow an appreciative or loving thought. Feel your energy expand as you hop onto an expansive thought-train. If you make this process a habit, you'll find more and more people attracted to you. Positive energy attracts people like magic! Negative energy repels, or at best attracts manipulators.

Of course, even when you get on a thought-train that takes you to a contracting, stressful emotion, you still have many options about what actions to take. For example, even if you feel irritated or impatient with your roommate's mood, you can choose to fully experience those feelings without saying or doing things that are likely to antagonize her.

Crisis Options: Stay Poised in a Crisis

How do you deal with a crisis? Are you afraid you might fall apart? Be aware that you have many options for responding. Here's an effective process for mastering yourself in a crisis.

- Slow down your physical and mental processes.
- Take a few very deep breaths.
- Have the intention of becoming grounded and centered.
- Go into slow motion as if in a slow-motion movie.
- See yourself in charge of the situation.
- Move very deliberately.
- Take action to handle the crisis, one step at a time.
- If frantic or harried thoughts come in, repeat the deep breathing.

You can use one or more of the relaxation techniques discussed earlier. The simplest technique is simply to pause and take a few deep breaths. Don't say, *I must relax.* Instead, start breathing deeply. In fact, avoid telling yourself that you *should, must* or *need* to do anything. Simply have the intention to follow these strategies.

Become very aware of the present moment. Have the intention to feel centered and grounded in your body and very present mentally. All this helps you to rise above any chaotic mind chatter. Feel your breathing slow down and your entire body slow down, including your thinking process. You must slow down enough to end the frantic rush to action and to take the necessary steps, one step at a time, to deal with the crisis.

Power Options: Use Self-Talk That Empowers

He made me so mad. . . . It made me so sad. When you talk this way, you tell yourself that you have no choices in how to view an event. You step out of your power and so give away your power to the person or situation who *made you mad.* This leaves a power vacuum that others who want power over people can sense from a mile away. You first become a victim in your own mind (*He made me mad*). Then you become a victim in someone else's mind, who thinks, *I can get this one to do what I want.*

Does a little self-talk really have that kind of power-draining impact? Yes. Everything you say to yourself programs the subconscious part of your mind about how the world is and how you should respond. If you've said *he made me mad* hundreds or thousands of times during your lifetime, you've programmed your subconscious to respond as if you're a victim. To change the program, stop yourself in mid-sentence or mid-thought and correct yourself: *I chose to see him as a threat and became angry or I thought he was belittling me, which triggered my anger.* Choose your own words, but be sure they reflect your power to choose.

Sometimes thoughts seem obsessive. When certain thoughts just won't go away, let them run their course, much as you process your emotions by letting them run their course. Don't beat yourself up because you've hopped onto a thought-train to the dumps. It takes time to change old thought patterns, and growth is always two steps forward and one step back. The step back usually provides the momentum to take the next two steps forward.

Criticism Options: Don't Take It Personally

The tendency to view other people's actions and criticisms as personal put-downs stems from the fear of some sort of personal failure. Why do women seem to take these things more personally then men? Perhaps because men have generally been more single-minded about their career goals. They are more likely to keep focusing on such questions as *What do I have to do, what do I have to* learn *in order to advance*? That focus makes it easier to keep things in perspective. When the intention to *learn* from our mistakes overcomes our fear of failure, we're less likely to take people's criticisms and actions personally.

It may help to view business as a game. First, what's your major goal in this game? Discovering the limits of your capability? Reaching financial independence? Making a specific kind of contribution to the planet? Once you're clear about your major goal and you let go of any tension-producing *need* to achieve it, you can relax and begin to enjoy the *process* of playing the game in order to achieve the goal. The actions of others become part of the challenge and complexity of the game, and you make your moves with your goals foremost in your mind. Your focus changes from avoiding the risk of failure and protecting yourself from failure to winning the game. Problem situations merely alert you to the need to take corrective action. You switch from agonizing over the fact that a problem was allowed to develop to getting on with the job of correcting the problem. Your ego is not on the line. After all, it's just a game.

Sourcing Options: Put Criticism in Perspective

Ask yourself about your critic's qualifications on the subject at hand, and consider the source. Suppose you were to take a visitor on a tour of your department and explain major departmental goals, organization, procedures, and controls. He sees some potential problem with the way you're running things and suggests some ways you could improve the setup. The range of possibilities about his qualifications to criticize and advise you is shown on this scale.

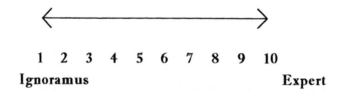

1 2 3 4 5 6 7 8 9 10
Ignoramus   Expert

Let's look at the two extreme possibilities. Possibility 1 is that your critic doesn't know a thing about running the business. In fact, he's so ignorant that he doesn't know the difference between a work schedule and an organization chart. In that case, if you allow yourself to become upset because of the criticism of a business ignoramus, you're acting even more foolishly than the person who criticized you.

At the other extreme, your critic may be a world-renowned expert on business organization. In that case, his observations are probably valid and his suggestions extremely valuable. In fact if you acted on those suggestions, you might become a top officer of the company in a very short time. To be upset by such criticism, then, would be inappropriate and self-defeating.

Most of your critics' qualifications will lie somewhere between complete ignorance and incomparable expertise. The point is that if you automatically respond negatively to feedback, you're showing that you lack self-esteem in that area of your life. Such negative reactions not only waste your energy, they tend to sidetrack you from your major goals. When you're criticized, ask yourself: What are the qualifications of my critic? What validity does this criticism have? Are ulterior motives involved? Can I use this feedback to help me reach my goals?

Do you welcome feedback? Ask yourself: Is it better for me to know what's going on in my department—the problems, conflicts, others' reactions—or not? If having all pertinent information, negative or positive, about what's going on in your area of responsibility is important to you, then your logical response to feedback will be, *Thank you. I'm glad you brought that to my attention. I'll look into it.*

Sometimes people will criticize you in such a negative, hostile way that it's difficult to remain emotionally detached. It may be appropriate to tell such a person that you appreciate the feedback but you *don't* appreciate the manner in which it was given. At the same time, it helps to keep in mind that the hostility is the other person's problem. She or he would react that way to *anyone* who represents to him or her what you do at the moment. It's a part of the individual's own conditioning and working out of his or her own life story and really has nothing to do with you personally. And, if you *still* feel strong emotions, you don't have to act them out. You can choose one of the substitute acting-out methods that follows.

Review Options: Look for Lessons and Growth Opportunities

As you grow in your ability to choose thinking or self-talk that results in expansive emotions, you'll sometimes slip into old thought patterns and take yourself straight into a contracting emotion. All is not lost. You not only have options for acting on the feeling, you can also choose to learn from the experience. You have the option of seeing how difficult people and emotional upsets actually help you learn about yourself and can accelerate your personal growth.

Pay special attention to people and behaviors that you don't like. Those traits and actions can show you the active parts of your personality that you think are too obnoxious to admit to and so you deny them. If you can begin to recognize them in yourself and admit to them, these traits and actions of *obnoxious people* can serve the invaluable purpose of showing you what you need to work on next in your personal development. When someone betrays you, for example, you'll probably experience a range of contracting emotions. At some point, ask yourself why you attracted such a person into your life. Is it because *you've* betrayed someone recently? Or wanted to? If so, you probably need to deal with betrayal issues within yourself. Or is it that you simply hold harsh judgments toward people who betray? Not one of us has completely conquered the tendency to make negative judgments of others, so we all need to work on empathy, compassion, and acceptance of others as they are. Maybe betrayal is coming up in your life at this time because you're ready to develop greater empathy and compassion for betrayers The bottom line: instead of hanging onto the contracting emotions of an event (such as betrayal), you can focus on the lessons for growth and self-understanding, which in turn trigger expansive emotions.

Action Options: Experience Feelings Without Acting-Out

As you master the techniques we've been discussing, *problem* emotions will become less and less a problem. Here's a strategy for constructively handling those *problem* emotions that do occur.

Accept your feelings. Be glad that you're able to experience the whole range of human emotions and that you're aware of being able to do so. Believe that a feeling isn't right or wrong, good or bad; it just *is*.

Let yourself fully experience your feelings. Be aware of feelings in the present moment. Don't begin focusing on guilt (about past experiences associated with a similar feeling) or worry (about what will happen in the future). Stay in the here and now by focusing on your senses—what you're seeing, hearing, touching, etc.

Choose not to act-out. Tell yourself that you're choosing not to act-out your feelings because to do so would be inappropriate and self-defeating.

Decide whether and when to give feedback. You may decide it's appropriate to *tell* the person who triggered the feeling what you're feeling. If you do this effectively, it's not acting-out, and the feedback can be constructive to that person. See the earlier discussion of managing anger.

If you can't give feedback calmly, postpone it. As a general rule, you don't have to respond immediately to anything. When your feelings are too overpowering for you to *experience them out* quickly, it's more professional to delay responding. You can act-out your feelings in privacy, if necessary. Later, when you're ready to deal with the problem situation, you can do so without having to deal with explosive feelings at the same time. To postpone gracefully, it helps to have some exit lines in mind. Your exit line is what you say before you change the subject or excuse yourself from the scene.

- *I'd like to check on a few things before I give you my answer* (or *respond to that, discuss that*).

- *May I get back to you at/on . . . ?*

- *Let me think about that for a while. I'll get back to you at/on. . .*

- *I'm glad you brought that up. I must leave for a meeting (or appointment) now, but I want to talk with you about this as soon as I return.*

Use substitute acting-out. Tell yourself that you'll enjoy acting-out your feelings in an appropriate way later. Sometimes just telling yourself this can defuse the situation enough for you to deal with it effectively at the time it occurs.

You can visualize throwing darts at a picture of the person on a dart board. (Some people even have dart boards in their office for this purpose.) Here are other substitutes.

- Any game that requires hitting a ball: Pretend the ball is the person or thing you resent and really smash it.

- Jogging or walking: Pretend you're stepping on the person you resent *if you need to!*

- Karate: Pretend your opponent is the person you resent (but don't get carried away!).

- Any physical exercise: You can work off the bottled-up energy of unexpressed feelings by reminding yourself while you're exercising that you're working out those feelings. Be aware of the situation and the resulting feeling you're now working out. You'll probably be free to rest peacefully once the tension and energy drain of unresolved feelings is eliminated.

- Hitting a large stuffed doll: Try to knock the stuffing out of a large doll, animal, or dummy, using either your fists or a baseball bat.

- A quick mental acting-out: Instead of visualizing the dart-throwing incident, you can picture yourself telling off the other person, kicking him or her in the seat of the pants, and so on. You may be able to work out the feeling in a few seconds and go on to deal with the situation calmly.

Expression Options: Express Feelings to a Trusted Friend

Another way of handling your emotions is to talk them out with someone. The more stressful your job, the more essential it is to have at least one trusted friend that you can *let your hair down* with. It's best if such friends are not connected with your job. Although business friends may understand the problems better than someone outside the company, it's risky to be completely open with them. True friends are rare. Most people are lucky if they have five or six at any one time in their lives. For the relationship to be truly mutually supportive, it should include these aspects.

- You can be yourselves with each other.

- You are interested in each other's well-being.

- You really listen to each other.

- You don't make judgments about each other's character, feelings, or behavior. (To avoid making judgments, think in terms of behavior that works or doesn't work, that appears to be constructive or destructive, rather than what is right or wrong, good or bad. Deal more with what is rather than with what *should* be.)

- You confide in each other about the joyous events in your life as well as the problem situations.

- You both feel more lovable and capable as a result of the friendship.

- You can trust each other's judgment about revealing shared confidences.

Frequently you can gain insights into problem situations and learn more about yourself by discussing things with a friend. Such discussions can also be very helpful in *experiencing out* any leftover, bottled-up feelings you may have. This type of friendship can help both parties keep a balanced perspective on life.

Research indicates that women have a knack for reaching out to close friends when the emotional going gets tough. Women's ability to rally round with a hot cup of tea, a little shopping spree, a heart-to-heart talk, a good cry, or a big hug seems to work wonders in healing those wounds from the slings and arrows of outrageous office politics. Men are often in awe of this power, and they would do well to try similar techniques, adapting them to men's ways of bonding and hanging out.

Applying Emotional Intelligence: Gratifying Customers' Emotional Needs

Future success in the business world lies not so much in selling products as in selling dreams that appeal to people's emotional needs. People are captivated by stories that appeal to their emotions. Companies are finding they must create stories about the firm and its products if they want to make them memorable and appealing. All kinds of companies are challenged to do this—whether they produce consumables, necessities, luxuries, or services.

Everyone in the firm must nurture these stories because good ones amount to the company's greatest asset. Because stories about the company and its products are so crucial, companies are learning to value the storytellers that create them. Storytellers are not limited to the creative advertising department. They need to exist throughout the company, especially at the executive level. At the top, if you want to win the enthusiasm of employees and the respect of the general public, you must create an appealing myth that weaves together the company's history and traditions.

Futurist Rolf Jensen [1999] defines six emotional markets where companies sell dreams and experiences that meet customers' emotional needs—along with the product or service that goes with it. Think about how your organization might profit from each one.

The Adventures Market offers safaris, theme parks, sports, and action/adventure films and programs. It meets customer needs for excitement, playfulness, fun, newness, surprise, curiosity.

The Love-Friendship Market offers gifts, such as perfume, flowers, candy, and knick-knacks, as well as opportunities to enhance togetherness, such as restaurants, entertainment, and home photography. Unique experiences are featured, such as the "genuine" Irish pub or the Bookstore-

Café offering "issues" discussions. This market meets needs for togetherness, belonging, and showing gratitude.

The Care Market offers pets and pet experiences, such as hotels that provide guests with "house dogs" they can take for walks, kennels that offer custom environments and experiences for your pet, and electronic pets. This market meets needs for caring, nurturing, empathy, compassion, devotion.

The Self-Identity Market offers products that proclaim the owner's identity, such as distinctive fashions, accessories, automobiles. Distinctive luggage may say "I'm a stylish, savvy world traveler." A SUV may say, "I'm a down-to-earth but adventurous guy," while a hybrid electric car may say, "I'm an environmentalist." This market meets needs for self-awareness, self-acceptance, self-love, and self-acceptance (as well as ego-pride and arrogance).

The Peace of Mind Market offers the comfort of the familiar, perhaps a feeling of small-town friendliness in a bank or boutique or retro nostalgia in a restaurant or bar. It meets needs for comfort, relief, certainty, calmness, and appreciation.

The Social Convictions Market offers green products and services, those that honor or protect the environment, animals, worker welfare, and human rights. Where the Care Market meets needs for caring, nurturing, empathy, compassion and devotion at the one-on-one level, this market meets it on the global level, with a special focus on commitment, conviction, and optimism.

Creativity Showcase
Using Emotional Intelligence
for Creative Solutions and Ideas

Some innovative solutions to current problems—for your information and inspiration—and as food for thought.

Problems in Residential Communities

Most families today live in fairly congested suburbs, towns, or cities. Home costs and maintenance are so high it takes the incomes of at least two people to survive. As a result, most children are raised in day centers till they're old enough for school.

Residential streets are often dangerous and children frequently have inadequate outdoor space for their activities. Traffic is often too fast and too congested to allow for relatively stress-free driving. Many residents must commute to work over long distances in heavy traffic. Sound familiar? These are the kinds of stressors that trigger contracting emotions, which in turn intensify your stress, making you more vulnerable to the financial and environmental stressors you're already encountering, creating a vicious cycle.

Innovative Solutions

Village Homes in Davis, California, was the pioneer community of its type. The developers, Michael and Judy Corbett, devised innovative ways to solve many typical problems of residential communities.

To begin with, they narrowed the streets and used the land instead for extensive parks and greenbelts, filling them with fruit trees, and providing agricultural zones among the houses so people can raise vegetables. Village Homes sells its organic crops of vegetables and almonds each year, helping to finance its parkland maintenance. Community organic farming helps residents lower their food bills.

The entire development is oriented toward the sun, and the homes feature passive solar design. Energy bills are up to two-thirds less than for comparable homes in the region.

Instead of costly underground concrete drains that add to housing costs, the Corbetts created natural drainage swales as part of a system of greenways, which provide for surface drainage of rain water. This plan allows the water to soak in, so the landscaping, most of which provides food, needs up to one-half less irrigation water.

Houses face each other across the greenways and cars are parked around back in garages off the narrow, 24-foot wide, tree-shaded streets. The street networks and the greenway networks enter the site from opposite directions like interlocking fingers, so they don't cross or form intersections. As a result, the greenways are safe from traffic, free and safe for children's activities. Narrower streets not only reduce random drive-through traffic, they save land, require less paving and maintenance, and produce less heat in summer. This, along with the many trees, helps lower cooling bills and makes the neighborhood cooler and shadier.

The center of community life is the greenways, which provide safe bike paths, pedestrian walkways, and plenty of space for children's activities and community events. Thanks to the vibrant "street life" of the greenways, criminal activity is unlikely. And in fact the crime rate is one-tenth that of neighboring areas.

Bottom line: The Corbetts understand people's emotional needs and their Village Homes community meets those needs better than most developments. As a bonus owners who must leave the area enjoy the highest resale prices of any area in Davis, and they sell their homes in one-third the normal listing time (Corbett 1981).

Creative Techniques
Based on Emotional Intelligence

CT 4.1 Empathy: Role Playing

Who are the key players in your problem-opportunity situation? Pick the most important player and pretend you are that person. Get inside her head or his skin. Walk around mentally in her shoes or in his body. See the situation from that person's viewpoint. Describe it as she sees it or as he feels it. How does this person want the situation to be handled or resolved? This requires the emotion of empathy.

- What insights does this suggest for you?
- Repeat the process for other key players.

CT 4.2 Empathy: Be-Its

Carrying the idea of role playing, a step further, you can not only pretend to be another person, such as a key player, you can pretend to be the problem, be the opportunity, be the company mission, be the current goal, be the future, be any aspect that may be important.

What elements, besides key people, are crucial to your problem-opportunity situation? In your imagination, be that element (be the product, be the customer, be the billing-shipping process, etc.). If you're being a product, imagine yourself as the source of the product, going through every step of becoming the finished product. If you're being an object that your company processes in some way, ask yourself such questions as "What can happen to me? Where should I go next? What if I went to the Accounting Department next?" Let your imagination play and run wild. What insights come to you? Write them down.

CT 4.3 Empathy: Be or Ask a Famous Person

Through your superconscious mind, you can have access to all the geniuses and important people who have ever lived and who will ever live. You can learn to tap into this information through empathy and intuition. Even if you don't believe in your ability to do this, try it. It's fun.

If you could pick the brain of anyone who has ever lived, who would it be? Think of a famous person—or any person you admire—a person you believe could understand and provide sound advice in this situation. Relax and turn all your attention to this process. Get in touch with all the qualities that you associate with this person. Use the emotion of empathy to tune into this person, to become this person. Now, as this person, review the problem-opportunity situation. How do you see it? What actions could you take? Which approach would be most effective? Write down any insights, ideas, suggestions.

CT 4.4 Empathy: Be or Ask an Outsider

Look for an entirely new take on the situation. Try these methods:

- Talk it over with a child and ask for ideas. Listen carefully. A child may still have the advantage of being open, spontaneous, curious, and flexible.

- Ask anyone who is outside the situation. An outsider's fresh take on the problem may bring new insight.

- Pretend your are a child, an outsider, even an alien from another planet. Imagine how this being would view the situation, ideas they might have.

CT 4.5 Emotional-Rational Grid (for products or services)

Step 1. Set up a 4-square grid . It should contain two columns and two rows (4 squares). Label the two columns "Emotional" and "Rational." Label the two rows "High Involvement" and "Low Involvement."

The "Emotional" column refers to products or services that appeal to the customer's emotions, situations where customers allow their emotions to strongly influence their purchase decision. The "Rational" column refers to products or services customers evaluate according to verbal, numerical, analytical, and factual criteria.

The "High Involvement" row refers to expensive products or services, situations where customers tend to pay a great deal of attention to the purchase decision. "Low Involvement" row refers to inexpensive ones, requiring decisions that customer view as relatively trivial and routine.

Step 2. List and number the products or services. What do you want to explore or evaluate? Maybe it's your firm's products, your competitors' products, or both. Give each product or service a number.

Step 3. Place on the grid. Determine where on the grid each product or service should go—according to whether customers see it as an emotional or rational, high-involvement or low-involvement decision.   If Product No. 1 is strongly related to an emotional response and is an inexpensive low-involvement product, place the "1" on the far left of that column and extremely far down in the low-involvement rows (far away from the high-involvement rows). If Product No. 2 is mostly emotional, but also has a strongly rational component, and it's a somewhat expensive high-involvement product (but not extremely so) place the "2" to the right of the Emotional column, close to the Rational column and in the middle of the high-involvement rows. These are illustrated in the sample grid.

There are a number of uses for this grid; for example:

- Evaluate and compare the various products or services that are currently on the market

- Identify problems where a market is over-saturated with a particular type of product or service

- Identify opportunities where there are holes or gaps in the market, where new or additional products or services are needed

You may also experiment with adapting this grid to other types of explorations, evaluations, and comparisons by changing the titles of the columns and rows.

Emotional	Rational
H I g h I n v o l v e m e n t *Product 2*	
L o w I n v o l v e m e m t *Product 1*	

Case Studies—Applying the Creative Techniques

In working on these cases, you may use creative techniques from any of the chapters. However, the creative techniques described in this chapter may be especially appropriate. Keep these self-questions in mind.

1. What problems do I see?

2. How can I probe beneath the surface to get at root problems?

3. What opportunities (hidden or obvious) can I find to take initiative, cut costs, and/or make money?

4. What creative alternatives can I generate?

5. As a consultant, what should I recommend as the best viewpoints and actions?

6. To answer these questions, what creative techniques can I experiment with to respond to this case? After completing the case analysis, ask: Which creative techniques produce the best results?

Case 3.1 ~~Career Change for Lisa Albright?~~ American Tours

American Tours is based in San Francisco and caters especially to tourists from Japan. The company is situated in a two-story office in downtown San Francisco with adjoining garage space for 100 vehicles. It has about 50 employees, including office staff, tour guides, drivers, and mechanics. American Tours provides individual and group tours of the City as well as such nearby sites as Napa Valley, Monterey Peninsula, Yosemite National Park, and Tahoe.

American works closely with travel agencies in Japan, especially Nippon Travel Company. American's responsibility for clients begins at the airport, when they first arrive, and ends at the airport when they depart to return to Japan.

American has been in business for 20 years, and 10 years ago there were seven firms competing in this Japanese tourist niche. Today there are only two, American and California Tours.

The company's focus has been on achieving customer satisfaction and maintaining a good relationship with Nippon Travel. To that end their goals include always picking clients up on time and resolving any client requests or complaints. In fact, an executive talks personally with the clients when things go wrong and confers with any client who is unhappy.

Jamie Yuen, founder and CEO of American Tours, is concerned about the company's future. Since the downturn of the Japanese economy, revenues and profits have dropped. He worries about how to boost the business. He worries that San Francisco's hotel rates are among the highest in the country. Many tourists are choosing other destinations, such as Los Angeles and San Diego. Jamie is not worried about competition from California Tours as much as rivalry from firms in other cities.

- What are the root problems facing American Tours?
- What opportunities is Jamie Yuen overlooking?
- How can emotional intelligence help Jamie and his executive team in dealing with this issue?
- What innovative actions do you recommend?
- Which CTs discussed in this chapter did you use in solving this case problem?
- Which CTs were most helpful and what ideas did they spark or inspire?

Case 3.2 Video Game Commercial

3D Adventure is a 13-year-old company that creates video games. One of their biggest competitors, **Megastar**, has a popular game called Jungle that features Grizmo, a large bear that engages in various battles in the jungle.

3D Adventure's latest hot game is called Tanks. Since 3D specializes in providing video material, they decided to create their own TV commercial for the Tanks product launch. As the team sat around, dreaming up ideas for the commercial, Otto Grant started laughing. "Hey, wouldn't it be a hoot if we showed our tanks attacking Grizmo the bear?" The other guys started laughing. They all liked the idea.

The team created the TV commercial as a vignette that takes place in a laundry room. It begins with the famous talking bear, Grizmo, talking to the audience. Suddenly a group of tanks shows up and begins chasing Grizmo around the room, trying to blow him up. By the end of the commercial, Grizmo has lost a paw and is on fire. The Tanks are victorious.

The Public Relations Department scheduled the TV commercial to be shown primarily on Saturday mornings during popular kid's shows. The Tanks commercial definitely caused a commotion. Megastar has sued 3D Adventure for $3 million dollars in damages. They claim that 3D violated copyright laws by copying Grizmo and using him in their commercial. They also claim slander of their product, saying the Tanks commercial implies their product is no good. As a result sales of the Jungle game have fallen off.

- What are the root problems facing 3D?
- What opportunities are they overlooking?
- How could emotional intelligence help them avoid these problems and capitalize on missed opportunities? What do you recommend?
- Which CTs discussed in this chapter did you use in solving this case problem?
- Which CTs were most helpful and what ideas did they spark or inspire?

Case 3.3 Career Change for Lisa Albright?

Lisa Albright has been working for Foremost Chemical for 12 years. She started as a part-time clerical worker when the youngest of her 3 children went into a preschool class. For the past 5 years she's been a full-time customer service trouble shooter. She coordinates with the 25 sales reps in her organization to make sure their customers get excellent service. All the sales reps are men; they all have college degrees; and most of them have degrees in chemistry or science. They all know Lisa, who's 38, and they generally refer to her as "the tall, good-looking redhead." They like her, even though she's a little shy—she has a reputation for getting things done and solving problems.

Customers include municipal water districts, which buy chemicals for water purification; the food service industry, which buys chemicals to use in processing and preserving food; and a few miscellaneous manufacturing firms, which buy chemicals for the manufacturing and cleanup process. Nearly all the purchase agents are men, and most of them see Lisa the same way the sales reps view her.

Lisa's manager Tom Silverman, calls her in to talk about her future with the company: "Lisa, I know you've been worried about making ends meet since your husband left. You know, you've learned an awful lot about this business and about our customers in the years you've worked in this office. I think you might do well as a sales rep—you have the opportunity to make more money. What do you say?"

Lisa was stunned. "Me? A sales rep? What kind of money are we talking about?"

Tom said, "Well, you'd have a base pay that's less than what you're making now, but you have a chance to make good commissions—maybe even double your pay."

"But I have a high school diploma. Period. What would the guys think? What would the customers think? And, you know, I've never sold anything! I'm pretty shy about meeting people."

"Well, you think it over, Lisa. If you want to give it a try, the job is yours."

- What problems or potential problems arise from this scenario?
- What opportunities?
- How would you address each problem or unmet opportunity?
- Which CTs discussed in this chapter did you use in solving this case problem?
- Which CTs were most helpful and what ideas did they spark or inspire?

Case 3.4 Mini-Mart Porn?

Mini-Mart Corporation owns 150 convenience foodstores in California, Oregon, and Washington. The company has carried such "men's magazines" as Playboy and Penthouse in the past. Recently their competitor, QuickStop, decided to discontinue handling such magazines.

Ellen Garcia is the **manager** of a Mini-Mart in Chico, California. She decides to stop selling these magazines in her store. She and her assistant manager Jim Jenson agree that in the interest of community standards, they should follow the lead of the QuickStop store in town and not sell these products. Ellen's husband, Joe Garcia, part-time store accountant (he also has other accounts), agrees with this decision.

Ellen feels pretty confident about making such a decision. She has been a Mini-Mart manager for seven years and has often won performance awards. Twice she has been named as Manager of the Year for her district. Her store has just completed the most profitable year it has ever had.

Mason Stewart, Mini-Mart merchandising manager, comes from Los Angeles to pay a routine call on the store and discovers that the magazines are not available. Stewart and Garcia have an extended discussion—and later an argument—about the necessity to follow company policy and stock the merchandise the company requires. The following day, after conferring with Rick Williams, executive vice president, Mason fires Ellen for insubordination and puts her **assistant Jim Jenson** in charge. Later, when Jim also refuses to carry the magazines, he is fired. Ellen's **husband Joe Garcia** resigns as store accountant.

Word spreads quickly throughout the community. A story about the incident appears in the *Chico News & Review*, and a few days later an Associated Press reporter calls Ellen for a telephone interview.

Ellen explains why she took the stand that cost her and her husband their jobs: "We Americans must stand up for decency. It's a patriotic cause." Ellen tells how she feels about recent trends, from soft-porn magazines to X-rated movies and home videos. "If we allow such trends to continue, America will hardly be a fit place to live. It's not just a religious issue for me, although my church does object to media porn. I'm thinking of community standards." She goes on to say that the philosophy behind the two magazines is "very destructive—basically that marriage and faithfulness aren't important." She adds, "They turn women into sex objects. They've begun using children in cartoons. We're giving up our livelihood in the cause of decency, in the cause of women and children who have suffered abuse, letting them know there are people who care." Ellen's husband Joe adds, "It was something we had to do. Money isn't everything. We're willing to take the consequences."

Christmas came a couple of months later and was tough on the Garcia family. Their daughter has a medical problem that costs them about $1,000 a month in medication, therapy, and care, but their medical insurance has been cut off. They're getting by on their small savings and Joe's limited income from his independent accounting work. Ellen and Joe tell friends, "We know in our hearts we did what was right."

- What problem or potential problems do you perceive?
- What opportunities—potential or unrecognized?
- How would you address each problem and opportunity
- Which CTs discussed in this chapter did you use in solving this case problem?
- Which CTs were most helpful and what ideas did they spark or inspire?

Self-Awareness Opportunities

SAO 3.1 What Feelings Do Your Stressors Trigger?

Purpose: To raise your awareness of the connection between certain stressors and related feelings—so you can process them effectively.

Note: You don't need to have artistic ability to do this exercise. The power of the exercise lies in your ability to imagine, to visualize. Your drawing can be very simple, crude, childlike, or symbolic. In fact, the power lies in the symbolism.

Step 1. Identify and draw your stressors. What stressors impact you now, in your current life? Make a drawing that symbolizes the stress in your life as follows:

- Draw a picture of yourself—it can be a stick figure, a symbol, or as realistic as you like.
- Symbolize in some way all the pressures and demands that you're aware of—using drawings, words, or other symbols.
- Show the intensity of each pressure, demand, or anxiety by drawing arrows, bridges, or other connections between the pressure and you. Indicate intensity by the size, thickness, darkness (or similar means) of the connections. Remember, even positive change can be stressful if you perceive it has a disruptive effect.

Step 2. Identify your feelings. For the first major stressor, get in touch with the feeling(s) you experience when you focus on that stressor. What feeling(s) have you felt when the stressor was especially active?

Step 3. Process your feelings. Process that feeling, using the process described in this chapter. Repeat for feelings related to other major stressors

SAO 3.2 Draw and Redirect Your Stressful Emotions

Purpose: To gain mastery of your stressful emotions so you can channel them into useful forms of self-expression.

Step 1. Identify a stressful emotion. Think of a stressful emotion that recurs in your life. It may be an emotion you have difficulty mastering, one that sweeps you up in its force, one that you act out in destructive ways. It may be an emotion that recurs in your dreams and is troubling to you.

Step 2. Draw the emotion. If you have difficulty seeing it as a symbolic or physical entity, do SAO 3.6, Observe Your Stressful Emotions. The emotion might look like a dark cloud, a tornado, a lightening bolt, a solid bunker, a shield, a smoking gun, a raging fire, an icicle, a vise or hand that squeezes—you get the idea. See the emotion as raw energy.

Step 3. Draw the channeling of the emotional energy. Draw a lead-shielded container around this raw energy-emotion. Now draw a mini-power plant. From this container of raw energy draw power lines and transformers coming out of the container and going to your house, to your brain or other body area, to your job, to a relationship—to anything you see as needing this energy. Every time you become aware of feeling this emotion, visualize it being transformed into positive energy that you can use to help achieve your goals.

SAO 3.3 Emotional Power Exercise

Purpose: To relax before a meditative visualization, before programming dreams and going to sleep, any time. This exercise is very simple.

- Think of a time when you felt unconditional love, when you received it or gave it. What feelings come up now when you recall this incident? How do you feel now? Identify your feelings, such as confident, optimistic, friendly, outgoing, calm, happy, joyful.

- Allow the feeling(s) to prevail throughout your body-mind as you go into meditation, go to sleep, or engage in some other activity.

Note. These expansive feelings have been studied and found to be connected with higher immune levels, healing, and wellness. On the other hand certain contracting emotions have been studied and found to be connected to low immune levels and illness. They include anger (hostility, rage), depression (sadness, self-pity, guilt, hopelessness), tension (agitation, nervousness, anxiety), and repression (denial of anxiety). When you feel stuck in one of these emotions, try this power exercise for a quick shift.

SAO 3.4 Worst-Case Scenario

Purpose: To regain a sense of peace and self-confidence during emotional upset.

Step 1. Do the process for getting at root fears discussed in this chapter

Step 2. As you work through that process, imagine the worst thing that could possibly happen in your current problem situation. For example, if it's a career situation, the worst thing may be losing your job. Imagine that you've lost your job.

Step 3. When you get to a *disastrous* bottom line, ask yourself:

- *Is this the end of the world?*
- *Will life go on?*
- *Can I survive?*

See yourself in that scenario (in this case, without a job). Fully experience the feelings that arise in connection with that picture. Get comfortable with your ability to deal with that scenario.

Step 4. Ask, what could be worse than this? For example, you can't find another job that's comparable to the one you now have. Repeat Step 3 for dealing with this new scenario.

Step 5. Keep going until you get to the worst thing that could reasonably happen.

For example, what type of job could you undoubtedly get? Could you deal with that low-level job, at least for a while until something more appropriate comes along? Become comfortable with this worst-case scenario.

You'll find that imagining the worst-case scenario will bring your fearful shadows and ghosts out of the closet into the realistic light of day. This process will bring you to a sense of competence for coping with whatever comes up. This in turn will bring a sense of peace and self-confidence that will serve you well in dealing with the current issue.

SAO 3.5 Put It in Perspective

Purpose: To help you put an emotional upset into perspective.

A. How Bad Is It?

Think about the current situation that has triggered some contracting emotions for you. Refer to the trauma scale showing various levels of damage that could occur to your body, ranked from top to bottom in order of perceived impact, pain, loss, etc. Which item on the trauma scale best corresponds with your current *traumatic* situation?

Trauma Scale:

1. Stubbed your toe	5. Lost your toe
2. Cut your toe, bandaid	6. Lost your foot
3. Stitches in toe	7. Lost your leg
4. Broke your toe	9. Paralyzed from neck down

B. Ten Years From Now

Picture yourself ten years from today. Picture any other persons involved in this situation. From that perspective, looking back to this time in your life, ask yourself:

- Ten years from now, how important will this problem be?
- Ten years from now, what response will I wish I had made?

SAO 3.6 Observe Your Stressful Emotions

Purpose: To help you become master of your emotions, to put them in perspective, to allow one part of you to move outside an emotion and observe it while another part of you fully experiences it, to contain raw emotional energy and then transform it into useful forms of self-expression.

Step 1: Create an internal observation room. When you sense the onset of one or more strong, stressful emotions, picture yourself in a mental room. Imagine yourself stepping back from the emotion and sitting down in an observation chair.

Step 2: Stack feelings in the middle of the room. As the first feeling comes up, imagine yourself placing it very carefully on the floor in the middle of the room. If other feelings want to come in, allow them to do so and carefully stack them one on top of the other.

Step 3: Carefully observe the feelings. Now take one feeling at a time—or the whole stack if that's what seems to be needed. Sit back and watch the feeling—its color, its shape, and the nuances of its emotional tones. Watch the feeling. Don't judge it or put it down but observe it. Some typical thoughts that might come up are

Oh, there you are again!

So, that's what you look like!

My, you're very dark today.

Step 4: Experience and let go. Allow yourself to fully feel the feeling in your body while the observer part you watches it in your mental room. When the force of the feeling has passed, let it go. If you have difficulty letting it go, ask that it be lifted. What you're left with is the energy that was being wrapped around the feeling.

SAO 3.7 Heal Painful Emotions and Beliefs

Adapted from the work of Tapas Fleming (1998)

All the meridian lines in your etheric body end at your third-eye acupressure point. All your chakra energy centers come together at the back of your head. Work with these key body points to shift your emotional energy. When you heal at the etheric body level, you automatically heal the physical body. The Tapas Acupressure Technique (TAT) is a very quick, simple process that is also very powerful. Mental focus is the key here.

Step 1. Practice the TAT hand position:

→ Your index finger and ring finger (1st and 3rd) find the indentations that "feel right" at the inner eye areas on either side of the bridge of your nose.

→Your middle finger (2nd) finds the indentation that represents the "third eye" between your eyebrows, just above your nose.

→Your other hand is cupped across the back of your head, just above the nape of your neck.

→Lightly touch and hold these acupressure points as you do the following steps.

Think of a problem situation you want to resolve—a situation, emotion, belief, trauma, allergy.

You are going to make six statements in relation to this problem. For each statement, your task is to just "be with" that statement. That's all. Simply focus your attention, be aware of clear intention, and notice what comes up. Then move to the next statement.

Ask yourself, On a scale of 1 to 10, how strong is this belief (trauma, condition)?

Step 2. State the Problem

Formulate a statement that expresses the problem in a way that feels right to you. For example, "I need for people to like me in order to feel good about myself." You may want to stress the belief by saying, "It's true that . . . Holding the TAT hand positions, make the statement several times. Then rest and be with it.

Step 3. State the Opposite

Think of the opposite condition. Formulate a statement that expresses that for you. The idea to focus on: "what happened has happened . . .I experience this condition . . . I hold this belief . . . and that's all right." Examples of an opposite statement are, "It's not true that I need people to like me in order to feel good about my self," or "I can feel good about myself even if people don't like me."

Holding the TAT hand positions, make the opposite statement several times. Then rest and be with it. These 2 steps may be all that's needed, but if the issue is deep-seated, you'll need more.

Step 4. Heal All the Origins

The next statement reflects your intention to heal all the origins of the belief, trauma, allergy, or other problem condition. You don't need to identify the origins, just intend to heal them. The statement might be, "All the origins of this belief (trauma, condition) are healing now."

Holding the TAT hand positions, make the statement several times. Then rest and be with it.

Step 5. Heal All the Energy Storage Places

This statement reflects your intention to heal all the places where this belief, trauma, or condition are stored—in your body, your mind, your life, and all the parts of you. The statement might be, "All the places where I've stored this belief are healing now—my body, mind, life, and all parts of me." Holding the TAT hand positions, make the statement several times. Then rest and be with it.

Step 6. Forgiving Yourself and Others

This statement reflects your intention to heal everyone you have ever blamed for this belief, trauma, or condition—including yourself. You may want to include your vision of the Creator in this statement, using your own words. A statement might be, "I forgive everyone that I've blamed for this belief (trauma, condition), including myself and the Creator.": Holding the TAT hand positions, make the statement several times. Then rest and be with it.

Ask yourself, *On a scale of 1 to 10, how strong is this belief (trauma, condition) now?*

If there is still some charge, work through the statements again. Repeat till the charge is gone.

SAO 3.8 Reversing Self-Sabotaging Thoughts

Adapted from the work of Peter Lambrou M.D. and George Pratt M.D., Scripps Institute (2000).

About 80% of the people who seek help with personal problems, when tested, show signs of negative electromagnetic energy flows. You can correct specific emotional states by working with the acupressure points in the etheric energy body to break up old programs and patterns. If you have not done an energy reversal such as this for a while, take a few minutes to work through this process for rebalancing general body energy and for rebalancing psychological thought energy within your body.

Step 1. Rebalance General Body Energy

Do this before the Emotional Acupressure Process (total time—3 to 5 min)

Purpose: To realign the body's electrical polarity (positive-negative electrical energy flow). Do this process before you do the Psychological Thought Energy process.

1. Seated, cross your left ankle over your right ankle (vice versa if more comfortable).
2. Extend both arms straight out in front of you.
3. Cross your right arm over your left arm (vice versa if more comfortable).
4. Rotate the palms of your hands so that they are facing; interlock your fingers
5. Rotate your interlocked hands down toward your stomach
6. Continue rotating inward so that you bring your hands up close to your chest, under your chin. Now you have crossed the center line of your body with your hands, arms, and legs.
7. *Focus on your breathing*: Inhale through your nose while touching tip of tongue to roof of mouth. Exhale through your mouth, resting tongue on floor of mouth.
8. *Focus your thoughts on the concept of balance. Picture in your mind an image that represents balance.*
9. Breathe in this manner for about 2 minutes, holding the "balance image" as consistently as possible.

Step 2. Rebalance Psychological Thought Energy

Purpose: To reverse negative electrical energy flows resulting from self-sabotaging thoughts. The electromagnetic energy of thought is believed to be the causal agent of emotional disturbance. If you verbalize a statement (thought) at least 3 times, you cannot avoid creating a thought field associated with that statement. The following 12 themes cover virtually all the subconscious self-sabotaging themes. Each statement begins with the positive thought, "I deeply and completely accept myself," followed by a self-sabotaging theme, and accompanied by an acupressure movement.

Chest Spot Rub: Find the "sensitive spot" by first locating the indentation between your collar bones, at the center of your body. Bring your fingers down about 3 inches and then to one side about 3 inches until you sense the "sensitive spot" in the chest area, above the heart and below the collar bone. Use the tips of your index and middle finger. With a counter-clockwise circular motion, massage or rub this chest spot firmly and quickly.

1. **All Limiting Patterns**

    I *deeply and completely accept myself—even with all my problems and limitations*.

    Repeat 3 times as you **rub the chest spot**

2. **Unsafe Future for Self**

    I *deeply and completely accept myself—even if it isn't safe for me to get over this problem*.

    Repeat 3 times as you rub the chest spot.

3. **Unsafe Future for Others**

    I *deeply and completely accept myself—even if it isn't safe for others if I get over this problem*. Repeat 3 times as you rub the chest spot.

4. **"I-Can't" Beliefs**

    I *deeply and completely accept myself—even if it isn't possible for me to get over this problem*. Repeat 3 times as you rub the chest spot

5. **Lack of Self-Permission**

    I *deeply and completely accept myself—even if I will not allow myself to get over this problem*. Repeat 3 times as you rub the chest spot

6. **Lack of Will Power**

    I *deeply and completely accept myself—even if I won't do what's necessary to get over this problem*. Repeat 3 times as you rub the chest spot.

7. **No Benefit for Self**

    "I deeply and completely accept myself—*even if getting over this problem will not be good for me*." Repeat 3 times as you rub the chest spot.

8. **No Benefit for Others**

    "I deeply and completely accept myself—*even if getting over this problem will not be good for others*." Repeat 3 times as you rub the chest spot.

9. **"Special" Problem or Blockage**

    "I deeply and completely accept myself—*even if I have a unique block to getting over my problems*." Repeat 3 times as you rub the chest spot.

10. **Holding onto Problems Now**

    I *deeply and completely accept myself—even if I want to keep this problem.*

    Repeat 3 times as you rub the chest spot.

Tapping technique: Using your index and middle fingertips, tap firmly 7 or 8 times.

11. **Holding On to Problems in the Future**

    I *deeply and completely accept myself—even if I will continue to have this problem*.

    Repeat 3 times as you **tap under your nose**, center line, above your upper lip.

12. Not-Deserving Beliefs

I *deeply and completely accept myself—even if I don't deserve to get over this problem*.

Repeat 3 times as **tap under your lower lip**, center line, above your chin.

SAO 3.9 Emotional Acupressure

Based on the work of Drs. Peter Lambrou and George Pratt (2000)

Purpose: To break out of problem emotional patterns by working at the etheric-body level with the acupressure points related to the body's holding patterns for specific emotions.

Prep 1: Do Energy Reversal *(total time: 5 to 10 minutes)*

Reversing Self-Sabotaging Thoughts (SAO 3.8)—if you have never done this work, or if you have not done the energy reversal process in a long while.

Prep 2: Practice These Techniques *(total time: 5 to 10 minutes)*

Tapping Technique: Unless instructed otherwise, use one or two fingers, index and/or middle finger, tapping firmly 7 times. Sometimes you repeat an intention as you tap.

Tap Sites:

With index or middle finger, feel into the niche or "sensitive spot" of each area as follows:

Eyebrow: Beside the inside edge of one eyebrow, in the space between eyebrow and bridge of nose

Outside Eye: Bone beside outer edge, or corner, of one eye

Under Eye: Bony circle under one eye at midpoint

Under Nose: Center point directly under nose and above upper lip

Under Lip: Center point directly under lower lip and above chin

Little Fingernail: Base of fingernail

Index Fingernail: Base of fingernail

Thumbnail: Outside edge of thumbnail, away from index finger. Tap with 2 fingers.

Back of Hand: Make a fist; find the indentation on back of hand between little finger and ring finger; release fist; tap the area with the tips of all 4 fingers of opposite hand.

Side of hand: Make a fist, palm facing you; rotate your fist outward so thumb is away from you, little finger is toward you. Find the side-of-hand area where the palm creases, just below the little finger knuckle; release fist. Tap on this "karate chop" area of the hand with 4 fingers.

Collarbone: About 1-2 inches from midpoint between collarbones find a niche or indentation

Under Arm: Reach around to area about 4 inches below opposite armpit; tap with 4 fingers

Rib: Either directly below the nipple where, on a woman, the base of a bra touches the ribs, or lower, where the ribcage begins about halfway between armpit and level of the navel;

Chest: Locate the indentation between your collar bones, midpoint of body. Bring your fingers down about 3 inches and then to one side about 3 inches until you sense the "sensitive spot" in the chest area, above the heart and below the collar bone. Rub the chest spot with a counter-clockwise circular motion of your first 2 (index and middle) fingertips. Rub firmly and quickly. This is the only acupressure point that is rubbed instead of tapped.

Eye Roll

Do the Back-of-Hand tap continuously as you do the follow eye movements. Keep your head level, facing straight ahead, and move only your eyes, not your head.

Eyes closed→eyes open slightly, looking down at floor directly in front of you→slowly trace an imaginary line with your eyes forward across the floor to the baseboard of the opposite wall→continue tracing the line up the opposite wall to where it joins the ceiling→trace the imaginary line back along the ceiling toward you to the point directly above; your eyeballs are now looking straight up.

Bridge Technique

Do the Back-of-Hand tap as you do the following eye movements, humming, and counting

1. Eyes open→eyes closed→eyes open slightly, looking down toward floor to your right→look down toward floor to your left→rotate eyes slowly in a full circle, from left to right, not skipping any part of the circle→rotate eyes slowly back again from right to left.

2. Hum about 5 notes of any tune, such as Yankee Doodle or God Bless America.

3. Count from 1 to 5.

4. Hum the notes again.

Prep 3: Assess Your Discomfort *(time: a few seconds)*

Assessment. Pick a number between 1 and 10 that represents the intensity or severity of your discomfort with this situation, using the following descriptors as a guideline.

1 - I'm feeling OK but not as relaxed as I could be

5 - My discomfort is very uncomfortable, but I can stand it

10 - My discomfort is extreme, the worst I can imagine, and I feel panicky and overwhelmed

Emotional Acupressure—Find Your Specific Problem Emotion

(time for an emotional process: +/- 5 minutes each)

Anger, bitterness, resentment

Assessment→Eyebrow tap→Little Fingernail tap saying 3 times "I feel forgiveness in my heart" (or similar statement)→Collarbone tap→Bridge→Repeat tap sequence→Assessment→Eye Roll

Anxiety over future events

Assessment→Eyebrow tap→Under Nose tap→Under Lip tap→Under Eye tap→Collarbone tap→Under Arm tap→Collarbone tap→Under Eye tap→Bridge→Repeat tap sequence →Assessment→Eye Roll

Anxiety, general, and worry, irritability, stress

Assessment→Under Eye tap→Under Nose tap→Under Lip tap→Under Arm tap→ Collarbone tap→Bridge→Repeat tap sequence→Assessment→Eye Roll

Disgust, revulsion

Assessment→Outside Eye tap→Under Eye tap→Under Arm tap→Collarbone tap→ Thumbnail tap→Bridge→Repeat tap sequence→Assessment→Eye Roll

Embarrassment

Assessment→Under Nose tap saying 3 times "I release myself from this feeling"(or variation)→
Collarbone tap→Under Arm tap→Collarbone→Under Rib tap→Bridge→Repeat tap sequence
→Assessment→Eye Roll

Fatigue, tiredness

Assessment→Eyebrow tap→Under Eye tap→ Collarbone tap→Back of Hand tap 50 times
→Bridge→Repeat tap sequence→Assessment→Eye Roll

Frustration, impatience, disappointment

Assessment→Eyebrow tap→Under Eye tap→Under Arm tap→Collarbone tap→
Little Finger nail tap saying 3 times "I let go of this frustration for my own well-being"
(or similar)→Bridge→Repeat tap sequence→Assessment→Eye Roll

Grief, sadness, sorrow, despair, hopelessness

Assessment→Eyebrow tap→Outside Eye tap→Under Eye tap→Under Nose tap→
Under Arm tap→Collarbone tap→Index Fingernail tap→Collarbone tap→
Back of Hand tap 50 times→Bridge→Repeat tap sequence→Assessment→Eye Roll

Guilt, remorse

Assessment→Under Lip tap→Index Fingernail tap saying"I feel forgiveness in my heart for my
own well-being" (or similar)→Collarbone tap→Back of Hand tap 50 times→Bridge→

Repeat tap sequence→Assessment→Eye Roll

Habits - compulsive, addictive

Assessment→Eyebrow tap→Under Eye tap→Under Nose tap→Under Lip tap→
Under Arm tap→Collarbone tap→Bridge→Repeat tap sequence→Assessment→Eye Roll

Heartache, love pain

Assessment→Eyebrow tap→Under Eye tap→Under Arm tap→Collarbone tap→

Little Fingernail tap while saying "I will love again" or variation→

Back of Hand tap 50 times→Bridge→Repeat tap sequence→Assessment→Eye Roll

Hiccups

Assessment→ Under Nose tap→Middle Fingernail tap→Index Fingernail tap→
Thumbnail tap→Side of Hand tap→Collarbone tap→Bridge→Repeat tap sequence→Eye Roll

Jealousy, envy

Assessment→Middle Fingernail tap saying"I am filled with peace and harmony"

(or similar)→Under Arm tap→Collarbone tap→Bridge→Repeat tap sequence→ Assessment
→Eye Roll

Jet Lag (Do once an hour during the flight)

Flying West: Eyebrow tap→Collarbone tap→Bridge→Repeat tap sequence→Assessment→
        Eye Roll

Flying East: Under Arm tap→Collarbone tap→Bridge→Repeat tap sequence→Assessment→
        Eye Roll

Loneliness

Assessment→Eyebrow tap→Under Lip tap→Side of Hand tap→Back of Hand tap 50 times
while saying at least 3 times "I am filled with hope" (or similar)→Bridge→
Repeat tap sequence→Assessment→Eye Roll

Nasal Congestion

Under Nose tap→Under Eye tap→Collarbone tap→Bridge→Repeat tap sequence→Eye Roll

Obsessive Thoughts

Assessment→Under Eye tap→Collarbone tap→Under Eye tap→Collarbone tap→
Under Arm tap→Thumbnail tap saying "I release these thoughts for my own well-being" or variation→Under Arm tap→Collarbone tap→Bridge→Repeat tap sequence→Assessment→
Eye Roll

Pain, chronic pain, tension headache

Assessment→Eyebrow tap→Outside Eye tap→Under Eye tap→Under Nose tap→
Collarbone tap→Under Arm tap→Little Fingernail tap→Collarbone tap→
Index Fingernail tap→Collarbone tap→Back of Hand tap 50 times→Bridge→
Repeat tap sequence→Assessment→Eye Roll

Phobias, general (fear)

Assessment→Eyebrow tap→Under Nose tap→Under Eye tap→Under Arm tap→
Collarbone tap→ Bridge→Repeat tap sequence→Assessment→Eye Roll

Phobias, specific (snakes spiders, claustrophobia, flying, etc.)

Assessment→Eyebrow tap→Under Nose tap→Under Arm tap→Under Eye tap→
Collarbone tap→ Bridge→Repeat tap sequence→Assessment→Eye Roll

PMS Symptoms

Assessment→Eyebrow tap→Under Lip tap→Under Eye tap→Under Arm tap→
Collarbone tap→Middle Fingernail tap→Back of Hand tap 50 times→Bridge→
Repeat tap sequence→Assessment→Eye Roll

Procrastination

Assessment→Eyebrow tap→Under Nose tap→Under Lip tap→Under Eye tap→
Collarbone tap→Under Arm tap→Collarbone tap→Under Eye tap→Thumbnail tap→
Middle Fingernail tap→Back of Hand tap 50 times→Bridge→
Repeat tap sequence→Assessment→Eye Roll

Rage

Assessment→Outside Eye tap→Under Eye tap→Under Arm tap→Collarbone tap→
Little Fingernail tap saying 3 times "I feel forgiveness in my heart for my own self-control and peace" (or similar statement)→Collarbone tap→Bridge→Repeat tap sequence→ Assessment→
Eye Roll

Regret

Assessment→Under Eye tap→Under Arm tap→ Collarbone tap→
Little Fingernail tap→Collarbone tap→Index fingernail tap→Collarbone tap→
Middle Fingernail tap saying 3 times "I release the past and focus on my life ahead" or variation→Back of Hand tap 50 times→Bridge→Repeat tap sequence→Assessment→Eye Roll

Rejection, hurt feelings

Assessment→Under Eye tap→Thumbnail tap→Under Arm tap→Collarbone tap→
Little Fingernail tap saying 3 times "I deeply accept myself and remain open to new possibilities" (or similar statement)→Collarbone tap→Back of Hand tap 50 times→ Bridge→
Repeat tap sequence→Assessment→Eye Roll

Shame

Assessment→Under Lip tap saying 3 times "I deeply and completely forgive myself and others and I accept a new beginning" or variation→ Under Arm tap→Collarbone tap→Little Fingernail tap→ Collarbone tap→Index Fingernail tap→Collarbone tap→Back of Hand tap 50 times→Bridge→Repeat tap sequence→Assessment→Eye Roll

Trauma, emotional

Assessment→Eyebrow tap→Outside Eye tap→Under Eye tap→Under Arm tap→Collarbone tap→Thumbnail tap→Under Arm tap→Collarbone tap→Index Fingernail tap while saying 3 times regarding anger "I feel forgiveness for him/her for my own well-being" or variation →Collarbone tap→Index Fingernail tap while saying 3 times regarding guilt "I feel forgiveness in my heart for my own well-being" or variation→Bridge→Repeat tap sequence→Assessment→ Eye Roll

Worst Case Scenario—If All Else Fails—A Comprehensive Sequence

Assessment→Eyebrow tap→Outside Eye tap→Under Nose tap→Under Lip tap→ Under Eye tap→Collarbone tap→Under Arm tap→Collarbone tap→Under Eye tap→ Under Rib tap→Little Fingernail tap→ Collarbone tap→Index Fingernail tap→ Collarbone tap→Middle fingernail tap→Thumbnail tap→Side of Hand tap→ Back of Hand tap 50 times→Bridge→Repeat tap sequence→Assessment→Eye Roll.

SAO 3.10 Heartfelt Stress Reduction

Purpose: To shift out of stress-related emotions.

When you experience feelings such as worry, frustration, agitation, recognize the feelings and process them. If you have difficulty releasing them, try this process:

- Concentrate the feelings in your heart.

- Concentrate all your attention on your heart.

- Pretend you're breathing with your heart. Breathe in through the heart.

- Think of something that triggers feelings of love or sincere appreciation.

- Channel that into the warm, loving emotional energy of your heart.

- Soak your contracting emotion in this warm energy.

- Hold that image in your heart for at least 10 seconds. This will calm your heart, and then your mind and body.

- Ask your heart the best way you can take care of yourself and still be able to do the things you need to do.

SAO 3.11 Clearing Out Contracting Energy

Purpose: To boost the power of your inner work.

Step 1: Focused Breathing. As you do your deep breathing to relax, say to yourself:

Breathe in . . . love
Breathe out . . . fears

Breathe in . . . love
Breath out . . . negative ego, negative judgment

Breathe in . . . love
Breathe out . . . pain from the past

Step 2: Visualization. To deepen the relaxation, use this visualization.

- Focus in your heart area.

- Bring in love/white light through the crown of your head.

- Bring it down into your heart area and let it fill your heart

- Let love and caring radiate out from your heart.

- Feel love, caring, connection, compassion, gratitude

- Open the eyes of your heart

- See beyond the trivial to the big picture

- See the pathway of your life

- See what needs to be next for you

SAO 3.12 Emotional Film Exercise

Purpose: To become more aware of how you experience various emotions in your body.

Step 1: **Find emotional films.** Plan to view one or more films that evoke strong emotions—both contracting and expansive. Select a film that you've seen that evoked extremely expansive emotions, as well as a film that evoked extremely contracting emotions. You want to experience as full a range of emotion as possible. You may choose to view only the most emotional scenes of each film for purposes of this exercise.

Step 2: Review Map of Emotions. Review the Map of Emotions in this chapter—to remind yourself of some of the emotions you might become aware of during the films. Have it in front of you as you view the films.

Step 3: Relax. Do some deep breathing. Become relaxed, focused, and centered.

Step 4: Experience your feelings. As you watch the film and an emotion comes up, do the following:

- *Movement*. Allow yourself to become so fascinated with the *movement* of the feeling that the *content* loses its importance.

- *Accompaniment*. What *comes with* the feeling . . . Self-talk? Images? Confusion?

- *Location*. Where is the feeling *located*? . . . Local? (in your stomach, neck, etc.)? Global (general, overall)?

- *Qualities*. What's the *quality* of the feeling? . . . Contracting? (cold, prickly, tight, etc.) Expanding? (warm, fuzzy, loose, etc.)

- *Form*. Does the *form* of the feeling appear to be . . . Solid? Particles? Waves?

- *Vibration*. What is the relative *vibration* of the feeling? . . .Fast? Medium? Slow? Faster, higher, thinner? Slower, lower, thicker?

Step 5: Assess. After you've watched the films and responded to the questions in Step 4, assess the overall experience. What insights or new self-knowledge did you experience?

References

Ackerman, Diane. *A Natural History of the Senses*. New York: Vintage Books, 1991, 309.

Braden, Greg. *Awakening to Zero Point*. Questa NM: Sacred Spaces/Ancient Wisdom, 1994.

Capra, Fritjof. *The Web of Life*. New York: Anchor Books, 1996.

Carr-Ruffino, Norma. *The Promotable Woman*. Franklin Lakes, NJ: Career Press, 1997.

Corbett, M. *A Better Place to Live*. Emmaus, PA: Rodale Presss, 1981.

Davis, Bennett, "A Mind of Its Own," *Ambassador*, February 1999, 22-26.

DeBeauport, Elaine. *The Three Faces of Mind*. Wheaton, IL: Quest Books, 1996.

Diener, Ed, Urbana: University of Illinois, Department of Psychology, 1991.

Durden-Smith, Jo. *Sex and the Brain*. New York: Arbor House, 1983.

Fleming, Tapas. *You Can Heal Now: The Tapas Acupressure Technique*. Redonda Beach, CA: TAT International, 1998.

Goleman, Daniel. *Emotional Intelligence*. New York: Bantam, 1995.

Jensen, Rolf. *The Dream Society: How the Coming Shift from Information to Imagination Will Transform Your Business*. New York: McGraw-Hill, 1999.

Lambrou, Peter and George Pratt, *Instant Emotional Healing: Acupressure for the Emotions*. NY: Broadway Books, 2000.

Pert, Candace. *Molecules of Emotion : Why You Feel the Way You Feel*. New York : Scribner, 1997.

Pollack, Willliam. *Real Boys*. New York: Random House Inc. 1998.

Wolger, Roger J. "The Signs of the Times and the Time of the Heart," *Journal of Family Life*, Fall 1995, 26-33.

Chapter 4
Motivational Intelligence
Passion for Life

Work as though you don't need the money. Anonymous

Your motivational intelligence is a function of your "emotional brain," or limbic brain. It's sometimes called the mammalian brain because all mammals have this type of brain. You're motivated when you *feel* passionate about something you really want. Motivational intelligence is all about what drives you to want something and what moves you to get it. This is the ultimate in creativity because it's about creating the life you want—and doing it in a way that fulfills your purpose for being here. It's about your life blueprint and is related to the etheric energy body that serves as your physical body blueprint. It's related to your abdominal chakra, sexuality, creativity, sorting out, choosing, and life purpose.

You can use your motivational intelligence to guide your life through a process of wanting and getting. The secret to this intelligence is becoming aware of what you love, desire, and want—which in turn offers clues to your underlying life purpose—what you came into physical life to learn and what you came to contribute. This life purpose fuels your passion for life, a precious gift. When your work is aligned with that life purpose, you'll often find yourself in the creative flow state.

Words to associate with this intelligence include *desire, wants, goals, drives, life purpose, etheric energy body, abdominal chakra, orange, tone re or D, emotional-limbic-mammalian brain.*

Myths & Realities

The culture conveys many myths about motivation, often to coerce people to follow cultural norms about duties and responsibilities.

Myth 1. It's selfish to focus on your own wants and desires.

The culture teaches that it's selfish or egotistical to want—that you shouldn't be "spoiled." Have you conditioned yourself to hide your deep desires, saying that it's selfish or egotistical to want? Instead, try learning appropriate ways to feel excited about, and even get, what you want. When you stop wanting, you begin to die.

One type of cultural heroine or hero is the selfless, altruistic, all-giving person. And in fact some of the happiest people *are* empathetic, compassionate, caring, and giving. But they're living this way because it fulfills them in a very real, deep way. They've made decisions about the ways they want to live in the world. So they are, in fact, acting out their wants, desires, and passions. Each person must reach this place in life—or not—in their own time and in their own way. The main point: your wants, desires, and passions are a treasure because they are a way of being that drives your actions, your doing. Instead of squelching your wants, channel them in ways that lead you in the direction you want to go. Make them work for you, not against you.

Wanting is the slow, burning fire that leads you ever more deeply into all your emotions. If you learn how to stay in, and move through, that emotional fire, you arrive at love—love of life, personal love, and compassion.

Myth 2. Please others; forget about yourself

This is a variation on the adage, "It's more blessed to give than receive. When someone close to you indicates they want something, do you immediately think you should satisfy that want for them? (Or feel guilty if you don't satisfy it?) Do you later conclude that they're spoiled and demanding? (And resent that?) How about respecting their wanting and then encouraging or helping them to do the work of getting what they want for themselves? This is a deep change you may need to make in order to respect your own desires and those of others.

Myth 3. If it feels good, it's probably bad for you

Do you have difficulty with wanting because you link it in your mind with pleasure? You want pleasure because pleasure feels good, but maybe you've been taught that pleasure is usually bad. Are you caught in the trap of staying in only one reality or one brain system, the basic brain of values and obligations? You don't need to choose between hard work and pleasure; you can have both. You can revise your beliefs and view pleasure as life-giving rather than greedy, lazy, or selfish.

Myth 4. Good people focus on their duty to family and society.

The culture says, "Do what it is your duty to do." You have responsibilities to your parents, family, society, etc.

In fact, at the deepest level you always do what you want to do in the long run. You find ways to avoid what you don't want to do, perhaps by being "too busy, too sick, too tired, etc." You may find that easier to get away with than actually admitting that you're going for what you *want*—unless what you want happens to be something that's condoned.

Search for what really excites you, for it's the only fuel that keeps you in love with life. To reach your personal potential for growth and success, you must go through a self-questioning process and arrive at a place where you've decided what *you* really want to do with your life. Then you can freely and joyfully take responsibility for creating a life that moves toward those goals you've adopted for yourself.

Don't try to fulfill someone else's idea of your purpose in life, your life's work, the responsibilities you'll assume, or your goals. If you try to do someone else's goals, you can never be truly committed. You'll always have some resentment about the situation. And if you don't, you're really in trouble! Surely you'll want to listen to the people who care most about you and your welfare. But you must make your own decisions in order to live life with passion and to achieve a sense of fulfillment from your achievements.

Find the place where your deep joy and the world's deep needs meet. If you do, your work will bring joy and satisfaction over the long haul, although there will surely be difficult days. Re-connect with your *own* desires, passions, your heart's calling—to regain your power. Get in touch with your life purpose and you'll boost your motivational intelligence.

Myth 5. Forget your wants. They just lead to frustration.

According to this myth, if you don't expect anything good to happen, you'll be happily surprised when it does and never disappointed when it doesn't. You can't control what happens to you. It's all up to God, fate, luck, your karma, etc.

You may conclude with your rational mind that what you want is not intelligent. You may think, "Why want it, when I know I can't have it?" When you think this way, what you *want* becomes less important than what you think is possible.

Fear of failure may keep you from fully living your desire. You must risk "failure" as a necessary price of going forward, of growth. If you want something, and learn a few simple techniques for creating what you want, you'll probably get it. Be very clear about the end results you intend to achieve, but don't cling to them. Focus on the *process* of living, preferring to achieve specific results but not desperately needing them. Don't become so fixated on the *goal* of getting a job or money or a lover that you forget to enjoy the process. Rather, hold the desire and passion and bask in the process of moving toward the goal. If you don't achieve that particular goal, you can still enjoy the process, and you can also learn a lot about yourself, others, and how to do it next time.

You've read about the latest scientific research that indicates you are *not* a victim of external objects and events. You do have personal power, which you can give away, but it can't be taken from you without your permission. A key to creating the life you want is to treasure your wants, tie them to a life purpose, and align your goals with that purpose.

How Motivational Intelligence Works

Motivational intelligence is about love, desire, wanting, and passion. It goes beyond your deepest conditioning about what you *should* want to what you came in to do in life—your life purpose. It gives you the strength to live and to break out of your self-sabotaging patterns and to form new self-empowering patterns. Unless you want things in life, and want them strongly enough to learn very specifically what it is you really want, you're likely to sabotage your own efforts, and finally destroy your life-passion, gradually losing interest in everything.

Motivational intelligence is the capacity to recognize what you want and what moves you to action. It's about listening to your inner self and observing what excites you, interests you, gets you going. It's making up your life in your own way, based on your own desires and passions, setting and achieving your own goals, not someone else's. It's using your sense of your own life purpose to guide yourself through a *process* of desiring and creating—over and over throughout your life.

You gain access to your passion through identifying your life purpose and following it. When you're standing in your life's purpose, when you're "on purpose," the passion is always there, and possibilities live everywhere. You feel powerful and capable of achieving your goals. So getting in touch with your passion will always get you out of your rut and onto a higher road. In this way, passion gives you access to your inner power.

The Wanting-Satisfying Process

To want is forever; satisfactions are temporary, according to Elaine DeBeauport [1996]. Wanting is the emotional process of expansion that goes on continually in the emotional brain. Satisfaction is the resting point in the process of desire.

Satisfaction is to wanting as conclusion is to thinking—a form of temporary closure. You can feel, and even express, many desires without satisfying them, and you don't have to criticize yourself for wanting. You don't need to act on every desire or rush to satisfy them all. Wanting and desiring are emotional indicators of what you've allowed yourself to be affected by. They tell you what you love. If you decide your wanting is not pleasant or life-giving or that it's too expensive, you can shift your focus to more life-enhancing desires. Use your rational and intuitive intelligences to give yourself reasons for shifting your interest. Use your basic brain of action to withdraw from this desire. Use your rational intelligence to notice that you don't feel good doing it and to quit.

What should you do when you feel dissatisfied?

- Realize that every time you satisfy a desire, you can rest and celebrate instead of criticizing yourself for wanting more

- Use your rational and intuitive intelligences to select the desires that are more in alignment with your life purpose and that make sense for you now.

- Use your rational and intuitive intelligences to establish your priorities, referring back to your emotional brain to see if that's what you really want.

- Use your basic pattern-parameter intelligence to rest or to act on something else.

The wanting-satisfying process will last forever and indicates that your emotional being is alive and well.

Coming from Deep, True Desire

You need to encourage that passion that comes from deep, true desire in order to strengthen yourself to live, to identify old patterns that either don't work or actually sabotage you, and to create new patterns that enable to you bring your goals into reality.

Which of your desires are superficial? Are you *conditioned* to want something or do you really want it, regardless of your conditioning? See the vital connection between conditioned patterns and wanting. Realize that you can want independent of your deepest conditioning.

Are some of your desires actually negative ego desires to be better-than, to merely impress others, or to feel less worse-than and therefore a special case? Negative ego will always eventually bring what you do *not* want. The key question to ask yourself: Do I want this for my own deep satisfaction? Would I want it even if others ignored or despised it?

Learn to identify your true, deep passions. Use this deep wanting to guide yourself away from old conditioned patterns that no longer serve you. Then enlist all your brain systems to building your motivational intelligence—vivid, wonderful visions and goals of your neocortex, supportive habits and patterns of your basic brain, and expansive emotions of your emotional brain.

Remember, when you are into your passion, you are totally here in the present moment. You are completely charged and focused. You are oblivious to distractions. You forget yourself, your troubles, your day-to-day life. You hitch yourself to something bigger. Sounds like the definition of creative flow, doesn't it?

Motivational Profiles: Six Types of Workers

A survey of thousands of employees [Herman 1995] suggests six types of workers ranging from those who focus primarily on the clock to those who focus on getting personal fulfillment from their jobs. How well do you think these people understand their own wants, desires, motivations, life purpose, and goals? How effectively do you think they go about satisfying these wants? Do any of these profiles describe your patterns?

Clock Punchers

- Ended up in current job by chance, not design
- Satisfaction level is lowest of all groups
- 75% would make a different career choice

- Typical demographics: female, no college, earn under $30,000
- Typical occupations: cashier, waitress, hospital orderly, etc.

Paycheck Cashers

- Priorities—good income, good benefits
- Not focused on stretching abilities or changing the world
- Happy in their cubicles
- Typical demographics: young, male, ethnic minority, no college degree
- Typical occupations: blue-collar, or non-professional white-collar jobs—factory worker, entry-level word processor, etc.

Ladder Climbers

- Priorities—job security, company loyalty
- Working way up to better job
- Typical demographics: female, modest education, good income; 48 percent earn more than $50,000
- Typical occupations: skilled blue-collar supervisor, middle manager, etc.

Risk Takers

- Want to get rich quick
- Always seek opportunities to make bucks
- Job hop, looking for better jobs
- Typical demographics: young, male, educated, successful; 40 percent earn incomes over $50,000
- Typical occupations: software entrepreneur, commission salesperson, etc.

High Achievers

- Leaders who take initiative
- Planned their career path early on
- Highest income group: 25 percent earn over $75,000
- Typical demographics: male, highly educated
- Typical occupations: professional—lawyer, surgeon, CPA, upper management

Fulfillment Seekers

- Want to make the world a better place
- Seek jobs where they can contribute
- Team players rather than leaders
- High satisfaction with their work
- Typical demographics: white, married,
- Typical occupations: teacher, nurse, social worker, public defender, etc.

How to Boost Your Motivational Intelligence

You can easily boost your motivational intelligence—the level of motivation you feel and the skill with which you use it to create the fulfilling life you want. You can begin by identifying your deep desires, what you're good at, your life purpose, the goals and activities to achieve that purpose, and ways to stay "on purpose."

Booster 1. Give Your Motivation a Quick-Charge

You can boost your level of motivation by falling in love with life and by identifying what turns you on and moving toward those situations.

Any Love Affair Will Do

Mary Oliver's poem "Wild Geese" speaks of the Web of Life and inspires a love of life.

> *Whoever you are, no matter how lonely,*
>
> *the world offers itself to your imagination,*
>
> *calls to you, like the wild geese, harsh and exciting—*
>
> *over and over announcing your place*
>
> *in the family of things.*

You need a high level of motivation in order to guide yourself and sustain your life within the all-pervasive Web of Life. You need it in order to fully participate in life itself. The secret is knowing that you are one with the Web of Life, one with the energy of all life. You *are* energy. You *are* life. Identify yourself with the Web of Life so you can take your rightful place within it. Live your emotions, and use your turn-ons to know yourself, to stay passionate, excited, truly and vibrantly alive.

If you identify with all energy, with the Web of Life, you'll feel that you belong, that you're a full-fledged member, and you can continually accept and receive energy. Become aware of how this Web of Life affects you and how you affect it. If the flutter of a butterfly wing in Japan affects the weather in California, what impact do your thoughts and actions have?

Your love of life is precious because it's your deepest connection with all creation. Use your love of this Web of Life to boost your motivation level. You know that what you love is what moves you most deeply, so find something to love. *Any love affair will do.* Love a sunset, a tree, an animal, a person, an idea, a cause, a career. It's your way of saying *yes* to life—honoring what's here, approaching it, penetrating it, surrounding and integrating yourself with it.

When you doubt or question life, you drain off some of your energy. Your rational mind can doubt and question any aspect of life. Your basic brain can wrap life into a package of duties and bury your energy under a pile of "shoulds." Your emotional brain can get worn out from dealing with all this. Free your emotional brain by encouraging yourself to *be* what you feel like being, to *do* what you feel like doing, to have what you most want. Free yourself to experience whatever feelings come up—happiness or anger or love or sadness. Process these emotions and discover what you really want.

Find Turn-Ons that Light Your Fire

What excites you? What kinds of situations, people, food, drinks, ideas, music, sexuality, challenges, work, art, sports, hobbies, weather do you really groove on? What kinds of recognition, flirting, compliments, rewards turn you on? Exactly what is it that gets you excited? Observe your reactions to life so you can know consciously what excites you. Keep asking yourself these kinds of questions:

- What makes me feel excited and expanded?
- What starts me trembling with excitement?
- What stirs me into motion?

Only this fuel can keep you motivated and really in love with life.

Desire is a deep, passionate, unclear feeling. It takes skill to observe it in all its subtleties. To feel and to observe are two different skills. Watch and observe your body to see what gets it to act What moves you to pick up the phone, plan a trip, write a letter, or go to see someone? What causes you to repeat that action over and over? Notice what stimulates you to move: is it good company, someone in need, money, a compliment, God, status, making love, childhood dreams, what?

This information provides clues to identifying your life purpose, what you want to learn in life and contribute to life. This information also can help you decide on the best approaches to take, the kinds of interim goals and rewards that will work for you, and the kinds of activities to plan for achieving those goals.

Use these turn-ons as the fuel to throw again and again on the fire of your motivation. The secret to conscious motivation is being willing and able to notice which turn-ons work for you and to find ways to create those turn-ons to continually fuel your fire. Feed that fire so it won't go out in the difficult times, so you can stay in the wanting, the longing, the desiring.

Booster 2. Find a Life Purpose

Your life purpose, and your motivators, are tied to what you like and what you're good at. Do you really know what they are? Can you list them quickly? If not, don't worry. Many people aren't clear about the kinds of things they're good at and really enjoy. They feel there may be many things they could do or would like if they only knew more about them or had a chance to try them—especially in the career area.

What Do You Like? What Are You Good At?

The only way to identify your skills and interests is to start with what you know now. Then, as you learn more about various jobs and careers, you have a basis for evaluating how well they fit your skills/interest set. At the end of this chapter you'll find the SAO called "What Do You Like to Do? What Do You Do Well?" It will help you identify your skills and interests.

Your most valuable resource can be people who are working in the field, industry, company, or position you are considering. Use your networking skills to locate these people and to arrange some informational interviews. Ask them such questions as:

- Where do you see the industry going in the next few years?
- Tell me about your career path.
- How did you get your job?
- What do you like best and least about your job?
- Could you describe a typical day on the job?
- What is the average salary for this type of position?
- What is the single type of thing I could tell you about myself that would help me get a job?
- Is there anyone else I could speak to? In a particular job or department? In another company?

Why Are You Here?

Underlying and surrounding what you like and what you're good at is your life purpose. Ask yourself:

- Why am I here?
- Why did I come into this world?

We all came here to learn certain lessons to make some kind of contribution to the world —your life purpose is composed of these two aspects. The SAO called "What's Your Life Purpose' is designed to help you get in touch with this. Once you get some sense of your life purpose, you'll begin to understand your primary motivators. Then you can assess all your goals and activities in the light of how well they align with your life purpose. It's a great way to keep you "on purpose."

> *Your life purpose, or mission statement, is a long-range overview*
>
> *of what you believe you want to do with your life*
>
> *—why you're here and who you are in the overall scheme of things.*

You may never have some specific experience that tells you, "This is your life purpose." George Bernard Shaw said, "Your life purpose is simply to help the purpose of the universe." This is a good starting point, but you'll want to get more specific than that

How can you realize what your life purpose is? If you had no life purpose, you wouldn't be here on Earth, so you *can* learn to recognize that purpose.

In the meantime, author David Spangler (1996) says that you may decide, "I don't know what tomorrow brings. I don't know which task I should undertake. I don't have a sense of my life purpose at this moment. But right now, here in front of me, there's someone or something to interact with. I can honor that person or situation, that place or object, and I can give my whole heart to it." This is a choice. You can choose to give your self and your passion in that way to call forth the good in someone or something else. In this way you create your own calling, moment by moment.

Over your lifetime, your life purpose will undoubtedly grow and shift, but there will be a consistent core or thread. That core is what makes your life purpose different from your goals, even long-term goals. When you become consciously aware of your life purpose, you can consciously set goals that are aligned and integrated with that purpose. Your day-to-day activities can lead you in the direction that seems right to you. People who have managed to "get it all together" in this way say their achievements became more meaningful to them. The work itself—and the resulting achievements—began to bring deeper satisfaction and joy.

When you're on purpose, you have a deeper, more sustainable source of motivation that keeps you working toward your goals. The line between work and play becomes fuzzy, because those activities that you see as part of your life's work, you also see as important, satisfying, and the source of fun and joy in your life. In addition, work that you love to do, you learn to do well, and the work that you do well is the most likely to bring in the money you want. Isn't it elegant that the work that brings you joy is most likely to bring you abundance? All it takes is getting in touch with your deep desires and how they reveal your life purpose.

Booster 3. Develop Clearly Stated Goals

Once you have some sense of life purpose, you're ready to move into the goal-setting process. This includes the precondition of allowing for abundance, then brainstorming the things you want and need to move toward achieving your life purpose. After that you refine and rank a short list of goals that are clear and specific.

Allow Abundance in Your Goals

Do you approach goals from a viewpoint of scarcity? Do you think, Since there are not enough resources for everyone to have all they need, then the more I get, the less there will be for someone else? Think of all the things that are perceived as scarce. Jot them down. If you analyze the world's resources—such as food, fresh water, housing, education, health care, money, time, energy, love—you may realize that we have adequate resources, and even abundance, if a critical mass of people were to decide to manage these resources properly.

The World Game Institute determined that within 10 years we, as a global society of humankind, could solve all major global problems and create a vital, sustainable economy for all people. We have the technology and we could raise the money if we managed our resources differently. The cost? About $ 250 billion a year for ten years. The amount spent on "defense" globally? About $750 billion a year. This is based on 1991 statistics provided to the World Game Institute by UNICEF, Worldwatch Institute, Rocky Mountain Institute, and World Resources Institute.

Surely we could collectively choose to have not only adequacy but sustainable abundance. Abundance thinking reflects individual beliefs or collective beliefs about the key resources in life.

- Take money—our creative energy becomes money; we can think of it as green energy.
- Or time—there are always 24 hours in a day; we have abundant time to achieve our top-priority goals once we clarify them and weed out the nonessentials.
- Or energy—all that exists in the universe is energy; the only problem is finding and using the best form of energy for each of our purposes.
- And love, which exists in our minds and hearts—the more love we give to ourselves and others, the more we tend to receive, and the more we have to give back again. The only limits are our fears that shield us from giving and receiving love.

When you come from an attitude of abundance, you can move more freely toward your goals. Since there's plenty for everyone, your successes don't need to be built on someone else's failures. Your having more doesn't mean that someone else has less. It's a win-win attitude: everyone can win. On the other hand, our culture also has a tendency to make heroes of greedy multi-millionaires and billionaires. The type of abundance discussed here is aligned with the concept of "right livelihood," earning a living in ways that contribute to humanity. It means going beyond the need for greed and sharing the wealth with those who help you to create it.

As you complete the SAO, "What Are Your Goals?," focus first on setting goals that tie in to your life purpose and the contribution you want to make. Secondarily, but with clarity, focus on the type of abundance you want for yourself—abundant relationships, abundant health, abundant joy, abundant material resources. When you're *on purpose*, doing what you're here for, the abundance will materialize in the best form for you.

Be Clear About What a Goal Is

The term *goal* as used here is synonymous with *objective* and is quite different from an activity in the following ways:

- A goal is a specific end result you want by some stated point in time.
- Activities are things you *do* in order to achieve your goal.
- You may *enjoy* an activity, but that doesn't make it a goal.

There may be a variety of feasible and acceptable activities that can help you reach your goal.

The activities are a means to an end. The end is your goal. That's why it's so important to separate goals from activities—so you'll be clear about what you're really after and feel free to consider alternatives for getting there.

It's also important to have a clear picture of your goals. Write them down. You're much more likely to achieve written goals than mental ones. They're more specific—and they're easier to remember, to update, to revise, and to mark off once they're achieved. And the marking-off increases your sense of satisfaction and your motivation to keep achieving.

Distinguish Between Specific and Vague Goals

Look at the differences between the vague and specific goals shown in Table 4.1. Most of us tend to carry around a mixed bag of *wants*. Many of them are vague; some we picture as activities instead of what we hope to gain *from* those activities. We usually wish we had these wants now, and we dreamily hope to have them some day. We must transform such dreamy wants into clear, specific goals in order to achieve them. How specific? Preferably specific enough so that on the target date you've set for attainment of the goal, you *know* for sure whether you've achieved it or how close you've come to it, and anyone knowledgeable on the subject could also tell.

Table 4.1 Vague Versus Specific Goals

Vague Goals	Specific Goals
To make more money	To earn $30,000 next year
To move up in the company	To be general manager of a regional branch by ...
To get ahead in life	To have an MBA degree by ...
To have more free time	To have at least one month of free time per year by ...
To travel more	To travel to the Far East for three weeks in ...

Distinguish Between Goals and Activities

In many cases, only you can decide whether a *want* is a goal or just an activity. Ask yourself, *Why do I want to do this?* If the act or process of doing something is what you desire, then it's probably a goal for you. If the activity is mainly a *means* to having something you desire, then it's not a goal for you.

For example: *Why* do you want more free time? Is it to have more time to pursue a hobby, develop a skill, travel? If so, then those activities are your goals and having more free time is a *means* to that end. On the other hand, you may want freedom to do things on the spur of the moment, to pursue whatever tickles your fancy from time to time. If so, then having more free time is indeed your goal.

Here is another example: *Why* do you want to have a masters degree? Is it to get a better job, make more money, or feel the personal satisfaction of having the degree, regardless of its other advantages? Suppose you find that the major reason you want a degree is to increase your earnings. You might find a number of alternate career paths or ways of becoming qualified for a particular career path that would take less money, time, and energy than getting a degree.

When you find it difficult to decide whether a want is a goal or merely an activity you enjoy that is a means to another end, try this:

- Get comfortable; relax as fully as possible.

- Close your eyes and try to visualize yourself once you have achieved your goal.

- How do you feel? Are you satisfied with that particular end result? Are you satisfied with the *way* you got it? Is anything missing?

- What would you have done differently if you could?

Sometimes visualizing end results and how you feel about them can help you decide what you really want. For example, if you visualize yourself holding a particularly desirable job *without* having gotten the degree, you may determine whether having a degree is your true goal.

Brainstorm, Refine, Rank Your Goals

After you spontaneously generate a random list of things you want in your life, the next step is to evaluate the list, sorting out activities from goals, adding goals you may have overlooked, rewriting them so that they are specific and contain time targets, and ranking them in order of their importance to you.   Most people find it helpful to categorize them by life area, such as career area, personal development, and private life. The SAO "Refine and Rank Your Goals" guides you through this step.

Booster 4. Plan Your Activities and Set Priorities

The next step is to consider which activities will provide the best avenues for reaching these goals. Write down any and all activities you can think of that might help you achieve your goals, taking one goal at a time. At this point, do not rank the activities. Again, fantasize, brainstorm, let the creative-child part of you take over.   Send your judgmental counterpart out of the room. Be daring. Be outrageous. When you've listed activities for all life areas, summon your critical, practical, reasonable side to help you select the activity that is most feasible and the most likely to contribute to your first goal. Rank that activity 1. Rank the second most likely activity 2, etc., down to the least likely activity. Repeat for each goal.

Does your list of activities boggle your mind? If so, start picking out the activities *you are willing so spend at least five minutes on during the next week.* Now remove from your list all activities you are *not* willing to spend five minutes on. Such activities may be important, but obviously they're not important enough to occupy your time right now, so you'll probably never get to them. Do some of your goals now have no activities listed for them? Go back and list other activities, then rank them and delete the impractical ones.   Keep going until you have for each goal a list of activities that are important to you and are things you are willing to begin acting on right away. Once you've completed all the Self-Awareness Opportunities to this point, you should be close to knowing:

- what you want

- what you can do to get it

- what you will do about it in the next week

Develop Short-Term and Long-Term Action Plans

You'll probably want a one-month action plan, a one-year plan, and perhaps a five-year plan. Think broadly as you complete the longer-range plans, focusing on goals rather than on activities.

To accomplish the most, make a one-month plan *every* month. Use it as the basis for your weekly and daily *To Do* lists. Compare months to see how you're progressing toward long-term goals. Finally, remember to reevaluate your decisions regularly to be sure that your goals reflect what you really want in life and that your activities are the best ones for getting you there.

Here's the total process you'll be following to get what you want in life:.

- setting goals and priorities
- developing specific action plans with prioritized activities to help you reach those goals
- periodically reevaluating your goals, action plans, and priorities

Make Your Plan a Reality

Now it's time to work your plan. Here are some general suggestions for bringing your mental plan into physical reality.

Envision and focus. Use relaxed concentration and visualization as a technique to command your inner resources so that all your actions tend to move you toward your goals, which gives you a powerful focus.

Act. Begin this week, even if you undertake only a five-minute activity for each goal.

Communicate. Let the important people in your life *know* about the goals they may be able to help you with. For example, let your boss or mentor know about appropriate career goals.

Get support. Make a list of the people who can help you and give you support as you work toward your goals. Decide the best way to enlist their aid. Include support systems in your plan.

Enjoy. Make the *process* of achieving your goals as enjoyable as possible. It's important to keep your eye on the end result you want, but it's also important to relax and enjoy yourself along the way. In fact, your enjoyment of an activity should be one of the criteria for selecting it.

Negotiate. Use your goals to help you achieve specific results on the job that will serve as the basis for negotiating promotions and raises later

Focus. Don't get so carried away with the *activities* that you lose sight of the *goal.* Use your action plan to chart activities; mark them off as they are completed and as the goal is achieved. As mentioned earlier, it helps if you keep a list of your top three or four goals handy and refer to it regularly. Some successful women keep their lists (or symbolic pictures of their goals) posted where they'll see them daily in their homes or offices.

Overcome barriers. Become a problem solver who can figure out how to overcome barriers to reaching goals. Don't let procrastination, interruptions, and distractions keep you from achieving your goals. Manage your activities.

Reevaluate. If you're having unusual difficulty in achieving a goal, ask yourself whether the goal is right for you. If it is, then reevaluate the activities you have selected and look for new ones.

Keep goals flexible. Your goals are not set in concrete. They're just part of a plan that can be changed as *situations* change.

Congratulate yourself. When you achieve a goal, remember to give yourself credit and reward yourself.

Keep setting goals. Once you have achieved a major goal, set another one to take its place. You say you've earned a rest? You don't want another major project for a while? Then your new goal might be to have a specific number of additional unstructured hours each week, month, or year to do as you please.

The object is to be clear about what you want and what you're doing with your time and your life—so that you're making clear choices rather than drifting.

Booster 5.   Overcome Typical Barriers to Success

Recognizing your life purpose and following that path is such a powerful motivator and life enhancer, why doesn't everyone do it?   Usually it boils down to fear of failure—or fear of success because success means change and change is risky.   Here are some typical "reasons why" you may not be creating the life you want.

Self-sabotage

Are you afraid of finding out whether you've "got what it takes," so you "forget" to mail the application, make the new contact, research the company?   Or when the time is ripe to move down that path, you suddenly just "must" clean out the garage or your closet, catch up on phone calls or e-mails to old friends, re-do your Christmas list?

By far the major way you sabotage your goals is by projecting your fears, doubts, and worries into your goal vision.   Only when you become aware of your self-sabotage patterns, and own up to them, can you start moving toward your vision.

Remedy: At the deepest level, your fears, doubts, and worries spring from self-limiting beliefs. Be aware: Your beliefs are never neutral.   They either move you forward or hold you back.   And you choose what you will believe.   See SAO 4.12 for getting in touch with these beliefs.

At the action level, all this putting off and distracting yourself is are just various forms of procrastination.   See the remedy for overwhelming paralysis.

If you believe there are opportunities in everything that happens, then possibilities will appear everywhere.

Analysis Paralysis

Do you analyze your life purpose to death, picking apart all its varying implications until you lose the heat of your passion?   Remedy: Focus on how fortunate you are to have a sense of your life purpose, feel the gratitude, and let it move you.

Overwhelming Paralysis

Do you turn your life purpose into such a huge project that you intimidate yourself into paralysis? Remedy: Take it one moment and one day at a time.   Set some easy, short-term goals and focus on those.   Let go of the need and focus on the preference.   Be happy just to make some progress every day, even if it's only five minutes of work toward a purposeful goal.

Make a list of your resources—people or organizations who could help you, advise you, mentor you, coach you; places you can go; things you can read, try, reference.   Ask, how can I use each of these resources to achieve my goals? Do I need a network? A team? Ask yourself what resources your associates need—what skills, interests, education, and other resources they need in order to contribute. Be willing to share resources.   Hooking up with others can get you moving in the right direction.

Perfection

You keep waiting for the perfect moment to take the plunge.   You must have just the right combination of energy, inspiration, education, freedom, money, time.   "Someday" is your motto.   See the remedy for "overwhelming paralysis."

Self-Deception

Do you say, "I can't afford it," or "I can't take the time or money to learn the skills," or "I don't want it anyway," and other little lies? The truth is you do want it, but you won't spend the money it takes, you won't change your priorities, and you won't make the little sacrifices you think the purpose requires. Remedy: face the facts and get your priorities in order.

Self-Devaluation

If you're *really* afraid of success or failure, you may even take to drinking, gambling, spending until you're deeply in debt, and other addictive behavior patterns. When your hidden agenda is to make yourself not good enough to achieve your life purpose, then you can find any number of ingenious ways to follow a path that conflicts with your true path.

Remedy: We may be getting into serious territory here. Think about some good professional counseling that will help you to overcome old negative programming and to build your self-esteem. See the SAOs in the Basic Intelligence chapter that deal with breaking out of old patterns.

Settling for Another Path

Are you choosing a path that's parallel to the real one? For example, are you becoming an art critic rather than an artist, a teacher rather than a parent, a nurse rather than a doctor, a legal aid rather than a lawyer?

Are you choosing a substitute path instead of the real path because of some stereotype? For example, what you really want to do is great paintings or great politics or great social work, but the real path seems "too arty" or "too goody-goody" or "too dirty." Maybe your parents said that artists starved or politicians were crooked or social workers were too self-righteous.

Remedy: Focus on the belief that when you are "on purpose," on the real path and following your passion," things do work out for the best and none of those negative self-limiting beliefs need apply to you. Try this approach: "Why shouldn't I go for what I really want? I can always settle for less if that doesn't work out. But, first, if I don't give it my best shot, then I've accepted defeat without even going for it."

Booster 6. Cross the Gap from Wanting to Having

Say you haven't been aware of your life purpose, and you haven't been achieving your goals. Try this attitude: "Where I am now is simply where I am now. The universe attaches no value judgment to it. The gap between where I am and where I want to be creates a healthy tension that can move me forward."

You won't move forward unless you stay clear and honest about where you are now. When you start to deny failure or pretend success or start to settle, you drain your "moving-forward" energy and momentum.

Try this: Focus on where you've been (that you don't want to be) and where you are now (that you don't want to be). Notice how that energy feels. Now focus on where you want to be, what you intend to have, what you're committed to moving toward and achieving. Notice how that energy feels.

Think about the quality of energy you feel when you're moving away from what you *don't* want. Doesn't it have a negative quality? This focus is not a powerful way of creating what you want in your life. Say for example you have a problem with owing money and you focus on solving that problem, which is getting rid of what you don't want, what you are *against*. Your focus on that problem can lead you to pay off your debt, but if that's as far as it goes, you're likely to repeat the pattern, accumulate debt again, and face a similar problem. That's because you're not generating a positive attractor energy that draws a positive outcome into your life.

In contrast, notice the quality of energy you feel when you're moving toward what you *do* want. Does it feel more positive and powerful? It is. Now when you approach a problem, such as owing money, you focus on what you want, what you are *for*, which is an abundant life without money worries. This focus also involves paying off your debt but it allows much more—such as recognizing ways to create a life free of money worries, one where money flows in freely and adequately. Now you are generating a positive attractor energy that draws abundance into your life.

Any time you notice yourself thinking about what you don't like, don't want, or are against, think about the reverse side of that coin and ask:

What am I *for*?

This concept is so powerful, it's worth writing on a card and posting it where you'll notice it regularly.

Booster 7. Keep Checking Your Motivation Level

To keep yourself on track, keep asking yourself, What's my motivation level now, on a scale of 1 to 10? If it's 5 or below, you need to take a new look at your goals and priorities. In the middle of a project, ask yourself,

- What am I feeling?
- What feedback am I receiving?
- How does it make me feel?
- What am I wanting now?

Use your feelings as a signal to readjust your plans, rather than ignoring them, which can lead to sabotage. Know what you really want—and you'll save time, money, and heartache. Invite your rational brain into more accurate, more efficient, and realistic planning. Feel the blocks so you can move around them or over them. Within these blocks may be the necessary energy and information you need to complete your project successfully. Consider these suggestions.

- Feel what it is that you truly want
- Experience the desire, love your longing.
- If your feelings are unpleasant or painful, keep the following in mind:
- Don't shift to *thinking about* the wanting or the doing
- Don't move away from *experiencing* your wanting at a gut level.
- Don't intellectualize or postpone it.

The only way to know how to want is to experience the wanting and let it motivate you.

Creativity Showcase

Using Motivational Intelligence
for Creative Solutions and Ideas

Some innovative solutions to current problems—for your information and inspiration—and as food for thought.

Problem—Wasted Time, Effort, Resources

Any human activity that absorbs resources but creates no value is waste. Some typical types of waste are:

- Products and services that don't meet customer needs.

- Production of products or services that no one wants so that inventories build up and surplus goods must be disposed of

- Processing steps that could be eliminated

- Unnecessary movement of materials or people from one place to another

- People at a later stage of a process waiting idly for people at an earlier stage to complete or deliver their segment

- Mistakes that need to be fixed

Innovative Solutions—Lean Thinking

Lean thinking is an innovative approach to preventing waste that has four inter-related parts:

1) Continuous flow of value, 2) as seen from the customer's viewpoint, 3) at the pull of the customer, 4) in search of perfection.

Paul Hawken (1999) tells how companies can use lean thinking. Sometimes they must motivate their clients to "pull for" a new lean approach. For example, Interface, an innovative leasing company, had to overcome the psychological stigma traditionally attached to leasing—that it means you're too poor to buy and that you end up paying more.

One asset that people never thought of leasing was the carpet on their floors. Wall-to-wall carpeting has traditionally been bought and kept till it develops worn spots and stains—usually about ten years. When a company replaces its carpet, workers must shut down the offices, remove all the furniture and equipment, tear out the old carpet, take it to the dump, lay the new carpet, and then move everything back in.

Carpet that was under furniture and equipment, in corners and other low-traffic areas, is till good. Therefore, many square feet of very good carpet are discarded along with very few square feet of worn carpet. This is major waste. It takes two pounds of fossil fuel to turn one pound of petroleum-based material into carpet, and additional fuel to transport new carpet to the customer and discarded carpet to a landfill. There it stays for about 20,000 years—along with billions of pounds of other carpet in landfills across the country. This situation calls for lean thinking.

Interface executives, headquartered in Atlanta, decided to start from scratch and re-think their entire mission and strategies. They asked, "What do business owners and managers really want in a floor covering?" The answer: Carpet to walk on and look at, not to own—and carpet that gives them the best value for their bucks. Interface found that the 80-20 rule applied to replacement needs—with 80 percent of the wear occurring in about 20 percent of the carpeted area.

They created a new floor-covering paradigm that motivates clients to lease, not buy. Instead of selling carpet, they lease floor-covering services. Here's how it works: Interface provides the carpet in the form of "carpet tiles." They take responsibility for keeping the carpet clean and fresh. When any area becomes worn, torn, or stained, they replace it with new, perfectly matched, recycled carpet tiles—and they do it overnight with no disruption of office routine.

The new carpet they developed is called Solenium, a new polymeric material for a new kind of floor-covering service. It can be completely re-manufactured back into itself. All the worn materials are completely separated into their components, fiber and backing. Each component is then remade into an identical fresh product. The manufacturing process produces virtually no waste.

Compared to typical nylong carpet, Solenium requires 35 percent less material to produce and is four times as durable. That means it uses seven times less massflow per unit of service, according to Interface engineers. Customers love it because it's highly stain-resistant, doesn't mildew, is easily cleaned with water, and offers better soundproofing. It combines the durability of resilient flooring with the acoustics and beauty of soft flooring.

Solenium's combination of improved physical attributes, when factored in with the service lease aspect of the paradigm (needing to replace only 20 percent of the carpet) results in a 97 percent reduction in the net flow of materials and embodied energy. In addition, manufacturers can produce it for less money and make a better profit.

This type of innovative paradigm shift lets us be kinder to Mother Earth and to future generations. It also allows us to motivate manufacturers, retailers, and clients to "think lean" by eliminating wasted time, effort, and resources.

Creative Techniques Using Motivational Intelligence

Every creative technique you can imagine is related to your motivational intelligence. That's because you must be motivated to actually use a creative technique before it can do you any good. The most important creative activities involving your motivational intelligence are those that help you get in touch with your life purpose, the big fire that runs your engine. Having a sense of life purpose also helps you to recognize and use all those little things that turn you on, that light your fire and keep your motivational intelligence growing. The Creative Techniques that follow will help you do that. The cases will help you apply your motivational intelligence to real-life situations.

CT 4.1 Creative Questions

In order to discover what your basic skills are (or those of a client or employee), ask the following creative questions. You can have more than one answer to these questions. Write down answers in the order they occur to you. Then go back and rank them. Keep in mind that the first answer that comes up is probably your No. 1 preference.

Problem Preference. What kinds of problems do I like to solve—those focusing on people, info, or things? Do I prefer problems with a main focus on the people in the situation? Their thoughts, feelings, desires, conflicts, learning, healing, etc.? Or do I prefer problems with a main focus on knowledge, information, and data? Or is it problems with a main focus on things, such as building, vehicles, equipment?

Question-Answer Preference. What kinds of questions do I like people to ask me? What types of questions do I like to answer? Questions about how to make things work? Or why people act a certain way? Or what a situation really means? Or what the person should do next? Other?

Knowledge Preference. What kinds of knowledge do I like to bring into a conversation or situation? Do I like to impart knowledge about what makes people tick? The history of something? How something works? How culture comes into play? How to do something? Other?

Conversational Preferences. What kind of conversation—when I overhear it—am I likely to want to join into, even to interrupt, because I'm so interested in the topic? (For example, when I'm at a party, in an airport, at a meeting, etc.) What clues does this give me about my passions?

Activity Preference. What are my favorite activities, hobbies, avocations, etc.? Most of these are also industries, so the question becomes, How can I fit this activity into a job or business?

Word Preferences. What are my favorite words? What kinds of words do I find myself using over and over. (Suggestion: Ask people close to you to notice the words you frequently use, especially words that they don't hear others using as often.) Your vocabulary often reveals areas that are close to your heart. Categorize the words to see patterns that could reveal a field of interest.

People Preferences. What kind of person would I most like to meet? What would make that person intriguing to me? The kind of work do they do? (What is it?) The kind of activities they're involved in? (What are they?) What they like and what they're good at? (What things?)

Reading Preferences. What kinds of magazines and books do I buy when I browse a newsstand or bookstore? Within those venues, what types of article attract my attention so that I'm likely to read them? What internet sites do I frequent? Suggestion: Look at your bookmarks to detect patterns.

Viewing Preferences. What types of TV shows do I watch? Pay special attention to programs that are educational and informative. Which shows or topic am I most likely to watch and enjoy? When I watch game shows on TV, which categories do I like for contestants to pick because I stand a good chance of getting the right answers and because I'm interested in the information in those categories?

Writing Preferences. If I could write a book (or if I were required to write a book but could pick any topic), what subject would I write about?

Review these answers for clues to your own interests—especially those you would like to develop further and do something about.

CT 4.2 List Your Passions

Note: Work on this technique after you have completed the SAOs concerning life purpose and goals.

Successful people who passionately love life and love their work are likely to have lists of things they want to explore, do, see, launch, write, or achieve before they die. For some it's a mental list, but written is best. For example, the best travel agents have a list of places around the world they want to see. Successful writers keep a list of topics they want to explore and possibly write about.   Business entrepreneurs have a list of new types of businesses they would like to research and perhaps launch before they retire. Professionals keep a list of career areas they would like to explore and experience.

- Make lists of topics you want to explore, goals to achieve, people to meet, places to see, etc.
- Put your No. 1 desire first and rank order each list.
- Draw or paste small pictures or symbols, in color, on your list, to spark a multisensory, emotional charge.
- Put the list where you'll see it regularly, renewing your awareness of it, but not where you'll see it so frequently that it becomes invisible to you.
- Revise it as your interests change and as you complete items.

Case Studies—Applying the Creative Techniques

In working on these cases, you may use creative techniques from any of the chapters. However, the creative techniques described in this chapter may be especially appropriate. Keep these self-questions in mind.

- What problems do I see?
- How can I probe beneath the surface to get at root problems?
- What opportunities (hidden or obvious) can I find to take initiative, cut costs, and/or make money?
- What creative alternatives can I generate?
- As a consultant, what should I recommend as the best viewpoints and actions?

To answer these questions, what creative techniques can I experiment with to respond to this case? After completing the case analysis, ask: Which creative techniques produce the best results?

Case 4.1 Steven's New Career

Steven, age 43, is thinking of a midlife career change. His lifelong career in the grocery business is not as fulfilling as he would like. After graduating from high school about 25 years ago, he completed two years of college work. His father and grandfather were in the grocery business in Houston, so it was natural that he worked in his father's stores from time to time as a young man. He also got some experience with another grocery chain before joining his father's firm full time.

Steven met **Vickie**, who was a regular customer at one of the stores, married her and two years later they had their first daughter, **Lila.** Two years later along came **Nancy,** and two years after that their third daughter **Marion** was born.

About this time Steven entered a venture with his father and bought a retail grocery store in Pinecone, a small town about 50 miles from Houston. Making a good living from Pinecone Grocery was usually a struggle. At one point the firm bought two more stores in nearby small towns, but neither of these stores generated lasting profits and were closed. The firm took a big loss when the grocers' cooperative they belonged to declared bankruptcy and closed. Another blow was the entrance of a huge Walmart grocery-department store into the market area. Finally, Pinecone Grocery was destroyed by a fire. Since it was under-insured, Steven was unable to rebuild. So ended a 10-year struggle.

At age 38 Steven was looking for a substantial job for the first time in his life. He was hired as a department manager for Mercado, a medium-sized chain of huge supermarkets that targets the Latino American community. Mercado Centrale, the store where Steven works, is located in central Houston.

He's been with Mercado for four years now. Lila, Nancy, and Marion are 18, 16, and 14—Lila is entering college this fall and the other two won't be far behind. Vickie has been employed from time to time but is currently not working as she's having some health problems.

The family still lives in Pinecone, so Steven has a very long daily commute to work. Still, he's hesitant to move to Houston with two daughters still in Pinecone High School—and he feels he can't really afford the move just now. He is, however, thinking of making a career change—creating a new career in an entirely different field. He consults a career counselor who asks him some questions.

Skills. Steven was asked what he thinks his key skills are and he jotted down these answers:

work quickly and am never one to lay back and wait for things to happen

not always perfect at getting all the details taken care of

tend to take action

like to work with people,

good at team building

have good organizational skills

like to work on solutions to problems by setting up strategies or action plans

take pride in my work

have a good work ethic

like to explore new challenges in business

Interests: When asked what he's most interested in, Steven replied:

Internet startups, ventures involving the internet and computers

real estate sales

other types of selling

history, archeology, and Spanish culture

Goals: To the question, What goals do you want to achieve? Steven replied:

to be independent, own my own business again

to gain financial stability

to get my daughters through college

to meet and spend time with people who are successful, genuine, self-motivated, and sharing to travel—see some sights around the country and the world, especially Mexico, Central America, and the Egyptian pyramids

to spend more time with family

Steven has been offered an opportunity by Robert, a business acquaintance who owns a real estate agency in Houston. If Steven will take the real estate courses he needs and pass the test to get his license, Robert will welcome him into the firm.

Steven is also very interested in some type of internet startup, but he doesn't have a bright idea yet, nor a business plan. However, he can get a loan of up to $75,000 once he comes up with a good idea.

- Which of these two career possibilities best fit Steven's profile?
- What opportunities are likely in each area?
- What problems could arise in each?
- What other types of careers, job positions, or startup businesses might fit his profile?
- Which CTs discussed in this chapter did you use in solving this case problem?
- Which CTs were most helpful and what ideas did they spark or inspire?

Case 4.2 Career Change for Lauren Alvarez?

Lauren Alvarez has been a sales rep for McDougal Food Supplies for 7 years. When she began, she had several disadvantages:

- She was the first woman sales rep in her region.
- She had no sales experience.
- Her background included a great deal of company experience but not the educational credentials of the other reps.

She discovered during the second year that she was being paid 30 percent less than other sales reps hired at about the same time.

In spite of these disadvantages, Lauren has become one of the top reps in the southeast region, which includes about 25 reps. She often wins awards for selling the most product. It wasn't until the company computerized sales records that she discovered she usually placed first in profits earned from sales. So not only did she sell a lot, she sold more of the products with highest profit margins.

Now, Van Meter Food Suppliers has just acquired McDougal's operations in the southeast region, and Lauren's not sure what the changes will mean for her. Everyone's anxious about the future. **Victor Seymour**, the branch manager of the Little Rock office, Lauren's manager, takes her to lunch one day and says:

"Lauren, I believe Van Meter is going to lower our bonuses and reduce our retirement stock options. I think those of us making the most money are going to lose on this deal. I have an idea for starting my own food supply company. What I really do in my job is get the supplies that you sales reps sell. What you do is sell those supplies to companies that process food. What **Pattie Goodman** does is handle billing, shipping, and other aspects of getting your orders processed and getting the product to our customers. I want you and Pattie to come in with me as equal partners. Let's do it for ourselves instead of doing it for Van Meter."

Lauren has never once thought about starting her own food supply business. She asks Victor if she can have a couple of weeks to think it over and he agrees.

Now, two weeks later, Lauren is still stewing and fretting over what to do. She has a good steady job with the company and is building a fairly good retirement plan because of the general stock options and matching funds the company provides. After all, she's well into her 40s now, and she's never been an entrepreneur. To complicate matters, a Van Meter vice president was in yesterday and acted as if he'd heard something about Victor's plans. He said to Lauren: "Well, these changes always create some chaos. I just hope no one in the region decides to go off and form a competing company. You know, we don't like that, and our suppliers know we don't like it. They usually won't sell to defectors if we let them know that we're unhappy. Anyway, Lauren, I know that doesn't apply to you. And I anticipate a 25 percent increase in your bonus beginning this year."

- What problems or potential problems arise from this scenario?

- What opportunities?

- How would you address each problem or unmet opportunity?

- Which CTs discussed in this chapter did you use in solving this case problem?

- Which CTs were most helpful and what ideas did they spark or inspire?

Case 4.3 Sell the Business?

Dennis Wong has been Vice President of Sales and one of 3 managing partners in Heartland Food Supply for 7 years. Dennis calls on purchasing agents in the food industry and sells them the seasonings, spices, preservatives, and other food additives they need for processing foods. It's been an exciting and successful 7 years. At the end of the first year, he and his two partners bought Mercedes company cars. At the end of the second year, they each took a $100,000 bonus. And bonuses have increased every year since.

Lately, though, the competition is getting tougher and tougher. Dennis' partner, **Shane Hudson**, President and buyer of the products they sell, asks him, "What's going on? Sales and profits are down a little for the first time. And you seem to have lost some of your enthusiasm for this game."

"Oh, it's just the same old thing—only more so. New guys trying to break into the market. They're willing to sell stuff at zero profit margin, just to take the customers away from us. The customers should know it can't last, but a lot of them go along for the ride anyway."

Shane says, "Well, a guy from Archer Supply called me the other day. I think they're interested in buying us out. Of course, they'd want us to run the business for a few years—and to train our replacements when we decide we want out. After all, what they're buying is our knowledge and contacts—the customers and the suppliers. We really have no physical assets--we just buy and sell product. I've done some research on what our type of business is worth, based on sales and profits—and I figure we can get at least 3 million—and may 6 million from Archer—or from some other supply company that wants to expand. What do you think? Should we sell?"

"Gee, I don't know, Shane. I've passed my 50th birthday. I'm not ready to retire, but I *am* getting a little tired of this particular rat race. Still, we've done awfully well. It's tough right now, but I think we can ride out these competitors, and when we do, it may get a lot better."

- What problems or potential problems arise from this scenario?

- What opportunities?

- How would you address each problem or unmet opportunity?

- Which CTs discussed in this chapter did you use in solving this case problem?

- Which CTs were most helpful and what ideas did they spark or inspire?

Case 4.4 A Banker's Dilemma

Linda is the mother of an 18-month-old child. She is a loan officer with Trust Bank. Linda had resigned from her previous job with World Bank because the maternity leave was inadequate for her to make the adjustment to a new baby. When she went to work for Trust Bank, it was with the understanding that it would not be a high-pressure position—no expectation that she would work overtime or make business trips. However, Linda is beginning to feel pressure to do just that.

Linda's job involves working with customers (and bringing in new customers) who have assets in excess of a million dollars. Most of the loans she makes to them are for real estate, either residential or commercial. This means Linda must have a network of contacts with realtors and appraisers. She receives a base pay of $40,000 and a bonus of 1% on the value of all loans she makes. She is evaluated by how the total value of loans she makes and the repayment rate on those loans—in other words, she must correctly evaluate clients' ability to repay the loans she grants them.

Linda approaches **Jan, her manager**, to tell Jan that she has decided she must resign in order to find a part-time job, about three days a week. She says, "My son needs more of my time and attention just now. I need to work, and I want to work, but I have decided to give his needs top priority for the next year or two."

- What problems or potential problems arise from this scenario?
- What opportunities?
- How would you address each problem or unmet opportunity?
- Which CTs discussed in this chapter did you use in solving this case problem?
- Which CTs were most helpful and what ideas did they spark or inspire?

Self-Awareness Opportunities

You make the road by walking it. Anonymous

SAO 4.1 What Do You Like to Do? What Do You Do Well?

Purpose: To get to know more about yourself by identifying your key interests and skills, and to organize these into career building blocks.

Instructions: Follow the instructions given in Parts A through D. Then Examine the Showcase examples and set up a similar sheet with seven columns for analyzing your own favorite activities— what you enjoy doing.

Part A. Interests—Activities You Like to Do

Step 1: What excites you? List 3 times in your life when you felt passionate and excited. Think of 3 special times when you could say "I did that and it feels good." Get started by writing the first one that comes to mind, and the other two will probably come back to you.

Step 2. What do you gravitate toward?   Ask yourself some probing questions, suggested by career specialist Richard Bolles (2000):

1. What kinds of problems do you like to solve?

a. Problems in which the main focus is on the people (or animals)—their thoughts, feelings, desires, conflicts, learning, healing, etc.?

b. Problems where the main focus is on knowledge, information, or data?

    c. Problems where the main focus is on things, such as cars, houses, pictures, etc.

2. What kinds of questions do you like people to ask you?

    a. What they should do next?

    b. What a situation really means?

    c. How to make things work?

3. What kinds of knowledge do you like to bring into a conversation or situation? A.

    a. Knowledge about what makes people tick?

    b. The history of something? How culture comes into play?

    c. How something works? How to do something?

4. What are your favorite words? What kinds of words do you find yourself using over and over. Ask people close to you to notice the words you frequently use, especially words that they don't hear others using as often. Your vocabulary often reveals areas that are close to your heart.

5. What are your favorite activities, hobbies, avocations, etc.? (Note: most of these are also industries.)

6. What's your definition of a "fascinating stranger"?   What do they like and what are they're good at? What kind of work do they do? What kind of activities are they involved in?

7. What kinds of magazines and books do you browse through or buy at newstands or bookstores? Within those venues, what types of article attract your attention so that you're likely to read them?

8. What internet sites do frequent? Look at your bookmarks to detect patterns.

9. If you watch game shows on TV, which categories do you like for contestants to pick because you stand a good chance of getting the right answers and you enjoy the information in those categories? What types of TV shows do you watch? Pay special attention to educational channels or other programs that are educational and informative. Which shows are you likely to watch?

10. If you were to write a book, what subject would you write about?

    Interpret your Answers: Questions 1, 2, 3: How many "a" answers did you give to these first three questions? This score reflects a people orientation. Your "b" score reflects your information orientation, and your "c" score reflects your technical orientation. Question 4: Which words fall into the categories of people, information, and technical? Which category has the highest score? Questions 5-10: How do your answers fit into the people-information-technical categories? Do other categories or patterns emerge? What do your patterns suggest about your key skills and interests?

Step 3: What do you like to do? Now that you've played with your likes for a while, summarize them in the first column of your seven-column table. Just randomly list them, as they come to mind, 20 things you most enjoy doing. Don't attempt to respond to the other columns until you have completed the first column.

Step 4: Why do you like those activities? Now find out what your "liked" activities have in common. Analyze each activity listed in the first column by responding to the other columns.

In column 2, opposite the first activity, place a dash (-) if you most enjoy doing this alone; a plus sign (+) if you enjoy this activity with another; or a slash (/) if either (or no preference).

In column 3, place an *I* for activities in which you experience intimacy, perhaps *I* + for deeper levels of intimacy.

In column 4, note activities that carry a risk factor with an *R*.

In column 5, write the approximate date you last engaged in the activity.

In column 6 identify the primary need filled by engaging in this activity; that is, what motivates you to get involved? A need to achieve (*A*), to exercise power (*P*), or to interact socially (*S*)?

In column 7, identify the types of skills or knowledge that you use when you engage in the activity. Write one word that symbolizes each skill or knowledge area used in this activity. Looking at all your activities, how do they fit with your "people, information, and technical" scores?

Step 5: Rank Your "Liked" Activities. Rank the activities in order of the degree of enjoyment you derive from each.

Showcase: Ashley's Favorite Activities

Ashley's Example	2	3	4	5	6	7
Favorite activities:	alone - other+	intimacy level	risk factor	last did	need met*	skills-knowledge used **
Entertain	+	i+		6/2	S	visualize
go to parties	+	i		5/13	S-P	communicate.-
hang out with close friends	+	i+		6/18	S	intuit
take photographs	-	-	r	6/2	A	communicate.-
travel	+	i	r	1/5-15	S-A-P	intuit
write letters, reports, diary	-	-	r+	6/18	A-P	visualize-act visualize-act
make presentations	+	-		5/20	A-P	communicate-org.
shop for collectibles	+	i		6/15	A-S	communicate-org. apply information

*A=achievement need   P=power need   S=social/belonging need

**Ashley realizes that her chief skills used in party-going and hanging-out are communication skills with a healthy dose of empathy and intuition. Her skills in writing and making presentations are also primarily communication skills, in these cases allied with the ability to visualize past and future events and to organize her thoughts and feelings about them. She sees the chief skills she uses in photography and travel as being able to visualize what she wants to do and achieve and to follow through. In shopping for collectibles, her chief skill is applying the information she has gained through study and shopping experiences. She can see a strong skill pattern of visualizing, communicating, and organizing—allied with a strong need for social interaction and intimacy, followed by achievement need, in low-risk activities.

She repeats this process in a separate list for what she does well. She finds that most things she does well are also on the favorite list. She identifies those activities that appear on both lists as her core skills—the ones to build a career around.

Part B. Skills and Knowledge—What Are You Good At?

Step 1: What Do You Do Well? If possible, complete this part a day or so after you complete Part A. Complete column 1 by listing, in random order, ten things you honestly do well; take no more than twenty minutes.

Step 2: What Do Your Skills Have in Common? Complete columns 2 through 7 as instructed in Part A.

Step 3: Rank Your Skills. Rank the things you do well in order of their importance to you, also considering your level of expertise in each activity.

Part C. Patterns and Insights

Step 1: What Patterns Can You Find? What interrelationships do you see among the different factors, such as alone/with another, intimacy, risk, need fulfillment/motivation, and types of skills and knowledge? What patterns seem to emerge concerning what you enjoy (interests) and what you do well (skills/knowledge)? Notice the dates column. Are you developing your most likely talents or neglecting them? Are these truly the interests and skills you most enjoy and that seem most important to you? Or do you wish they were, or believe they should be? If so, where do these wishes and beliefs originate? From family? Friends? Teachers? Describe the interrelationships and patterns in writing. From this deep inner source comes your passion for your work and for life.

Step 2: What Insights Pop Up? What insights emerged from this exercise? State in writing how these insights affect your image of yourself, what you want in life, and what talents and contributions you have to offer.

Part D. Career Building Blocks

Look over your interests, skills, patterns, and insights. Identify some common building blocks of skills and interests that could form the foundation for a career. Take several sheets of paper; consider each page a block. Give each block a label, and within it list the types of interests, skills and knowledge that apply. Play with your blocks, moving them around in different combinations and configurations to fit various types of jobs and careers. Remember, each of your skills are transferable skills—they go everywhere with you. It's up to you to recognize them and use them. Ask yourself, "Where would I be happiest using these basic skills? Remember, you'll be most effective where you are the happiest. Each of your skills is potentially a marketable skill. It's up to you to find the company and situation that needs this skill. So once you identify your package of transferable, marketable skills, it's a matter of doing some research and informational interviewing to determine how your skills would fit in with some company's needs or a set of customer needs.

SAO 4.2 What's Your Life Purpose?

Purpose: To help you determine your life purpose.

Process: The three steps in this process all center around getting in touch with aspects of your childhood and family situation. First, get in touch with your control strategies, which will block you in achieving your life purpose. Second, identify what you came here to contribute. Third, identify what life lessons you came here to learn. We all came here to contribute and to learn lessons—your life purpose is composed of these two aspects.

Step 1: Identify Your Control Strategies

Bring your particular control drama and resulting control strategies into full consciousness. What are you doing to manipulate for attention, for energy, for control? These manipulations and strategies begin in childhood. A control drama is the soap opera episodes you played out. It's the dialogue, the he-said she-said, the actions and reactions involved in getting attention, energy, and control. The control strategies are specific behaviors you use within this drama.

Identify your childhood family's control dramas. Go back into your past, your early family life, and see how your control habits were formed. Seeing how they began will bring your way of controlling up to the conscious level.

Your family members were no doubt operating in a control drama themselves, trying to pull energy out of you as a child. That's why you had to form a control drama in the first place. You had to have a strategy to win energy back.

It's always in relation to our family members that we develop our particular dramas and strategies. But once we recognize the energy dynamics in our families, we can go past these control strategies and see what was really happening.

Examples of control strategies**:**

- Withdrawing, sulking, withholding approval or affection
- Demanding, dominating, taking center stage
- Attacking, accusing, blaming, nagging, making wrong
- I did you wrong but it's OK because I have a conscience and I feel guilty . . . or because I worry about you
- Lashing out and then withdrawing
- Saying yes and going along but resenting, waiting to get even . . . or saying yes but feeling sorry for me or feeling that I sacrifice for others
- Being incompetent, naive, sick, or otherwise weak and needing help
- Demanding perfection of self, or of others, or both
- Taking charge, doing the work, being the leader—to be sure everyone does it my way

Key questions:

- What did your mother do to get attention, to get energy, to control? What was her control drama? How did you react to that?
- What did your father do? How did you react?
- What did your sister(s) and/or brother(s) do? How did you react?

Step 2: Identify what you came here to contribute.

Reinterpret your family experience from a personal growth viewpoint and discover who you really are.   Once you become conscious of your control strategies, then you can focus on the *higher truth* (or contribution) of your family members, the silver lining that lies beyond the energy conflict. This higher truth can energize your life, for it can help you know more about who you are, the path you are on, what you are doing here.   When you discover your life purpose, you can begin to move beyond your subconscious control strategies and more consciously create the life you want.

To discover your real self, consider the belief that the real you began in a position between the higher purposes of your mother and your father. Consider the possibility that you were born to them for this reason: to take a higher perspective on what they stood for. Your path is about discovering a truth that is a higher synthesis of what these two people believed. Your life purpose is about somehow combining the two approaches your parents took.

Example: Ashley was amazed when she first connected her life purpose—to be a management teacher—to the fact that her father was a manager and her mother was a teacher.

Key questions: (Tip—first, write freely about everything that comes to mind. Next, go back and edit, sift, and refine until you get your answers down to a few words.)

- Why was I born to this particular family? What might have been the purpose?

- (Every person, whether consciously or not, illustrates with her or his life how she or he thinks a human being is supposed to live. Try to discover what each of your parents taught you—the higher truth, or contribution, of each).

- Who was my father? What was his message to me? His higher truth or contribution?

- What was my mother's underlying message? Her higher truth or contribution?

When I put the two higher truths together, What do I get? What is my higher truth?

This is what you came here to contribute.

Example: Ashley's mother was an advocate of equal rights for all persons, regardless of ethnicity, gender, lifestyle, and other differences. Ashley's father was able to give unconditional love to all his family and friends. Ashley realizes that her contribution as a leader/manager/teacher is to show how unconditional love toward all types of persons represents the type of healing needed in today's world.

Step 3: Discover Your Life Lessons—What You Came Here to Learn

While your parents were conveying their higher truths, they simultaneously conveyed issues they needed to work through.

Key questions:

- Looking at your mother's life, what could she have been done better? What would you have changed about your mother? That's one part of what you yourself are working on.

- Ask the same about your father's life. That's the other part you are working on.

- Put the two parts together. ***This is your life lesson***—what you came here to work on as the next step in your evolution, your life purpose.

- Put this life lesson into the form of a question: *How can I learn to . . .?*

This is your basic life question.

Learn to also ask current questions that tie in with this basic life question. The "what next?" type of questions are important because their answers keep you on track.

Example: Ashley's mother was an extremely critical person and had an uncontrollable temper. When it flared, she became abusively negative, judgmental, and hostile. Her actions made her family feel she was temporarily insane. Her life lesson was to learn about judgment and anger. Ashley's father had a self-esteem problem. He was very intelligent, powerful, and loving but never fully moved into his own power. Ashley realizes that her life lessons are about negative judgment of herself and others and moving into her own power as a woman.

Step 4. Alternate Search

Are you having difficult identifying your life purpose and life lesson? If so, try this alternate approach that doesn't depend on parent memories but incorporates relationships with all the important men and women in your life.

Your Feminine Side

- Who are the women in your life—past and present—who are important? List 5 or 6 women.

- What are some strengths of these women? List them and then notice types of strengths that most of them have in common.

- What are some weaknesses of these women? List them and then notice types of weakness that most of them had in common.

These are the feminine strengths and weaknesses you came in to work with—to build on the strengths and to work on the weaknesses.

Your Masculine Side

- Who are the men in your life—past and present—who are important? List 5 or 6 men.

- What are some strengths of these men? List them and then notice types of strengths that most of them had in common.

- What are some weaknesses of these men? List them and then notice types of weakness that most of them have in common.

These are the masculine strengths and weaknesses you came in to work with—to build on the strengths and to work on the weaknesses.

Now combine your feminine and masculine strengths. How do these suggest your life purpose—what you came to contribute? Then combine your feminine and masculine weaknesses. How do these suggest your life lesson—what you came to learn?

Step 5: On a card write your life purpose and life lesson.

Make it easy to remember your life purpose and to speak about it when appropriate. Write a brief one-liner, "My life's purpose is . . . ." Do you feel empowered when you say this? Is it easy to recall this line? If not, rewrite it until it's easy to remember and you feel empowered when you say it. Then print it on a card, with colorful embellishment and symbols if you like.

Keep this card on hand in a place where you'll notice it from time to time—as a reminder that keeps you on track when you need to remember goals and priorities.

SAO 4.3 What Are Your Goals?

Purpose: To begin the process of identifying those goals that are most important to you.

Step 1: Your Mission. Write your personal mission statement (life purpose) in one sentence.

Step 2: Your Goals. Keeping in mind that a goal is a specific end result, list your five most important goals. Include goals related to family, career, and personal development

SAO 4.4 Refine Your Goals

Purpose: To help you weed out activities from goals, to make your goals as specific as needed, to identify all the goals that are important to you, and to prioritize them so you become clear about which are the most important to achieve.

Step 1: Distinguish between goals and activities. Look at the list of goals you made in SAO 4.3. How many are actually activities? Eliminate them.

Step 2: Redefine your goals to make them more specific. Select the following items that reflect your goals and fill in the blanks to make your goals specific. At this point, don't rank or evaluate their practicality or relative importance.

Rank:

_____ To have $_____ in assets by _____
                                    (date)

__3__ To be____HeadProfessional____ by __2008__
             (job position)   (date)

_____ To have a relationship with_____ in which we
                              (description of person)

_____ by _____
        (feel, believe, do...)   (date)

_____ To weigh _____ by_____
                 (pounds)   (date)

__2__ To have a ___B.S_____by__2004__
             (degree or certificate)   (date)

_____ To retire with $_____ a month income (or equivalent) by _____
                                                                (date)

_____ To have_____ days of free time per year by _____
                                                     (date)

_____ To learn_____ by _____
             (specific skills or knowledge)   (date)

_____ To travel to_____ in _____ for _____
                                          (date)   (length of time)

__1__ To spend__7__ hours a _____week_____ in mutually satisfying
                           (days, week, month, year)
         activities with_____family_____
                        (description of person(s))

Other goals:_____

Step 3: Brainstorm. List other goals that don't fit into the preceding categories. Be as outrageous as you like. Use the enthusiastic, creative-child part of your personality to brainstorm. Send that critical, practical part of you *down the hall* till later. Make your goals as fantastic or as simple as you like. Anything goes!

Step 4: Evaluate and rank. After you've freely and wildly listed any goals you can think of, start asking which one of all your goals is the most important (include all goals in Steps 2 and 3). Put the number "1" in the space to the left of that goal. Continue the process for the second most important goal, the third, and so forth until all are ranked. Do you want to delete any goals? Can any outlandish ones be modified or combined to make them more realistic? Are they all specific?

Step 5. Categorize by Life Areas. What are the major life areas that are important to you? For most people they're career, personal development, and private life. Sometimes goals overlap, and that's great, but pick the category that's most relevant to the goal at this time. Having goals in all areas helps you to focus on your need to create a balanced life.

SAO 4.5 Add Power to Your Goals

Purpose: To help you increase the power and effectiveness of your goals.

Step 1: Visualize a Passion Pyramid

Imagine a Passion Pyramid that looks like this. Think about your life purpose and visualize being on that path. What's your passion factor? Pick a number:

0=Hot-Hot, 9=Hot, 8=Turned-on, 7=Excited, 6=Enthusiastic,=5 Interested,

4=Possible, 3=Lukewarm, 2=Little interest, 1=Almost no interest, 0=no interest

Now think of each long-term goal and your passion factor, then each short-term goal's passion factor, then your planned activities, and finally your current do-list. Do you need to make some changes to ramp up your passion factor?

Step 2. Visualize end results

During a quiet time, relax deeply and imagine being "on purpose," actually achieving your top-priority goal, and living the end result of having that goal.   Focus on what you are doing, having, and most of all *being*; that is, how you feel, how others feel, how relationships are affected. Note any conflicting feelings or thoughts that come up—thoughts about barriers to achieving the goal or about payoffs for not achieving it. Repeat for each goal.

Example: Need help making your vision more powerful? Try this technique. Imagine you are looking through a glass door. On the other side is a beautiful life, just the life you want. See the scenery, the people, your home, your life there. Become aware of where you're standing now, your life now with its events and with your beliefs. Grab the handle and open the door but don't go in yet.

Notice how welcome you feel, the sounds and sights and breeze and scents. Look around and see everything you want—all the parts of your dream vision—family, career, friends, personal development. Now, look back at where you've been and around at where you are. Then look in front of you, all around, at where you want to be. Know that all you need to do to get to this other side is to feel strongly the intention to do that..

Ask yourself, "Do I want this? Is this my intention?" If yes, then step forward and step in. Now you're in the land of possibilities, where goal visions come true. Trust that now you're standing in your life purpose, your intention, your commitment. How does it feel?

Step 3: Check the source of each goal.

Are you sure this is *your* goal? It is very important to establish this. If you are trying to achieve a goal because someone else thinks you should, you can never give it the full level of commitment, passion, and enthusiasm you give to goals that come from deep within you. The achievement of others' goals can never bring you the joy and fulfillment you deserve, and you will never reach the same level or quality of success as you will with your own goals. So analyze each important goal in this light. Have you chosen this goal because it's what you think someone else would admire? For example, a parent figure, spouse, influential friend, teacher? Or is it truly what *you* want in your life?

Step 4: Apply the energy/emotional level test

If you have difficulty ranking a goal—or if at any point in the goal-setting or goal-implementing process, you are pulled between two alternatives—try the following analysis. First, be sure you have developed an adequate foundation for making the decision, through self-analysis of your life purpose and deepest desires and through gathering the information you need. Then ask yourself the following questions.

- Do I feel energized when I think of a particular choice?
- Do I sense a drop in my energy level when I think of the choice?
- Which option has a special glow around it when I picture it? An emotional attraction?

Then ask yourself, if the decision were based solely on emotion, which alternative would I choose? You will probably experience the greatest success when you go for the alternative that energizes you and brings up positive feelings, such as a sense of freedom, well-being, growth/expansion, or enthusiasm.

Step 5. Ask, What else is possible?

Keep asking that question each time you set up a goal vision. Get at least three or four other possibilities beyond the goal vision before you stop. This process will help you to include all the elements you really want in your vision.

Think ahead to the point when you will have your goal vision—say a year from now. As your Future Self, look back over the past year.

- How was it for you?
- What did you achieve?
- How were people involved and what happened in relationships?
- What would you change?

Look at all the goals you achieved. Ask, What would make my life easier? What would make it more magical and exciting?   How can I link together all my goals in a more creative, magical way?" If you want to live every day with passion, take a look at your life purpose—then design a project or set some goals, that seem bigger than your life, a project or goals that you're not sure how to achieve.

Step 6: Turn old blocks into new cornerstones

For each major goal, examine your current and past beliefs and attitudes, thoughts and feelings, decisions and choices. Are any of them likely to block your success in achieving the goal? What new beliefs and attitudes could you adopt that would support this goal? How can you change your thoughts, letting go of nonproductive ones and focusing on positive ones that enhance your chances of success? What old decisions—about yourself and others or your place and your roles—might be inappropriate now for what you want to achieve? What actions (based on your beliefs, attitudes, thoughts, feelings, and decisions about you and life) have you made in the past regarding goal achievement? What new action choices might be better?

- List Goal No. 1.
- List current beliefs, attitudes, and so on, that conflict with achieving your goal.
- Identify new ones that would support it and list them.
- Repeat the process for each major

SAO 4.6 What Activities Will Achieve Your Goals?

Purpose: To generate activities leading to achievement of your top goals in each life area.

Step 1: List Career Goal 1. Then list at least four activities that would lead to the achievement of Goal 1.

Step 2: List Career Goals 2 and 3 and their activities, as you did for Goal 1.

Step 3: Repeat the process for personal development and private life goals. After you have listed activities for *all* goals, rank the importance of the activities listed for each goal.

SAO 4.7 Test Your Parameters

Purpose: To increase your comfort level with those goals and activities you're attracted to but that seem too bold and risky. To take the first steps toward being an effective risk-taker, stepping out beyond your current parameters and fears to create the life you want.

Step 1: Risky Activities. What are some activities you generated that attract you but that you feel are too bold or risky to try? List them. What other activities can you think of that might be too bold or risky? Add them to the list.

Step 2: **Reducing Risk Factors**. Pick the least risky activity. Are there ways you could reduce the risk factors?   List them beside the activity.   Repeat the process for the remaining least risky activity.   Repeat for all the activities you've listed, dealing last with the most risky activity. *For example*:

- The risk of going back to school for a degree could be reduced by starting with one evening course.
- The risk of investing in the stock market could be reduced by investing in a mutual stock fund that has a good 10-year performance record.
- The risk of asking for a raise could be reduced by gathering documentation showing your specific achievements that translate into higher profits for the firm.

Step 3: Risky Goals. What goals can you think of that attract you but that you feel are too bold or risky? Repeat Step 2 for those goals. *For example:* What is most risky about the goal *to become an executive* (or lawyer, doctor, news anchor, and any other career goal)? Is it, *being the target of criticism and political infighting*? If so, what are some good sources of information about handling criticism and office politics? Would getting good information increase your political savvy and reduce the risk factor?

SAO 4.8 What Are Your Most Productive Career Activities?

Purpose: To help you identify your most productive career activities.

Part A. Ask Career Questions

By now you should have a specific type of job in mind as your key career goal. You should also be able to describe your ultimate career goal—the top position you're aiming for. To help you identify the activities most likely to help you reach that goal, look at these questions. (Note: See John Wright's *The American Almanac of Jobs and Salaries* for some of your answers.)

- What type of company do you have in mind? Can you pinpoint a specific company?
- What type of degree, courses, or other training will you need?
- What specific skills and knowledge will be required? At what level of ability?
- What kinds of people could tell you more about the job, help teach you what you need to know, help you get your foot in the door, help you gain favorable visibility within the company, introduce you to people who can help?
- What jobs will you need to hold in order to prepare yourself for your *ultimate* career goal?
- What functions do you need to have experience with?
- How do these functions link up with each other? (For example, what are the links between production and sales, sales and marketing?)
- Can you get some actual job descriptions your target company has prepared for these jobs?
- Which staff positions would give you the best chance of moving into a line job?
- Which line jobs provide the basic experience you'll need?
- Once you have a career plan, who can give you the most helpful evaluation of its effectiveness?
- Is the plan workable in view of the other top priorities in your life?

Followup: Use your answers to help complete the remaining SAOs regarding goals.

Part B. Brainstorm with a Friend

Brainstorm with a partner about ways to achieve a particular goal. What types of activities might work? If your goal is to go to Paris, what do you need to get there? How can you get the time, the money, and any other resources you'll need? Next, work on your partner's goal.

Part C. Create Mutual Support with a Friend

Discuss a key goal with a friend. Tell her the specifics of the goal and the actions you plan to take. Verbalizing your commitment, as well as writing it down, tends to strengthen it. Your friend should also share one of her goals with you. Set regular dates to discuss what actions you actually took and how they worked out. Two nationally known authors recently explained how this process worked for them when they were each writing their first books. They agreed to phone each other every Friday to discuss their progress. Each wanted to be able to tell the other that she had moved along in her project. If Thursday arrived, and she hadn't written all week, she was motivated to write something rather than admit on Friday that her project had been neglected.

Part D. Make Your Goals Visible

Find methods of keeping your goals up front, of staying focused, or making them real to you.

Pick three top goals: Write them on a business card, along with the target dates. Put the card where you will see it many times a day: tucked in your dresser or bathroom mirror, in the clear-plastic window of your wallet, on your desk calendar, or in another visible place.

Draw vivid symbols of your top goals, using colored pens or pencils if possible. Put them on a card and display them as discussed in 1

Showcase: Ashley's Life Purpose

Purpose: To give you an example of how the life purpose exercise is applied and to help illustrate the relationship among life purpose, goals, and activities.

After Ashley completed the self-awareness opportunities for identifying life purpose and setting goals and activities, her results looked like this. The elements of Ashley's life purpose look like goals and in a sense they are, but they are actually a long-term mission statement—or even a lifetime goal. Notice the ways in which her life purpose overlaps into all three life areas and leads to an integration of the three areas. You may not see this degree of integration in your life purpose, at this point in time, but it's not unusual for the areas to become more integrated over time.

Ashley's Life Purpose: Leader/Manager/Teacher

Career area: To develop leadership and managerial expertise in the business world. To continually learn about the ways of this world and grow from these experiences.

Family/friends: To build loving relationships of many kinds—family, personal, professional.

Personal development: To continually learn about the philosophical and spiritual aspects of life—what life is all about.

Integration: To help others learn the types of things I've learned and am learning. To bring together my learning in the business, personal, and philosophical/spiritual areas of my life to enrich all areas.

Ashley's Top Three Goals in March, current year

1. To complete my MBA degree by December.
2. To negotiate a promotion to sales manager, based on my MBA, by December.
3. To find and join, or establish a women's personal growth group by June.

Ashley's Top Three Activities to complete this week

1. Complete report on workforce diversity for management class.
2. Contact 12 customers in order to meet sales goal for this quarter.
3. Attend evening seminar on women's roles in creating community.

SAO 4.9 Action Plans

Purpose: To prepare an action plan to help you focus on top-priority goals and activities for the coming month.

One-Month Action Plan

Step 1: From goal to do-list. List your top-priority career goal. Under it, in order of importance, list the major activities, with their target dates, that you plan to complete this month. Put the most important activity on your To-Do list for *today* and keep it on the list until you have accomplished it. If you haven't acted on this activity within seven days, go back and reevaluate your goal and activities.

Step 2. Repeat the process for career goals 2 and 3.

Step 3. Repeat the process for any top-priority personal development goals and private life goals that you want to include.

Longer-Term Action Plans

Step 1: List the top three career goals, with target dates, you plan to accomplish in one year.

Step 2: Repeat the process for your personal development and private life goals.

Step 3: Make longer-term plans, such as three-year, five-year, or ten-year plans—using the time frames that make the most sense for your life.

SAO 4.10 Bringing Life-Purpose Goals into Your Reality

Instructions: Do this 5-minute process several times a week until your goal becomes reality.

Step 1. What specific goal do you want to create now, one that is in alignment with your life purpose? Think of a scene or symbol that represents the essence of this goal.

Step 2. Become very relaxed, using techniques that work for you, eyes closed. Imagine your goal scene as if it has already happened. See the people involved, what it's like. Feel the feelings involved.

Step 3. Imagine a universe that is black, no light. Now a clear white-light star appears in the void. Send your goal scenario or symbol into the center of the star.

Step 4. Imagine your brain as a beautiful blue-violet shiny crystal, a spacious crystal that reflects and magnifies anything that comes into it. Bring the goal-star in through your third eye into the inside of this colorful crystal brain. Watch as the goal-star is magnified and reflected throughout this beautiful blue-violet crystalline place.

Watch the goal-star explode—expanding, energizing, merging throughout your mind and body. Watch it explode a second time, experiencing this process. And a third time.

Step 5. Imagine your heart center as a beautiful emerald green shiny crystal, a spacious crystal that reflects and magnifies anything that comes into it. Let the goal-star drop down into this green crystalline heart center. Watch as the goal-star is magnified and reflected throughout it.

Watch the goal-star explode—expanding, energizing, merging throughout your mind and body. Focus on your commitment to making this goal become a reality. Feel the energy of your heart and the merger that occurs between your heart, the goal, and the star. Watch it explode a second time, experiencing this process. And a third time.

Step 6. Allow the goal-star to rise up from your heart center into your brain center and out through your third eye, into the dark sky again. Put it out into the universe and let it go.

SAO 4.11 Life Purpose Followup

Purpose: To re-visit your life purpose from a different angle and apply it to an important goal.

Remember, motivational intelligence is about knowing and following your wants and desires. Ultimately, it's about achieving your purpose in life

Step 1. Look for additional clues to your purpose. Ask yourself these kinds of questions:

- What fulfills me? What thrills me?
- What is a passion for me?
- What lights me up?
- What am I willing to commit to?

- What would I love to be doing? To achieve?

- What would make me thrill to get up in morning?

Listen to your inner self. Meditate for at least a few minutes every day (when you awaken or as you fall asleep, for example) with your life purpose or goals question in mind and listen for your future. Discover who you can become.

Step 2. Verbalize your answers. First to yourself, then to others. Put them in writing.

Step 3. Visualize a plan. Once you get in touch with what your life purpose seems to be (it's okay if you're not absolutely sure), ask, How can I go about making my contribution? Achieving what will fulfill me?" Decide on a major project or achievement. . In the example below, opening a new business is the end goal. What is your end goal? Close your eyes and visualize.

- Picture your passion pyramid.

- Picture your achievement at the top.

- See your goal, exactly how it looks, who's there—sense how it feels.

- Visualize yourself in that place. It's done. Declare it. Know it.

- Give that a date.

- Now, ask, "What did I do right before that?" In the example, "finding a location" is the activity. Name your activity and give it a date.

- Before that? In the example "getting financing" comes just before the end goal. Name yours and date it.

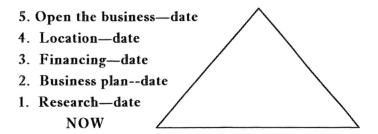

5. **Open the business—date**
4. **Location—date**
3. **Financing—date**
2. **Business plan--date**
1. **Research—date**
   NOW

Work your way back down the pyramid to now. In the example, the steps backward are "developing a business plan" and "researching the field."

Now create a second pathway down the other side—as your Plan B, to provide options.

Step 4. Do it in writing. Now that you've visualized the achievement process, put it in writing. Draw the pyramid on a sheet of paper. Make each step a brief statement, a one-liner, or a picture—anything that's a powerful symbol and reminder for you. Hang the picture where you can see it every day. Consider making a separate picture of the step you're currently working on and placing it where you see it often. Focus primarily on the current step, with the overall plan in the background.

Step 5. Bring it to work. Bring your life purpose to work. If you're not passionate at work, ask yourself what traits or characteristics you can bring to your job that will allow you to express more passion there. Is there a part of your life purpose that you can bring into a work project or task?

Step 6. Make a "Vision Board." Look for pictures in magazines and brochures that turn you on because they symbolize some aspect of your goal vision or life purpose. Cut them out, collect them for a while, then create a collage on a poster board. Now you have a powerful visual image of the life you want to create. Keep it where you see it regularly. This helps to bring your ideas from the higher, finer energy levels into the denser physical energy level—to make it physically "real" to you.

SAO 4.12 Break Out of Self-Sabotage

Purpose: To become aware of self-sabotaging (S-S) beliefs and to overcome them.

The gap between where you are and where you want to be is made up of the beliefs and attitudes that block you or don't support your getting there.

Step 1. Identify your Want-Have gaps. In each major area of your life that seems very important to you now, identify where you want to be in terms of specific goals and where you are now. Notice the types of gaps between what you want and what you have.

Category	Where I want to be	Where I am now
Personal development	With a Girlfriend	Single
Career	Head Prof.	Waiter / Bartender
Family	Spend more time	Maybe 2 / week
Friends	Spend more time	Maybe 2 a week
Health	Very Healthy	→
Leisure	Relax & Go out More	Lots of work
Community	More Involved	Not involved at all
Other:		

Step 2. Identify your beliefs. Using the typical S-S beliefs shown in the table below to prod your thinking, identify your own S-S beliefs about where you are and where you want to be.

Step 3. Reverse to S-E beliefs. Ask yourself, Is this belief real? In fact all your beliefs are ideas you have accepted or created, so you can create new beliefs in a heartbeat, once you decide you can and will. Simply turn around each Self-Sabotaging belief from an "I-can't" type of belief to an "I-can" belief. For example: I *can* find the money (time, resources, energy) for my top priorities. When you change your self-sabotaging belief, you change your self-talk about your goal vision from "unlikely or impossible" to possible and probable.

Step 4. Find the fear of change underneath. How many of your S-S beliefs reflect a fear of failure? Fear of success? What you call fear may be your body's resistance to the act of changing – to dealing with the new and unknown. Fear of change, fear of moving closer to your goal vision, and fear of actually getting what you've always wanted are the types of fear that are self-sabotaging and limiting. They keep you imprisoned in your old patterns.

You know that in life the only constant is *change*. So face your fears and see them as a sign that you dealing with change. If you are experiencing no fear, you are simply not out there trying! See fear as a measurement tool that indicates the extent to which you are leaving your old "don't-want" situation behind as you move toward the "do-want."

- In meditation and in your daily life, focus on trusting in what you want. Visualize yourself releasing the part of you that's afraid of making your goal vision come true.

- Keep speaking your goal vision. Keep seeing and speaking the possibility.

Typical S-S Beliefs	My S-S beliefs about where I am	My S-S beliefs about where I want to be	New S-E beliefs

I don't have enough:
     money
     time
     resources
     skills
     knowledge
     energy
I'm not:
     successful enough
     good enough
     capable enough
     I'm too young/old
     I'm too set in my ways
     I'm in the wrong place
     I've already missed out
I can't learn it—it's too:
     difficult
     technical
     esoteric
Others will:
     envy me
     resent me
     try to use me
	Time
	Skills
	
	Capable Knowl
	
	Esoteric
	
	Envy me
		Time
		Skills
		
		Capable Knowl
		I'm too set in my ways
		
		Esoteric	

Step 5. Intensify Your Intention and Commitment. Do you have beliefs like these?
- I'll be stuck with this decision, can't change this decision, can't go back, etc.

- I might be wrong, look foolish, fail, etc.

These are some typical beliefs that block intention and commitment to achieve a goal. Think of intention and commitment as something you do with every cell of your body, that you do with your heart and your gut, down to the marrow of your bone. Don't settle for half-way measures.

Once you fully intend to create your goal vision and commit to it as a top priority, you immediately start moving faster toward it. The next step becomes clear. At that moment all sorts of things begin to happen. A whole stream of events flow from that decision, all kinds of meetings and "coincidences" and resources that you never dreamed would come to you. A brave, bold decision contains within it genius, power, and magic. Make that decision now. Think of intention and commitment as tools to move you forward. Change your beliefs to supportive ones; for example:

"This decision will move me forward and open up new possibilities."

Step 6. Just do it. Ask, "What will I do or be in my goal vision that I'm not doing or being here and now?" Begin to do and be everything on your lists.

Step 7. Identify your "if only" barriers. What else is keeping you from achieving your vision? Ask yourself, "What is the 'if only I had . . .'" that's blocking me? Identify it. Then start doing the activities that will take you to your goal vision anyway. Develop alternative activities. Be creative. Find a way to start now.

What other "If only" do you have? When you feel a block, ask "What's real here?" Write down what you are thinking and telling yourself about what's real. What stories are you making up that drain power from your goal vision? What is it that you don't trust? List what you do trust and what you don't. Create empowering beliefs to counter your untrusting beliefs.

Bottom line: Be clear about what you want. Do everything you know to do. Be present. Be here now in every moment, enjoying and living your life. Relax, be in nature, find what helps you to feel serene and at peace. When in doubt ask: Is this what I want to do now? Is this part of my life purpose? Do I feel passion around this?

References

De Beauport, Elaine. *The Three Faces of Mind*. Wheaton, IL: Quest Books, 1996.

Carr-Ruffino, Norma. *The Promotable Woman*. Franklin Lakes NJ: Career Press, 1997.

Hawken, P., A. Lovins and L.H. Lovins. *Natural Capitalism: Creating the Next Industrial Revolution*. Boston: Little, Brown, 1999.

Herman Group, The. Employee Survey for Shell Oil, 1995.

Maisel, Eric. *Fearless Creating*. New York: Putnam, 1995.

Oliver, Mary, "Wild Geese," in *Dream Work*. New York: Atlantic Monthly Press, 1986, p. 14.

Spangler, David. *The Call*. Riverhead Books, 1996.

Wieder, Marcia. *Making Your Dreams Come True*. New York: Harmony Books, 1999.

Chapter 5
Associative Intelligence
Relationships, Relationships

Exquisite freedom is the primary characteristic of the associative thinking process.
Elaine DeBeauport

A man noticed how the steam from a boiling pot raised the lid of the pot enough to make it clatter. He connected steam and energy, an association not normally made, a new association. The result was the steam-powered engine that enabled the industrial revolution. Your associative intelligence—your ability to see relationships between things, how one thing associates with another—is one of your most powerful intelligences. It's mainly about putting together what is, in a new and different way. It's a key to your creative intelligence.

You use your associative intelligence to directly perceive something, to freely associate one thing with another, or to link two ideas together in your mind. Thinking in this way is often the first step in moving from rational left-brain thinking to right-brain thinking, which also includes your sensory and intuitive intelligences.

Through Associative Intelligence you link your body's lower-level and higher-level vibrations within your heart center. You relate the specific, the details—your attractions, repulsions, emotions, desires—with the general, the big picture—planetary and universal concepts, principles, and ideals. You go into neutral, move into the higher frequencies of nonjudgmental acceptance, unconditional love, and compassion for "what is." You rise above the need to label, categorize, add to or take away from what is, using direct perception to just "be with" what you encounter. This is sometimes known as heart chakra energy, as well as the causal energy body—strongly affecting how you create your life.

Words that will help you understand what your associative intelligence is all about include: *similarities, comparisons, relationship to, connection with, analogies, similes, metaphors, causal energy body, heart chakra, green, tone fa or F, neocortex, right brain.*

Myths & Realities

Most of society's many myths about associative intelligence revolve around keeping things and people labeled and in their proper places.

Myth 1. A place for everything; everything in its place.

This type of belief works fine for keeping a room neat and orderly, but when you extend it beyond that, it can block your creative drive. One of the greatest and most readily available sources of creative ideas is connecting two things that aren't supposed to go together—putting one thing in a "place" that belongs to another thing. For example, burrs that you pick up from weeds don't "go" on your trousers—it's the wrong place for them. But the idea for velcro came from the insight that the burr-fabric connection could be translated into a great fastener. Keep an open mind about where things go, the "right" place for a thing, which things fit together, and other types of associations and connections.

Myth 2. A tiger doesn't change its spots. You can't teach an old dog new tricks Once a loser, always a loser.

These are all ways if placing people in rigid categories and assuming that they'll always belong there. Actually, everyone is constantly changing. No one is exactly the same person from one minute to the next. True, recognizing a person's habit patterns and parameters—limits and territory—is helpful in understanding their behavior and even making predictions about it. But assuming they can't or won't change is carrying pattern-parameter techniques too far. Associative intelligence is about being willing to see people and things in new ways. It's sometimes about seeing the essence of who a person is, beneath the surface appearance and behavior. It's about giving people a chance to show they're moving and growing. It's can be about reviving dead relationships.

How Associative Intelligence Works

Associative intelligence works to increase your creative intelligence by relating the wide variety of things you encounter to the big picture, the Web of Life. It relates all kinds of strange things making new connections and linkages.

Relating to the Big Picture

You've learned about your basic-brain intelligences, as well as your emotional-brain intelligences. Now you're ready to explore the intelligences of your highest-level brain, the neocortex, which has two distinct halves, often called right-brain and left-brain, as symbolized in Figure 5.1. They are connected by a bridge of nerve fibers called the corpus-collosum. Your left brain is associated with the right side of the body (left-brain, right-handed) and is the seat of your rational intelligence, which we'll discuss in a later chapter. Your right brain is therefore associated with the left side of your body and is the seat of three important intelligences: associative, sensory, and intuitive. All these right-brain intelligences have a capacity for catching glimpses of a larger whole, a greater truth, a bigger perspective. All have a sense of timelessness, of being able to access all time in the now. All include getting a sense of the whole before focusing on the parts.

Taking Charge. Have you allowed your rational mind to be the master of your life? Now you can make it your slave, your tool. You can step into your rightful place. Your whole self, your creative self, your higher self can be the master. You do this by using your right-brain intelligences as new-idea generators and your rational brain as evaluator and implementer.

Integrating Right and Left. Creative intelligence is *not* a matter of using either the wholistic right brain or the sequential, rational left brain, but of using both as partners in the creativity process. Instead of *either-or*, it's a case of *both-and*. In most situations, you'll want to let the right-brain processes run free without interference from your rational left-brain. After your wholistic right-brain has, sensed, intuited, connected, and associated with all kinds of things and generated a batch of ideas, your rational left-brain can come in to ground your ideas in physical reality. You'll use it to organize the new ideas, to evaluate them, and to put them to work in the world of consensus reality.

Figure 5.1 Neocortex Intelligences

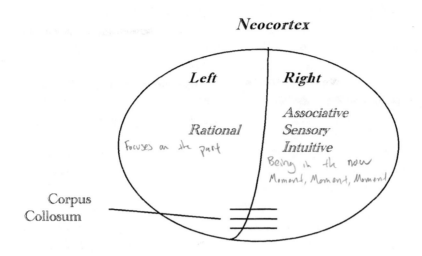

Discovering New Connections

When you're using your rational intelligence, you connect ideas or actions in a step-by-step linear sequence—who, what, where, when, why, how, verbal symbols, math symbols, either/or. Western culture fell in love with this straight-line way of thinking.

When you use your associative intelligence, you freely make connections without regard to sequence. In the process of connecting one known idea with another, you may come up with just the brilliant new idea you need. Here, instead of a straight line is a free-form process—direct perception of the person or object, discovery, multiple connections, dynamics among and between persons and objects, both/and, no limits, abundant ideas and discoveries.

Associative thinking is associating, linking, relating, connecting with whatever and whomever you want. Its main quality is total freedom. It can free you to make an immensely larger number of connections, bringing to life other unused areas of your brain. These new connections will increase your intelligence and can provide the first step toward accessing the *unused* 90 percent of your brain power.

This intelligence is about dynamics, multiple connections, direct perception, and discovery. De Beauport notes three functions that make associative intelligence a key factor in generating creative responses to problem-opportunity situations:

1. *Direct Perception.* When you directly perceive something, you relate to the person, object, or situation as-is without applying labels, symbols, concepts, conclusions, or evaluations.
2. *Free Association.* When you freely process a situation, you make connections without being distracted by sequence or cause-and-effect. Instead you search among images and thoughts in a state of mental freedom.
3. *New Arrangements.* You link and rearrange associations, make new connections, and relate things in different ways and by different methods in order to make new compositions.

Direct Perception

Every word in our language is a symbol that stands for something that has its own reality, its own existence. When you experience a symbol for something, that is a substitute for directly experiencing the actual thing.

You use your rational brain to think mainly with verbal and mathematical symbols. Associative intelligence gives you a choice: you can either relate to symbols of people (employees) things (espresso coffees) or situations (lunch meetings in the cafeteria) and link them in various ways, or you can associate directly with the person, object, or situation. Direct perception serves as an entry into all the intelligences of the right brain. When you perceive directly, you can free yourself of the left-brain rational labels, assumptions, conclusions and concepts and relate to an entity from many different angles or viewpoints. You're free to see the complexity of what you're experiencing before you have to relate to the accepted symbol for it. You can decide where to focus your attention.

When you think of associating things, you probably think of linking them together. This linking is much more powerful if you're first able to *de-link* the words, symbols, labels, stereotypes, and assumptions from that person, object, or situation. When you do this, you're better able to "just be with" that entity in its being-ness. You free yourself of pre-conceptions and assumptions about it. You bypass the cultural and gender labels, stereotypes, concepts, assumptions, and symbols. You take in your direct experience of persons, things, and ideas as if they are brand new.

Now you're free to be with that entity's reality—to notice and associate with any aspect of it— not just those aspects triggered by labels or symbols of it. Now you're free to associate continually with the reality of that entity according to your own perceptions, desires, and creativity in the moment.

Figure 5.2 Perceiving Things Directly

Look at the image in Figure 5.2. Try de-linking—forgetting about—all the words, labels, stereotypes, and beliefs you normally connect with this type of image. What you see here is a symbol for a living being, of course.

Imagine that you're looking at the original living cat. Focus fully on being here now in this present moment—no past and no future, just the now. Imagine just "being with" this being as if you had never seen anything like it before. Be totally open to letting it be exactly what it is. This is direct perception. It's requires "being here now"—in the present moment.

In the next few days, as you encounter various people and animals, try perceiving them directly. Start building a habit pattern of direct perception.

Associating Things Freely

Innovation comes from a new way of seeing, making a new guess about what will work. Although most of the "scientific method" is rational, what makes it powerful is the associative process of looking into the unknown, catching glimpses of new ideas, and associating them with known ideas, arranging and rearranging ideas into new patterns.

The artistic process is similar. For example, a painter focuses on a subject, looks for new ways to express what she sees there, arranges and rearranges these new perceptions until she finds the "right" design. Associative thinking is essential for scientists, artists, business persons, and everyone involved in creative thinking.

When you change your patterns, your routines, or your habits, you usually trigger a new way of seeing. Ideas come pouring in and collide, making new connections. When you take any kind of trip—even a day trip—to a new place, you get out of your rut. You come back a different person. It may be a tiny difference, but those differences can add up to innovation.

Making New Arrangements

When you link together in new ways the people, places, ideas, concepts, things, colors, foods, or smells that you perceive, you're using associative intelligence. Your mind freely wanders and roams all over your known experience and unknown imaginings, free from the limits of cause and effect. You're free from the rational need to assess, measure, judge, or reach a conclusion, free to begin a voyage of discovery.

You make meaning by linking together your glimpses of ideas and flashes of insight, your mental maps of things. You play with these ideas, moving them around, linking them together and seeing how they connect with a problem-opportunity situation you're working on. You explore their nuances, their subtleties, their mysteries to discover something new about them. You try them out in various patterns or arrangements—until you find new meaning.

How to Boost Your Associative Intelligence

Okay, swinging door. What can I do with that? Comedian Charlie Chaplin
Okay, five notes. What can I do with that? Musician Bobby McFerrin

When I see a gadget, I imagine how I can use it for something else.
I'm always trying to get things to do what they're not supposed to do.
Creativity has to do with the way you carry on your life.
   Author Isabel Allende

Associative intelligence is looking at what's there and doing something different with it. You can boost your associative intelligence by playing with new ways of using things, and linking them together in new ways. You can apply it to the way you learn—how you gain new information and expertise. You can practice it through the way you create new relationships and revive old ones.

Booster 1. Play with Links   ~~Right Brain Study Skills~~

"Word play" is powerful. Putting together bizarre and ridiculous combinations of things makes you laugh. Both absurdity and wit give you a quick way to overthrow the tyranny of the right way, the status quo, the given, the known. For example

- Look at the wall and rename it chair
- Stare at a rug and call it kitty

This can break the connection you've established between the thing and your words for it. It can push you into thinking in the picture language of the sensory-visual intelligence.

Even more powerful than word play is "picture play"—moving pictures around in your mind, making new connections among them—because it's closer to direct perception Your most creative inspirations may come to you not in words but in visual images.

"Activity play" is also powerful, especially when you combine it with "picture play." For example, Einstein often asked questions that linked together two or more unrelated activities. As he mentally answered the questions, he formed mental pictures of the activities; for example:

- What would be like to ride a beam of light and at the same time look back at a clock?
- What would happen if I dropped a coin while standing in an elevator that was dropping?

This play at combining activities is a key feature of creative thought. It's thought at a stage that comes before you connect your pictures with words or numbers. It can lead to new insights that you can later find the words or symbols for—to communicate them to others.

Try using these kinds of associative play to understand relationships in a new way.

Booster 2. Learn on the Right Side

Because our schools have traditionally viewed learning as almost completely a rational, left-brain activity, most people continue to limit their learning activities to the rational. Stop to think about your learning process. By far, the most prolific learning period of your life was from birth to age 5 or 6. Did you really learn primarily by rational thinking? Kids learn by associating Mom's touch with her voice with comfort and survival, etc. Kids pick up nonverbal information before they learn the language, using their intuition to determine who's okay and who's not.

To boost and speed up your learning capacity, and therefore your creative intelligence, use your right-brain as well as your left-brain. For example, a book is a very rational learning tool, but you can also use right-brain methods for grasping a book's information. Try the following suggestions.

Read in New Ways
- Read the pictures and graphics before you read the words.
- Before reading the main text, scan the non-text materials, such as headings, subheads, tables, graphs, sidebars, opening quotes—to get a sense of the overall organization plan, the key ideas, and the information that merits special treatment by being highlighted in tables, graphs, or boxes. This gives you a sense of the priorities and relative importance of various topics.
- As you read the main text, pay attention to how it relates to the pictures, graphics, and other non-text materials and make the connections between them.
- If there's a summary at the end, review it *before* you read the main text, to get a sense of the bottom line.
- Consider skipping around in the text if that would help you get a better grasp of the materials.

React to Information in New Ways
- As you read, bring the materials alive by relating them to your own experiences.
- If the material is abstract, ask yourself these kinds of questions:
  What does this statement really mean?
  How does it apply to real-life experience?
  How would this concept or idea work in my life?
  How would it look, sound, and feel in this real-life situation?
- Visualize concrete examples of each abstract concept.
- As you read (or hear someone speak, if it's a lecture), visualize how the information applies to life in general and to your life in particular.
- Discover new ways to link new information to the things you already know.

Booster 3. Relate Creatively to People

Much of your creativity relies on building collaborative, synergistic human relationships. You often must work with a team of people in creating innovative responses to problem-opportunities. Also, in business the goal of your creative efforts nearly always involves customers or users of a product, process, or service. And you virtually always must sell your innovation to the right people in order to make it a success.

Finding creative ways of dealing with people is a brilliant skill that enriches your career as well as your personal life. You know that rational thinking focuses on making evaluations and coming to conclusions. It requires skepticism, continuous doubting, and questioning. While this approach can work quite well for evaluating your own ideas, it's hardly the best approach for building relationships with people. How to win friends and influence people has always centered around paying attention to them, focusing on their concerns, not your own, and relating to their concerns by showing that you've had similar experiences, so you can relate to theirs.

Relate Beyond Rational Limits

When you use your rational intelligence to form and maintain relationships, you severely limit your possibilities for building a wide range of exciting, interesting friends and associates. Your rational mind relates by:

- Trying to understand people by adding up what they've achieved, what they own, how many friends or contacts they have, and other external measurements of human worth
- Dealing with people based on their "place" in a social group, an organization, or the society in general, the status trap
- Dealing with people based on cultural myths, stereotypes, labels
- Identifying parts of human beings, summarizing these parts, then proceeding to criticize them and doubt them based on this incomplete information and resulting conclusions
- Assuming that having met someone or spent time with them means you completely know that person
- Criticizing, doubting, and concluding, which results in judgments that are actually mental traps.

These traps severely limit your "voyages of discovery" of other people.

In contrast, when you use associative intelligence to relate to people, you perceive them directly instead of by their name, label, or other symbol. How do you want to be perceived? Don't you hope that people will get to know the real you, hopefully your best self? Do you want to be judged on some isolated mood or action you took? You know that a mood and resulting action is not "you." It's just a temporary energy flowing through you—unless you keep repeating it until it becomes a rigid pattern that your friends can accurately predict. Give people a fair chance. Try taking the first steps toward friendship, and love, with the associative intelligence techniques of directly perceiving, linking, associating freely, and making new arrangements.

Relate by Direct Perception

The associative technique of directly perceiving people as unique beings is a rare and well-appreciated quality that can help you relate to who a person really is. It opens you up to really finding out about a person, like turning a fresh page, a blank unknown that's ready to be filled in. When you start with a blank slate, you're inspired to find out how to fill it. If you start with labels, stereotypes, and assumptions, you think you already know most of it. This is really a type of arrogance on your part.

Direct perception is a great approach to meeting someone new. It can also be very powerful for shifting a stuck relationship with someone you've known a long time. Try tossing out all your past conclusions and judgments about an old friend and be with that person as if for the first time.

Relate by Free Association

This is a de-linking process. De-link your labels from the person. To help you make a fresh start, a new approach, try thinking about the person's body as billions of cells in constant motion and change, an endless possibility of discovery.

1. See that some of the person's energy is obvious, and much of it is hidden, aspects that you can only glimpse.
2. Ask yourself, What can I intuit here? What can I relate to? What affects me, moves me, interests me, intrigues me?
3. Realize you can't really "know" others. You can't measure them, or completely understand them, but you can catch glimpses of them.
4. Ask yourself, "What's going on? What's happening with this person?"
5. Begin by finding something, any little thing, that pleases you, that you can relate to.

When you focus on what *kind* of person someone is, you judge, label, and conclude. This closes your mind to what's really happening with this person and in the relationship the two of you are having. When you focus on what your relationship together will *be*, how you *are* together, you're able to freely associate with the person and to notice how the relationship is moving along. You can focus on the energy or communication that develops between the two of you, whether it

- feels more like rapport or like reporting information
- is open and agreeable or blocked and tense
- is abundant or minimal
- is clear, high quality or full of static and interference

Begin the contact with a process of free association. Then move on to finding links, and continue it by looking for other associations, ways to relate to one another.

Relate by Linking

Associate what you find out about a person with your own interests and experiences. Express appreciation of what you find in the other person and share something of your related experience. This gives you a link to connect and bond with the person. Finding those connections also motivates you to continue exploring, to learn more about the person. These connections are the conversational links for making that exploration fun and charming. It allows you to participate in the give-and-take of meaningful conversation and to show that you understand and can relate to the person's interests and experiences.

When you use associative thinking, you can use a process to explore, discover, find some aspect you can appreciate in every person you meet—and use that aspect to forge a new relationship. You can feel comfortable in meeting anyone or going anywhere. With this tool you can creatively re-invent old, stuck relationships and inspire them with new life.

Your rational mind may come in to judge what's "missing" in the other person. When this happens, you don't have to conclude, separate from, or destroy the budding relationship. Instead, you can shift out of your rational thinking into an associative process. See the person as a fresh page free of labels or judgments. See the person as a new combination of energy that has never before been this exact configuration. (It's true!) Search for something, anything, that's interesting, pleasant, or admirable. Just get a glimpse. Focus on that, give it detail, express your interest ,and make the connection. Remember, "You don't have to buy the whole package (the whole person). You can love the glimpses that you really like and leave the rest" [DeBeauport 1996].

Creativity Showcase
Using Associative Intelligence
for Creative Solutions and Ideas

Some innovative solutions to current problems—for your information and inspiration—and as food for thought.

Problem—Wasted Land, Grass, Grain, and Animals

Cattle ranching operations in the American West and Midwest are facing numerous problems. Grasslands have been over-grazed, they say, so ranchers must increasingly buy or raise feed for the livestock. In fact, about one-third of the cereal grown on the planet is fed to livestock, and the proportion has been growing. Animals turn only about 5 to 45 percent of this grain into meat—not a very efficient use of cereal. Cattle grazing is also hard on the land. In fact one-third of the original topsoil in the United States is gone, and much of what remains is low quality. Topsoil is eroding much faster than it's being formed—and doing so at a faster pace each year. Yet topsoil-intensive grains are being converted into feedlot fat that most people don't want to eat. This is a major waste of land, grass, grain, and animals—not to mention money, time, and human energy.

Creative Solution—Natural Rotation Feeding

Think of creating a painting, says rancher Charles Opitz (see Hawken 1999). Imagine that the canvas is the land you have, the paint is the green grass you hope will grow on it, and the brush is the livestock that needs to graze the grass. How you manage your livestock's grazing patterns determines how green the grass will grow—how your painting will look.

And the way animals naturally graze is the key to creating a green-grass painting. The analogy describes a new method of rotational grazing pioneered by Allan Savory. Working in Africa, he watched the huge herds of wild animals that are native grazers of Africa's grasslands They don't permanently harm the land. Cattle herded by tribal people do moderate damage, and cattle herded by white ranchers destroy the land. Curious, he investigated the grazing patterns. He found that native animals become hemmed in and agitated by prowling predators, so they graze in a relatively small space for a short time. Their hooves dig into the grass and dirt, leaving deep prints, which catch dung, water, and seeds, ingredients of next year's grass crop. The animals move on quickly and don't return until the following year, when the grass has re-grown. Grasslands worldwide typically co-evolved with grazing animals and actually cannot remain healthy without them.

Savory based his rotational method on this natural pattern and introduced it successfully to American ranchers. Much of the U.S. rangeland commonly considered over-grazed is actually under-grazed but grazed in the wrong way. When cattle, and other livestock, graze for shorter and less-frequent periods in a particular area, ranchers actually produce a better product—lean, organic, free-range animals.

Dairy cows that graze this way yield slightly less milk than confined cows but at far lower capital and operating cost. Therefore the dairy makes higher revenues per cow. The cows walk around finding their own food and depositing their manure within a paddock, then move on to another paddock area most every day, so the grass can recover.

Ranchers need to understand the best time for livestock to harvest the grass, at its nutritional peak, and the optimal time period for letting the grass recover. Manure needs adequate time to return to the soil, closing the nutrient loop without producing toxic runoff. Grassland management greatly reduces the plague of nitrogen runoff—35 times less than the runoff from corn-and-bean fields used to make cattle feed. In fact, this is the main source of the nitrogen runoff that's smothering sea life in a huge area of the Gulf of Mexico—a patch about the size of New Jersey and growing.

Taking care of our soil is essential to taking care of our planet, ourselves, and our future generations. Soil is truly amazing. It provides fertility, stores water, holds it and later releases it, decomposes wastes, removes litter, transforms wastes into nutrients, cleans and filters toxins, and plays an integral role in the cycling of nitrogen, carbon, and sulfur—the grand cycles that affect every aspect of our climate.

Biologist Evan Eisenberg (1998) explains that "One teaspoon of good grassland soil may contain 5 billion bacteria, 20 million fungi, and 1 million protoctists" That means a square yard of soil would contain unimaginable numbers of these creatures plus maybe 1,000 each of ants, spiders, wood lice, beetles and their larvae, and fly larvae; 2,000 each of earthworms, millipedes and centipedes; 8,000 slugs and snails; 20,000 pot worms, 40,000 springtails, 120,000 mites, and 12 million nematodes. In an acre of soil, the weight of this below-ground life forms equals about 12 horses. (Hawken 1999)

These soil micro-organisms turn everything that falls on the ground, or grows in the ground, back into nutrient flows. Eisenberg uses a flea market metaphor to describe soil activity

Soil is like a flea market, an economic free-for-all in which all buyers and sellers pursue their own interests. Every scrap of merchandise—broken, salvaged, repaired, second-hand, or seventh-hand—is mined for its last ounce of value. Decay is good business because there are nutrients that can be extracted and energy that can be gained from the breaking of chemical bonds. The net effect of this activity of the soil biota is vital to life above-ground at street level—not because nature originally made it that way, but because the various forms of life above and below ground have co-evolved together.

Creative Techniques
Based on Associative Intelligence

CT 5.1 Associations

Write down a word or two that may or may not represent your problem, your situation, or some aspect of it. Then write down another word that comes to mind, that you associate with the first word. Now write a third word that you associate with the first word. Keep going, listing related words till you have a nice list. Review your list, looking for insights to hidden problems, opportunities, solutions, options.

CT 5.2 Free Associations

Write a one-word summary of your problem or situation. Looking at that word, write down the first word that comes to mind. Look at the second word and write down the first word that comes to mind. Keep going till you have a nice list. Look at these words. See how each of them gives you some insight into the situation. Can you use any of these words to draw analogies that could lead to a solution or new idea? Notice words that stand out for you and use them to brainstorm new associations, ideas, or solutions. You're looking for thoughts that might in turn lead to solutions or unrecognized opportunities.

CT 5.3 Qualities and Attributes

Review your problem or situation. What qualities or attributes are important? For example, if physical qualities are important, list qualities of size, weight, mass, color, odor, speed, etc. If social qualities are important, look at rules, leadership traits, communication aspects, etc. If psychological qualities are important, you might look at appearances, perceptions, motivations, symbolism, needs. If business aspects are important, consider qualities of function, cost, finance, service, maintenance, etc. List all the qualities or attributes of the problem, object, or situation. Systematically analyze each quality or group of qualities, trying to change them in as many ways as you can. Play with them to see how you could modify them, replace them, eliminate them, add to them, etc. Review the qualities you end up with, looking for the best ideas, options, solutions.

Especially good for generating new ideas and options.

CT 5.4 Quality Association Chain

List all the qualities or attributes of a problem, object, or situation. Now, free associate on each quality or group of qualities in order to generate new ideas. Study these combinations or ideas to determine which are most workable. Especially good for generating new ideas and options.

CT 5. 5 Combine and Play with Qualities and Attributes

After you have defined the problem, draw a large circle, like a clock-face and insert the numbers 1 through 12 around the clock-face. In the center write the problem definition as a brief statement or question. Identify 12 qualities or attributes of the problem or situation. Write a one-word symbol of each of these 12 attributes beside the 12 numbers on the clock-face.

Begin with the 1 quality. Brainstorm, free associate, or mind map any thoughts that come up about this attribute. Move on to quality 2, work on it, and continue until you have generated ideas for all 12 qualities.

What qualities can you combine? Perhaps you can see some likely combinations. If not, choose to combine some attributes at random. Play with the combining process. For each combination, either brainstorm, free associate, or mind map, or do all three processes. Continue until you feel you have enough ideas.

CT 5.6 Associate with Poems, Songs, Etc.

Make up little poems, songs, etc. that throw a new light or humorous slant onto the situation. Some people use such well-known songs as Beverly Hillbillies, Trouble in River City (from the Music Man), and Dixie to parody current problems. Ask yourself what insights the song or poem suggests. Especially good for recognizing problems and opportunities.

CT 5.7 Associate through Analogies

A direct analogy involves finding out how an object, item, or person is like other things that you are familiar with. For example, computer memory storage (unfamiliar) is like a beehive with the bees stashing stuff in specific little cells (familiar). Indirect analogies are often expressed in terms of how a pair of interrelated things (clock-hand to a clock) are like a pair of similar related things (indicator needle to a speedometer). Some examples are:

> A page is to a book as a screenful is to a computer monitor
> A peach is to a peach tree as a child is to a parent
> Blades are to a fan as a propeller is to an airplane
> A spider is to its web as a weaver is to the fabric

To associate through analogies, try this process:

- Consider two things that are essentially dissimilar and by a direct analogy show how they have some similarity. You can use anything—animals and how they function, equipment or toys and how they function, weather and how it functions.

- How can you apply certain facts, knowledge, or technology from another field to your current problem situation? For example, can you use facts from biology—such as how animals or plants function—to get new ideas?

- Create some analogies for your situation or problem. Ask yourself what insights the analogies suggest for finding opportunities, hidden problems, or solutions. This is a good technique for generating options.

  Note: A **personal analogy** *involves pretending you are the person, object, or item—it involves the emotion of empathy and the tool of imagination—becoming the item. See the "be-it" creative techniques in the emotional intelligence chapter.* **Symbolic analogy** *involves developing a "shortcut" expression of the issue at hand, a key word, and using one or two analogies that are related to this key word, in order to brainstorm. Example: "The situation is cut-throat—it leaves us gasping for a breath of life; our profits are bleeding through this gaping wound."*

CT 5.8 Associate through Metaphors

"A seawave of change." "Cooking the books." Metaphors usually treat one thing as if it were something else so that people can see a resemblance they would not ordinarily perceive. A metaphor is a figure of speech that links together two different universes of thought—oceans and economies, cuisine and accounting.

Metaphors stimulate the imagination, appeal to the emotions, give vivid life to a challenge, transform the intangible into an image that you and others can more easily grasp. Metaphor allows you to compare and link the literal reality around you with the figurative reality of your imagination, your emotions, your intuitive possibilities, your dreams, and your ability to dare to dream them. Metaphors are great for helping a team to share a particular vision.

Create some metaphors for your situation or problem. Ask yourself what insights the metaphors suggest for finding opportunities, hidden problems, or solutions. Especially good for generating options.

CT 5.9 Associate through Similes

"As cute as a ladybug." "Sparkling, like a sun-struck pond." Similes show how things are similar, usually by using such terms as "like" or "as." Create some similes for your situation or problem. Ask yourself what insights the similes suggest for finding opportunities, hidden problems, or solutions. Especially good for generating options.

CT 5.10 Associate with Random Words

Open the dictionary (catalog or other book) to any page and point to any word. Write the word on a sheet of paper. Repeat this process until you have listed at least 20 words. For each word, ask:
- How does this word relate to the situation?
- What does it suggest?
- How could it bring me insight, new ideas, or otherwise help?
- Jot down ideas.

CT 5.11 Associate with Two Words

After you have identified the problem-opportunity and expressed it in a brief statement, pick two key words from the statement, usually the action verb and its object (to increase sales, to reduce costs). On a sheet of paper, enter the two words as labels for two columns (for example, a column labeled "increase" and one labeled "sales.") Under each labeled column head, list alternative words that are synonyms, similar words ("add to, augment, expand, extend, grow.")

Using the first word from the first column, combine it with the first word from the second column. What insights or ideas does this combination suggest? Now combine that word with the second word from the second column, the third word from the second column, until you've used all the words in column 2.

Go to the second word from the first column and one by one combine it with each word in the second column, being open to new ideas and writing them down.

Now that you've exhausted all combinations of the words in both columns, what new insights, ideas, or suggestions do you have?

CT 5.12 Associate with the Energy Sources

Are there physical elements involved in your situation or problem?
- Trace each one back to its original source. All physical things can be traced back to the natural resources they are made of.
- What other applications do these physical elements have?
- What other resources could be used to produce these physical elements?
- Does tracing the physical elements back to their energy source show you how certain elements of the problem are related?
- What new ideas or solutions do these relationships suggest?

CT 5.13 Associate with an Ideal World

Write a little story telling what your problem-opportunity situation would be like if you could create it any way you wanted.

- What would the ideal situation be?
- Compare the existing situation with your ideal situation. What is the gap between ideal and actual? What are the differences?
- Why are those differences there?
- What problems or opportunities do the differences suggest?

CT 5.14 Associate through Murphy's Law

Murphy's law says, "If something can go wrong, it will." Examine the current situation or visualize an action plan you've developed to deal with it. Brainstorm all the things that could possibly go wrong. Look for potential problems, or actual problems that may be there but are not obvious. Example: equipment breaks down, a key person doesn't show up, key information gets lost, etc. List all the potential problems worth considering and what you'll do to prevent or handle them.

CT 5.15 Associate through Hidden Opportunities

If something can go right, it will? Examine the current situation and how current developments and trends may play out in the future.

- What opportunities are people overlooking?
- How could the organization make money? Gain market share? Capture new customers? Increase customer satisfaction? Provide better service? Etc.
  This technique is especially good for recognizing problems and opportunities.

CT 5.16 Focus on One Item (product, service, other) to Associate

- Pick a product, a service or other item that you want to change.
- List the qualities or attributes of this item.
- For each quality, do a free association, listing all related items that come up.
- How does each free association apply to changing the item or solving the problem? What ideas do the free associations, in combination, suggest?

CT 5.17 Associate the Input-Output Qualities (of products or services)

For the product or service that you are exploring, do the following:

- Determine the system input, the desired output, and the limiting requirements or specifications.
- Brainstorm ways of bridging the gap between the input and the desired output, given the limiting requirements or specifications.
- Use the qualities or attributes of the input to suggest solutions.
- Ask, "Can these qualities lead to the desired output in any way?" Keep asking until you've exhausted the possibilities.
- Evaluate the ideas that you've come up with.

CT 5.18   Associate with Possible Uses (products-services)

Explore a product, service, or object by naming all the possible uses for it—even the most outlandish and far-fetched. This process can yield several types of results; for example:

- A powerful brand name for the item
- Ways of marketing the item
- New, related items the firm could offer

CT 5.19   Relational Words Checklist—for product-service

Identify the product, service, or item that you want to change or alter in this problem-opportunity situation. Apply the words from the following checklist to this item. Review the results to see what insights, ideas, or suggestions come to mind.

Checklist

about	by	multiply	submerge
above	bypass	near	subtract
abstract	complement	not	symbolize
across	dissect	now	thicken
add	distort	of	through
after	divide	off	throughout
against	down	opposite	till
along	during	or	to
amid	eliminate	out	under
among	except	over	toward
and	extrude	past	transpose
around	flatten	protect	unify
around	fluff up	repeat	up
as	for	rotate	when
at	freeze	segregate	where
because	from	separate	while
before	help	since	with
behind	how	so then	upon
below	in	soften	who
beneath	integrate	squeeze	why
beside	into	still	widen
between	invert	stretch	within
beyond	join	subdue	without
but			

CT 5.20   Related Products, Services, Items

First think of all the businesses that are related, even remotely, to the one you're considering in this problem-opportunity situation. Now think of businesses, products, services, or items that are related to those. What new products, services, or items could your firm develop in any of these businesses?

CT 5.21 Reverse And Un-reverse

State the problem-opportunity situation, using an action verb. Then take the opposite, or antonym of that verb and apply it to the situation. Looking at it in that way may give you new ideas. Now take the new ideas (un-reverse) back to the original problem statement.

For example: "gaining customers" becomes "losing customers." What does that suggest? That you should be willing to lose customers that cost you more in company resources than you actually gain? Would this free up time for gaining really lucrative customers? For paying more attention to the most profitable customers you currently have?

CT 5.22 Improvement Checklist—for products-service

Identify the product, service, or item you want to change or alter. Set up four squares or columns with these words at the top of each: "Try:" "Make:" "Think Of:" "Take Away or Add:" Apply each of these processes to your item. What insights, ideas, or suggestions did you get? Write them down.

Case Studies—Applying the Creative Techniques

In working on these cases, you may use creative techniques from any of the chapters. However, the creative techniques described in this chapter may be especially appropriate.   Keep these self-questions in mind.

1. What problems do I see?
2. How can I probe beneath the surface to get at root problems?
3. What opportunities (hidden or obvious) can I find to take initiative, cut costs, and/or make money?
4. What creative alternatives can I generate?
5. As a consultant, what should I recommend as the best viewpoints and actions?
6. To answer these questions, what creative techniques can I experiment with to respond to this case? After completing the case analysis, ask: Which creative techniques produce the best results?

Case 5.1 Eclipse Salon in Burlingame

Eclipse Salon is breaking even but is not really making money for its owner, **Carol.** She created the salon two years ago by leasing a space in an attractive new building in downtown Burlingame. She hired an architect and contractor and had the interior of the building finished to her specifications. At the time Carol was leasing a styling station at a nearby salon, paying $750 per month and bringing home about $3,000 per month.

Eclipse is designed for a maximum of 12 stylists and/or nail technicians. Carol set the rent for stylists at $750 per month and for nail techs at $500. She needs to bring in $3750 a month in order to break even on her expenses, which are as follows

salon rental (5-year lease)	$2,200
loan repayment	1,000
utilities	200
insurance	50
cleaning service, misc. supplies	300

If Carol rents 4 stations to other stylists and counts her own need to pay rent somewhere as the 5th rental, this provides the $3,750 she needs to break even.

When Carol first opened the salon, she was very selective about who she accepted as tenants and coworkers, and within 5 months she had the 4 tenants she needed to break even—having turned down several applications. (She now wishes she had been less selective—especially since she ended up with a problem tenant anyway.) Therefore, for the past 1 ½ years, Carol has paid the salon's bills, but her income has been approximately the same as it was before she started the salon. It consists of money she brings in from her styling services to her personal clients.

As soon as there were 5 people working in the salon, Carol realized that having 12 people would overcrowd the salon, and the ideal would be 10 people—8 or 9 stylists and 1 or 2 nail technicians. She's been working to bring in 5 more tenants for 1 ½ years now.

The Rita Issue. A year ago, she did bring in 2 young stylists but they left after a couple of months. Carol suspects that Rita was a strong factor in running them off. Rita has not been easy to deal with. A former salon owner herself, she displays fairly extreme mood swings and is probably a drug user. Carol would like to end the relationship, which she can legally do because she rents the stations on a month-by-month basis. But where Rita goes, Ramona goes—they're bosom buddies, having worked together for 12 years. Carol is afraid she won't fill their spots and would face operating at a $1,500 loss every month.

Receptionist Issue. A major barrier to attracting stylists to the salon is the fact that Carol does not provide a receptionist to answer the phone and schedule appointments. Each station has its own telephone outlet, and each stylist answers her own phone and schedules her own appointments. Stylists who have become accustomed to this method like it because it gives them complete control over contact with clients and work schedule. At the same time it avoids much political infighting among stylists over new clients—walk-ins and call-ins. Carol handles those and rotates who gets them in as fair a way as possible. There have been no complaints in this department.

On the other hand, stylists who have always had receptionist service are reluctant to give it up and therefore refuse to consider renting a station at Eclipse. Receptionist pay ranges from $1,500 to $2,000 per month. Salon owners who provide this service must figure this expense into their total monthly overhead and set their rentals accordingly—so that in effect stylists pay their fair share of the receptionist's salary.

Product sales. This revenue is a small factor in Carol's income—she thinks of it as money to take care of the extras. On gross sales of a hair or nail product, 50 percent goes to buy it and 50 percent is profit. When the other stylists sell products to their customers, Carol pays a 10 percent commission, so she makes a 40 percent profit on those sales. She has 3 display racks of products along the front wall, about 36 feet of shelf space.

Station Rentals. Stylists who can pay a rent of $750 a month are those who already have a clientele in the area. Therefore, they come from other local salons. Recruiting must therefore be done in the local area, either by word of mouth, in person, or through advertising. Carol has run ads in the local newspaper several times, with no results. She had a tacky "Stylist Stations Available" sign in the window for a while with no results.

One alternative Carol has thought of pursuing is to attract stylists who have recently moved to the area or just graduated from cosmetology school. She could agree to charge them a reduced rental until they can build a clientele.

This month, **Sylvia**, a nail technician with a very limited clientele in the area, began renting a station at $300 month, with the agreement to begin paying $500 in 6 months, after she's built a clientele.

Two young hair stylists have indicated they'll start leasing in January at $750 a month, but Carol has little confidence that they will follow through.

Carol is grateful that she's paying her salon bills and not losing money, but she feels she's spinning her wheels. Why start a business if you can make the same income renting from someone else—and avoid all the responsibilities and hassles of being an owner?

- What are the major problems and opportunities here?
- What should Carol do next?
- Which CTs discussed in this chapter did you use in solving this case problem?
- Which CTs were most helpful and what ideas did they spark or inspire?

Case 5.2 Lightning Bats

Joe Benvenuto began playing softball about 8 years ago, when he was working in the data processing department of a trucking company. One fateful night he was asked to sub for one of the company's team players. He swatted three home runs that night and before long he was traveling 20 weekends each year to softball tournaments all over the U.S. He began wondering if a superior bat could help his game.

His friend **Chris Demato** has the same question. They begin working together to develop their own type of bat, a special aluminum model. They name it Lightning and start Lightning Co. They soon find that plenty of other players are wondering the same thing, for when they place an ad in *USA Today*, they get the first flurry of orders.

Chris wants to function as a silent partner, so Joe runs the company. He grows it by doing most of the important management tasks himself. But the part of the job he's always loved most is R&D—continually experimenting with various bat shapes and materials to keep improving the performance of the product. After all, Lightning is the most expensive softball bat in the world and people expect plenty for their money.

Within 5 years, Joe finds that his management tasks are so time-consuming that he must get up at 4 am if wants to put in a conventional workday before early afternoon. About 2 p.m. he begins his three-hour stint in the batter's box of a nearby public park—swinging at softballs served up by his private pitcher, driving them to a fence 320- feet away. Typically, he'll swing at as many as 200 pitches each session. Between pitches he calls the company engineers by cell phone, rapping about how the bat might be modified. The next afternoon, he gets a slightly modified version of the same bat. Then it's back to hitting again. Joe believes there's no book you can read that tells you how to develop a good bat because it's not an exact science. He finds that the best way is to coax new bats to emerge is in small daily increments of trial and error.

Lightning bats are more than a simple cylinder of aluminum. The company is now selling a patented double-wall bat that features two thin layers of aluminum. The thickness doubles to about six inches at the average bat's "sweet spot," the place on the barrel that provides a ball with the most pop. With a bigger sweet spot, a player can hit the ball harder and with far more consistency. Now the race is on to develop bats with advanced materials such as carbon fiber, graphite, and strong aluminum alloys code-named CU31, EA70, and SC500. Competitors are nipping at Joe's heels.

Joe decides to develop a new bat designed for hardball leagues. To test the various stages of this new bat, he hires **Vic Mazetti**, a hardball player who stands 6 feet 5 inches and weighs 250 pounds. Joe says, "The hardball guys who play on Friday nights just want to hit the ball."

The company is now bringing in about $10 million in orders each year and has grown significantly each year of the 7 years it's been in existence.

- What potential problems and opportunities do you detect?
- What should Joe Benvenuto do next?
- Which CTs discussed in this chapter did you use in solving this case problem?
- Which CTs were most helpful and what ideas did they spark or inspire?

Self-Awareness Opportunities

SAO 5.1. Right Brain or Left Brain?

Purpose: To assess which types of intelligence you currently rely on the most: your left-brain rational intelligence or the right-brain intelligences (associative, sensory, intuitive).

Instructions: Circle the letter that best represents your usual response to the situations described. When you have responded to all the statements, follow the instructions at the end to compute and interpret your score.

1. When meeting someone, I usually show up
   a. early   b. on time   c. a little late   d. late

2. Sticking to plans usually makes me feel
   a. safe and secure
   b. mostly comfortable, satisfied
   c. a little bored
   d. constricted, like I'm locked in a very small closet

3. When someone interrupts me, I usually find it
   a.   very frustrating   b. annoying   c. normal, no big deal   d. stimulating

4.   At the beginning of the work day, I usually
   a.   make a list of things to do and plan my day around my list
   b.   make a do-list but may deviate from it
   c.   have a few things in mind that I want to accomplish
   d.   shuffle through piles of stuff to do and then decide what to do first

5. Day dreaming is
   a. waste of time
   b. one way I relax and goof off
   c. sometimes productive
   d. the best part of my day

6. When faced with a decision, I usually
   a. weigh all the options and make a decision based on the facts
   b. weigh the options, notice my instincts, and make a decision based on the facts
   c. weigh the options and facts, then go with my instincts
   d. go with my instincts

7. When learning how to use a new piece of equipment, I usually
   a. read the instruction manual carefully before beginning
   b. look at the manual, especially the pictures, then jump in and get started
   c. get started, and if I run into trouble, check out the manual
   d. jump in and wing it

8. When it comes to time, I prefer to
a. depend on my good sense of time but frequently check the clock
b. depend on my good sense of time
c. ignore what time it is, but check the clock when necessary
d. not know what time it is and not wear a watch

9. When someone gives me directions, I usually prefer them to
a. tell me verbally, step by step, what to do or how to get there
b. primarily tell me step by step but also give some visual landmarks
c. primarily give me visual references but also give me brief verbal directions
d. give me visual references—how things should look, what to look for, etc.

10. At any one moment, if you ask me about it, my checking account is likely to be
a. balanced to the penny
b. pretty well balanced
c. I'm not sure—it's been several weeks since I balanced it
d. I don't know—I don't keep a running balance

11. When I'm shopping, and I see something I really want, I usually
a. buy it only if I have plenty of money to spare
b. buy it if I'm caught up on all my bills
c. charge it if I have not bought too much already this month
d. charge it and hope the charge is approved

12. When faced with a stupid rule or instruction, I usually
a. follow instructions
b. follow instructions but complain
c. try to get it changed before I do anything
d. bend the rules, do it my way

13. When telling a story to a friend, I usually
a. cut to the chase, give the facts
b. stick with the main facts but jazz it up a little
c. tell it in a very animated way
d. tell it in an animated way and maybe get sidetracked

14. I feel that risk taking is
a. to be avoided when possible
b. to be avoided unless I can see my clear to succeed
c. necessary if I want to achieve and should be based on the probability of success
d. part of life; go for it!

15. When it comes to my personality, my typical pattern is
a. loyal and dependable
b. loyal and fun-loving
c. fun-loving and dependable
d. fun-loving and funny

16. On weekends, I usually
a.   make a "to-do" list and focus on getting things done
b.   focus on getting things done but also relax and have fun
c.   relax and have fun but try to get a few things done too
d.   do what I want when I want, including doing nothing, if possible

17. On vacation, I usually
a.   have read books about my destination area and have a list of things to do and see
b.   mainly make a plan and stick with it but leave some time to play it by ear
c.   mainly play it by ear but have a few plans in mind
d.   wing it, play it by ear

18. When it comes to making decisions, I usually
a.   decide right away and stick with it
b.   take some time to decide and stick with it
c.   take some time to decide and keep the door open to change my mind
d.   put off making a choice and often change my mind

19. When I have been faced with major changes in my life, I usually found it
a.   terrifying
b.   pretty scary or tense
c.   rather interesting
d.   exciting

20. My work place usually looks
a.   uncluttered, shipshape
b.   mainly uncluttered—a few personal or "loose" things lying around
c.   fairly busy—work, favorite things lying around
d.   very busy, cluttered

21. When it comes to paperwork, I usually like to
a.   file it
b.   mainly file it but leave out a few piles
c.   primarily pile it; when I must, file it
d.   pile it

22. When faced with an overwhelming task, I usually
a.   do it full blast till finished
b.   work on it spasmodically till finished
c.   waiver between working on it full blast and trying to forget about it
d.   either jump in and stick with it or postpone it and hope it goes away—no in-between

23. When it comes to finding things, I'm usually
a.   good at it because I believe in a place for everything and everything in its place
b.   pretty good at keeping track of things with the occasional lapse
c.   fairly regularly I lost keys, a phone number, etc.
d.   almost every day I spend some time looking for keys, papers, etc.

24. When it comes to remembering things I must do, I
a. usually remember every detail
b. usually manage to figure it out
c. sometimes lose track
d. what was the question again?

25. When it comes to long-range plans, I
a. usually plan months, even years ahead
b. often make a few plans for next month or year
c. usually play it by ear but sometimes plan for next month or year
d. like to keep my options open and play it by ear

26. People probably describe me as
a. usually level-headed (unemotional)
b. mainly level-headed but sometimes emotional
c. mainly emotional but often level-headed
d. emotional, passionate, or moody

27. Here is my work style, in a nutshell:
a. I concentrate on one task at a time; I'm easily overwhelmed by multiple tasks
b. I'm able to juggle a few things at once but prefer focusing on one project at a time
c. I like to juggle more than one project at a time
d. I thrive on juggling several projects at once; I get bored working on only one thing

28. For touchy matters, I usually prefer to communicate by
a. writing a memo
b. sending a memo but also asking to meet face to face
c. meeting face to face and following up with a confirming memo
d. meeting face to face

29. When reading a book, I usually
a. start at the beginning and work my way through to the end
b. read the contents, then read only interesting chapters in a systematic way
c. start at the beginning (or end) but then jump around to other parts
d. jump in with whatever looks most interesting

30. When asked a question, I usually
a. try to give the right answer; I figure there's usually a right or wrong answer
b. try to give the right answer but realize some issues are too complex to have right or wrong answers
c. ask myself if there's a good answer to the question
d. try to figure out where the question is coming from

31. When asked for my opinion, I usually
a. think before I speak
(b). think first, although occasionally I blurt out what's on my mind
c. say what's on my mind, although sometimes I stop and think first
d. say what's on my mind

$a = 12 \times 2 = 24$ Left Brain
$b = 12 \times 1 = 12$ $+ \; 36$
$c = 5 \times 1 = 5$ Right Brain
$d = 2 \times 2 = 4$ $+ \; 9$

32. When it comes to major projects, I usually
a. stick with it till finished
b. stick with it but sometimes drop out
(c). get bored, tired, distracted, or otherwise drop out, but sometimes stick with it
d. get bored, tired, distracted, or otherwise drop out

Computing your score:
- Add up separately your "a," "b," "c," and "d" answers, giving you 4 separate scores.
- Multiply as follows: "a" score x 2, "b" score x 1
- Add these two "a" and "b" sums together. This is your left-brain score.
- Multiply as follows: "c" score x 1, "d" score x 2
- Add these two "c" and "d" sums together. This is your right-brain score.

Maximum score on either side: 64

SAO 5.2 Create Analogies, Metaphors, Similes

Purpose: To practice using your associative intelligence.
Instructions: For each of the following words, brainstorm as many analogies, metaphors, and similes as you can within ten minutes. You're trying to think of images, symbols, ideas, of things that are similar to, like, descriptive of the listed word. Suppose you wanted to convey to someone who was unfamiliar with the listed word the full meaning of the word, or a wide range of meanings of the word. What words could you use? Be creative. Be funny. Be awesome.

Body

Computer

Corporation

Culture

Freedom

Magic

Market

Morality

Transportation

Virtual corporation

Wings

References

Carr-Ruffino, Norma. *The Promotable Woman*. Franklin Lakes, NJ: Career Press, 1997.

De Beauport, Elaine. *The Three Faces of Mind*. Wheaton, IL: Quest Books, 1996.

De Bono, Edward. *Serious Creativity: Using the Power of Lateral Thinking to Create New Ideas*. New York: HarperCollins, 1992.

Hawken, P., A. Lovins and L.H. Lovins. *Natural Capitalism: Creating the Next Industrial Revolution*. Boston: Little, Brown, 1999.

Higgins, James W. *101 Creative Problem Solving Techniques*. New York: New Management Publishing, 1994.

Eisenberg, Evan. *The Ecology of Eden*. New York: Alfred A. Knopf, 1998.

Chapter 6
Sensory Intelligence
Visions, Tones, Body Awareness

Dance as though no one is watching. Anonymous

Sensory intelligence is about relating to the world and learning through your senses—seeing/visual, touching/moving/kinesthetic, hearing/aural, and smelling/tasting/olfactory. Since it involves relating to the physical space around you, it's sometimes called spatial intelligence. The aspect that's most vital to your Creative Intelligence is your internal visioning ability. Vision, imagination, and insight are also powerful links to soul information and your soul-level energy body. Its energy center within your chakra system is your brow, or third-eye, chakra.

Kinesthetic intelligence includes finding your way around—motion, movement, athletics, sports, and artistic expression through movement, such as dance, ballet, and the artistic movement aspects of acting and other presentations.

Aural intelligence includes relating and learning through listening—through the sounds that resonate through your body, through soaring with beautiful music and expressing yourself through music.

Olfactory intelligence includes relating and learning through your sense of smell and taste and includes artistic expression through preparing and appreciating foods.

Visual intelligence includes relating and learning through what you see externally and internally—through your powers of visualization and imagination. It includes artistic expression through the visual arts and appreciation of visual arts.

Key words to associate with sensory intelligence are: *image, imagination, fantasy, visual, musical, tones, chords, dancing, movement, motion, athletics, smelling, tasting, third-eye chakra, soul energy body, blue-violet, tone la or A, neocortex, right-brain*

People vary in their patterns of taking in information. Most of us actually receive a mixture from all the senses but rely most heavily on one sense above all others. For most the dominant sense is vision, the images they take in. For some, it's the sounds, verbal and musical, that they hear. Some rely mainly on touch and body movement, while others focus on odors or fragrances. Creative people often perceive or think in cross-over terms. For example, if the smell of new-mown grass brings up the color green in your mind, you are crossing olfactory with visual. Such cross-over is called synesthesia.

13

Myths & Realities

The culture tends to de-value the amazing power of your imagination more than any other sensory intelligence. Yet your imagination is so powerful in firing up your creative intelligence!

Myth 1. It's only your imagination.

This common cultural myth says that your imagination doesn't count. It's the realm of the immature and mentally unstable. It's too chaotic and unruly, as are the ideas emerging from it, to be accepted as respectable, dependable, or valuable. It follows that imaginative storytelling, even the future scenario, is not worth much. As a child your imaginative ideas were probably discounted and de-valued, so why should you give it much of your attention and energy? Why should you value and work with the ideas your imagination spins out?

This is really sad because your greatest creative power resides in your ability to imagine and visualize. Experts in this subject have concluded that *anything* you can imagine has the possibility of being brought into physical reality. It's just a matter of time, energy, and resources.

Myth 2. You're just fantasizing. Get real!

This is related to the imagination myth but it goes further and divides the world into the unreal (free and wild mental exploration) and the real (thinking and acting in accordance with the belief of cultural consensus.). Fantasizing is even more far-out than imagining and therefore takes you a little closer to the "loony-bin."

Everything that you bring into your physical reality, you create first in your mind. If you want to develop creative responses to increasingly challenging problem-opportunity situations, you must generate a wide range of ideas. Remember, you use your rational intelligence at appropriate steps in the problem-opportunity resolution process. But the other intelligences, such as visual intelligence, are just as important; in fact, they're irreplaceable for the exploratory and idea-generating steps in the process.

Myth 3. Stop daydreaming.

The myth is that daydreaming is a waste of time. It's equated with idleness and loafing, and the assumption is that daydreams have little connection with doing and achieving things in physical reality. We are a culture that values "doing" as proof that we're achieving. Many of us forget that our creative geniuses have always been "daydreamers," as well as night dreamers.

How You Experience Sensory Intelligence

When you're using the rational part of your brain, you probably express your ideas in words, using such terms as "I think." When you use the sensory part of your brain, you probably express yourself in terms of seeing images or hearing tones, as indicated in Table 6.1.

Table 6.1 Comparisons of Rational and Sensory Modes

Rational Intelligence	Sensory Intelligence
"I think"	*"I see, I hear, I feel, I smell, I taste"*
intellectualizing	*imagining*
studying	*meditating*
planning, analyzing data	*visualizing*
thinking in words	*thinking in images, pictures*
"What are the causes? Effects? Reasons why?"	*"What will it look like? Feel like? Sound like? Smell like? Taste like?"*

Auditory Intelligence

Good listening requires both patience and auditory intelligence. Active listening involves patience, giving the person time to get the message across. When you are an alert, active listener, you're able to listen for long time periods, take in the words people say, along with their tones of voice, and make quite comprehensive or in-depth meanings from what you hear. If you're impatient, on the other hand, you may react before you've had time to grasp the message or the meaning the person is trying to convey.

You may be an alert listener of sounds in the outer physical world. You may be able to connect and interpret a variety of sounds. You may hear not only the sound but its connection to meaning. Auditory intelligence is connecting inner meaning to a sound you receive from the outer physical world.

Musicians rely on auditory intelligence. They hear sounds and music in the outer physical world and can integrate them on the inner level. They hear musical themes, variations, sounds, tones, and combinations on a purely inner level without necessarily receiving input from the outer level. They can translate those inner sounds into musical notes and play the music back. Other musicians can read their music and play it.

You may hear suggestions, words that seem to come from a deeper level within you. You may sometimes speak of "listening to my inner voice." The two levels of auditory intelligence are:

1. Hearing sounds or words from your outer physical world—alert, active listening that depends on how well you focus and link various sounds with meaning.

2. Hearing sounds or words from your inner world—experiences that depend on how well you relax and open up to listening within.

Creativity Showcase

Swimming with Dolphins:

Using all the brain-tones to activate brain cells, other cells

Joan Ocean, a psychologist who lives in Hawaii, believes that dolphins, who are members of a pod family, communicate as one, using "pod mind." This means that all of the dolphins, at the same time, understand each other's thoughts and feelings. Joan thinks this intuitive ability develops in societies like the dolphin pod, where there are no secrets, where everything can be known, and where there's a strong sense of caring for each other.

In addition to accessing the pod mind, the dolphins also communicate through sound. They make very high-pitched and very low sounds. They can chirp and make sounds that seem like laughing. Many of their sounds are beyond our ability to hear, but will still affect our bodies if we come nearby.

A few years ago Joan began to swim with the dolphins for three and four hours every day. A dolphin pod normally consists of over 200 dolphins. Once she began swimming regularly with them, they always included her in their pod and included her in their swims.

She began to realize that swimming in close proximity to them was changing her metabolism. Their tonal language sounds are frequencies that would enter her body and affect the frequency of her body. She would move into a type of altered state of consciousness, which she now believes is the normal state of dolphin consciousness. For her it was very peaceful and serene—like an active meditation. In that state she felt as though she could swim forever.

Joan says that dolphin information can help us to go beyond our old limiting social and cultural beliefs. It can help us understand that we're capable of a lot more than what we think we are. For instance, our minds have capabilities that we're not using. Joan said, "The dolphins sometimes sonar our brains and see that a lot of the parts of our brains are inactive. They must think we're sleeping because our brains are very quiet and inactive in many ways. They encourage us to use more of our brains. When we swim with them, they use a tonal language to stimulate our brains—and all the cells of our bodies" (Roberts 1999).

Many people who swim with dolphins come away with a decision to give up their old lifestyle, the belief in the old Protestant work ethic that you have to work hard in order to succeed. The dolphins don't believe that. Their success is based on certain vibrational frequencies that we call "love." To the degree that you're able to create that vibrational frequency in your body, you will draw to yourself great happiness—and everything that would enrich your happiness.

Joan is a psychologist, who felt she was very good at her work. After she met the dolphins, she mentioned her experiences to her clients, and some of them wanted to join her swims. What happened was these clients overcame the difficulties in their lives within a couple of days instead of needing weeks of counseling. Joan believes a big part of her clients' healing had to do with reconnecting with nature. Most of us are cut off from the natural world in our daily lives. Yet, it's such an important part of our health and well-being. After being with the dolphins, people make a decision to be closer to a more natural way of life.

Kinesthetic Intelligence

When you do well in an individual sport such as dancing, skating, skiing, or swimming, you're using kinesthetic intelligence. When you have developed this intelligence, you have these kinds of experiences:

- Feeling comfortable in your body in relation to the space around you.

- Being free to guide yourself spatially rather than respond to rules or other players, as required in team sports.

- Synthesizing connections on an inner level

- Communicating this inner level by the movement of your body, by kinesthetic ability. This movement may be graceful, artistic, and highly skilled

Olfactory Intelligence

Think of the power of fragrances to bring back full-blown memories of your past experiences. Remember the smells you loved or hated, smells from nature such as honeysuckle blooms or fresh-mown grass. Remember the food fragrances of bread baking or onions frying. How about the sexual impact of odors and fragrances? Research indicates that you must be comfortable with the way a person smells, even the most subtle smells, in order to create a close or intimate relationship.

Most of what you taste when you eat or drink is actually what you smell. These two senses are intimately intertwined. Good cooks know this when they experiment with new recipes. As they put together the ingredients, they smell the various spices and herbs they might use, connecting each in the imagination with the final dish to be served. *Mmmm, smells like dill would be great in this sauce. Curry? No, too strong.*

What you smell affects your health. Pleasant smells and positive thoughts can boost your immune level and therefore your health. Unpleasant smells and negative thoughts do the opposite. Scientists recently found a direct causal link between changing moods, which can be affected by odors, and the immune system [Dodd 1998]. When people smelled rotten meat, their antibody levels dropped steeply (antibodies fight disease organisms). But the smell of chocolate prevented the suppression of the antibody. Women's immune responses varied less than men's, but their reactions to smells was greater.

Visual Intelligence

Visual intelligence includes imagining, or visualizing situations, processes, objects, methods, anything. It includes planning visually and visioning the future. It's essential for good storytelling and for creating future scenarios. It's a mental process that activates your neocortex at a more profound level than associative intelligence. You can use it to gain access to more information about your inner processes and therefore your own being.

Before humans learned to use written language, they expressed themselves through pictorial images on cave walls, serving bowls and baskets, etc.

When you look for things and see things with your eyes open, you're using your sensory intelligence in an external physical world. You may do a drawing based on what you see. You may use your visual intelligence to size up a situation quickly, to take in data that you see, and to assess various aspects of a complex situation—by studying it visually.

Sensory intelligence, including visual intelligence also takes place on an internal level. Rich visual imagery can also be a thinking process. You may visualize something that you've never seen on the physical plane and then communicate it to others by drawings or by translating images into words. You may use verbal description, metaphor, and similar methods to communicate your inner image.

Vision as a Brain Function

Your brain function is highly specialized. You process your perceptions, color and movement, and form in separate brain regions, for example. Also, your visual system is not designed to make absolute judgments about what you see but rather to make comparisons. How you perceive the brightness of an object, for example, depends on the intensity of light that surrounds it, and how you perceive its color depends on the color of surrounding objects. And, visual perception is reconstructive and creative. The image that falls on the retina of each eye is two-dimensional, but you live in a three-dimensional world so your brain must reconstruct that world. We're just beginning to learn about how holographic, three-dimensional scenes materialize via laser beams and how they can be reconstructed from a tiny snippet of the whole scene.

Here's the bottom line: your visual system uses many pieces of information to reconstruct a scene. The visual information that comes into your eyes is invariably imperfect, yet you form in your brain a logical and complete visual world, although it's not clear just how you manage to do this. What scientists have concluded is that you create images in your brain by using visual information, and by drawing on visual memories. You construct a coherent image, but not necessarily the one that's "out there." Your other brain systems operate in a similar fashion. For example, your memories are often reconstructive, reflecting the coming together of many past experiences. Your visual system is not faultless, nor is any other part of your brain, but your brain constantly works to give you a logical, consistent, and coherent view of the outside world [Dowling 1998].

Visual Language

Combining words with images produces better problem solving, encourages learning, increases learning speed, and allows for more complex expression. Thanks to the Internet, a new language—visual language—is growing and spreading around the globe [Horn 1998]. We don't realize how pervasive this new global visual language is because it's called by so many different names by different professional groups:

- *business graphics* and *information design* (technical writers)
- *idea sketching* or *mind mapping* (teachers)
- *signage* (architects)
- *computer aided design* (engineers)
- *charts* and *graphs* (scientists)
- *graphic design* (advertisers)

Some important applications of this visual language are:

- Externalizing creative problem-solving
- Displaying problem analysis and multiple viewpoints
- Exploring deeper connections and feelings, such as shared visions of the future
- Making group processes visible
- Presenting multiple viewpoints
- Enabling people to understand complex issues
- Resolving complex issues by making them more visible. For example, an information mural can display the many aspects of an issue and keep a group on track

- Revealing cross-boundary issues that we need to work on

- Facilitating cross-cultural and international communication. For example, several hundred cartooning conventions are now understood globally.

Visualizing and Vibrant Well-Being

Visual intelligence is so powerful that it can boost or harm your immune system and therefore your ability to function effectively. Studies indicate that you can affect your resistance to disease by visualizing pleasant experiences [Doss 1998]. The antibody immunoglobulin is found in saliva and protects against respiratory infections. Within 20 minutes of mentally reliving pleasant experiences, the antibody doubled. After 45 minutes, it increased even more, and after three hours it increased by 60 percent. Conversely, when people mentally relived traumatic or guilt-ridden experiences, the antibody level dropped.

Depriving yourself of the need to visualize is not productive. Research indicates, for example, that children who spend too many hours watching television, computer screens, and video games, lose much of the ability to mentally image. Loss of this ability, in turn, often leads to hostile, even violent, feelings and actions. The practice of visualizing, or daydreaming, may be related to dreaming, which we know is essential to maintain balance and sanity. Research also indicates that such waking imaging boosts children's rational intelligence (Tarlow 1999).

Images, Thoughts, and Feelings—Equally Powerful

Images are configurations of energy, just as thoughts and feelings are. Elaine DeBeauport

Energy can form itself in many ways, such as a picture (image), a sentence, or a feeling. An image is a mental configuration just as surely as a thought is. One is expressed as a picture, the other as a sentence. Both can conform to consensus reality or not.

Society discounts internal images as fantasy, hallucination, "just your imagination." Some images reflect external consensus reality, while others are pure inventions of something that has never been known in the human world. But even fantasy or hallucination are harmful only if you begin to believe they're part of consensus reality and won't let them go. To boost your creativity, you can view both thoughts and images as mental configurations that you can either verify with consensus reality, or not. You can move beyond rational prejudices against visualization to build this powerful intelligence. DeBeauport asks:

- What if society were to value visual thinking as highly as rational thinking?

- What if we educated and developed ourselves in both intelligences?

- Then would we value the artist as highly as the intellectual?

- Would film and television be regarded as highly as literature?

The scientific method of discovery actually depends upon a good imagination. When you're doing research, you use your visual imagination and intuition at some stages and your rational intelligence at other stages. For example, since your brain can't see what it's not prepared to see, you must prepare it with possibilities so it can see new ideas. You *imagine* a model or system of interaction that is new and desirable or a bringing together of people, things, or ideas in a new way. Using some sort of imaginary model, you set up hypotheses, which are guesses about how things work. Then you gather information to test the validity of your guesses.

The scientific method relies on the hypothesis, or guess, which is an *image* of the possible. You *imagine* a hypothesis that might reflect a truth and then proceed to use approved processes for verifying whether it is true. Your *imagination* may create and evaluate many hypotheses or *images* before finding one that can be verified and that proves to be useful. This process of continually projecting images is sensory-visual intelligence at work.

Your imagination can be richer and more creative than anything you see externally. For example, images that you create inside your mind as you read a book are often more rich, vivid, and powerful than those you see on the screen when the book is made into a film. When you read a book, you are the producer and director of the visual images that portray the story you're reading. You have more freedom than a film director to create any images you want.

Visualizing and the Planning Function

Imaginative visualizing is a form of planning. It may be used together with analysis, which focuses on the factual data that's currently available to you. You use visual intelligence when you focus on seeing an inner picture of how something might turn out in the future. This is a powerful way to rehearse future plans, to notice gaps and errors, and to adjust your plans for success.

You can create more beautiful and useful products, services, processes, and buildings if you first visualize them through drawings, pictures, simulations, and models. You can try out different versions, compare them for beauty and effectiveness, and select the ones that work best. Computer programs have greatly enhanced this process.

When you use this intelligence, you become involved in imagination, fantasy, and hypothesis. You can form mental images to improve your brain power, to enrich your life, and to guide you in your daily life. Images are information that you can use in whatever range of reality you decide to visit: the imaginary, the subtle, or consensus reality.

How to Boost Your Sensory Intelligence

You may receive intuitive messages through your senses. Most people do, but people vary as to which sense connects most often with intuitive intelligence. And some people receive most or all of their intuitive messages as a wholistic "sense of knowing," which doesn't seem to involve any of the senses. If you are like most people, however, you can boost your intuitive intelligence by boosting your awareness of sensory messages, especially those that seem to come from "within." In other words, messages that are *not* clearly from your external environment, such as the ringing of a doorbell, the sight of a person at the door, the touch of her hand in a handshake, or the smell of her cologne. Your inner senses include:

- seeing visual imagery, as a thinking process
- hearing sounds, music, tones, themes from within
- hearing messages, information, from an inner voice
- smelling and tasting by imagination
- thinking about certain body movements and feeling them in your mind, playing them out or practicing them (psycho-cybernetics)

Booster 1. Expand Your Sensory Experiences

Pay attention to your senses and find ways to experience them more fully every day. Television can be stimulating, in moderation, if you watch creative fare that engages your imagination and expands your sensory experiences. Unfortunately most programs do the opposite, relying on deadening repetition of a few tired formulas, filled with clichés. Producers often use ever-increasing gore and violence as a substitute for creative, intelligent programming.

Over-exposure to such programs, especially in your younger years, can actually deaden your sensory intelligence. Research suggests that children who spend hours looking at television and computer screens experience alterations in their brain waves. Researchers interpret such alterations as the loss of internal imaging capacity. In turn they associate this loss with more aggressive and violent feelings experienced more frequently by these children than by those who engage more a greater variety of sensory experiences, i.e. hands-on, interactive and physically active learning and playing.

Booster 2. Become More Sensual

Enjoy sensual experience—the breeze on your skin, the fruit on your tongue, the lover's touch on your lips—let them entice you and work their full magic. The experiences in Table 6.2 can give you some ideas. Let even the unpleasant sensory experiences interest you—the weird smells, little pains, messy sights. Raise your awareness of the whole range of your sensuality.

Table 6.2 Sensory Highs

Falling in love	Friends
Falling in love for the first time	The beach
Laughing so hard your face hurts	A hot shower
Your first kiss	Sleepovers
A special glance	Being part of a team
Getting mail	Playing with a new puppy
Taking a drive on a pretty road	Having someone play with your hair
Hearing your favorite song on the radio	Sweet dreams
Lying in bed listening to the rain outside	Hot chocolate
Hot towels out of the dryer	Road trips with friends
Walking out of your last final	Swinging on a swing
Chocolate milkshake	Going to a really good concert
A long distance phone call	Spending time with close friends!
Getting invited to a party	Riding a bike downhill
Butterflies, fireflies, humming birds	Hugging the person you love
Laughing till you cry	Running through sprinklers
A good conversation	Laughing for absolutely no reason at all
A care package	Laughing at an inside joke
Laughing at yourself	Balmy summer nights
Midnight phone calls that last for hours	Getting out of bed in the morning and
Watching the sunrise	rejoicing because you're alive!

Remember, everything you create or do happens first in your mind. So when you develop your inner senses, you give a powerful boost to your creative intelligence. For example, you expand your skills in:

- observing and exploring the world
- learning about the world by making connections between what you see, hear, touch, smell/taste, both externally and internally, and what you think.

- expressing yourself—through artistic creations based on what you see, hear, smell/taste or body movement you feel within, to produce a painting, a song, a dance, a great dinner, a new business project, etc.

- opening up to receive intuitive information

Be willing to fine-tune these senses. One way to do that is to practice synthesthesia, the crossover of sensory input. Ask yourself these kinds of questions:

- What color is that sound? That word? That image or picture? That fragrance?

- What color is that touch, that physical movement (for example, a leap, a twirl)?

- What sound-tone is that color? That word? That image? That odor?

- What sound-tone is that touch or physical movement?

- That sound has what feeling?

- That image triggers that word?

A feeling may elicit also a color, sound-tone, fragrance, touch, or physical movement. A word may elicit a picture, a color, a sound-tone, an odor, a taste. Every one of the senses can cross over with any and all of the others.

Allow more input from your outer world. Try these techniques:

- When you listen or read, visualize what the words are saying—see the experience, events, processes, people, relationships, etc.

- Draw quick sketches of how things look, where this would help you make it real, concrete, and memorable.

- Work with sensory input in your inner world. Meditation is a way of listening beyond your negative ego, rational-mind yadda-yadda. With practice you can learn to differentiate between ego-chatter and deeper-level information.

- Deeper-level information can help you put your current life and concerns into a bigger framework, the larger picture. You see clearly what's trivia and what's important. Your priorities fall into place. You engage in a higher-level thinking process that can lead to visions for what you and others can create in the future.

- Use this inner learning to boost your level of expectancy, your active belief in "I can."

- While in meditation, work with visualizations to express this inner learning in the outer world. For example, set related goals and visualize the goals as already achieved.

Booster 3 Try Creative Culture Shock

As a creative person—whether your niche is in business, science, academia, or the arts—you need to continually cultivate new awarenesses You need to clear your mind of old habits and search for input that's really new, that triggers creative insights—over and over and over Your biggest block to regaining that beginner's mind, the one that welcomes new ideas, is your belief that you already know it. It's the "been there, done that" syndrome You need to continually regain the curiosity and wonder you had as a little child—the "wow, that's amazing" attitude.

There's no better way to unblock your mind—to get back to that blank-slate beginner's mind—than to travel to strange parts of the world If you don't have the time and money to go in person, try the next-best thing. Travel in your imagination by immersing yourself in the strange worlds you can find in books, films, and the Internet. You'll find a cost-effective glimpse into the values, mindsets, and imaginations of other cultures. Buy yourself a ticket to a refreshingly, shockingly alien environment that assaults all your senses Start with the one that seems most exotic and alluring to you at this moment.

You must keep looking outside for fresh input—whether it's in wildly varying fields of inquiry, talking to kids or old folks, taking up new hobbies or sports, whatever works to keep you moving mentally. You need to *know* what you don't know You need to contact what is really new for you, and recognize it as such through your beginner's mind. You can't leave to chance this fresh input and the powerful awarenesses that results from it. You need to plan for freshness in an intentional, systematic, and ongoing way. And then keep making new associations and connections between things—seeing new, weird, and wonderful analogies and relationships.

Booster 4 Allow the Magic

You've learned that such emotions as gratitude, forgiveness, curiosity, and wonder empower the creative process. They're magic.. Let's look at wonder for a moment. This emotion arises from a sense of enchantment. And here's where your senses play a definite role. The garden has long been a metaphor for paradise, and beautiful gardens enchant us all. We're enchanted by seeing beautiful colors and forms of flowers, trees, grass, birds, and water in pools and fountains. We're enticed by their fragrance, their touch, their sounds.

Enchantment comes from opening up to nature—how it speaks to you, what it teaches you. It comes from allowing the wonder of the innocent child to return and to stay always within you. So open up to the enchantment your senses can bring to your life—not only from nature but from all your experiences. Here are some examples:

Kinesthetic touch Rapture over the sensuous feel of handmade things; of fabrics, sculpture and furniture; of moving your body in sport, dance, or any activity; of moving through life; of enchanted travel. Think of a time when your bodily sensations were vivid and divine, such as floating, soaring, gliding.

Sound and silence Groove on the music of enchantment. Think of a time when you heard sounds, other than words, that had a vivid impact on you. Allow the enchanting power of music, chimes, and singing bowls to reverberate through your body.

Images Glory in the beauty of nature and art. Think of a time when the beauty of the scene before you took your breath away.

Smells and tastes Relish food and its preparation, presentation, and enjoyment. Think of a fragrance or odor from your past that was enticing and vivid. Allow into your awareness all the related memories connected to this sensory memory. Think of a taste, something delicious that you ate, or tasted through the atmosphere (such as salt air), that had a vivid impact on you.

Booster 5 See Your Visualization Power

Imagination is internal visualization. Imagination may function most powerfully during meditation, when external distractions are minimized. So use your imagination!

Your right hemisphere will develop along with your left. You will energize both hemispheres and constantly expand the network of connections in your neocortex. You'll improve your memory and possibly your enjoyment of all your experiences.

Imaging or inner visual thinking is its own form of thinking. When you're exploring a topic or communicating about it to someone, use the term "I see" as well the term "I think" to express the information. Both processes register in your memory and you may remember the image more vividly than the word. You have many ways of accessing your memory. When planning a new project or event, it can be just as important to ask, "What will it look like?" as to ask, "What is the cause" or "What is the effect?"

Every time you hear yourself saying "I think," imagine yourself also saying "I see" or "It looks like" and create a mental picture related to that thought.

If you hear yourself saying "I think" when you're really imaging, rephrase your statement to reflect reality. Conversely, if you finding yourself saying "I see" when what's going on internally is actually a thought, rephrase the statement to "I think." Then convert this thought into a picture and express what you see.

Periodically, as you read something, take a moment to visualize it Even better, draw some images, either to help you grasp the material more deeply or to include in your writing to help readers grasp the information. Sketch relationships and images that help you understand the material, make it real, connect it to related information, show various types of relationships, etc.

Before you begin to write something, visualize it—how it looks, relates, connects, flows. After you have written, go back and review Imagine that you're the reader or audience for this bit of writing. Visualize the story or information as that reader would probably be able to do. Notice important gaps and opportunities for enlivening the visual experience.

Sketch and doodle any time you feel like it. When you're learning about a new topic, seek out pictures, films, videotapes, and other visuals that can help to crystallize the concepts in your mind.

Any time you're listening to others, especially when they're conveying information or instructions, visualize how that information would look in physical form. See people using it or carrying out the instructions. Imagine the results.

Meditate for Deeper Messages

To practice internal visualization, close your eyes to prevent visual distraction and you may create more powerful images. The more relaxed your body becomes, the deeper you can go into your inner self. Actively imagine a person or a place until you feel as if it is in your presence. Stay still and quiet until images come that are not activated by your will. Let images present themselves on the screen of your mind. Let them pass by without becoming attached to them. Remain quiet and still, focusing on the screen of your mind without losing your concentration, and more images and colors will present themselves Smells may also come. You tend to get more profound and comprehensive glimpses within your inner being when your eyes are closed than when they're open.

Every time you meditate, focus more deeply into this inner space of thin and rapid wavelengths, and other dimensions of life will occur. Focusing on an inspirational person that represents to you love, forgiveness, appreciation, and wonder can help you deepen into the thinner wavelengths.

Create the Life You Want

You can use visual intelligence to program your day or any future event or project You can create images of the possible before it happens. Research on psycho-cybernetics has documented the power of mental rehearsal—over and over gain since the 1950s. That's why virtually all the world's top athletes and artists use such techniques.

See yourself giving an important presentation, for example, presenting the information, answering questions, relating to the people who will be there. This practice can help you to feel secure with the people and the event before experiencing it in your external reality. Visualizing the future allows you to realize what may be missing from your presentation or project. You can imagine how to change your presentation or fill in the missing parts of the project. You get to see and play the game ahead of time, rehearse it, adjust your action plan, refocus your attention, or change the plan.

You may want to visualize an ordinary day as peaceful, loving, connecting with others. You can enter the day more consciously, alert to what you need to do, seeing how to make it the kind of day you want, aware of what needs adjusting or how you might be more flexible, etc. This practice can lead to a day that is less stressful, and more fulfilling, creative, and joyful. Here are some suggestions:

- Focus on the event or project as if you are watching a film.

- Visualize each step of the event or project as it unfolds.

- If you're not satisfied with a particular part, go back and imagine how it could be most effective and fulfilling Try some creativity techniques to come up with new ideas. about how to handle this aspect. Now visualize it again.

- Allow yourself to be affected by this picture and have the intention to create it most effectively.

- Focus especially on the end result you want and the feelings you have about that. Experience the feeling tone between you and others who are involved.

- On the other hand, be open to the idea that it could unfold even more effectively than you have imagined, and allow yourself to be flexible when the event actually occurs. Be willing to let go of the exact results you've visualized, to put it out in the world mentally and trust that "this or better—for the highest good of all" will emerge.

Use Past Experience to Boost Future Success

You can use this powerful visualization process to re-live the past in order to boost your future success. You can use your imagination to build on past successes and current strengths. In the past you have experienced moments of great strength, great health, great flexibility, etc. You can bring these moments and situations back to your consciousness and allow yourself to be affected by them in the present moment. You can also learn lessons from past "failures," which are really just learning experiences, and you can go back and heal old wounds that still block you. Try these techniques while you're in a relaxed meditative state:

- Recall past successes that give you the confidence and the informational reminders for succeeding in your current projects and relationships. Pull up all the sensory information about how that past success felt emotionally as well as what you heard, saw, touched, smelled and tasted.

- Learn from past experience what not to do. The only reason to go back to old hurts and "failures" is to ask, "What lesson did I learn? What if I could do it over?" Take the lesson and let go of the idea of "failure."

- Re-experience past hurts that are still creating problems in your life—rewrite history, in ways that free up your creativity. Give yourself what you needed at that point in your life. (See suggestions in the basic pattern-parameter intelligence chapter.)

Use Expectancy to Boost Your Creative Power

Expectancy is vision, the capacity to imagine and see a better tomorrow. Positive expectancy can help you visualize a better future—and to actually bring it about. Expectancy is a new vision of the future, different from what you're living in the present. You can convert these images of the future into a way of guiding your life. You can train your mind to focus actively and consciously on positive future images. You can actively construct the vision that you want to bring into reality. You may want to change some of your images as you go along, but your current vision can serve as your guiding star.

Remember, your brain is energy—and when you consciously guide this energy, you can create great things. When you don't do it consciously, your subconscious ego does it without your awareness. Here is the paradox you must work with: you can create more of the kinds of things you want in life if you consciously guide your own energy. On the other hand, you're usually interacting with many people and events in the Web of Life, and co-creating with them. You must also work with their energies and be flexible in allowing events to unfold in all their wondrous complexity.

The future can be a state that you first envision in your mind, which then happens or not, depending on many factors. We can all participate in helping to create a better future. To visualize the future is a capacity of your mind. Use it consciously.

Creativity Showcase
Using Sensory Intelligence
for Creative Solutions and Ideas

Some innovative solutions to current problems—for your information and inspiration—and as food for thought.

Problem—Compromised Designs

Most architects, engineers, and other designers are taught that design is the art of compromise. It means choosing the least unsatisfactory trade-offs between many desirable but incompatible goals. But this type of thinking is faulty. In fact, when designers take a wholistic approach to achieving design goals, they may not have to compromise at all.

There are $6 trillion worth of U.S. houses with thermal efficiency that rests on this type of flawed thinking. The cost of building and maintaining these homes could be greatly reduced, and huge quantities of energy could be diverted to other uses.

Creative Solution—Whole System Engineering

J. Baldwin broke through the traditional design vision one day as he watched a pelican catching a fish. He realized that nature runs a design laboratory here on earth by seeing that everything is continually improved and rigorously re-tested. The result is life forms that work. Those that don't work become extinct. Nature does not compromise. Nature optimizes. A pelican is not a compromise between a seagull and a hawk. It's the best possible pelican, the optimal bird for its ecological niche. That implies that the pelican lives within an ecosystem where everything else is also optimized as it co-evolves along with the pelican. A change in the pelican or in any part of the ecosystem could have great impact on all parts of the system, because all its parts are co-evolving and working optimally together.

Baldwin began to realize that an engineer can't design an optimal fan except as part of an optimal cooling system integrated into an optimal building design that's well-integrated into its site, neighborhood, climate, and culture. The more integrated all these parts become, the more they co-evolve to work optimally together, the more the design trade-offs and compromises become unnecessary. He started applying this vision to his design work. The traditional thinking is that to save resources or energy, such as when you install super-insulated windows, you must spend more money up front. But Baldwin found he could actually spend less money up front by integrating all the smaller savings so that they worked together.

For example, when the building's insulation is thick enough and its windows energy-efficient enough, just these two parts working together can eliminate the need for a furnace or air conditioner. When you install an entire heating-air conditioning system, that costs more than the better insulation and windows cost, up front, not to mention a lifetime of savings in utility bills. Add passive solar orientation, more efficient appliances, and other improvements and you greatly expand the savings

Baldwin realized that many designers actually make a system less efficient while making each of its parts more efficient because they don't link up the components in the right way. If you don't design the parts to work with each other, they're likely to work against each other.

He also believes in doing things in the right order or time sequence so as to maximize their favorable interactions. For example, you need to replace the office lighting, and you also need to replace the air conditioner. If you do the lights first, and replace them with cooler lighting, you can make the air conditioner smaller. Michael Corbett of Davis, California, uses these principles too. He says, *You know you're on the right track when your solution for one problem accidentally solves several others.* (Hawken 1999).

Creative Techniques Based on Sensory Intelligence

CT 6.1 Sensory Exploration

Focus on your problem-opportunity situation Begin to sense it, using each of your physical senses in order to explore all aspects of the situation

How does it look? Imagine—literally, figuratively, symbolically Allow new insights Write them down Repeat this process for the other senses:

- What do you, or others, hear? What sounds do you connect with the situation?
- How does it smell?
- What does it taste like?
- How does it feel, by touch, kinesthetically?

How can you more fully experience all aspects of the problem-opportunity situation? For example, if you are working on improving a service or product—or creating a new service or product—how can you live with current services or products that might be competitive? Test them yourself . Use them in your own life. Broaden and deepen your experience with this type of situation. What insights does this experience suggest?

CT 6.2 Listening: Ask for Input

- Who are the stakeholders in your problem-opportunity situation?
- How can you best elicit ideas, suggestion, information, or input from them?
- What process can you use that will inspire or motivate them to contribute?

- How can you be sure they feel rewarded for contributing, even if their idea cannot be implemented at this time?

CT 6.3 Listening: Keep an Open Mind

When someone discusses a problem-opportunity with you, be aware of opening up your mind to new possibilities. Listen to all ideas, including "far-fetched" ones for possibilities they may open up for you. As you listen, envision the possibilities that could be related to the idea the person is discussing.

- For one week, pay special attention to open listening. Keep a record of your experiences.

CT 6.4 Listening: Music

You need a great diversity of experiences to boost your creative intelligence. Music stimulates the right side of the neocortex (sensory, associative, intuitive intelligences) It also tends to put the left brain (rational) to sleep. And different styles of music stimulate different parts of the right brain. So keep an open mind and you'll find some renditions you like in virtually every music genre. Then listen to as many different styles of music as you can with the exception of heavy metal or hard rock, which has a dissonance that is incompatible with creativity and health.

Experiment with playing various types of music in the background as you go about various activities. Research indicates that certain classical music, by such composers as Bach and Handel, increases the ability to learn and to function more intelligently. New Age music tends to facilitate relaxation, meditation, and a peaceful state of mind. Some is designed to help you produce the alpha and theta brain waves of meditation. Popular, rock, jazz, and similar types of music may pep you up, inspire you, or have other effects you need and want.

Remember, music vibrates quite thoroughly throughout your liquid, spatial body, and your energy bodies, making a significant impact. You resonate with the musical vibrations you're exposed to.

- Experiment with various types of music as you work or study during the coming week. Write about your experiences.

CT 6.5 Visualization Practice

You can't do anything well unless you can focus. Practicing focus strengthens your visualization process and the right hemisphere of your brain. Here are a couple of things most everyone can visualize. Try these now. Then ask, What can I visualize that will help me with my current project?

Visualize a route you take regularly—either to your home or to your place of work or other location. See how many turns and road signs you can remember. Write the directions for someone who is not familiar with any of the streets.

Visualize your home. See how many features of each room you can precisely describe. Instruct someone who has never been in your home how to get in and find your watch (or other item) you have put away. Put this in writing. Seeing the process and expressing it verbally are quite different skills.

CT 6.6 Visual Stimulation

Visual stimulation is great for triggering new ideas. It's also powerful for holding in your mind your intention to create something new.

Collect magazines, brochures, and catalogs that have colorful pictures, including ads, that delight your imagination. Likely choices include travel and fashion magazines, travel brochures with inspiring destinations, and colorful catalogs of jewelry, clothing, and home furnishings.

Clip pictures that appeal to you and that seem in some way connected to what you want to create in this situation. Don't limit yourself—when in doubt, clip it—range free and wide rather than tight and small. You may also find key words, sentences, and even brief articles to add to your creative collection.

Decide how you will put together and use these clippings, both to trigger new ideas and to symbolize your intention to create something new. Possibilities include:

- **Make a collage** on any size paper or poster board using paper glue. Or use a cork bulletin board and push pins. Play with arranging the clippings in various patterns before you actually glue. Do you want to add your own lettering or drawings? When you've finished your collage, place it where you'll see it frequently. Each time you see it, be conscious of its symbolism, meaning, and impact for you.

- **Make file folders**, using some cataloging system to identify the type of clippings in each folder. Place your clippings in the folders. Set specific times to go through the folders, to remind yourself of your vision and to inspire yourself. Add to the folders on a regular basis until you bring your vision into physical reality.

- **Other methods** might be posting one picture at a time on your desk as you work, on your bathroom mirror, on the cover of your notebook, or on the dashboard of your car. What other methods might fit your lifestyle?

CT 6.7 Visualize: Idea Collage

As insights, flashes, and ideas come to you (or your team), jot them down on post-it notes or index cards and keep them in a box where you can easily refer to them. Periodically take them out and arrange them on a bulletin board, desk top, or table top. Rearrange them and play with them, looking for relationships, patterns, combinations, and new ideas.

CT 6.8 Visualize: Drawing Pictures

When you are trying to identify or define a problem-opportunity, visualize it and draw pictures of it. This process can help also in generating alternative solutions or action plans once the situation is defined.

- Try drawing with the hand you *don't* use for writing. This helps you to engage both sides of your neocortex brain.

- What insights does each picture suggest?

CT 6.9 Visualize: Mind Mapping

Mind mapping builds on the fact that your brain works primarily with key concepts in an interrelated and integrated manner. Here's how to show these relationships visually:

- Write a brief definition of the problem, opportunity, or item in the center of a piece of paper and draw a circle around it.

- What are the major aspects of this problem-opportunity? Write each one on a main line drawn outward from the central circle, like main thoroughfares running out from the city center.

- What are sub-aspects or key qualities of each of the major aspects? Write these on branches (similar to streets) running off the main thoroughfares.

- Use your ingenuity to add other visual signals, such as different colored pens for major lines of thought, circles around thoughts that appear more than once, connecting dotted or colored lines between similar thoughts, etc.

- Study your mind map. What new relationships do you see? What insights, ideas or solutions do they suggest?

CT 6.10 Visualize: Ask "What If?"

Firms often use "what if" scenarios to formulate strategic plans and contingency plans. This is especially helpful for testing and evaluating action plans, but you may find uses for it at all stages of the problem-opportunity process.

For each aspect of your plan, ask "What if (worst case scenario) happens? What would happen? How could we respond?" Do this for the best case scenario, and for all scenarios that you believe have a reasonable possibility of occurring.

CT 6.11 Group Visualizing: Picture Stimulation

Select pictures from various magazines, catalogs, or other sources and present them to the group. Depending on the size of the group, you can present them in an album, a file folder, a bulletin board, or a projector in the form of transparencies or slides.

- People examine each picture and describe it, while someone records the descriptions on a flip chart or chalk board, where all can see it.
- Use each line of the description to generate new ideas. Record these ideas separately.
- Repeat for each picture.
- Review ways to integrate the new ideas.

CT 6.12 Group Visualizing: Idea Display

- The team identifies the problem-opportunity situation and defines it in a brief statement. Members individually write as many ideas as they can on post-it notes or index cards. Take 5 to 10 minutes and each member tries to generate 15 to 20 ideas.
- The facilitator collects the cards and redistributes them so that no member has her or his own cards. Encourage the use of humor in sorting the cards and discussing the ideas.
- One member reads a card aloud. All members look for cards in their stacks that contain related ideas and read these aloud. The group gives this set of cards a name that captures the essence of the thoughts represented. This becomes an *idea set*.
- The next member reads a card aloud, and the process is repeated. Repeat until all cards are categorized into idea sets.
- The idea sets may be combined into all-inclusive groups.
- Play with the idea sets—connecting, arranging, and rearranging—to stimulate ways of responding to the problem-opportunity situation.

CT 6.13 Group Visualizing

Here is a structured detour into creative visualization that can be used to accelerate creativity.
Example of use: The group is planning its annual trade show. Members are somber and methodical. They need a creativity jolt.

Step 1 The team leader asks the group to remember a favorite scene from a movie. Ask people to mentally recall and record that scene, with any thoughts or associations that occur to them. Give them a few minutes to recall and then to jot down some notes.

Step 2 The team leader mentions her own favorite scene as an example. Then she maps, where all can see, some free associations between her scene and the current situation.

For example, her memory might be the jump-to-light-speed scene from Star Wars.   The spaceship reminds her of sitting in an airplane.   That in turn reminds her that she flew in from overseas yesterday.   She's jetlagged, she thinks, and although the sun is streaming through the window, for her it 's really 11 at night, and she'd prefer a midnight snack to the lunch sandwich she's about to face This free association leads her to the idea, "What about adding food concessions to the trade show? Anyone for pizza?" Her demonstration sparks the imagination of team members.

Step 3 Hopefully, the favorite movie scenes of the group span a wide range, but eventually members are usually attracted primarily to one scene or theme. As members of the group add their own memory of the details of the preferred movie scene, they also begin to make connections to the subject of the meeting (such as planning a trade show).

A favorite movie is only one type of detour. Other types of scenes may be more inspiring for your group's particular project. You can use any type of scene or topic that's interesting enough to bounce people's minds out of a narrow focus. When you focus on *the* problem too intensely, you narrow your thinking to the tried-and-true.   This blocks your access to the vast storehouses of subconscious and superconscious imagery and experience Topics can be as wide ranging as

- memorable meals
- most vivid childhood experience
- greatest sporting event
- first love

Case Studies—Applying the Creative Techniques

In working on these cases, you may use creative techniques from any of the chapters. However, the creative techniques described in this chapter may be especially appropriate.   Keep these self-questions in mind.

1.   What problems do I see?

2.   How can I probe beneath the surface to get at root problems?

3.   What opportunities (hidden or obvious) can I find to take initiative, cut costs, and/or make money?

4.   What creative alternatives can I generate?

5.   As a consultant, what should I recommend as the best viewpoints and actions?

6.   To answer these questions, what creative techniques can I experiment with to respond to this case? After completing the case analysis, ask: Which creative techniques produce the best results?

Case 6.1 ArtRock Versus VROOM

Phil Cushway started his own business about 15 years ago. His firm is called ArtRock and sells Rock 'n Roll memorabilia. When he started, it was just Phil and one employee. All they needed was a place where to store their merchandise so that it would lay flat and stay dry. Phil now has 30 fulltime employees on the payroll and a large warehouse-office facility.   ArtRock prints Rock 'n Roll posters for shows around the country. Its creative team is constantly creating new collectible merchandise.   ArtRock has a working relationship with many different artists and bands.   This makes it much easier for Phil to land hard-to-get licensing contracts. ArtRock currently holds some exclusive licenses for very big names, such as Jimi Hendrix. That means they hold all the rights to the posters and memorabilia they create using those big names.

ArtRock generates most of its revenues from its inhouse retail mail order catalog and from wholesale orders from large stores and other mail order companies. Everything has been going well. The ArtRock catalog was ranked No. 1 and Billboard magazine ranked the ArtRock website as the No.1 Rock 'n Roll website. Phil has been expanding his business every year. This has been possible because his management philosophy is to give the creative team all the flexibility they want. Therefore ArtRock has consistently generated new products that sell remarkably well.

All of this changed eight months ago. Suddenly a mail order company called VROOM started outselling the ArtRock catalog and taking away long-standing customers. The company started its collectible merchandise catalog business three years ago and finally began to turn a profit a few months ago. VROOM has always sold ArtRock's proprietary collectibles, among other items. Now that their business has increased, VROOM has become one of ArtRock's strongest wholesale clients, recently accounting for about 20 percent of its wholesale orders.

Jack Vroom, the owner, is one of Phil's long-time personal friends. In fact when Jack was creating a business plan and starting up VROOM, he relied on Phil's experience, and he thinks of Phil as a mentor. Now that Phil is losing significant market share and revenues to Jack, he wonders if he has created a monster. Maybe he won't be able to compete effectively with VROOM without cutting his ties with Jack.

Phil is considering cutting out VROOM, no longer selling ArtRock's proprietary merchandise to them. That would hit VROOM hard. Without ArtRock's products, VROOM would lose the bulk of the merchandise it currently features in its catalog. Most of these items are proprietary and cannot be copied due to ArtRock's exclusive licensing and manufacturing agreements

Phil has a business dilemma. Should he cut off VROOM and lose one of his biggest accounts? He also has a moral dilemma. How should he deal with a competitor who is also a long-time friend?

- What are the root problems you see operating in this situation?
- What opportunities is Phil overlooking?
- How would you address each problem or unmet opportunity?
- Which CTs discussed in this chapter did you use in solving this case problem?
- Which CTs were most helpful and what ideas did they spark or inspire?

Case 6.2 ABC Co in Asiana

ABC Company, a large US personal hygiene and cleaning products manufacturer, has been shipping container-loads of product for sale into a large Central Asian country. for the past two years (We'll call the company Asiana; it's a part of the former USSR) This year they introduced a household cleansing powder into the area for the first time. The ABC representative office in Asiana (we'll call it ABC-Asiana) contracted with a major **U.S. steamship line** to bring the product in 40-foot shipping containers to a European port by water. The containers then go by rail to the final destination in Asiana. The containers are 40 feet long, 8 feet wide, and 8-1/2 feet high.

The problems are occurring in Asiana, the country of destination. There are delays in getting clearance of the shipments through the customs officials of Asiana. There are delays in getting the product delivered to **ABC-Asiana's rented warehouse.** These delays are resulting in costs to ABC Company for storage of the *loaded containers* at the railhead while the company is waiting for the customs clearance. ABC must also pay "demurrage charges" to the steamship line if they do not return the containers, empty, back to the railhead within 7 days of their arrival at the final destination.

Customs clearance problems

1. The ABC-Asiana often does not receive documentation, the paper work on the shipment, from the US office in time to give it to the *local customs house brokers* before the cargo arrives.

2. The customs-clearance process often does not begin until after the cargo arrives.

3. The documentation sometimes arrives on time, but is incomplete and ABC-Asiana must take time to get the missing information before proceeding. The U.S. dollar values on the invoices which arrive by mail with the documentation sometimes do not agree with the values on the invoices which arrive with the cargo inside of the containers.

Delivery problems

1. Delays in customs clearance, as described above, cause delays in delivery.

2. The warehouse does not have enough room to accommodate all of the incoming cargo, which, over the past 2 months, has arrived in lots of 28 40-foot containers 2 to 3 times per month.

3. The steamship line's local agent does not have enough trucks.

4. The warehouse cannot handle (i.e., receive, unload and send out) more than two or three 40-foot containers per day. One cause is the lack of loading dock space. Another cause concerns problems in getting a representative of the local chamber of commerce on hand to monitor the unloading of each container at a bonded warehouse facility. Local law requires such monitoring.

The warehouse is a Korean/Asiana joint venture. It is a customs-bonded facility (a bonded facility guarantees the customs process is legitimate). ABC company feels they need to use such a facility for security reasons, even though the cargo is usually fully cleared by customs before it arrives at the warehouse.

However, the warehouse is currently holding 28 container loads of uncleared cleansing powder in bond for ABC. There is a discrepancy in the way the product was described on the railway bills and in the documentation sent to the representative office by the U.S. office. The cause of the discrepancy: At a border station between Europe and the Former Soviet Union, the railway bill was translated from German into Russian by the *railway agent of the steamship line*. The translator called the cleansing powder something other than what it was and, at the final destination, the cargo was seized by customs. This problem is currently being resolved in court in Asiana

ABC Company has temporarily stopped importing the cleansing powder into Asiana because there is enough on hand there to satisfy local demand for several months. They also want to get the court case resolved. They feel they need to use this time to solve the customs clearance and delivery problems before they start importing again.

Note: In the destination Asiana city, there are no other bonded warehouses that are up to ABC's standards. ABC's warehouse is planning to open an additional, larger facility in the near future. It is not clear, though, whether they will have additional dock space.

According to local law, customs clearance may be performed up to 10 days before the date of arrival of the cargo, up to the point of inspection of the cargo by the customs authorities. In other words, clearance documentation can be prepared in advance, but customs still has the right to inspect the cargo upon arrival. Customs also has the right to take up to 12 days after the arrival of the cargo to complete their inspection and sign the documents for release of the cargo.

The **steamship line's local agent** can handle (meaning, pick up loads, deliver them, and return empties) between 5 and 7 containers per day, including those of ABC company. The steamship line has about 30 other customers in the destination city besides ABC company.

Only one **chamber of commerce representative** is assigned to any given facility ABC's warehouse facility serves 9 other clients besides ABC.

- How can ABC company prevent the delay in the customs clearance process?

- How can ABC company prevent other delays of their shipments to Asiana?

- What other problems and/or opportunities do you see here? What would you do?

- Which CTs discussed in this chapter did you use in solving this case problem?

- Which CTs were most helpful and what ideas did they spark or inspire?

Self-Awareness Opportunities

SAO 6.1. Expressing Your Thoughts and Feelings Visually

Adapted from the work of Barbara Ganim and Susan Fox, Visual Journaling, *Quest Books 1999*

Purpose: To become more aware of your visioning and imaginative power and to practice expressing your thoughts and feelings in a visual way.

Step 1: Set a focused intention

When you set a focused intention, you send all the cells in your body the message that you have a clear goal behind the actions you are about to take. This helps your body to overcome resistance to change. Some examples of intentions are

I intend to understand the root of this problem.

I intend generate at least three creative solutions to this problem.

I intend to select the best solution for this problem.

Step 2: Relax and visualize.

Use your deep breathing and other relaxation techniques. Then visualize the situation or person you want to learn more about. If appropriate, re-experience an event or emotion that you want to learn more about or to express more fully. Focus on the strongest physical sensation you're experiencing now within your body. Imagine what this sensation might look like if it were a color, shape, or form—or all three. What would best express it visually?

Step 3: Draw your inner images.

Draw freely and quickly—to express, not impress. Above all, don't judge what you draw. When you finish, respond intuitively to the following questions—allowing your first response to be valid.

- How do you feel when you view the drawing?

- What does it reveal about the problem? About the solution? About how you feel? About your emotional tone? What do the light or dark, bright or somber colors reveal? The shapes or images?

- How do you feel about the colors? What impact do they have on you?

- Does anything about the drawing bother you? If so, write about it.

- What do you like best about your drawing? Write about it.

- What have you learned about the problem or about your feelings from this drawing?

- Are these feelings connected to a specific issue, person, or concern? Write about it.

- Does understanding your feelings help you deal with the issue? If so, how? Write about it.

Take the attitude that you don't have to solve any problems now, though you may. Just enjoy understanding more about the problem and your feelings or being able to express yourself more fully.

Step 4: Get information from your drawing.

Get information by asking your drawing some questions. Look at the drawing as a whole and ask, *What are your trying to tell me about myself or my life?*

Pick one aspect of the drawing, such as one image or one color and ask, *What are you doing in this drawing? What are you trying to tell me about myself or my life?*

Pick another aspect and repeat the questions, until you have worked with every major part of your drawing. If an answer seems especially important, focus on it and ask it for more insight.

Step 5: Explore connections.

If you sense a relationship between the messages you receive from your drawing and other events in your life, past or present, ask yourself these questions:

- Are the feelings I expressed in this drawing similar to feelings I've had in what other situations?
- The messages I get from my drawing are connected to which life trends or personal patterns?
- Which messages might apply to some of my current life situations?
- How does this drawing help me understand who I am or who I could be?

SAO 6.2 Sensing Information: Feeding Intuition

Purpose: To practice using your senses to receive intuitive insights.

Instructions You can practice and develop the ability to receive intuitive insights from your higher consciousness—so that you can use them at will. The major barriers are believing you don't have imagination or intuitive ability and trying to *make* the messages come. Relaxed focus is the key— *allow* the messages to come. Let go of the need to make them come and be open to letting them in.

Step 1: Breathe

Slow down your breathing process, taking more and more time to breathe in, hold it, and breathe out. Feel your body and mind slow down.

Step 2: Relax

Continue with one or more additional relaxation techniques that work for you, such as those suggested in the Basic Intelligence chapter. Aim to reach the alpha state of deep relaxation.

Step 3: Go Into Higher Consciousness

Focus all your attention in your feet. Hold it there. Then, step by step, focus your attention in your ankles, calves, thighs, and on up through your body to the crown of your head. Imagine that above your head is a magnificent Higher Self, Soul Self, Intuitive Self, Creative Self, higher consciousness, or some aspect of yourself that is much larger than your physical self. Allow your consciousness to move up into that Self Become comfortable hanging out there for a few moments.

Step 4: Ask a Question

Ask this Self a question that's concerning you, such as *What should I do about. . . ?   What's going on with . . .?   How can I . . . ?*

Step 5: Receive a Message

Be open to the various ways intuitive messages typically appear—how your various inner senses may be the vehicle.

Hearing words in your head

You'll have to practice, and note the results, because this intuitive channel can be confused with ego-mind thinking. Sometimes the verbal messages are soft and brief, other times they're loud and repetitive. It may help to focus inside your head in the area just above your ear level.

Seeing pictures, colors, or symbols in your mind's eye

Focusing inside your head in the area just above your eye level may help. You may sense visions indirectly, or you may see them like a movie. You may see colors or geometric shapes or other symbols instead of picture. Visual messages are certainly noticeable, but you may not know how to interpret them. Dreams are intuitive visual messages, so a good dream interpretation book may help you [Bethards 1995] with these waking visualizations. Ultimately, it's your image and you must decide what it means.

Feeling, sensing in your body

Intuitive messages sometimes come as feelings, most often in the stomach-abdomen area. It may help to focus on that area when you want to pick up an intuitive message about a person you're with. Feeling messages can be confused with negative ego-related, fear-based feelings. Hindsight can help you learn to distinguish among feelings. For example, looking back some time later, what did your strong feelings about that person really mean?

A sense of knowing

Sometimes intuitive insights come as a sense of knowing what's going on or what will happen. You may feel it throughout your being, especially in your mind, but it's not purely verbal. If the message is loud and clear, you'll know what to do. But it may come as a subtle flash or a glimmer. You must learn to notice these and to trust this type of knowing

Try asking your Higher Self some questions; for example, "Does that little flash of insight mean I will get the job?" "Does this mental image mean I should partner up with Jim in order to win the new account?" Be open to the answer—get a sense of a "yes" or "no" inner response. Then check it out, see what actually happens when you follow the advice. That way, you can learn to recognize and trust this intuitive knowing.

SAO 6.3 Kinesthetic Arm Testing

Purpose: To receive subconscious and superconscious information that is carried in the body.

Preparing questions for kinesthetic arm testing

Step 1: What question do you have about your life—such as, what to do next, what choice to make, what direction to take, etc.?

Step 2: Convert your question: What do I want to have in my life that I don't now have?

Step 3: Ask, How do I want to feel when I have this thing in my life?

Relax, close your eyes, and visualize an "end results" scene where you already have this thing in your life. Get in touch with the feelings you want to have and how the results look and play out. You may want to refine the specific results and feelings that seem best in this visualized scenario.

Now you are in touch with the ultimate results/feelings that you want. Think of at least 3 or 4 "next steps" that could move you toward those results and feelings you want.

Step 4: Formulate 3 or 4 "test statements" about your next step in terms of achieving those results/feelings: " . . . *is the next step in having* (specific results/feelings) *in my life.*"

Examples:

Test statement 1: *Focusing on learning as much as possible is the next step to having a great job that I love and feel fully committed to.*

Test statement 2: *Relaxing and being with family and friends is the next step to having a great job that I love and feel fully committed to.*

Test statement 3: *Working in my field for the next 3 months is the next step to having a great job that I love and feel fully committed to.*

Preparing to arm test with a partner

Find a partner to work with. When you are testing your statements, you are the Testee, your partner is the Tester. Then you can reverse roles to test your partner's statements.

- Pair up - Who will be first Tester, Testee?

- Both: Remove any head covering and all metal objects from your body (jewelry, coins, glasses, large belt buckles, jackets with large metal zippers).

- Tester: Be professional, impersonal

- Testee: Relax and move into a neutral attitude. You are not trying to exert your will or opinion; you are allowing information from the universal web of life to flow through your etheric-energy body. Your intention is to hold your arm parallel to the floor, but you will allow your body to respond to the information.

Step 1: Testee, close your eyes, relax, go into neutral, and hold out one arm parallel to floor

Step 2: Think of certain images or make certain statements

Step 3: Tester: place 2 fingers (forefinger, index finger) on top of testee's arm just above the wrist. When testee is ready (is holding an image or has just made a statement), press down on testee's arm

Practicing with your partner

Hold these images in your mind as your partner performs the arm test for each one. The "a" images normally result in your arm collapsing to your side, while the "b" images results in a firm bounceback.

a. Someone you fear or despise	b. Someone you love very much
a. Revenge	b. Forgiveness
a. Swastika	b. American flag
a. Hitler	b. Mahatma Ghandi
a. Stalin	b. Mother Teresa

Testing your statements

Your partner arm tests you as you make your statement:
" . . . *is the next step in having* (specific results/feelings) *in my life.*"
If a statement is true, your arm will hold after a bounce, if not, your arm will fall all the way.

Have 3 or 4 other options ready so you can test them.

Here are some other types of test statements people like to arm test:

- *It is safe for me to explore . . . .*
- *. . . is a good way to phrase this inquiry.*
- *. . . is the best choice (or plan) for me.*

References

De Beauport, Elaine. *The Three Faces of Mind*. Wheaton, IL: Quest Books, 1996.

Dodd, Vikram, *The Guardian* (London), as reported in *San Francisco Examiner*, November 22, 1998. Study conducted by David Warburton, professor at Reading University, England, for Associates for Research into the Science of Enjoyment (ARISE).

Dowling, John E. *Creating Mind: How the Brain Works*. New York: WW Norton & Company, 1998. See the chapter on vision.

Franquemont, Sharon. *You Already Know What to Do*. New York: Putnam, 1999.

Hawken, P., A. Lovins and L.H. Lovins. *Natural Capitalism: Creating the Next Industrial Revolution*. Boston: Little, Brown, 1999.

Horn, Robert E. *Visual Language: Global Communication in the 21ˢᵗ Century*. Bainbridge Island, WA: MacroVU Press, 1998.

Roberts, Joseph. "Communicating with Pod Mind: An Interview with Joan Ocean," *Common Ground* (a journal published in Vancouver BC), August 1999.

Tarlow, Mikela and Philip. *Navigating the Future : A Personal Guide to Achieving Success in the New Millennium*. New York: McGraw-Hill, 1998.

Chapter V
Intuitive Intelligence
Connections to All

No problem is solved by the same consciousness that created it.   Albert Einstein

Intuition is knowing from within, knowing without referring to logic or reason. It's "the direct knowing or learning of something without the conscious use of reasoning; immediate apprehension or understanding" (Webster's). Intuitive knowing speeds up the creative process, as it's your direct connection to your spirit energy body, which connects with the Web of Life and the universe beyond space-time limitations. This is your highest-level intelligence, incorporating all the others and related to your crown chakra, the one with the highest frequency.

Intuitive intelligence is inner knowing that comes with apparent ease and elegance. We often refer to an intuitive message as a hunch, gut feeling, or inspiration. You're born with intuition but it's like a muscle. You either use it or lose it. It's the intelligence that's most essential for creativity. Intuition is also related to spirituality. It can give you clues to your inner destiny, your future. The greatest use of your intuition and your creativity is creating the life you want, the life that is most fulfilling for you and makes a contribution to the Web of Life.

In dealing with the world rationally, you hold it constant by means of categories you formed in the past. Through intuition, you grasp the world as a whole, in flux. All the other intelligences feed into your intuitive intelligence—what you know from your senses, from the deeper limbic system of feelings, and from the basic brain of action. These connections are woven into words, numbers, images, sounds, colors, shapes, insights, feelings, and actions. Your intuitive brain somehow puts together all the information and experiences you've ever come in contact with and are willing to access.

Your intuition takes in information from your basic intelligence—about moving toward or away from things, establishing boundaries and behavior patterns—and uses it along with other input to provide you with inner knowledge about whether to say "yes" or "no" to such decisions. You can access this higher intelligence to identify which patterns and boundaries are no longer productive for you and which new energies you should move toward.

When you use emotional intelligence to develop the feelings of empathy and compassion, your intuition can integrate these feelings with other information, such as higher-level desires from your motivational intelligence, and create an exquisite form of empathy, expanded boundaries, and attunement with the world.

Words to associate with intuitive intelligence include: *inner knowing, between the lines, wholistic, beyond time-space, universal access, global-inner connections, ESP, psi, spiritual energy body, crown chakra, red-violet, tone ti or B, superconscious, right brain, neocortex.*

Myths and Realities

The many cultural myths about intuition tend to discount its value. Typical myths center around the belief that intuition is neither rational nor reliable.

Myth 1. Intuition is irrational and unreliable.

Western society has not traditionally encouraged the use of intuition in everyday life, nor has it tried to teach intuition. The myth is that intuition does not conform to any logical process that can be replicated and depended upon to be reliable. The reality is that you cannot measure with rational techniques and standards a process that is wholistic, timeless, and dependent upon the inner life of the practitioner.

When you use your intuition to solve problems and make decisions, you're in good company. Recent research indicates that the higher your position in an organization, the more you must rely on soft data and intuition in making decisions. Most top-level decisions involve broad policy matters rather than operational details, depend on future events, and have such general implications that you cannot depend on hard facts and figures alone in reaching them. As innovation becomes more and more the measure of survival and success in business, intuition plays an ever-larger role. Although effective executives certainly won't ignore relevant facts and figures, they must also take into consideration the feelings and opinions of other people, information gleaned from the company grapevine, and their own intuition about future probabilities.

For at least 30 years, research has confirmed that business leaders rely on intuition. For example, after they conducted ESP experiments for ten years, two professors at the University of Pittsburgh's School of Engineering established that higher-level executives have higher levels of ESP and are more likely to use it in their work than lower-level personnel [Douglas and Mihalasky 1974]. Also, a *Harvard Business Review* survey of business managers and executives revealed that higher-level executives say they often rely on ESP [Nierenberger 1989].

A nationwide survey of 2,000 business, government, and academic leaders was conducted in 1982 by Professor Weston Agor, University of Texas at El Paso [Nierenberger 1989]. He concluded that top-level leaders rely more on intuition than do lower-level managers. Moreover, women consistently score higher than men in intuitive ability. And Asian managers score higher than Westerners. The women were more reluctant to admit using intuition, however, fearing that it would be viewed as a sign of weakness. Agor did a follow-up study of the executives who scored in the top 10 percent in intuitive ability. Virtually all said they use intuition in making the most important decisions, though many said they do not reveal this fact to their colleagues.

Over 100 U.S. universities now offer courses in parapsychology, including Princeton and Duke, and many professors who teach these course are studying executive ESP. Some of the reputable private research institutions doing research on leadership and ESP are Stanford Research Institute (SRI) in Menlo Park, California, The Mobius Society in Los Angeles, McDonnell Laboratory for Psychical Research in St. Louis, and the Institute of Noetic Sciences in Sausalito, California.

Some people are startled to discover that top executives depend on intuition so much. It's not surprising to others who believe that intuition is actually the result of a process of tapping your own experiences and information stored in your personal subconscious memory and also Web of Life experiences and information that exist in superconscious mind. This information is analyzed and synthesized instantaneously because intuitive mind is wholistic and timeless, bypassing the slower, more tedious rational mind processes. In other words, intuition may be more of a short cut to problem-solving and decision-making than a completely different process.

Myth 2. It's only women's intuition.

Just as emotions are known as "women's territory" in our culture, so is intuition. And since anything in women's territory has been traditionally considered second-class, inferior and therefore discounted, this means that intuition has been de-valued in our culture.

You've seen that research indicates that business women rely more on intuition than the men do. Those who succeed are likely to realize that many men also rely on intuition but they express it in businesslike ways. You may hear successful business women say, *My feel for the marketplace . . ., My gut reaction . . .,* or *My best estimate . . . .* Such women find that their intuitive insights are more likely to be accepted when they express them in terms that men are comfortable with.

Myth 3. Intuition and intuitive people are weird.

Since Western culture has traditionally not accepted intuition as a valid way of thinking, intuitives and psychics are usually viewed as "outsiders." It's too bad. Society is so insistent that we conform to its norms. Yet Creative Intelligence (intuition, genius, etc.) is a measure of how far we're willing to deviate from the norm.

How Intuitive Intelligence Works

You are an intuitive person—at least you were as a child. You may now be conditioned to ignore intuitive messages, but you can regain the ability. You can use your intuitive intelligence in every aspect of your business and personal life.

Answering Rational Questions. You can use it to get answers to the rational "who, what, where, when, why, and how" questions; for example:

- What next? What should I create or do next in this project? In my life?
- Why is this coming up in my life?
- What decision should I make in this situation?
- Who can I connect with on this project?
- Where should I do this? When is the best time to move on this? How can I achieve this goal?

Enriching Your Life. You'll use your intuitive intelligence in these ways and many more:

- to enhance your day-to-day work life—and all your relationships
- to work with teams—and with people in general
- to develop a greater vision and exercise leadership based on that vision
- to increase the depth of intimacy you're comfortable with—intimacy with yourself and others
- to change your life in ways you want; for example, to stop smoking, break out of old habits and ruts, change careers, commit to new relationships, take risks
- to get in touch with your life purpose
- to guide your decisions and choices
- to find your unique niche in the community—and the activities that are part of your purpose
- to create a future that's in line with your purpose
- to assess the intuitive energy within your body and beyond your physical body

You'll find many, many ways to develop your intuitive intelligence. You'll find enough ideas here to take you a long way, but because your intuition is without limit, you can grow and develop it throughout your life. The fun never has to end.

Connecting to the Web of Life

Intuitive intelligence is the ability to tap your unspoken knowledge of the entire world. The atoms of your body hold the knowledge of all that is (holographs), all that has been, and all that will be [Polanyi 1960]. Your connection to the Web of Life is what powers your intuitive intelligence.

A unified theory of living systems is the basis of Fritjof Capra's work (1996). We know that all living organisms are ultimately made of atoms. What makes them "living" versus nonliving is a web network pattern of interactions and relationships. The pattern of life is a network pattern, capable of self-organization—self-regulation through feedback about our actions, and learning from our "mistakes." Living systems are always cognitive systems—knowing, conscious. Living is itself a process of cognition. All living organisms are conscious, are knowing, and do "think."

Perception is what you make of what's "out there." There is no absolute "out there" environment. There is only what you make of it—and that changes as your internal patterns of relationships change—as your believing-thinking-feeling-acting change.

The mathematics of complexity allows us to model the network interconnectedness of all life. Dynamical Systems Theory (DST) describes these highly complex systems.

DST→Chaos Theory→Branches of Fractals = Branches of DST→
a language to describe nature's complex, irregular shapes

Nature is relentlessly irregular and nonlinear, and the inanimate world is much more nonlinear than we thought. Most of the real world is nonlinear. DST deals with quality and patterns, not with quantity and substance. We must go beyond rational, linear thinking in order to deal with reality.

How do you perceive reality? If you're like most people, you create abstractions of separate objects, including a separate self. Then you believe you belong to an objective, independently existing reality full of lots of selves, fragmented objects. You probably extend this fragmented view to the whole human species, dividing it into different nations, races, religious, and political groups. You may believe that all these fragments—in yourself, in your environment, and in society—are really separate. This alienates you from nature and from other people.

But when you shift your conceptual focus from objects to relationships, you're able to realize that identity, individuality, and autonomy do *not* mean that separateness and independence are all there is. That's just a piece of the reality pie. If you were to regain your experience of connectedness with the entire Web of Life, your intuitive intelligence would return. Your creativity would blossom. If you're part of the web, you can tune into all parts of it. If you can see time as an abstraction, you can tune into all that happens in all times [Capra 1996].

Receiving Intuitive Messages

You can receive intuitive messages in many ways. Your pattern is unique, and you can also boost your openness to all the ways of intuiting and increase your intuitive intelligence in those ways.

Through Basic-Brain Dreams and Body Messages

Dreams can be prophetic and play a role in your intuitive development. Dreams are part of basic intelligence, which you incorporate into your intuitive intelligence. Some dreams are Big Dreams that carry important information for you. You know now how to program your dreams to get answers to questions and to keep a record of them. You've had some experience at interpreting your dream messages. Hopefully, you're learning to trust your dream messages. You're ready to move on to some new ways of interpreting and using your dreams, as discussed in the Self-Awareness Opportunities segment of this chapter.

Notice messages from your basic brain, body messages such as an energy increase or decrease, a sudden attraction to or recoiling from something, or sudden nausea. Ask yourself, "What is my body trying to tell me? What message is it feeding into my intuition?"

Through Emotional Intelligence

Notice sudden changes in your feelings about a situation. Intuitive messages sometimes come as feelings, most often in the stomach-abdomen area. It may help to focus on that area when you want to pick up an intuitive message about a person you're with. Ask yourself, "Does this feeling seem to come from my negative ego? My subconscious? The superconscious?" Emotional messages can be driven by ego-related, fear-based feelings—concerns about whether you're better-than or worse-than others, what others think of you given that judgmental framework, and similar issues. Hindsight can help you learn to distinguish among feelings. For example, looking back some time later, what did your strong feelings about that person really mean?

Through Sensory-Visual Awareness

Intuitive messages may come by seeing pictures, colors, or symbols in your mind's eye. Focusing inside your head in the area just above your eye level may help. Visual messages are certainly noticeable, but you may not know how to interpret them. Dreams are intuitive visual messages, so a good dream interpretation book may help you with any type of picture or symbol [See Bethards 1995]. Ultimately, it's your picture and you must decide what it means.

You can enhance your intuition through imaging or visualizing. Record on paper the shapes and images that come to your mind during a period of deep relaxation and/or meditation or zoning. This might result in a mandala, symbolic geometry, or other meaningful diagram.

Through Kinesthetic Awareness

Intuitive messages may come as a muscle contraction or other internal body movement. It may come as inner awareness of body movement, such as drifting, floating, soaring, or falling. Notice and ask yourself what this awareness means. Your may also put yourself into "the zone" or a moving meditation by such movement-in-space as dance, sports, or similar body motion.

Through Aural Awareness

Intuitive messages come to many people through words they hear in their head. You'll need awareness, practice, and evaluation of such inner hearing because it can be confused with negative ego chatter. Ask yourself, "Is this a better-than or worse-than type of message? Is it based on contracting emotions?" Sometimes the verbal messages are soft and brief; other times they're loud and repetitive. It may help to focus inside your head in the area just above your ear level. Ask for guidance from your Intuitive Self, your Higher Self, or other helpful source. Focus on the intention "for the highest good of all persons involved."

You may encourage intuitive insights and receive intuitive messages through mentally toning or hearing inside your head, or through a variety of tones, chords, or songs. You can expand this by combining it with other sensory input. Let's take toning. The three chambers of your body are head, chest, and pelvic chambers. Through your head you can "tone," discovering sounds that vibrate certain parts of each of these three chambers. You can progress from toning to a broader range of sounds. After a while you can add movement by carefully listening to your natural sounds and following the impulses that arise from those resonances.

Through Olfactory Awareness

Certain odors, fragrances, and tastes may trigger strong associations for you, memories from the past, and other senses, emotions, and thoughts. Notice especially smells and tastes that have a vivid, sudden, or dramatic effect on you. Ask yourself what message may be implied here.

Through Associative Intelligence

Intuition often comes as a synchronistic experience—a coincidence or series of coincidences, when connections materialize and events fall into place. Notice these happenings and ask yourself what they mean and what hidden messages they hold. Also notice situations where all options but one seem to disappear and times when an unwanted or unhappy experience turns out for the best.

Through Inner Knowing

An inner knowing message comes as a hunch, an awareness that events are flowing in a certain direction, a sudden relevant remembrance, an insight, or a sudden "aha." These are especially nice because they usually need little interpretation, but you must learn to notice them, pay attention to them, and act on them.

Sometimes intuitive insights come loud and clear—or in a subtle flash or a glimmer—a sense of knowing what's going on or what will happen. You feel it throughout your being, especially in your mind, but it's not purely verbal. It's the flashes and glimmers you must learn to notice, and you must learn to trust this type of knowing. Try asking yourself some questions that you can later check out, so that you can learn to recognize and trust this knowing. For example, when you've had a little flash about what's going on, ask yourself, "What did that flash really say? What does it mean? What does it tell me about what's going on and what is about to happen?" If you're not sure, ask for guidance from your Intuitive Self, Higher Self, or other guide.

How to Boost Your Intuitive Intelligence

Your intuition is just below the surface of consciousness. You just need some techniques to switch your awareness to that below-the-surface level so it can rise up into your conscious mind. To begin with, prepare yourself by adopting beliefs that open you up to your intuition. Then notice and work with your various mental states, ranging from the rational-active through various levels of meditation to the dream state. Meditate every day to tap into subconscious and superconscious levels. Spend as much time as you can in beginner's mind and mindfulness. All these techniques help you to maintain a mind that's aware and open to new ideas. Practice using your intuition every day, beginning with small predictions and messages and graduating to more important problem solving and decision making.

Booster 1 Adopt Beliefs That Nurture Intuitive Intelligence

The intuitive process is about receiving information in a way that's different from the way you get it when using rational or associative thinking. You get it at a speed that's faster, from a level that's deeper. The intuitive process involves the deeper accessing of your being. You receive waves picked up by your brain. The signals often come in quantum leaps rather than coming in recognizable continuous waves. You cannot direct the intuitive process but you can prepare for it and you can develop it by adopting three beliefs:

1. *Belief in a larger reality*—that there is a larger reality than the one you perceive with your senses.

2. *Belief in self-observation and change*—that you can mentally observe your thinking and your actions, learn from this self-observation, and make decisions to change your thinking and actions.

3. *Belief in connection*—that you can connect or attune with the vibrations or resonances of others and with the Web of Life and that attunement can bring you intuitive information.

Belief in Larger Realities

You can think of this larger reality in many ways—as the universe, the cosmos, source, nature, God, Goddess, All-That-Is. This all-encompassing reality must be one that you can believe in and can trust to be loving, kind, and safe, regardless of how your immediate environment may seem. To develop this belief, begin by focusing on a larger horizon, and then allow yourself to move toward it. You goal is to trust or think your way into, feel, or experience a largeness, an all-pervasiveness, a love so alive that it expands your limits until you lose your ability to describe it.

Find a belief system .Make it one that enables you to search ever-greater horizons. Relate your larger belief system in something all-encompassing to your everyday, limited existence.

Develop your capacity for wonder. Begin by admiring something, by being able to be surprised, and by experiencing a state of wonder. Experience gratitude for the wondrous.

Believe that everything is possible. Begin to trust your guesses and your hunches. Include them in your conversations. Allow yourself the freedom to guess.

Belief in Self-Observation

Love all your glimpses of all-that-is and continue your search into infinity. Ask, "Who am I?" Wait for the response. Continue to ask that question again and again. Continually ask yourself and continually observe your responses. By focusing deeply within your brain, you enter rare vibrational levels.

You can also observe your thoughts, images, emotions, and actions in your everyday life. By focusing on your inner life first, by observation and meditation, you can find guidance in those thinner inner ranges that help you to attune, harmonize, and heal your body-mind as it operates in the denser realities.

Observe your mind. Watch your mind when your thoughts are forming and let the thoughts come through even if they are not complete.

Belief in Connection

See how you are embedded in the Web of Life. Be willing and able to tune your body-brain-mind system in relation to your observation of yourself and all that surrounds you. Attunement is caring for your body-mind system as an instrument. You protect it from outer harm and continually tune the parts of your system in order to be able to play the entire range of vibrations.

Practice continuous self-observation so you can activate your thoughts, feelings, and senses. In this way you sensitize yourself to life all around you. You can then attune yourself to others, listen and receive, intuit or know from within. You can practice attunement by listening and responding with sensitivity to people, animals, plants, rocks, or any other forms of existence in nature.

It is you who tune in the program with your antenna-mind, whether you tune into the trivial or the great, the expansive or the contracting, the fine or the gross. You can choose to tune yourself into any station on the entire range of energy vibrations in which you are embedded. You create your reality partially by what you choose to select, to focus or concentrate on, to attune with.

Attunement is becoming "one" with whatever station you are tuned into, and ultimately with the Web of Life itself. "At-one-ment" is a way of expressing the deep state of consciousness that can result from tuning in and receiving.

Attunement is also the practice of shifting into alternate states of consciousness, alternate mental states, or alternate intelligences. It is your job to tune in. You can choose the wavelength you wish to be on and receive whatever enters that range.

Relax. Learn to use deep breathing to slow down your brain waves and body processes in as many situations as possible.

Value silence. Give yourself the joy and serenity of silence as often as you can.

Receive. Learn to receive. Change your energy from active to receptive. Learn to accept whatever you receive without making judgments or saying to yourself that it's not what you were looking for. Accept it anyway. Intuitive intelligence is not about directing but about receiving. Value whatever you receive.

Booster 2 Tune Into Varying Brainwave Frequencies

You learned in Chapter 1 that your various states of mind can be defined by the measurement of your brain waves, as shown in Table 7.1.

Table 7.1 Intuition and Brainwave Cycles

Intuitive Level	Experience	Brain State	Cycles Per Second
Intuition low	Rational, active	Beta	13 to 25
Intuition high	Drifting, light meditation or hypnogogic-before/after sleep	Alpha	8 to 12
Intuition very high	Deep meditation	Theta	5 to 7
Intuition very high	Dream state during sleep	Delta	1 to 4

In the beta state, the rational, active level, the brainwave cycles have a dense, rapid frequency. The meditative states progress in depth of relaxation, from alpha to theta, while retaining mental clarity, and the brainwave cycles become thinner and less frequent, until you reach delta, which goes through the dream state to the deepest level of sleep

In certain key moments of your life, the thinnest wave vibrations become as practical as the most dense. If you want to stop dividing and separating yourself from other people and from the Web of Life, open up to the entire vibrational range of energy in every person. Then you'll start connecting.

Booster 3 Meditate Every Day

Meditation is the best path to building intuitive intelligence, according to most writers who have studied the subject and are highly intuitive themselves. You have nothing to lose in this process because at the very least it boosts your health as a stress management technique. Relaxation and stress relief can be your first meditative goal. The second goal is to allow and enjoy these periods of silence, when you let the joy of being alive wash over you. With that aliveness and in that silence comes the voice of intuition—the body flash of intuition, and the knowing of intuition.

All you really need to excel in this process is the willingness to trust that you *are* intuitive and the willingness to practice meditation and other intuitive processes. Trust and practice are the keys. You can do it! Aren't you curious about your intuition? Encourage that curiosity. Practice trusting in your intuition, practice acting on it, and have fun with the whole process. Let your intuition invite you into your greatness—and don't be afraid to respond to it.

Booster 4 Move Into Mindfulness

"In the beginner's mind, there are many possibilities. In the expert's mind, there are only a few" says Zen teacher Shunryu Suzuke [Jamming 1996]. You boost your intuitiveness by getting back into the "beginner's mind." You empty your mind in order to return to the first innocence of the child.

One way to do this is to let go of the need to solve a problem or generate new ideas, to distract yourself. You redirect your concentration to subjects that don't carry the burden of anxiety, subjects with no connection to the task at hand. Mentally, take out a "fresh piece of paper." Shift your mind from the task-fixated self that's harboring doubts and fears to a nonthreatening but vivid world of playing ball, dancing, singing, cooking, or anything you really want to do, can get caught up in, and enjoy doing. You achieve mindfulness by escaping the heavy, single-minded striving of most ordinary life.

Intuition comes in after you free yourself of old, limiting mindsets. That's when you allow new information, like a new melody, to come into your awareness. It flowers after you open yourself to new information and surprise, after you've played awhile with various mindsets, viewpoints, beliefs, and attitudes, after you've focused more on the *process* of creating something new than on the actual end results. This intuitive information may be full of surprises, and it may not "make sense." If you resist, and evaluate it on rational grounds, you can silence a vital message.

Purely rational understanding serves to confirm old mindsets and rigid categories. How do you stay open to experience? When your mind is set on one thing or on one way of doing things (often mindlessly determined in the past), you blot out intuition and miss much of the present world around you.

Booster 5 Practice Intuition Every Day in Every Way

Get in the habit of practicing intuition through using it to solve problems and make decisions—about everything from finding a parking place, to knowing the best time to telephone a friend, to playing the stock market (not using real money at first, of course).

Play Intuitive Games

Make up fun ways to test your intuition. For example, play an "artificial dreaming" game with a friend. Make up a story about your partner. Look into the future and see your partner's possibilities. Play with choices. Ask yourself, "What would happen if . . . ?" Notice pictures that come, feelings that come. Watch especially for scenarios that evoke elation and enthusiasm. Then follow up to see how much of this actually happens and keep a record of your accuracy. Play the same game, making up stories about your own future.

Use Intuition to Solve Problems

To boost your problem-solving ability through intuition, pay attention to these suggestions:

- Acknowledge the power in your intuition
- Articulate what you want to know
- Formulate an intention
- Get in touch with what you don't know.

You can think of the space between what you know and what you want to know as a *knowledge gap* that you want to fill with intuitive information. Try re-framing your problem-opportunity as a basic question that reflects the knowledge gap. You can view the gap as an electromagnetic line that will magnetically attract intuitive information to it. Information from all sides of the line will be drawn to it. Your goal is to mentally hold that gap without filling it in with your biases, prejudices, or old ways of thinking. If you're open to it, information *will* be attracted into that magnetic space. Wait for answers to be attracted into the mind-space you've created. You may need to meditate once or many times, holding your question in mind. You may need to detach and play.

You'll increase your intuitive intelligence by opening up to symbols. They can be very powerful because they can trigger a connection to your inner wisdom. One technique is to adopt symbols that are powerful for you. For example, you can find a geometric shape to focus on and let it fill your mind as you say to yourself, "My intuitive mind will fill me with answers."

If a symbol comes up in your mind, ask yourself, *What does this symbol mean?* If an answer comes easily, in a flash, it's probably intuition. You don't have to analyze it, figure it out, or work at it. If it doesn't come easily, you should wait and try another time when you may be more open, more relaxed.

Use Intuition to Make Decisions

Think of your intuitive ability as the inner knowledge of whether to say yes or no, move toward an energy or away from it. Develop a sensitivity to both the "yes" and the "no." Again this incorporates basic intelligence.

Survey all your options—the alternative decision paths you could take. Use your imagination to picture yourself actually going down a particular decision path, living out the decision. Allow your intuition to guide you in how this would play out, how it feels, how it looks, how comfortable or "right" it seems. Do this for each major alternative you're considering.

Recognize Your Hits

Learn to recognize the intuitive hits that you get. For example, ask yourself, What does an intuitive message feel like? Where is there energy that points to intuition? Where is there a certain vitality? Notice patterns. Learn the language—the symbols Slow down, be curious, play. Intuition works best when you place no pressure on yourself to be intuitive. So find ways to relax. Relaxed and open—that's the combination you want. Be aware of what's going on around you. Increase what you can notice, what you can find. Open up, be alert to all. Recognize synchronicity, meaningful coincidences. These are calls to action, signs to take notice.

Practice is the most valuable way to boost your intuitive intelligence only if you review and assess your intuitive hits. After each successful outcome, review the mental, emotional, and physical clues you relied on in following an intuitive idea. This will help you establish which ones are valid, for future reference. If your hunch turns out to be valid, you can chalk it up to intuition. If not, it was wishful thinking, knee-jerk reaction, or some other subconscious process, usually triggered by negative ego concerns. Intuition comes from the superconscious, a higher level of information. Write down your predictions. Later, look back to review and assess your accuracy and to learn how your intuition speaks to you. Review and assessment is the way you learn to distinguish valid intuitive information from other types of information.

Booster 6 Adopt a Range of Workable Techniques

Senior executives apply intuition to identify problems, to streamline routine jobs, to pull isolated facts together, to balance purely logical analysis, to solve problems faster, and to judge character in job interviews, according to a Harvard Business School study [Weintraub 1998]. But how do these executives build their intuition and tap into it? Here are some specific techniques for tapping your intuition—morning, noon, and night. See the SAOs at the end of this chapter for detailed suggestions.

- When you awake, review your dreams for messages

- Prepare for the day; for example, ask, "What's important for me today?"

- Tune into your body, asking for information

- Shift modes and activities when you need inspiration—to refresh and renew your mental state

- Listen to music—experiment to see what's most conducive for you.

- Exercise vigorously to "cleanse" your mind and body and allow new awareness and sensitivity

- Take the 20-minute focused walk (see CT 7.1).

- Notice flows of energy within you and around you

- Notice what's going on beneath the surface—with people and events.

- Trust your "little feelings" and hunches about people, places, things, plans.

- Detach and play—play with words through metaphors, analogies, and other forms. Literally play at anything that may take you into the intuitive zone.

- Draw sketches and build models of new products, using various materials

- Study pictures of all kinds to find new approaches to a problem.

- Practice using intuition to solve problems and make decisions.

- Keep a running record of your intuitive hits.

- Meditate—with focus and purpose. Do it so often that your life is often a "walking meditation."

- Review the day, in the evening, to process the events, to learn lessons, and to think about what you want for tomorrow.

- Program your dreams, at bedtime, asking for dreamtime answers, information, experiences.

- Play games, have fun. Be playful and childlike. Collect toys—symbols, figurines, rocks, crystals, chimes, music tapes, pictures. Allow intuition to come in.

Recognize Your Blocks to Intuitive Intelligence

Typical beliefs, attitudes and actions that block your access to your intuition include focusing on the quick fix, becoming attached to one way of doing something, avoiding life's experiences, not respecting boundaries—your own or others, and coming from negative ego.

Block 1: Focusing on the Quick Fix, the Easy Answer

Some people believe that unless they get instant ESP or instant intuitive tools dropped in their lap from heaven, then they're simply not intuitive or intuition isn't real. The reality is that you *are* intuitive but in your family and culture your intuition may have been squelched or denied. You must "do the work" of opening up and tapping into your intuitive intelligence. Hang in there through the growth cycles. If it seems you're right back where you started weeks or months ago, look again—this time you're surely at a more self-aware level.

Block 2: Becoming Attached

Have you become too attached to a favorite technique or tool for getting things done? Or to a particular way of doing something (the one way)?   Or to a certain form that results should take? If so, then you've probably closed your mind to other techniques, tools, methods, and forms. That means you've closed off many of the possibilities for achieving the results you need or want.

Find ways to let go of need and to advance to the level of preference. If you can sincerely think in terms of "I want" or "I prefer," rather than "I need," you can also let go of related attachments to technique, form, etc. Value direct communication with the superconscious level so you can tap into the bigger picture. This will help you to let go of contracting fear-based emotions and move beyond trivia to larger life-purpose concerns.

Block 3: Avoiding Life's Experiences

Are you in the habit of using addiction, denial, or drama as techniques to avoid the possibility of experiencing fear, pain, or other contracting emotions? If you're desperate to avoid facing what's going on in your relationships and in your life, you may use these avoidance techniques in order to distract yourself from

- staying grounded and centered
- fully experiencing the emotions that come up
- taking the journey within to your true self—where enchantment, wonder, and magic can occur

You can become addicted to most anything as a way of avoiding what's going on in your relationships and in your life—from addiction to television to talking on the telephone to collecting friends to eating chocolate. You can become addicted to creating dramas, soap operas, cheap thrills, and convenient romances as a means of denying your suspicion that your life has little purpose or meaning because you're not on track. Look at the level of melodrama in your life and ask yourself how much of this you are creating and why.

Block 4: Coming from Negative Ego

False intuition can come from a need to "make" the solution work or the event to happen rather than a relaxed intention or preference or a knowing that this is the way.   You may be coming from the negative ego part of you, which often tries to control people and situations to "make" things happen the way you want. That part of you is also good at hypocrisy, so it may easily fool your "rational" self into believing that you're not really trying to control others. Control games involve mixed messages, rationalizations, denials, and cover-ups. Your negative ego may be an expert at playing the rescuer and other codependent roles, projecting its own contracting emotions and motivations onto others.   There's a distinct difference between "instant knowing" and knee-jerk responses.   Knee-jerks tend to have a flavor of desperate urgency.   That's a contracting emotion, typical of negative ego.   The emotions of intuition are expansive, such as serenity or enthusiasm.

The Rescuer or Martyr Syndrome

The rescuer role is one that tends to make others depend on you rather than developing their own inner strengths and skills.   It may involve false humility ("Oh, it was nothing,") sacrifice (That's ok, I don't really want a life.") or a Messiah complex ("I must sacrifice in order to save these people.").   Part of the syndrome is to hang out in such contracting emotions as excessive worrying—about other persons, and guilt—over "not doing enough."

Projections

Your negative ego harbors a range of contracting emotions that drive certain motivations and actions.   It loves to project these upon other persons in your life.   When you project, you attribute to that person the thinking, feeling, desires, future, etc. that your negative ego is experiencing.   You can point to the other person as having certain problems, mentally keeping the spotlight away from your own similar problems.

Block 5: Not Respecting Boundaries

Are you in touch with your own boundaries—your personal life space, your aura?   And do you require people to respect that space as your own?   Do you in turn respect the personal boundaries of your intimates and associates?   Not respecting boundaries can lead to codependence that is not mentally or spiritually healthy.   It can lead to wanting to possess another person or allowing them to feel that you are "theirs."   It can also lead to misplacing the authority, and therefore the responsibility, for what happens in your life.

The mentally healthy goal is to be author of your own life, and therefore your own "authority" for making the final decisions that affect your life.   When you take responsibility for your own life, you move into the driver's seat, where you belong.   Healthy relationships are about giving and receiving, nurturing and being nurtured, supporting and being supported.   They're not about possessing or controlling another person.

In addition to one-on-one relationship boundaries, recognize cult and guru situations, where you're expected to give up important aspects of your life in order to "belong."   Demanding such sacrifice violates your boundaries.

A very powerful way to bond with another person—at whatever depth and level you decide is appropriate—is to visualize the two of you in terms of your energy centers. The seven major energy centers and the major roles they play in your life are shown in Figure 7.1.   When you visualize, connect one or more of your energy centers with energy cords; you're bonding at the superconscious level.   Following through at the conscious level becomes almost automatic.   But first, be sure to get in touch with the boundaries of your personal energy field, your aura, and that of the other person. Don't merge energy fields, which implies intrusion, codependence, possession, etc.   Instead bond one or more energy centers.

Figure 7.1   Personal Energy Fields: Boundaries and Connections

Chakras *Energy Power centers*	*Your Space,* *Boundary*	*Other's Space,* *Boundary*

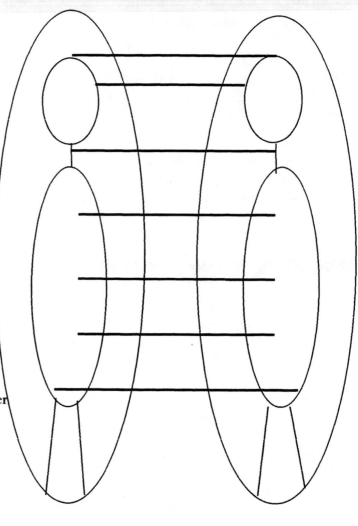

Crown - Spiritual Intuitive Power

Brow – Visioning Soul Power

Throat – Mental Rational Power

Heart – Associative, Causal Power

Stomach – Emotional Power

Abdomen – Motivational
          Etheric Power

Base of spine – Basic Physical Power

Theoretical Relationships:

Intelligence Type	Energy Body	Chakra	Color	Tone	Function
7 Intuitive	Spirit	Crown	Red-violet	ti, B	Being, connecting to spirit
6 Sensory	Soul	Brow	Blue-violet	la, A	Visioning, insight, imagination
5 Rational	Mental	Throat	Blue	so, G	Thinking, expressing thoughts, communicating, personal will
4 Associative	Causal	Heart	Green	fa, F	Linking higher-lower vibrations, centering personal growth, unconditional love
3 Emotional	Astral	Stomach	Yellow	mi, E	Feeling, emotions as sensors, control, personal power
2 Motivational	Etheric	Abdomen	Orange	re, D	Body blueprint, life purpose, sorting out, choosing, sexuality, creativity
1 Basic	Physical	Spine	Red	do, C	Survival, safety, security, territory, family, community, vitality, joy of living

Overcome Intuitive Blocks

You can overcome the blocks to intuitive intelligence through such remedies as developing a higher level of awareness and intention, learning how to move from the subconscious state of mind to the superconscious, where you can receive guidance, and protecting your mind and body.

Remedy 1: Develop Higher Awareness and Intention

The easiest way to begin a process of breaking these negative-ego cycles is to notice the ego hi-jinks and control games of your friends. Just be sure you carry this awareness the necessary step forward to noticing your own. Confront your hopes and fears as honestly as you can. Be up-front with yourself. Stay on the path toward knowing yourself, which is a lifelong journey of personal growth that is always spiraling upward. Here are two helpful techniques:

1. As you do your intuitive work, especially when visualizing goals and end results, verbalize this intention: "With harm to none For the highest good of all." This will help to align you with your Higher Self and the superconscious Web of Life.

2. When you work on shifting your beliefs and attitudes, and when you look to your intuition for guidance about what to do, ask yourself, "What am I *for*?" It's so easy to focus on what you're against, what you want to fight against in the world. It's so much more powerful to focus on what you want to create, what you stand for.

Remedy 2: Move from Subconscious to Superconscious

How do you know whether the inner messages you identify are really intuition? One way is to ask yourself, "Is this coming from my subconscious or my superconscious?   To begin with, the more you align your worldview with the superconscious, the more accurate your intuition is likely to be.

As your worldview expands, your intuition expands.

When you're experiencing life with strong inputs from your subconscious, what you experience may be a sense of separation and isolation. To compensate you may go into negative ego thoughts, feelings, and actions—focusing on superficial appearances and better-than worse-than issues. You may feel stuck in your current situation, unable to make decisions about moving forward because you're just not sure what you want to do. Your feelings tend toward the contracting emotions, and fear is the underlying feeling, as shown in Table 7.2.

When you're experiencing life in close connection with your superconscious, what you experience tends to be a sense of wholeness, connected to the Web of Life. You feel in touch with your Higher Self, that bigger part of you. Your life seems to flow and decisions come easily from a sense of wise knowing. Your feelings tend toward the expansive emotions, and love is the underlying feeling.

Remedy 3: Receive Superconscious Guidance

To build your intuitive intelligence, it's clear that you need techniques for tapping into your superconscious mind and receiving guidance, information, and support from that source. You already know how to do that, but let's review.

1. *Relax*—do your deep breathing and other relaxation techniques.

2. *Become alert and aware*--Be Here Now in the present moment.

3. *Align*—bring in superconscious energy through your crown chakra and earth energy through base chakra.

4. *Attune*—imagine you're becoming at-one with your superconscious, your Higher Self, your Spirit energy body, so that you're strongly connected with the Web of Life.

5. *Focus*—get in touch with your desire. What is your question? Be clear, specific. This creates an energetic magnet that draws in answers from the superconscious.

6. *Ask*—specifically ask for help, advice, information. Believe that answers will come

7. *Release*—let go of the need for a particular answer to come in a specific way.

8. *Allow*— be willing to accept any answers or hints that come, in whatever form they take.

9. *Recognize answers*—be open to the many ways that messages may come—words, pictures, symbols, omens, inner mind, outer reality, flashes, glimmers. Learn your intuitive language.

10. *Record*—write down the messages—verbalize, write, record on tape, draw. This makes it real!

11. *Feel gratitude*—be willing to validate the experience. Gratitude is a powerful emotion for establishing a path to intuitive knowledge, a path that will become well-used if you acknowledge all the intuitive hits you get.

12. *Implement*—use the information as a creativity boost.

Table 7.2 Experiencing the Subconscious and Superconscious

Subconscious Mind	*Superconscious Mind*
Separated	Whole
Isolated	Connected
Negative ego	Higher self
Stuck	Flow
"Decision Paralysis"	Fluid movement
Don't know	Wise knowing
Contracting emotions	Expansive emotions
FEAR	LOVE

Remedy 4: Protect Your Intuitive Body-Mind

In early childhood, most people have unusual experiences of direct perception. Some have out-of-body experience, others are in touch with "friends" from other realms or levels of reality, still others have a healing touch with others. Looks of disbelief and concern from parents are usually sufficient for most of us to close off access to such intuitive pathways. What would all intelligence be like if we could protect these pathways in early childhood? If you were an especially intuitive child, you probably became so fearful of being "different," or even insane—and therefore of losing the love, warmth, and security you needed to survive—that you would no longer allow yourself to open up. How can you now strike a healthy balance—allowing yourself to develop the full range of your intuitive and creative intelligence while still functioning effectively in consensus reality?

When you open up and tune in, you experience a vulnerability. Your defenses and blocks come down. Here's how to protect yourself.

Center yourself in love

One safeguard is unconditional love, the warmth that comes when you tune into love, feel it, and express it, and the feeling of security that comes with being surrounded by a loved one. Center yourself in love, in your heart center.

Ground yourself in nature

You are a physical human being currently existing in physical, material reality with others in your culture who are living a similar reality, called consensus reality. Stay in touch with nature and keep in mind how your intuitive intelligence and inner reality are connected with your time here within the consensus reality.

Surround yourself with expansive energy

If the intuitive capacity is developed without love, or without superconscious awareness, it can be used to interfere with other lives rather than attune to other lives. This misuse of power is sometimes called evil or black magic. Evil can occur when people use their power without respect for others. How can you protect yourself? Each day, or whenever you feel the need for protection, do a brief meditation.

Relax, go into a meditative state. Mentally bring in pure white light through your crown and let it fill your entire body, every cell. Let the white light radiate out into your aura to your personal boundary and fill it completely. Be aware that the white light is a protective shield, letting in all that's beneficial for you and shielding you from all that's harmful. If you feel the need for a little extra protection, mentally surround the edge of your aura with deep blue light, forming a border around the white light.

Listen to Your Body's Intuitive Messages

You want to maintain a high level of physical wellness and energy, and therefore to heighten your creative intelligence. Of course you do—and you will if you learn your body's intuitive language, listen to it, and act on it at an early stage. If you fail to act, your body will keep sending ever-more-urgent messages until you're forced to notice, as discussed in the chapter on Basic Intelligence. The moment you notice an anxiety signal, stop and ask your body, "What is the message?"

Advanced Intuition Techniques

Advanced techniques discussed here are based on the proven human capability to transcend time and physical space. They include remote viewing, future prediction, sending mental energy, and out-of-body experiences.

Advanced Technique1: Remote Viewing and Prediction

We have the capability of transcending time and space, mentally tapping into the future and mentally communicating with people throughout the world. Why do most people deny this capability?

In our culture we have the illusion that time is linear—a line running from the past to the present and out into the future, but from the right-brain perspective, all is now. We usually view events as occurring one after the other, sometimes as cause and effect, but always in a straight-line continuum of time. This naturally leads us to the conclusion that time flows in only one direction, from past to present to future.

Actually time flows in all directions. Think of a complex web of events and possibilities that lies just beneath the surface of this apparent linear flow. Think of the strands of this web tying together all events—past, present, or future, creating a holistic construct that we call reality. The past is not fixed, actually. It keeps changing whenever we look at it anew. The present that we're conscious of is actually a fraction of a second in the past. The future is in flux, depending on the actions we take now. When we pull on any of those strands of the web, we shake the whole thing and change the very fabric of reality as we understand it.

Here's the truth according to quantum physics: everything exists now—past, present, and all possibilities for the future. It's all accessible to each one of us at any time. This means there's a vast storehouse of information and paths that can connect our mind to that source. Some call it the akashic record, meaning "place of all knowledge." Others call it a library that you can access simply by acknowledging its existence and being open to receiving information that's in it.

You're always evolving in wisdom and maturity. In this present moment, you can meditate back in time to an event when your child self or your adolescent self was hurt. You, as the wiser adult, can help your child see the situation differently and handle it differently. You can heal that child or adolescent. You can also meditate forward and imagine your Future Self, which is wiser and more mature than your present self. You can receive support, wisdom, love, and healing from your Future Self.

You—and all of us—are making up reality as you go, in keeping with your intent. Intent acts as a sort of magical cord that strings all the elements together. It's what makes remote viewing work. Imagination is the seat of creativity, directly connected to what will eventually happen. You are capable of seeing or envisioning what you will eventually experience, because you're sending yourself the information that you will come to know in the future. Since all time exists now, including the future, whenever you come to know something from the future, you can pass it back into the now.

Practice predicting what's going to happen in order to tap into your future and use it. Predictive ideas, while subtle, are very powerful. Thoughts are what drive events. Don't look at the future with attitudes shaped by the past. Keep an open mind when you predict.

Advanced Technique 2. Giving Readings

Your intuition may now be coming through loud and clear much of the time. If not, you'll probably reach that stage at some point. People with open, intuitive channels sometimes pass along their "knowing" to friends or associates who ask them to share their insights. You may decide that this is a service you want to provide, and you may see this as a way to continue building your intuitive skills. Giving readings does raise some ethical questions. Here are some suggestions.

When in doubt, do nothing.

Don't play God or interfere in someone's life. Don't say anything negative. Remote viewers, who "see" people and objects at distant locations, have no right to interfere with the process of people's lives. Let their lives unfold in the way they were meant to be. It's their adventure, not yours.

Revisit your notions of "disaster"

If you see something "dire" or "disastrous," remember that everything that happens has value. We're all on a journey. Our suffering has meaning as well as our joy. Our spirits live on forever, so what could be bad? If someone asks a responsible intuitive such questions as "When am I going to die?" the answer is something like "Oh, let it be a happy surprise."

Assess your motives

If what you hope to gain by giving certain information is to feel special, loved, powerful, or otherwise be rewarded, keep quiet. Your negative ego is probably interfering. If your urge is at all driven by a need to retaliate, provoke, or express passive-aggressiveness, or if you don't really understand exactly what your motives are, be quiet.

Recheck your data

When research subjects get 65 percent of answers right on psi tests, it's considered impressive. No matter how strong your signal, acknowledge that you could be wrong. Deliver information in a way that makes that clear. You can ask your body to answer yes or no to a question. Highly kinesthetic people use these signals:

- "Yes" feels like a subtle opening, expanding, or relaxing of the innards.
- "No" feels like a contraction or withholding, a tightening or tensing inside.

Ask, "Is there something I need to do with this?"

Ask yourself if you really need to do something with the information you just received. Ask it even if someone has asked for the information and you got a strong hit that makes sense. Ask yourself if giving this information could impede or limit the person's choices, foster unhealthy dependence on you, or drive behavior in unfortunate directions? If so, keep quiet.

Intervene meditatively

If you decide not to speak up about your "dire" prediction, you can still visualize a positive outcome in a meditation. But even then, meditatively ask permission from that person. Also, focus on the following intention when you intervene: "with harm to none, for the highest good of all."

Finesse it or phrase it positively

Therapists frequently use a finesse strategy—especially when the person will probably view the information as negative. For example, instead of giving him the information directly in conversation, keep it for background information. When he mentions something related to the information, you can pick up on it, inserting the it in a nonthreatening way. Instead of "I sense you will be fired," you wait till he mentions something about his job and say, "I sense some problem there."

You could phrase the information as a question and be willing to be wrong. "You're not in danger of getting fired, are you? Well, this is just a hunch and I'm not sure where it applies." Be sure to clarify the person's option choices. "I sense that you also have strong skills in another field." You can put "bad news" in a personal growth context to help the person discover his own options. "You seem to be ready to move on to a new phase of your career."

Drop out of your head, into your heart

Move out of a rational mode. Bring your consciousness into your heart area. In your heart you're likely to evoke authentic feelings of love, compassion, and gratitude. You pump up your intuitive ability and strengthen your trustworthiness.

Advanced Technique 3: Sending Mental Energy

Do we affect each other by sending mental energy? Many studies, such as those at Duke University Medical Center indicate that we do. For example, heart patients were asked if they wanted others to meditate or pray for them. Those who said "yes" became the experimental group. People who meet regularly in study groups to pray and meditate were given information about the heart patients and included them in their sessions. The groups included Protestants in North Carolina, Buddhists in Nepal and France, and Carmelite nuns in Baltimore

All were lay persons except the nuns. Comparisons were made between the experimental and the no-prayer control group and the results presented at the American Heart Association's 1999 meeting. The prayed-for group had 100 percent lower incidence of complications.

Related experiments include laboratory studies with bacteria, yeast, and fungus. When people meditated and visualized the bacteria increasing, they did. When people meditated and visualized the bacteria decreasing, they did.

This indicates that there's more going on than people getting better because they believe others are pulling for them. The bacteria did not know that people were pulling for them—or against them. It would seem that when people have the intention to create an end result, they can bring about desired results.

This brings up an ethical issue. If focused intention can harm bacteria, cancer viruses, HIV, etc.—as studies indicate that it can—couldn't it also be used to harm people? Or if not harm them, simply interfere in their lives without permission? When you tap your intuition and create mental scenarios that affect others, how can you avoid harm? One way is to mentally ask permission of others. Visualize their personal boundaries and mentally respect those boundaries Another is to repeat the affirmation mentioned earlier: "With harm to none and for the highest good of all." Ask your Higher Self to guide you in carrying out that intention.

Advanced Technique 4: Traveling in the Astral Body

Are you one of the many people in the world who has had an out-of-body experience (OBE)? If not, you should at least be aware of the phenomenon, which is related to intuition and creative intelligence. OBEs are an unusual gift, though they seem natural and even ordinary to those who experience them on a regular basis. Author Lyall Watson in his book *The Romeo Error* lists famous authors who reportedly experienced OBEs. They include Ernest Hemingway, William Wordsworth, Emily Bronte, George Eliot, Alfred Lord Tennyson, D. H. Lawrence, Virginia Woolf, Bernard Berenson, Arthur Koestler, George Meredith, and Arnold Bennett.

Research indicates that about 5 percent of people have had at least one OBE [Smith 1998]. Authors of this research concluded that demographic factors have no bearing on who has these experiences, but there is a significant connection with past meditative or mystical experiences. However, the research of Dr. Celia Green of the Oxford Institute of Psychophysical Research makes one wonder if young people are not more in touch with the OBE phenomenon than others. She surveyed undergraduates and found that 34 percent had at some time had an OBE.

One study of 100 people who have experienced OBEs revealed the following:

- 50 percent have seen their bodies from the outside
- 30 percent traveled in the OBE state
- 5 percent acquired information via ESP while having an OBE

In another study by the Society for Psychical Research in England, of the people who had had just one OBE, 75 percent had seen their own body during the experience and 10 percent saw a silver cord connecting their physical and spiritual bodies.

Specific brain-wave frequencies may enhance the ability to have an OBE. Jack Houck's 1994 study revealed that when a person's predominant EEG frequency measures 7.81 to 7.83 Hz, there's likely to be a Mental Access Window (MAW) to OBEs. This is between the deep meditation and hypnagogic drifting-into-sleep states for most people. Interestingly, the MAW frequency is also the same frequency range in which slight oscillations in the earth's magnetic field occur.

Houck studied psychics and geniuses and found that their EEG frequency falls naturally within the MAW range, even when they're fully awake and active. This may explain why many famous authors have experienced OBEs.

Houck made a recording of an input signal at exactly 7.81 Hz. He listened to the EEG unit in one ear and at the same time listened to the 7.81 Hz recording in the other ear. After a few minutes of relaxation, the two sounds became very similar—and then he experienced a full-blown OBE. Since then, 45 people have used the device and about half reported a full or partial OBE. Those having spontaneous OBEs reported that their perceptions were organized and coherent, not fragmented and isolated like those encountered in a drug-induced state.

People from many cultures throughout history have reported OBEs, referring to them in a variety of ways, as shown in Table 7.3.

Table 7.3 Out of Body Experiences Across Cultures & Times

Culture	*Terms for OBE*
North American Indians	Loosing the bounds of the soul
Egyptians	BA
Tibetans	Displacing the soul, Power of the Delog
India	Samadhi, Sidhi powers, Trong jug
Jacqui Indians	Brujo or witch flying
Greeks	Ecstasy
Australian aborigines	Seeing at a distance
Zulus	Opening the gates of distance
Amazon Indians	Induced by the Ayahuasca vine
Shamans	Induced by the "ritual of the irrational"
Pagan tradition	Induced by witches with herbal extracts

Most ancient cultures, including the Greeks believed that a nonphysical body, often called the soul or psyche, could move rapidly through time and space. Data on 60 different ancient cultures show that 54 of them had some knowledge of the OBE state. Egyptians, Tibetans, and Greeks believed that the soul existed as a double of the physical body and was able to fly. The experience of seeing one's double has been extensively reported. During an OBE, the self that's separate from the physical body seems to contain all of the individual's personality, consciousness, will, even logical thought. Even though consciousness is primarily outside the body during the experience, there is a sense that it's also in the physical body, only to a lesser degree at the moment.

Theosophical thought of the turn of the century in the United States and Europe viewed the human as a complex creation consisting of multiple bodies, each one more subtle than the one preceding it. Seven great planes of existence produced seven corresponding bodies. The astral body is able to travel on the astral plane. The higher the plane, the more causative it is in creating eventually the dense vibrations of the physical body. The astral plane produces a less-dense body.

In tribal shamanic tradition, OBEs are usually attained only by the tribal shaman, who has reached a higher level of consciousness than other members. Therefore, the shaman is able to mentally travel to earthly places as well as to the world of the dead or spirit world. Siberian tribes of the 1700s and 1800s, believed that humans can acquire the ability to have OBEs if they have mastered both their physical and spiritual selves.

Creativity Showcase

Using Intuitive Intelligence
for Creative Solutions and Ideas

Some innovative solutions to current problems—for your information and inspiration—and as food for thought.   Compare this with your own local experience.

Problems—Urban Blight, Transportation Nightmares

In 1971 Curitabo, Brazil, had most of the problems plaguing similar cities that had grown into metropolitan areas: traffic congestion, pollution, inadequate public transportation, crime, poverty, the homeless, and never enough money.   And in 1971 a new Mayor took office—Jaime Lerner who has been called   "cheery, informal, energetic, intensely practical, with the brain of a technocrat and the soul of a poet" (Hawken 1999).   We might add to those traits "intuitive" and "innovative," a leading-edge architect, engineer, urban planner, and humanist.   His intuitive and creative intelligence have made all the difference to the people of Curitabo.

Intuitive Web of Creative Solutions

Lerner and his staff continually asked, What is the best way to approach and solve the problems facing our people?   Listening to intuitive flashes from within—and listening to the people—they came up with new ideas for solving urban problems.

To begin with, they avoided solving problems in isolation, one at a time.   They tried to get all the important problems on the table first to, see how they were related.   For example, traffic was becoming a major problem.   But Lerner's team did NOT turn Curitabo's fate over to traffic engineers.   What they DID do was acknowledge and intuit the complex urban dance between land use and the people, between the space they had to work with and the movement of people within that space.

They worked with the dance of abundance and poverty, of nutrient flows and wastes, of health and education, of jobs and income, and of culture and politics.   They sensed all of these as intertwined parts of a wholistic design—a web of needs and wants to be met within the whole of city government.   And they found all sorts of hidden connections among the problems and potential solutions.   They were able to create a web of solutions so successful that many say it is magically intuitive.

Lerner credits Curitabo's best-known innovations to the principle of "growing along the trail of memory and of transport."   He says his team intuited that memory is the identity of a city, and transport is its future.   They saw transportation as more than a way for people to get around.   And they used it to guide land-use and to control growth patterns in a way that influences where people choose to live and where they choose to go, as well as how they get there.

Land Use

City officials first replaced the central historic boulevard in the center of town with a pedestrian mall, with attractive cobblestone streets, kiosks, and streetlamps. One of the first pedestrian malls in the world, it now includes 20 downtown blocks of bustling shops, art galleries, sidewalk cafes, restaurants, and recreational activities.

They based zoning rules not just on the tax base, political pressures, or developers' proposals—but on practical considerations such as water drainage, wind patterns, climate, and cultural-historical factors. Both in the inner city and the suburbs, the city has built affordable housing, schools, clinics, day-care centers, parks, food distribution centers, and cultural and sports facilities. The goal is to maximize convenience and community, and to minimize the need to travel. They blend low-income housing into the rest of the city as a way to promote equality and social interaction among all groups.

Traffic and Transportation

Experts say Curitabo has the finest public transportation system in the world. And it's entirely self-financed from fares, equal to about 45 cents U.S. The city provides the streets and stations, and everything else is provided by ten private firms. They're rewarded not by how many people they carry but how many miles of route they cover. This gives them an incentive to reach out to all residents and to avoid price wars over routes already well served.

Bus jams are unknown, as is bus vandalism because of widespread civic pride. Because the system meets people's needs so well, 75 percent of commuters use it, even though 28 percent of users have cars. Bikers use 100 miles of separate bike paths integrated with streets, buses, and parks. Special buses and taxis accommodate the disabled, many of whom travel to 32 specialized schools.

How did Lerner's team achieve this miracle? In the beginning, they chose to adapt existing streets for improved traffic flow, instead of building huge freeways. They created five interlinked growth axes, each consisting of three parallel streets. The middle thoroughfare carries express buses both ways, flanked by local traffic. The other two, one block to either side, are one-way express streets to and from downtown. This system achieves the performance of a huge freeway nearly 200 feet wide but spreads it over three existing adjacent streets. This innovation has been copied by many cities.

They started their new bus system with the buses the city had on hand and went on to create, with Volvo, a completely new kind of bus designed for people, comfort, economy, and rapid flow. Now more than 1,250 buses of 9 types are matched to the specific needs of the people so as to minimize empty seats. The metro area is linked by 245 integrated routes of 12 color-coded types, and by 25 terminals.

On the express routes, buses pull up alongside a "tube station"—an elevated glass tube parallel to the bus lane, that allows people to step directly onto (or roll wheelchairs onto) the bus. Departing passengers leave through the opposite end of the tube. Rush hour express buses leave once a minute, operating the traffic lights to maintain their priority. Each lane of express buses carries 20,000 passengers per hour, as many as a subway system, but at 100 times less cost. Compared to traditional buses, they carry three times the average passengers-per-hour—and it takes less than one-third the number of buses to do the job.

Water and Green Space

The success of the land-use plan depended on water. Curitabo lies between two major rivers and contains five smaller ones. In the 1950s and 1960s people started settling in floodplain shantytowns, and the increased paving of the city was causing worse floods through the city center. The staff decided to quit fighting nature and exploit the water as a gift. They turned riverbanks into parks, used small ditches and dams to form new lakes and made each the core of a new park. They turned unused streamside buildings into recreational facilities. When people complained about the park's loud lawn mowers and leaf blowers, city leaders brought in a city shepherd who grazes a flock of sheep, turning surplus grass into income for social programs.

Community groups arose to preserve and use the parks. City officials banned impervious paving of open space, provided permanent protection for vegetation in the low-density one-third of the city, and gave tax relief to owners of woods and gardens. All these measures allowed the rainwater to soak in where it falls. To further contribute to the greening of the city, Curitabo planted hundreds of thousands of trees, which serve as the city's lungs, cleaning the air and blocking noise.

Industry and Community

Well situated for commerce, Curitabo began building an Industrial City on 16 square miles of land six miles from the city. They also built low-income housing and services for a complete community, so employees could live nearby. Then they recruited 500 nonpolluting industries that now provide one-fifth of area jobs.

User-friendly, customer orientation is the goal of all municipal departments, many of which are headed by women managers and/or architects. These people-oriented, managers placed satellite city halls in the suburbs and in larger bus terminals. These offices provide information on training, business loans, job opportunities, and other city services. Telephone hotlines and internet websites also provide this information.

Curitabo leaders spend 27 percent of the budget on education. Curitabo has a 95 percent literacy rate, the highest in Brazil, and the lowest first-grade failure rate. They provide Lighthouses of Knowledge, each a 7,000-volume library, throughout the city with the goal of having one within walking distance of every child's home. The City recycles virtually everything, including buses, which become mobile job-training centers, where over 10,000 people a year get free job skills training.

Intuitive Creative Intelligence

By such intuitive ideas as working with nature, not against it; making the scale of solutions match the scale of problems; frugally using resources; re-closing broken loops; and designing toxicity out, health in—Curitabo creates a sustainable society as well as a sustainable economy.

Lerner says the central political principal has been to respect the people, because they're really the owners of all public assets and services. That means running a city government that is transparent, honest, and accountable. His staff intuited that if people feel respected, they'll assume responsibility to help solve the problems. And the poor, hungry, illiterate, and apathetic will recycle themselves into actively contributing citizens.

Lerner and his team love solutions that are innovative, intuitive, simple, fast, fun, and cheap. They experiment and improve as diligently as any high-tech startup. That means risks, so their failures are frequent, hard lessons are continually learned, and their struggles to improve are never-ending.

After 12 years as Mayor, Lerner went on to become governor of the state. His successors have continued the principles and style he set in place. Meanwhile, Lerner has been approached about running for President of Brazil.

Creative Techniques Based on Intuitive Intelligence

CT 7.1 The Focused Walk

When you are wrestling with a problem and not making progress, take a 20-minute walk. Briskly walk for 10 minutes away from your home or office. Turn around and walk back. Before you leave, focus on the exact problem you want to solve, a specific question you want to find the best answer to. To boost the effect, make up a little sentence stating what you want. This becomes your "mantra" as you walk, a few words you repeat over and over. Phrase it in symbolic language, if that makes it more powerful or fun for you. Repeat it over and over as you walk. Try singing it, using any simple little tune you remember or make up. Then you can walk to the rhythm of your mantra. As you walk, make gestures that symbolize your mantra. When you return, write three pages on any topic, even if you write over and over "I don't want to write." You'll end up writing intuitive messages. This is especially helpful when you feel frustration or anger about your project.

CT 7.2 Brainstorm—Group Technique

Brainstorming is usually done with your team, which should select a facilitator and a recorder. The facilitator helps the group define the problem-opportunity, preferably before the brainstorming session, so each member will have time to mull over the situation. Express the problem-opportunity situation in a brief statement.

Group members volunteer ideas, insights, suggestions, solutions, and any other expression they consider helpful to moving toward an eventual action plan, following these agreed-upon rules

- No judgments are made about any suggestions during the brainstorming phase.
- All ideas, even far-fetched "wild" ones are welcomed and respected.
- The goal is to generate a large quantity of ideas; quantity is more important than quality during this phase.
- During the session ideas may be combined, piggybacked, or refined—ideas may pop up and evolve, since one idea often triggers another.
- At the end of the session, the team takes a break and returns then or at a later date to further process and evaluate the ideas.

CT 7.3 Brainstorm—Brainwriting

Identify the problem-opportunity situation; express it in a brief statement. Group members sit in a circle and decide on a time period for individually writing down their ideas as they come up (at the top of a full sheet of paper or notebook).

At the end of the time period, each member passes his or her written ideas on to the next person, and that person piggybacks on the original idea, writing on the same piece of paper, again within a specified time period.

At the end of the time period, members again pass on the paper for the next person to piggyback upon. The group may use three or more rounds of brainwriting.

When the rounds are completed, each member reads aloud the ideas on the paper she or he is currently holding. The group decides how to further organize and process this information, perhaps using a rational creative technique.

CT 7.4 Brainstorm—Brainwriting Pool

Identify the problem-opportunity situation; express it in a brief statement. Group members sit in a circle and decide on a time period for individually writing down at least four ideas as they come up (at the top of a full sheet of paper or notebook). Remember, it's quantity, not quality, that counts in this phase.

When a member runs out of ideas, he or she places the paper in the "pool" at the center of the table. Members then choose a piece of paper from the pool and piggyback on those ideas. Eventually every member should exchange his or her paper for one in the pool.

Each member reads aloud the ideas on the paper he or she is currently holding. The group decides how to further organize and process this information, perhaps using a rational creative technique.

CT 7.5 Brainstorm—Five Minute Pool

Identify the problem-opportunity situation; express it in a brief statement. Group members sit in a circle and take five minutes to individually write down three ideas in three columns (at the top of a full sheet of paper or notebook).

After five minutes, members pass their three ideas to the next person, who piggybacks on those ideas and develops new ones, writing them beneath the original ideas. Repeat the process until every team member has contributed to every other member's original ideas.

Each member reads aloud the ideas on the paper he or she is currently holding. The group decides how to further organize and process this information, perhaps using a rational creative technique.

CT 7.6 Brainstorm—Eight Grids

Identify the problem-opportunity situation; express it in a brief statement. Decide which aspect of the situation to brainstorm. Prepare nine sheets of paper, each with a grid of three columns and three rows, resulting in nine squares.

Write the problem-opportunity statement in the center square. Now there are eight surrounding squares. Team members then think of eight related ideas, applications, solutions, issues, etc. Write these eight ideas, one to a square, surrounding the central statement, labeling them "A," "B," etc.

These eight ideas become the basis for generating eight additional grids. In the nine-square grid on a separate sheet, write idea "A" in the center of the grid ("B" becomes the center of another nine-square grid and so on through "H.")

Participants brainstorm related ideas, issues, solutions, applications, etc. for idea "A." Then continue on to idea "B" and so on through "H."

Review each of the eight grids and decide how to further process and evaluate them, perhaps using a rational creative technique.

CT 7.7 Brainstorm—Integration

Identify the problem-opportunity situation; express it in a brief statement. Each member writes down a response to the statement. Two members each read an idea aloud. The other members try to combine these two ideas into one. A third member reads her or his idea aloud and the other members try to integrate it with the previous idea. The team continues this process as long as they believe it is moving toward positive results. Members then discuss the results.

CT 7.8 Brainstorm—Idea Display for Entire Project

This technique is especially helpful in generating and deciding on alternatives when dealing with complex problem-opportunity situations. The team's ideas are displayed as they work on the project so members can begin to see interconnections, how one idea relates to another, and how all the pieces might fit together. It takes brainstorming several steps further in order to organize and deal with complex issues.

- The team brainstorms the problem-opportunity situation. Express it in a brief statement. This becomes the *topic header* at the top of the display.

- The team next brainstorms the purpose of this project—why you are working on it, why it's important, and/or the end result or goal(s) you want to achieve. Express the major purpose in a brief statement that becomes the *purpose header*, with other purposes displayed under it as subheads.

- The team brainstorms all the major aspects, issues, opportunities, or solutions to the situation. Each one becomes a *header*. Related ideas will be displayed under that header.

- Finally, there should be a *miscellaneous header*, under which the team will post stray ideas that don't quite fit under any other category.

For complex projects, the team may want to do a brainstorming process and display for each phase of the project, such as 1) planning the entire project, 2) generating new product-service-process ideas, 3) organizing the resulting action plan, 4) communicating the action plan.

The planning display will contain all the major ideas related to solving the problem or capitalizing on the opportunity. It forms the blueprint for the actions that follow. Each major idea becomes a *header*, and ideas generated under that heading become *subheads*.

The ideas display is an expansion of some of the ideas contained in the planning display. For example, a header from the planning display might become the topic header for the ideas display, and each of the subheads under that header in the planning display would become headers in the ideas display. Then ideas brainstormed in each category become subheads.

The organization display responds to such questions as: *What are the tasks that we need to get done? When do they need to be done? Who will do them?* In this phase the team takes the goals and plan established earlier, and the ideas that have been generated, and breaks them down into group goals and tasks and individual goals and tasks. The team can actually add the answers to these questions to the appropriate locations on the planning display and the ideas display.

The communications display responds to such questions as: *Who needs to know about this action plan? What do they need to know? When do they need to know it? What media will we use to communicate the information?*

CT 7.9 Individual Brainstorming and Team Voting on Ideas

Step 1: Identify the problem or opportunity that the team will address. If the problem or opportunity is not clear, the leader or the team may decide to use a brainstorming process for this step.

Step 2: Brainstorm ideas for solving the problem or for taking advantage of the opportunity— by asking team members to individually allow ideas to come up and to jot them down as they occur.

Step 3: Record all ideas of team members in round-robin fashion by writing them on a chalkboard or flipchart. If members are connected by computers, key them in on the computer for all to see on their screens. When a member has no more ideas to contribute, he or she passes. The round robin continues until everyone passes.

Step 4: Explore all ideas, one at a time. Team members ask questions of the originator of the idea, who then explains and clarifies the idea. Team members may add to the idea, connect it with another idea, or "play off of the idea" in any appropriate way. The purpose of this step is to clarify ideas and to use them as takeoff points for additional ideas.

Step 5: Vote on ideas after adopting a voting method. Each participant can write the 2 or 3 or 5 ideas that he or she considers most applicable, ranked in order of preference. The ranking can be placed either on a piece of paper, which is passed to a vote-counter, or into a computer program that will add it to a "best ideas pool." The top-rated 5 to 10 ideas may be discussed and voted on again.

This process is a good way to get full participation from all members of the team without any members dominating the process and without any team members feeling intimidated or shy. If computers are used for this process, then the ideas, questions, explanations, and votes of team members may remain anonymous. If computers are not used and anonymity is preferred, members can be advised of the problem/opportunity before the meeting and can anonymously submit solutions to be discussed at the team meeting.

CT 7.10 Immerse Yourself in Ideas

Collect all the information, insights, suggestions, ideas about your problem-opportunity situation, using every technique and method you know. In one sitting sift through all this information, including pictures and other visuals, experiences, and feelings.

Now put all this aside with the awareness that it will be incubating within you, cooking up new creative ideas. Shift your attention to completely different issues and activities. Let go of the need to solve this problem.

Allow your intuition to work with this information at its own pace and in its own way. Be open to various ways your intuition may reveal new ideas to you, including brief visual flashes, glimmers of ideas, murmurings of words of insight as well as brilliant, clear pictures or words that relate a complete idea.

CT 7.11 Shift from Rational to Intuitive Mind

Your intuitive mind alerts you by sending precognitive warnings in the form of images, dreams, gut feelings, etc. To recognize these signs, you must learn to shift out of your rational mind into your intuitive mind.

Step 1: Define your issue or problem-opportunity

If you can clearly define the real issue or root problem-opportunity, you're more likely to get good results from the process. Form a question that focuses only on one problem or issue. For example, "What production method should we use?"

Intuition usually works best in response to a simple, focused question, so don't mix together several issues in the question. Be clear whether you prefer a variety of options or a simple yes-or-no answer and phrase your question accordingly. "How can I make the most of my travel time in July?" asks for a variety of options. "Should I go to the Rome conference in July?" sets up a yes-or-no response.

Step 2: Relax and center your attention

Start with deep breathing to slow down your bodily functions and move to a slower brain wave. Become still. Allow your intuitive intelligence to take over while your rational intelligence becomes inactive. Center by focusing all your attention on an imaginary point of light between your eyes. You can bring the light into the center of your head and down into the center of your heart. You can listen to peaceful music. You can focus on a geometrical shape or a mental picture. You can focus on quieting words such as "I am . . . serene," "peace . . . be still," or "ohm."

Step 3: Let got of physical tension and open up

Once your mind is quieted, relax your body through one or more of the SAO techniques for "Be-Here-Now Consciousness" or "Deep Relaxation" in the Basic Intelligence chapter.

Step 4: Elicit intuitive imagery

Which intelligences do you bring in to play with your intuition? Your sensory intelligence—the five senses of seeing, hearing, smelling, tasting, touching? Your emotional intelligence—feelings of joy, sadness, anger, etc.?

Step 5: Interpret the imagery

If your senses or emotions bring to mind certain images, pictures or fleeting glimpses of something, what does that imagery mean in your current situation? How does it help to answer your question? Try amplification and word association techniques.

Amplification: start with a central image and continue to associate words and images with it until a significant meaning falls into place, or an "aha!" recognition pops up.

Word association: Starting with an original word that came to you and that seems significant in some way, think of other words that you associate with the original word, and write them down, perhaps with connecting arrows.

Imagining a graph: Imagine a line graph, bar graph, pie chart or similar visual that can indicate answers to your question.

Imagining a traffic light: Imagine a traffic light and see what signal it gives you: red for "no," green for "yes," and yellow for "wait."

Step 6: Take Time out

If you don't come up with something that seems "right" or significant, take time out to let the question incubate in your subconscious mind. Become occupied with other activities, especially activities that you can become wrapped up in. Getting into flow is helpful.

Step 7: Return for insight and implementation

Even if you got a significant answer to your question, often that answer will stimulate more questions. Notice if any come to mind and use the intuitive process on them. Then it's time for your rational mind to kick into action to resolve the issue or problem.

CT 7.12 Tuning Into the Customer

This is a technique to focus on what your customers would welcome in the way of products, services, or processes-for-delivery of goods or services. The purpose is to connect intuitively with customers and to receive intuitive messages.

Formulate three or four key questions The questions below will give you some ideas, but you'll probably have some questions unique to your situation.

- What do my top customers really want?

- What new product or service would delight them, even though they're not aware of a need yet?

- How much would they be willing to pay for this?

- How do they want to hear about it? How do they want it promoted?

- Where and how do they want to buy it? Through whom or what? Under what conditions?

- Which customers are really the target market for this new product or service?

Relax and allow yourself to enter a meditative state. Recall your key questions, one at a time. Imagine yourself attuning and connecting with your customers. Open up to intuitive messages. Afterward, write down any information that came up.

CT 7.13 Council of Advisors

Think of who you would choose as a council of advisors for dealing with this issue—people you admire, would trust, who would be knowledgeable and wise in this area. Visualize these people sitting around you. Connect with them. What are they thinking and saying? Ask them specific questions and listen for answers.

CT 7.14 Decision Making—the Open Door

- Relax; then imagine the decision alternatives that are facing you.

- Imagine that each option is a different door. Visualize them as doors. Make each a different color, design, size, whatever mental images seem right to you.

- Scan the doors. Which door opens up? That's the alternative to take.

CT 7.15 Become One With

- Think of the intuitive question you want to ask, the intuitive information you need.

- Become one with the person or situation you want to be intuitive about.

- Your heart is a center of intuition. Reach out and connect with that person or situation and take it into your heart.

- What do you feel in your heart about it?

CT 7.16 Symbolize the Situation

Focus on a problem-opportunity or question. Imagine that you have an intuitive answer and imagine an object that feels right as a symbol for that answer.

- Ask yourself, what symbolizes this situation? Get in touch with one specific symbol.

- Mentally hold that symbol in your hand. Feel its weight. Get in touch with the details of what it looks like.

- Listen to what the symbol might be saying to you.

- Bring it close to your nose and smell it. Taste it. Swallow it. Eat it all.

- How does it feel in your body?

- Now amplify the symbol by getting in touch with its attributes. Go over the qualities, the traits, the details, the characteristics of this symbol. Notice your feelings about these qualities. See if an "aha" insight occurs.

Your body know what's best for you, and it can give you clues about what's good for you and what's not. This is a way of getting in touch with your sensory, bodily intelligence and letting it feed into your intuition.

Case Studies—Applying the Creative Techniques

In working on these cases, you may use creative techniques from any of the chapters. However, the creative techniques described in this chapter may be especially appropriate. Keep these self-questions in mind.

1. What problems do I see?

2. How can I probe beneath the surface to get at root problems?

3. What opportunities (hidden or obvious) can I find to take initiative, cut costs, and/or make money?

4. What creative alternatives can I generate?

5. As a consultant, what should I recommend as the best viewpoints and actions?

6. To answer these questions, what creative techniques can I experiment with to respond to this case? After completing the case analysis, ask: Which creative techniques produce the best results?

Case 7.1 Entertainment Inc.

George Carson is working as a **management consultant** in Washington, D.C. A colleague Nina Franklin mentions that her uncle's company is looking for someone to establish a local franchise for its discount dining-card business. George looks into it and decides to invest in the franchise for the Maryland-Washington, D.C. area.

The Entertainment Inc. concept is fairly simple. Most restaurants have little cash for advertising or publicity, but they do have food and drink to trade. George, as head of the local Entertainment, Inc. franchise, offers to pay a restaurant cash up front. In addition the restaurant gets a free mention on George's website and a listing in his bimonthly publication of participating restaurants. In return they give George a 50 percent discount on food and drink purchased by cardholders who are members of Entertainment Inc. In a typical deal George would give the restaurant owner $5,000 cash in exchange for $10,000 worth of food and beverage "inventory" to be sold over time to cardholders who come in for dinner.

Customers who join Entertainment Inc. get a discount dining card that entitles them to get 25 percent off the menu price of participating restaurants. George gets his investment back via the membership fee each member pays for joining. George makes his operating expenses and profits from the difference between the 50 percent restaurant discount and the 25 percent discount George gives the member cardholders. One part of his expense is a royalty deducted by Entertainment, Inc., the franchiser.

Two years after starting his business, George experiences some problems that cause him to nearly run out of money. His sales reps have been accepting almost any restaurant that wants to participate. Why shouldn't they? George pays them a commission for each one they sign up. But it's turning out that some of the restaurants are not very popular with customers. When almost no one eats there, George gets almost no 25 percent commissions from discounts at those unpopular restaurants, yet he's given them several thousand dollars cash up front. Also, some restaurants are not very stable. In fact, one restaurant recently went bankrupt holding $35,000 of George's money, and that really hurt. A few restaurants have taken George's money but now they're refusing to honor the Entertainment Inc. discount card when a diner presents it. This is making cardholders angry and a couple of them are suing in small claims court.

George has a long talk with his **assistant Jean**. "You know, restaurants are rarely run by MBA's," Jean says. "That's right," George agrees. "There are many talented and capable people running restaurants, but their business decisions tend to be based on emotion and relationships. That puts us in a bind. We're giving these guys our money up front, and we have to live with them until we get our money back."

- What do you see as the major problems and opportunities here?
- What should George do next?
- Which CTs discussed in this chapter did you use in solving this case problem?
- Which CTs were most helpful and what ideas did they spark or inspire?

Case 7.2 Dorothy's Business Venture

Dorothy is a 35ish woman who lives in San Francisco. She has just completed her graduate degree in counseling and special education. Prior to obtaining her masters, she had a successful career as a legal secretary and attended law school for three years but did not take the bar exam.

Her background is in disability policy and counseling, Americans With Disabilities Act and assessing and training assistive technology—which could be helpful both to corporations in complying with the ADA and to persons with disabilities. (Assistive technology is any type of device that enables a person with a disability or other functional limitation to perform a job more easily. For instance, a person with a vision impairment could have a braille keyboard or voice output on a computer. A person who has a hearing impairment may have a flashing light to indicate a telephone call coming in on a TDD machine)

She has her Certified Rehabilitation Counseling certification (which is sort of like a national license), two certificates in assistive technology, and a certificate in hypnotherapy. (Hypnotherapists assist clients in achieving a relaxed state or a trance state and then using certain processes that can help them resolve personal problems)

She has also done Feng Shui consulting and studies the I Ching (these are two ancient Chinese practices that have withstood the test of centuries to help people find balance in their lives) and feels these two sciences are relevant to vocational counseling and adjustment to disability. She has two individuals who would like to work with her—**Alex Yuen,** who is fluent in Japanese and **Way Ling,** who is fluent in Cantonese and Mandarin. In checking out the yellow pages, Dorothy finds vocational and career counselors who offer services only in English or Spanish.

After reviewing possible positions in public employment and interviewing with several private firms, she has decided to open her own counseling/consulting business.

- How should Dorothy go about establishing a successful business?
- What steps should she take?
- How should she position herself and build a clientele?
- Which CTs discussed in this chapter did you use in solving this case problem?
- Which CTs were most helpful and what ideas did they spark or inspire?

Self-Awareness Opportunities

SAO 7.1 Meet Your Intuition

Purpose: To make your intuition real to you, and to become comfortable with it.

   Step 1. Relax. Do deep breathing, relaxation, and go into a meditative state.

   Step 2. Make a Creativity Retreat. Imagine an ideal place—where you can just be totally natural, be yourself, be safe, secure, peaceful, and serene. This place is your special space; it's just for you—whatever you want it to be and wherever you want it to be. You might want to call it your Creativity Retreat Feel yourself there. What does it feel like emotionally and physically? Design this place just for your comfort, your creativity, your serenity. Get in touch with your five senses.

* What do you see—visually? Experience it in detail.

* What do you hear? What sounds?

* What do you feel sensually—on your skin, under your feet, in your hair, etc? Be specific.

* What are the fragrances—the smells and tastes you experience?

   Step 3. Invite Your Intuition. Now, find a comfy spot within your Creativity Retreat to sit or lie. Get comfortable. Take a deep breath and invite in your Intuition. Let go of any previous ideas about Intuition—be open to experiencing your Intuition in any form it wants to take.

* Let it take a form that's real for you—person, animal, symbol, fairy, elf, other mystical being.

* Allow various images to arise. Which image comes up first? Which image most wants to stay? Which image seems more right than any other?

* What does your Intuition want to be called? Give it a name.

* Invite it by name to come in and visit with you.

* When you know that your Intuition is present with you, mentally say *Hi*.

* Ask your Intuition if it has anything to communicate to you.

* What comes up? Do you perceive words? ideas? pictures? colors? movement ? feelings? Allow, listen, open your heart, open your mind

* Accept what you get as valid, and file it away in your memory bank

* Thank your Intuition for coming to you.

   When you've ready, picture the room, and then open your eyes.

   Step 4. Record. Write about your experience and any information you received.

SAO 7.2 Resolving Problems

Purpose: To practice bringing intuitive knowledge into physical reality.

   Step 1. Acknowledge the power of your intuition. Think of time in the past when your hunches or intuitive flashes have been highly effective in handling a problem situation.

   Step 2. Write a brief statement of what you want to know in relation to this situation.

   Step 3. Write a brief statement of your intention in this problem-opportunity situation.

   Step 4. Get in touch with what you don't know but need to know in order to resolve this situation in line with your intention—the knowledge gap.

   Step 5. Go into a meditative state and ask your intuition to fill in that knowledge gap.

Think of that gap as an electromagnetic line that will magnetically attract intuitive information into it from all sides. Hold that space without filling it in with your biases, prejudices, or habitual ways of thinking. Intuitive information will be attracted into that magnetic space. Be patient. Wait for answers to be attracted into the mindspace you've created.

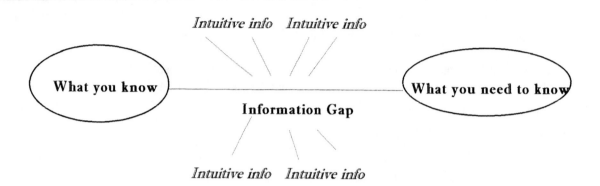

If you feel that nothing is coming in, look around and find a geometric shape to focus on. Let it fill your mind. Say to yourself, "My intuitive mind will fill me with answers." Frame the problem-opportunity as a basic question; for example, "How will customers view this new product?"

You may receive information as a symbol. Open up to symbols. They can be very powerful because they can trigger a connection to your inner wisdom. Ask yourself what this symbol means. If an answer comes easily, in a flash, it's probably intuition. You don't have to analyze it, figure it out, or work at it. If it doesn't come easily, you should wait and try another time when you may be more open, more relaxed.

If you still don't get the information you need, Close the meditation with a feeling of confidence that the information will come in its own time. You may need to let go, distract yourself by doing routine, relaxing things, especially those that you love to do, and be open to intuitive flashes. Return to the issue in meditation later. Don't give up. Stay as relaxed as you can.

SAO 7.3 Making Decisions

Purpose: To tap intuitive intelligence when making important decisions

Step 1. The Decision and Options. Get clearly in mind a decision you need to make—or a situation you need to work on. Then focus on the alternatives you're considering. Narrow them down to the two or three best options.

Step 2. Relaxing. Do deep breathing, relaxation, and go into a meditative state.

Step 3. Visualizing. Imagine you're walking down a path.

- Notice the scenery—the season, weather, time of day, sights, colors, sounds, smells.

- Imagine beauty all around you, that you're really enjoying this walk.

- Keep walking and go over the decision or the situation you're working on. Recall the two or three best options. Mentally list them and number them.

- Continue walking and enjoying the scenery.

Step 4. Seeing The Paths. Become aware of the path you're walking on. Looking ahead you can see that it splits into two or three paths—and each path takes you to one of your options.

- Come to the place where the path forks. Stop!
- Number the paths in any way that's comfortable for you. Be clear about how each path looks and which option it represents.

Step 5. Going Down a Path. Take a deep breath. Let it out slowly. Now pick one of the paths to follow and slowly walk down it. Notice how you feel.

- Where is this path taking you?
- How comfortable are you on this path—on a scale of 1 to 10?
- Does this path feel right? Take the time you need to explore this path and notice what comes up.

Step 6. Experiencing Other Paths. When you finish, return to the fork in the main path.

- Repeat the process for the second path and second alternative.
- Return to the fork in the main path
- If you have a third alternative, follow the third path and experience it.
- If you don't, just hang out with the experience you had on the two paths.

Take another deep breath, let it out slowly. When you're ready, open your eyes.

Step 7. Recording. Jot down your experiences.

SAO 7.4 Decision Making—Your Future Self

Purpose: To tap intuitive intelligence when making important decisions

You need to make a decision and want to consult your intuition. Relax into a meditative state and visualize the following:

- You see a beautiful beam of light—so big and so strong that you could ride on it. Hop on. Let the beam of light take you to a place in the future where you've already made the decision.
- See yourself in the body of your Future Self. Feel how relaxed your body is because you've already made the decision.
- Look around to where your hands and feet are. What do they look like? Now look around you. Where are you living? How are things going? How has this decision affected your life?
- When you have the information you need, get back on the beam of light and come back, bringing with you the decision your Future Self has already made.

SAO 7.5 Dream Interpretation

Purpose: To reach a deeper understanding of the meaning of your dreams.

You've already practiced programming your dreams, recalling them, writing them down, and interpreting them. You're ready to advance your dream interpretation skills to pick up intuitive information.

1. Give your dream a title
2. What's the dream about? What's the bottom line, your capsule summary of this dream?
3. Draw a picture, or pictures, that represent the important aspects of the dream.
4. Look and listen for symbols. What symbols need to be amplified?
5. Amplify symbols through word association, listing of attributes, etc
6. What intuitive messages come through?.

SAO 7.6 Remote Viewing

Purpose: To practice tuning in to persons, events, or things that are remote, getting information that you can't perceive directly with your senses, but must perceive intuitively.

1. Relax and go into a meditative state, quieting your mental chatter so you can be more receptive to intuitive information and can separate it from ego-talk

2. Let observations come in without jumping to conclusions. Remember, your mind tends to fill in missing pieces of a picture, based on your assumptions, on what you expect to see. This habit can blind you to new or surprising information.

3. Close your eyes. Imagine opening them at the "target area," seeing the type of person or situation that you want to get information about. You may at first see nothing. Be still and allow. Don't try.

4. You may see a jumble of shapes or vague impressions. Allow them to take shape. It isn't like watching television or movies. Much of the information may arrive in pieces that don't necessarily fit together. It can also come in words, feelings, smells, or tastes.

5. When you're ready, speak about what you're seeing.

6. When you open your eyes, sketch and record your impressions.

SAO 7.7 Remote Viewing—Partners

Purpose: To experiment with getting information about people you don't know and who are absent.

Preparation Phase:

1. Pair up. Decide which one of you will be Partner A and which will be Partner B.

2. A and B: Write on a card the name of a person you know well—a person your partner doesn't know.

3. List on the card that person's main traits or qualities, in rank order of strength or importance (don't let partner see what you've written).

4. Place the card face down in front of your partner.

Remote Viewing Phase:

Reaching a Loving Intuitive State

• Do your usual deep breathing and relaxation techniques, grounding, centering, bringing in protective white light through your crown, letting it spread through your body and aura.

• Imagine being surrounded and protected by a magic cushion of intelligent, vibrating energy that draws to it all the love and sweetness ever sent your way—every smile, good wish, gesture of gratitude.

• Imagine the loving people from your life showing up to guide you and wish you well, a personal cheering section. This can include powerful ancestors, guardian angels, power animals, and all kinds of symbols and spirits. This opens your heart, pumps up your psi ability, crowds out ulterior motives. (As a bonus, it increases your immune function and lowers blood pressure).

Round One:

Partner A: Focus on your "card person" as completely and exclusively as you can, while Partner B tunes into the person intuitively. Picture the person, "be-with" the person

Partner B: Tune in to Partner A's "card person." Allow impressions to come up. Be open to ideas, pictures, glimpses, a "sense of."

Round Two:

Partners A and B: Switch roles, A. Repeat the process, focusing this time on Partner B's "card person."

Followup Phase:

1.   To A and B: Write your impressions on your partner's card in front of you.

2.   Turn over the card and compare the two sides. Compare the traits your partner wrote from the remote viewing phase versus the traits you wrote about the person you know.

SAO 7.8 Intuitive Reading Practice—Partners

Purpose: To give an intuitive reading and to get feedback

Instructions: Work with a partner in a quiet place.

1.   **Flow.** Get into the flow state. Relax, focus on your breathing, allow it to flow, feel gratitude, which brings about feelings of self-confidence and love. Think to yourself, "I can trust my inspiration."

2.   **Caring.** Feel yourself as part of the Web of Life, connecting with all that is. Imagine yourself feeling attuned to your partner's energy. Let your heart reach out and touch your partner, connect strongly with your partner at the heart level.

3.   **Image.** Allow a memory (or symbol or scenario) to come up.

4.   **Meaning.** Ask such questions as, "What does this have to teach me, to tell me? What does this image say to me? What does this mean?"

5.   **Reading.** Share the intuitive information you perceived with your partner.

6.   **Feedback.** Ask your partner what this information means to her or him. If your reading contained some predictive information, follow up later to see what happened.

You may want to extend the process to future dreaming.

SAO 7.9 Future Dreaming—Partners

One way to practice intuition is through "future dreaming." If you're working with a partner, your intention is to make up a story about your partner. Go through the "flow" and "caring" steps outlined in "Intuitive Practice with a Partner."

- Look into the future and see your partner's possibilities.

- Play with choices. What would happen if . . . ?

- Notice pictures that come up, and feelings that come up Watch especially for scenarios that evoke elation and enthusiasm.

- Share your reading with your partner.

- Get feedback from your partner.

You can also do future dreaming for your own life.

SAO 7.10 Intuition Practice: Daily Play

Purpose: To build your intuitive skills by playing with it on a daily basis in a variety of ways..

Instructions: Pick one item each week to work with.

Practice is the fastest way to alter your fixed ideas about reality. Follow these rules:

Don't cheat. Pay careful attention to specific times, dates, amounts. Write down every unusual occurrence. Don't throw away your notes. Never stop practicing.

1. Before you go out in your automobile, picture the exact parking space you will take. Drive to it with the intention of parking there. Don't be put off if it doesn't work all the time. Record those times that it does work.

2. Before you meet with a group of people, write out a list of 10 to 20 random words on a card—words you wouldn't expect to hear in most conversations. Leave the card where you'll be sitting, and as the conversation progresses, check off the words as people say them. You may be surprised at how many get checked off.

3. Before you leave home, note the exact time you will arrive somewhere.

4. Before you shop, decide what the exact total will be on your grocery bill.

5. Pick the date and time of the next rainfall.

6. Before you go to sleep, decide what time you'll awaken in the morning. Don't set the alarm.

7. Relax, go deep, visualize a friend that you haven't contacted for a while. See what comes up. Repeat the process for two more friends. Write down the significant images, words, feelings, other types of information that come up about each of the three friends. Contact your friends and ascertain the significance of this information.

Write down your experiences and turn them in.

SAO 7.11 Intuition Practice: Play the Stock Market

You can practice applying your intuitive intelligence by investing in the stock market. First, do it without actually putting up your hard-earned dollars. Keep a record of your stock investments—how much money you make or lose over a specific time period.

Make Some Preliminary Picks

First, think of fields that interest you—the media, internet, biotech, fashion, other. Then think of specific corporations within a field that intrigue you, appeal to you, spark some interest within you It's important to engage your motivational intelligence in this project. To spark your thinking, browse through an issue of *Business Week* or other business periodical. Make a list of a dozen or so potential corporations or mutual funds. You can check the business section of your local paper, or the *Wall Street Journal*, to be sure that these corporations are sold on a public stock exchange.

Another approach is to go online to get information about hot stocks. Marketplayer.com has free charts showing which stocks are breaking out to 52-week highs on higher-than-normal trading volume. In addition this website has powerful programs you can use to screen potential stocks, using more than 100 variables. Another good place to find predesigned trend screens is wallstreetcity.com. Quicken.com screens for the fastest-growing companies in terms of sales and earnings.

After you choose a few stocks, focus on one at a time and imagine yourself invested in it. See how it feels. If a stock feels totally comfortable, think about finding something more exciting. Find a stock that feels comfortable but also a little daring and outrageous, a bit of a stretch in a direction that intrigues you. Pick three to five such stocks, or mutual funds, and write their names on index cards or sheets of paper.

Intuit the Trends

Intuitive coach Nancy Rosanoff recommends the following process. Put three to five stock cards face down and mix them up. Do a relaxation process. When you are fully relaxed, imagine that you are connecting with a universal source of information. See an image or symbol of this source and feel a flow of energy from this source into you.

Pick a card without knowing which stock it represents. Eyes closed, imagine this stock represented by a blank line chart with specific days, weeks, or months across the bottom. Watch or sense the line graph as it moves across the days, weeks, or months. Allow it to move up or down, showing you what's going to happen. Alternatively, imagine an arrow that points up, down or across, or imagine the words "up," "down," or "neutral." Open your eyes. On the blank side of the card, draw the graph or arrow you saw or sensed, or jot down the word. Repeat this process for each stock.

Compare the results for the various stocks. How do you feel when you see the name of the stock and how well it did in your visualization? Do this exercise with three to five stocks each day. You'll soon be able to sense the growth energy of stocks just by hearing their names. Let your rational intelligence feed into your intuitive intelligence by doing some selected reading that will help you understand trends in the fields you have selected. The key to this skill is to avoid running the show with your rational mind, and relaxing to allow your intuitive mind to do its thing.

Meanwhile, read the stock market reports to see whether your stocks actually go up, down, or stay about the same. Make notes, with dates, on each stock card. Track your progress to see how well your intuitive intelligence is building. If you want to improve, try variations on the visualization techniques.

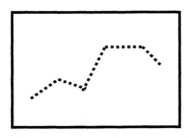 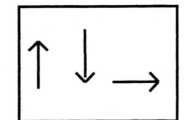

Mon   Tue   Wed   Th   Fri

Pick Your Stocks

When you're ready, pick three to five stocks you want to actually invest in. Decide how much you would invest in each, and write that amount on the stock card. You may want to do some pretend investing before actually taking the plunge. Play with timing, when to buy and when to sell. Just before the right time occurs, you may feel tremendous tension. Stay with it until the tension eases and the answer becomes clear. If in doubt, wait. Wait till the energy shifts and the path is obvious. As soon as you make a decision to buy or sell, write it on your card with the date.

Once you gain confidence in your ability to play the stock market, you're ready to put up some real money.

References

Capra, Fritjof. *The Web of Life*. New York: Anchor Books, 1996.

Day, Laura. *Practical Intuition*. Derry, NH: Broadway Books, 1997

De Beauport, Elaine. *The Three Faces of Mind*. Wheaton, IL: Quest Books, 1996.

Dean, Douglas, and John Milhalasky. *Executive ESP*. Englewood Cliffs, N.J.: Prentice-Hall, 1974.

Durden-Smith, Jo. *Sex and the Brain*. New York: Arbor House, 1983.

Emery, Marcia, "The Intuitive Healer," *Intuition*, Jan/Feb 1999, 8-13

Green, Celia. *Out of Body Experiences*. London: State Mutual Book & Periodical Service, 1989. Dr. Green is a professor at Oxford Institute of Psychophysical Research.

Hawken, P., A. Lovins and L.H. Lovins. *Natural Capitalism: Creating the Next Industrial Revolution*. Boston: Little, Brown, 1999.

Improving Your Intuition film produced by Intuition Network, San Rafael (Jeffrey Mishlove), distributed by Adler Media Production (45 min)

Kao, John. *Jamming: The Art and Discipline of Business Creativity*. New York: HarperCollins, 1996

Hammond, Holly. "Time Traveler. *Intuition*, Jan/Feb 1999. Joe McMoneagle worked with the CIA for 20 years as a remote viewer. He is currently a science associate, Cognitive Science Laboratory, Palo Alto, CA.

Muldoon, Sylvan Joseph and Hereward Carrington. *The Projection of the Astral Body*. (1929, reprint 1968). Alexandria, VA: *Projection of the Astral Body*. Time-Life Books, 1990.

Naparstek, Belleruth. *Your Sixth Sense*. San Francisco: HarperCollins, 1997.

Nierenberger, Gerard I. *The Art of Creative Thinking*. New York: Simon and Schuster, 1989.

Peirce, Penney. *The Intuitive Way*. Hillsboro, OR: Beyond Words Publishing, Inc. 1997.

Polanyi, Michael. *Personal Knowledge*. Chicago: University of Chicago Press, 1960.

Rosanoff, Nancy. *Intuition Workout*. Santa Rosa, CA: Aslan Publishing, 1991.

Smith, Angela Thompson. *Remote Perceptions: Out of Body Experiences, Remote Viewings, and Other Normal Abilities*. Charlottesville, VA: Hampton Roads Publishing, 1998. Includes information on the series of OBE studies done by psychologist John Palmer and colleagues.

Watson, Lyall. *The Romeo Error*. New York: Doubleday, 1974. The author lists famous people who reportedly experienced OBEs.

Weintraub, Sandra. *The Hidden Intelligence: Innovation Through Intuition*. Woburn MA: Butterworth Heinemann 1998.

Resources:

Intuition, a bimonthly magazine published by Intuitive Media, Inc., San Francisco,CA. intuitmag@aol.com

Chapter 8
Rational Intelligence
Building Upon Strengths

It is by intuition that we discover. . . and by logic that we prove.

Henri Poincare, mathematician

You already know that Western culture glorifies rational intelligence and either ignores or discounts most of the other intelligences. That doesn't make rational intelligence a bad thing. It's a glorious human gift, said to function at the relatively high frequency of the mental energy body and the throat chakra. This is the seat not only of thinking but also communicating and expressing your thoughts. So your rational intelligence is to be respected, but you'll want to use it to boost your creativity, not undermine it.

When you're involved in rational activities, you may be engaging in critical thinking, setting up hypotheses about what's true in reality, gathering information, categorizing and organizing it, criticizing information or processes or ideas, doubting and questioning, setting strategies to achieve goals, devising standards to measure achievement, selecting instruments to measure validity or achievement, reviewing information, comparing, judging, assessing, controlling, evaluating, reaching conclusions, and making recommendations. Your rational mind likes tightness and order. This all sounds familiar, doesn't it? These are activities we rely upon when we study, take examinations, tackle problems, do research, and develop and complete projects.

Words to associate with rational intelligence are *logical, sequential, intellectual, step-by-step, mathematical, scientific, I.Q., SAT, GMAT, mental energy body, throat chakra, blue, tone so or G, left brain, neocortex.*

Myths & Realities

Most of the myths about rational intelligence involve carrying to an extreme certain rational techniques, which are priceless when used in the right time and place, but self-defeating when overdone or misused.

Myth 1. Organize! Organize! Organize!

Organization is great—at the right time and place. You need to get a handle on large masses of data or objects, and organizing them into categories helps you do something constructive with them. This is a valuable use of your rational mind. Unfortunately, most of us overuse and abuse this ability, leading to the mindlessness of stereotyping and entrapment by category. Mindlessness sets in when you rely too rigidly on categories and distinctions that you created in the past; for example, the concepts of:

- either masculine or feminine
- either old or young
- either success or failure

9

You build your own categories based on the realities you pick up from others and the shared realities of the culture. Then you can become victim of your categories, blind to the fact that they are constructs, ideas, just one "take" on what reality is.

Remember, the creation of new categories is a mindful activity. Placing things in new categories where they "don't belong" can be mindful and creative.

Myth 2. Been there. Done that. Don't need to go there again.

You take in basic pattern-parameter information and lessons, forming boundaries and habits that work for you. Your rational mind helps you to do this at a high level of efficiency—through comparisons, critiques, assessments, reasoning, and conclusions. So you go on automatic much of the time. No need to reinvent the wheel with each decision. If you didn't handle life's routine matters while "on automatic," you'd never have the time and freedom to explore new, creative ideas. On the other hand, you must avoid automatic behavior that blocks your creativity.

How Rational Intelligence Works

Your rational mind is an extremely important part of the creative process. What you'll want to remember is that it's only a part. When you're working on a creative project, you'll use your rational mind for certain stages   You learned about the creative problem-opportunity process and its six stages in Chapter 1. Look at it again in light of the role your rational mind plays in this creative process— using the Kid Fun case from that chapter as an example as you move through the problem-opportunity stages.

Summary of Kid Fun Case

Stevie Ruiz, age 13, is president of Kid Fun, a company owned in equal fourths by Stevie, his mom, his dad, and Luis Martinez, the CEO. The company makes toys, which are invented by Stevie and his mom Donna. Kid Fun's initial product Water Talkie was Stevie's idea. Water Talkie can be used while snorkeling and allows users to talk with underwater partners.

Stevie's mom Donna had some previous success in marketing inexpensive novelties. She had developed "The Formula" for making money, which she describes this way: You start with an inexpensive product idea, something that costs under $2 to make and retails for around $10. You put dynamic packaging with that. You sell in very high volume. Finally— and this is the step that most people don't follow—you go out to get a large order before you start to manufacture your product. And it's critical not to depend on the retailers' ability to sell the product. You must make the right agreement when you take the order from the retailer: "You buy it, you own it; we don't buy back product that you can't sell." It's very important that inventors do that, so the retailer is motivated to find ways to generate sales of the product—not just stick it on the shelf and see what happens.

Once a prototype and packaging for Water Talkie had been dreamed up, Stevie and his mom sold 50,000 units to Toys R Us.

Case questions:

• What potential problems and/or opportunities do you think Kid Fun faces now?

• What kinds of products should Kid Fun develop next? In general? Can you think of some specific toys that Kid Fun should consider?

• What specific recommendations would you make as a consultant to Kid Fun?

Stage 1. Analyzing the Environment

No situation occurs in a vacuum. You must always ferret out those occurrences and trends going on around you that represent significant opportunities or threats. In Kid Fun's case, these include other toy manufacturers, especially pool toys, trends in what kids are attracted to and what they're doing these days, the entire retailing scene, including the Internet and e-commerce.

Key Question:

What are the ongoing opportunities, threats, comparisons with competitors, and other environmental issues?

Process:

First purely creative, then rational-creative. You'll begin by exploring the environment and generating ideas about how the environment is affecting your situation and how the situation in turn is affecting the environment, using all your intelligences except the rational critic. When you've generated enough ideas about what's going on in the environment, then use the rational process of reviewing, organizing, evaluating, and selecting the ideas to take to the next stage of the process.

Rational Activities:

- Look at the whole situation
- Raise doubts and questions about it
- Ask why

Stage 2. Recognizing Problems and Opportunities

At this point Kid Fun seems to have many opportunities and no problems. The main job of the players in the company is exploring the numerous opportunities—now and in the foreseeable future—sifting through them, and selecting the best bets for focusing their money and attention. Especially important are opportunities for new products and determining which products will appeal to kids. Here the main asset is Stevie. If he's really excited about a toy, chances are other kids will be also.

Key Questions:

What problems need solving? What opportunities need attention? Again, begin by exploring and generating ideas about where the problems and opportunities lie, followed by the rational process.

Rational activities:

- Look at the whole situation
- Raise doubts and questions about it
- Ask why
- Make logical links between cause and effect

Stage 3. Identifying Root Problems, Opportunities, and Assumptions

Kid Fun players must be careful to uncover hidden assumptions about the marketplace and how future products will fare there. Can they assume that since Water Talkie is a pool/water toy, their future toys should also be pool toys? Is that their niche? They must explore all reasonable opportunities to add to their product line—the various types of products they could develop—and the array of channels to distribute and retail their products.

As a new company, Kid Fun does not have enough money to expand rapidly, which may limit the ability to take advantage of market opportunities. If Kid Fun principals decide that generating adequate financial backing is a problem, they must explore the many sources of funding that could be made available.

Key Questions:

What is the underlying or root problem that we need to address? What hidden assumptions do we have that may be faulty? What opportunities are we overlooking?

Process:

First purely creative, then rational-creative. Again, begin with exploring and generating ideas about which of the issues you explored in Stage 2 are actually problems or opportunities that need further exploration—as well as possible assumptions that are faulty. Follow with reviewing, organizing, evaluating, and deciding which ideas to take to the next stage.

Rational activities:

- Ask why

- Review ideas about problems, opportunities, and assumptions

- Make sequential, precise, and logical connections (This contrasts with the associative intelligence you use to make more general, relational, and random connections.)

- Organize ideas in a logical way

- Evaluate ideas about problems, opportunities, and assumptions

- Select the best information and ideas for generating new solutions or responses to the problem-opportunity situation

Stage 4. Generating Alternatives

Kid Fun principals must now organize all the information they've gathered, analyze it, sift through it, make associations and connections, listen to their senses, their emotions, and their intuitive messages

Key Question:

How many creative ideas, solutions, or plans can we come up with that address this problem or opportunity?

Process:

First rational-creative, then purely creative. Organize all the information and ideas to get a handle on them. Then explore the information, make random associations, and remain open to emotional, sensory, and intuitive input in order to generate ideas.

Rational activities:

- Observe the situation, breaking it down into all it relevant parts

- Observe all the data in detail

- Find reasons why this problem-opportunity situation exists

- Create a new whole, a new solution or invention

- When you find the critical difference, what is missing, go on to create alternatives

Stage 5. Choosing from Alternatives

Kid Fun principals must select the best method for financing future operations. In fact, they decided to keep the firm private and swing a loan from the banker who had financed them from the beginning.

They brought in a business plan that described three new products Stevie had designed. All are water toys because Kid Fun players decided that is their best niche for now.

- Pool Peepers is a water mask designed to let the wearer see out. People looking at the wearer will not see a water mask but a face mask that looks like a lobster, frog, or dragonfly.

- Pool Pogo is another product that kids will like but parents must be sure it won't damage the pool.

- Bin-Aqua-Lars, underwater binoculars The issue is how far apart to position the lenses.

Key Question:

Which plan has the best chance of bringing us the most success in this situation?

Process:

Rational. This stage is all about evaluating and deciding—it's purely rational.

Rational activities:

- Search out and test the alternatives
- Make logical links between cause and effect
- Make detailed connections and order them in a sequential manner
- Give reasons to substantiate everything you say
- Be exact
- Explain step by step until you arrive at a conclusion.
- Reach a solution or a new invention.

Stage 6. Selling, Implementing, Evaluating, Following Up

Kid Toys must sell this plan to their banker. They must sell their toys to retailers. They must get the toys perfected, manufactured, and delivered to retailers on time. They must continually evaluate how well the toys are doing, whether improvements are needed, how to improve, how well satisfied their customers are. They must do the same kind of followup with other key stakeholders in the business, such as their retailers, suppliers, shippers, and banker.

Key Questions:

- What can we do to get the people we need behind this plan?
- What do we need to do to make it work?
- How can we get the best results from this plan?
- What feedback mechanisms do we need to set up in order to evaluate how well the plan is doing? Do we have a good Plan B or C if Plan A doesn't work out as we expect?
- What can we do to minimize the risk factor and to boost the success factor?

Process:

All four steps in Stage 6 require exploring and generating ideas, a process that is first purely creative, then rational-creative.

Step 1. Selling the action plan—explore ideas for selling the plan, generate ideas and select the best ones.

Step 2. Implementing the plan—explore ideas for carrying out the plan, generate ideas for how to do it and select the best ones.

Step 3. Evaluating the results of the plan—explore ideas for the kinds of feedback you need to best evaluate how well the plan is working. Gather evidence, observe the effects of the plan, analyze the causes for good and poor results, search more deeply and more specifically for cause-effect relationships. In this way evaluate the overall plan and each of its aspects.

Step 4. Following up to improve the plan—based on the evaluation of plan results, explore ideas for solving the problems and taking advantage of newly discovered opportunities, generate new ideas for modifying the plan and select the best ones.

Rational activities:

- Ask why and find reasons why
- Gather evidence
- Observe the effects of the plan
- Analyze the causes for good and poor results
- Search more deeply and more specifically for cause-effect relationships
- Evaluate the overall plan and each of its aspects.

Kid Fun has in fact grown rapidly in the past two years. They secured over $400,000 from their banker. Sales quadrupled last year, with accounts increasing from 18 to 125, including 250 Kmart stores and 600 Target stores, as well as stores in seven foreign countries. Foreign sales now make up about a third of total sales. Very helpful are sales in South America, Australia, and Southern Africa, where the seasons are reversed. This means summer-season sales of pool toys are spread out over the entire year. So far as overhead, Kid Fun still has no full-time employees. The four principals do nearly all the work, and other duties are either contracted out or handled by part-time employees.

Typical Rational Mind Activities

In summary, Your rational mind is an extremely important part of the creative process. What you'll want to remember is that it's only a part. When you're working on a creative project, you'll use your rational mind to:

Doubt, Criticize, Ask Why

- Look at the whole situation
- Find reasons why this problem-opportunity situation exists
- Raise doubts and questions about it
- At each stage of the process, ask why and find reasons why
- Evaluate ideas about problems, opportunities, and assumptions
- Continuously question until you discover critical differences between things.

Investigate, Research

- Gather evidence
- Observe the situation, breaking it down into all it relevant parts
- Observe all the data in detail
- Observe the effect of a situation, analyze the causes, and each time search more deeply and more specifically for cause-effect relationships
- Analyze the causes for good and poor results
- Search more deeply and more specifically for cause-effect relationships
- Explain the causes step by step until you arrive at a conclusion.

Organize, Reorganize

- Organize ideas in a logical way

- Make sequential, precise, and logical connections (This contrasts with the associative intelligence you use to make more general, relational, and random connections.)

- Make detailed connections and order them in a sequential manner

- Make logical links between cause and effect

Create, Innovate

- Select the best information and ideas for generating new solutions or responses to the problem-opportunity situation

- When you find the critical difference, what is missing, go on to create alternatives

- Search out and test the alternatives

- Create a new whole, a new solution or invention

Review, Follow up

- Be exact

- Give reasons to substantiate everything you say

- Evaluate the overall plan and each of its aspects

- Observe the effects of the plan

- Review ideas about problems, opportunities, and assumptions

Many of these rational activities involve doubting, criticizing, asking questions, and being objective rather than personal. These are valuable rational activities that can lead to trouble when done in the wrong place and time.

About Doubting, Criticizing

When you're being rational, any conclusion must be subject to doubt. You search for the critical difference that will provide the next logical step in order to continue the investigation. By questioning and doubting, you use your rational thinking to create a dynamic, open process that leads you on to continuous discovery.

About Asking Questions

When you need to know something, your rational mind begins asking the reporter's questions: who, what, when, where, why—and how. The answers to these questions give you an analysis of the situation and help you to understand what you're facing. In this way you come to understand the different aspects of the problem, which enables you to start resolving the situation from various points of view.

About Being Objective

Rational intelligence allows you to separate yourself from immediate action on a problem or an emotional reaction to it. Asking analytical questions helps you to distance yourself from the problem, become more "objective" about it. Abstract thinking allows you to set up theories about cause and effect, hypotheses or guesses about what would happen if you changed one or another aspect of the process or the situation. With analysis you look at all parts of the problem and get data about it. Then you put together all the relevant data and make order in such a way that you reach a new understanding of the problem. You assume that for every existing situation, there is one, several, or many causes.

How to Boost Your Rational Intelligence

Your rational mind is essential to creative problem solving and to responding to opportunities in a creative way. The question you must continually answer is, How can I use my rational intelligence most effectively? The answer always involves balancing the rational left-brain with the wholistic right brain so that you don't get trapped in rational-only thinking.

Booster 1. Balance Doubting and Criticizing with People Skills

Doubting and criticizing are important rational activities for certain steps in the creative process. They can enable you to sift through a myriad of options and arrive at the best plan of action for your particular problem-opportunity situation. On the other hand, you must beware of making the Doubtful Critic part of you the one you use in all your interactions with the Web of Life, especially in building personal relationships.

Problems

You know that the creative process involves building creative relationships—with clients, customers, your work team, and people within the company who must approve your innovations, use them, or sell them. Ask yourself whether you're overdoing rational intelligence in your personal relationships. Your many years of rational training in academia, and perhaps in a business or professional life, have formed a mind lens that you look through. Do you see the world primarily from a rational mindset? This can be devastating for building human relationships. Your negative ego finds your rational mind very cooperative in running its better-than worse-than program. Here's one way it works:

- You encounter a person

- Your immediate mental question is some variation of "Is he better-than I am or is he worse-than. (Variations include better-than Tom, Dick, Harry, or my ideal man.)

- You probe for important traits or qualities that help to answer your question.

- You come to a conclusion about the person.

- If it's a favorable conclusion, you still have an automatic tendency to criticize and doubt—to look for better-thans and worse-thans.

- You take the other person apart as coldly and specifically as you would take apart a piece of equipment or a business problem.

Are you likely to form a warm, nurturing, supportive relationship with this mindset? And if this is your primary approach to people, don't you, in turn, assume that other people pick you apart in the same manner? You use your own "better-thans" to feel better about yourself—temporarily—but deep down you know there's always a "worse-than" around the corner, waiting to pounce. Ever wonder why so many people in our modern culture are isolated and alone, off in their own little cocoons, perhaps with immediate family and two or three close friends—if that?

This kind of rational criticism and doubt can wear away your self-esteem until you give up and prefer numbness or an impersonal world. You may decide it's better to ignore others and to control your life through focusing on acquiring things or solving problems instead of trying to forge a broad array of personal relationships. Let's face it. The rational mind is not skilled at living joyfully with people.

Remedies

To balance your negative ego's Doubting Critic, use the people skills you've built, using your associative and emotional intelligences. Remember the associative intelligence skill of direct perception that you practice—the ability to just "be with" a person, without needing to add anything or take anything away from that person or the experience. This is actually a form of "unconditional love," worth its weight in gold, when it comes to relationships.

Remember also your skills at identifying those contracting emotions that seem to feed your Doubting Critic. Could they include one of these? Annoyance, blame, resentment, hostility, anger, powerlessness, regret, guilt, ego-pride, judgment, dislike, pity, disgust, contempt, revulsion, condemnation, arrogance, defensiveness, doubt, worry, anxiety, resignation, rejection,, mischievousness, confusion, caution, vulnerability, embarrassment, shyness, self-pity, suffering, dread, desperation, shame, loneliness, fear.

Identify the primary emotion, go into it and feel it fully. Be willing to let it go into other emotions anywhere on the emotional map, including going into deeper, more-contracting feelings. Be willing to let it go once you've fully processed it.

Remember what happens when you process and release contracting emotions? You free yourself to move into one or more of the expansive emotions, such as curiosity, excitement, admiration, empathy, love, happiness, and joy. For all of us, these emotions are an *up*, a *high*, and they motivate us to reach out to others, to share and interact. You become more open to new possibilities in relationships. You're more willing to take chances, to do something new and challenging, because you're focusing on the bright side of people and situations.

Booster 2. Balance Being Objective with Real Life

Rational thinking traditionally calls for being objective so that you don't confuse your personal opinions, emotions, and bias with what happens in consensus reality. You'll find it helpful to use objectivity when the situation calls for rational thinking. However, if you get in the habit of always "thinking at a distance" you may create blocks to your creativity. Always go back to a balance between the sequential, logical left brain and the holistic, connected right brain. Keep in mind that true knowledge must come from relationship—from knowing the wholeness of life and the wonder of life. Remember that all things are interconnected in the Web of Life.

Deal with Paradox

Remember too that "reality" is often a paradox. Nobel physicist Neils Bohr said, "The opposite of a profound truth *can* be another profound truth" [Capra 1996]. For example: "People are deeply caring and compassionate with other humans" and "Among animals, only humans deliberately torture and kill others from their own species." Also, "Energy vibrations materialize as waves" and "Energy vibrations materialize as particles." It depends on who's watching and what they want to see or expect to see. Practice holding in your mind both sides of a paradox, letting both be true.

Reconnect the Parts.

When you analyze you "think things apart" in order to study the parts. Remember to "think them together" again—to synthesize all the information you've studied into a whole picture.   You may need to connect both ends of paradoxes to get that picture.

Abstract thought involves theoretical, hypothetical concepts and ideas that are not necessarily grounded in applied experiences. Such thinking may be idealistic and transcendent. Abstract thinking therefore is very important for certain stages of the creative process, tying in with your imagination and the visions that you create. By itself, abstract thinking is only a small part of human intelligence. It's usually not the sole basis for your everyday decisions and actions, which are never completely rational but are always colored by emotions. Your thoughts are always embedded in your bodily sensations and in those processes that contribute to the entire range of human intelligence.

Ground Yourself

After you have used your rational mind, always come back into your body, your senses, and your intuitive messages. Ground theory and abstract relationships in your own experience by asking yourself such questions as "How does this play out in reality? In people's actual experiences?" Think of examples from your own experience, or imagine how a theory would work in real life.

Booster 3. Balance Automatic Routines with New Ways

We've discussed some of the advantages and disadvantages of categorizing data and objects in order to organize them and effectively handle them in your mind. Related to this is routinizing your recurring situations that call for problem-solving, decision-making, and action. You save huge amounts of energy when you go "on automatic" in repetitive situations.

Problem: Over-Routinizing

When you're on automatic, you take in and use only limited signals from the world around you without letting other signals penetrate. This is good unless you fail to notice new elements that could change the situation. Then automatic behavior could limit your self-image, your decision-making, your creativity, and your success.

Limited Self-Image. If you decide you know all about yourself, your boundaries, and your patterns—that they're fixed and done with for life—you'll be stuck with a limited, narrow self-image that can't grow.

Limited Decision-Making. Have you fallen into a routine decision-making process rather than selecting the best process and making your own decisions anew each time the situation changes? If so, you may get mindlessly seduced into activities that you wouldn't otherwise engage in. For example, the famous study on obedience to authority, which was done by Stanley Milgram at Stanford, showed that normally kind people could be extremely cruel. Participants administered painful electric shocks to people because they thought it was what other participants were doing. It was what they were "supposed" to do.

Limited Creativity. Do you ever let automatic routines take over instead of being mindful and taking personal responsibility for results? This can prevent you from making creative choices. Routines can lead you to attribute all your troubles to a single cause, which in turn narrowly limits the range of solutions you might seek. For example, do you blame your school failures on your teachers or your work failures on your boss? If so, you're more likely to repeat these and similar failures than people who take some personal responsibility for results. They're likely to see many possible explanations for their situation and to try some new, creative solutions. If you have an addiction and see the cause of your problem as purely genetic, you're likely to give up the self-control—and resulting creative ideas—that could lead to recovery. A single-minded explanation blocks you from paying attention to valid information that doesn't fit in with your "reason why."

Limited Success. Carrying this automatic syndrome a step further, repeated failure may cause you to give up. Research indicates that such "learned helplessness" then generalizes to situations in which you could in fact exercise control. If you keep failing at school, you may assume you'll fail at that new job you're interested in. You feel a sense of futility that prevents you from reconsidering the causes of the school failure. You remain passive toward the new job opportunity, even though you could handle the job with little difficulty.

Remedy: Keep an Open Mind

In reality you'll be most creative and successful if you develop rational habits and techniques while keeping an open mind to new information and a willingness to try new ways. If you're mindfully engaged, you'll actively attend to changed signals. Your behavior is likely to be more effective.

When you're open to different viewpoints, you begin to realize there are many viewpoints other than our own. There are as many find gradations of viewpoint as there are observers. For example, has a friend ever accused you of incorrect information, and you disagreed? He may have thought he was being frank. Suppose you opened up to an awareness of many perspectives of the situation you were giving information about. Could you accept that you both may be right? If so, you might be able to concentrate on whether your information conveyed the story you wanted to tell—or had the impact you wanted it to have (rather than concentrating on defending it). As a result, you gain more choices in how to respond, more options. And change becomes more possible for you.

Booster 4. Watch Out for Rationalizations and Projections

Your rational mind excels at rationalizing and projecting. You'll want to use it to help you be more creative, not undermine your efforts.

Rationalizing

When you rationalize, you give rational reasons for something. You intellectualize the causes for certain effects. Rationalizing, used correctly, is a powerful engine of the reasoning process. But if you give this power to your negative ego, it will use it to make all kinds of excuses for you. You'll be able to convince yourself that no matter now irresponsible you've been, no matter what a mess you've created, or co-created, things are not "as they seem." You can convince yourself of absolutely anything if you really want to and if you allow your negative ego to take charge. This is such a common occurrence that psychologists use the term "rationalization" to mean denying, avoiding reality, and making excuses.

The first step in avoiding rationalization is simply being aware and alert to the tendency. When you think you may be rationalizing, ask yourself, "Am I taking responsibility for creating this situation? Or am I denying, avoiding, or distorting what's really going on here?"

Projecting

In the intuitive intelligence chapter, you learned that your negative ego loves to project its own "stuff" upon other persons in your life, attributing to them what you are thinking, feeling, or wanting while in that negative-ego mode. You can point to another person as having certain problems that in actuality you are experiencing. This temporarily takes the spotlight off your own need to face your problem and "clean up your act." This is another one of those human tendencies that's so common psychologists have labeled it "projection." When you find yourself criticizing another person, ask yourself, "How does her problem reflect my own tendencies? Does his problem bug me because I haven't faced a similar issue in my own life?"

You'll want to watch out for rationalizations and projections, so you can minimize self-sabotage and keep opening yourself up to the expansive emotions that attract creative possibilities. On the other hand, remember that these are normal human tendencies. Don't make them wrong. Instead, see them as creative blocks. If you smile at your human frailties, you're likely to be able to move beyond them into more productive ways of using your rational intelligence.

Creativity Showcase

Using Rational Intelligence
for Creative Solutions and Ideas

Some innovative solutions to current problems—for your information and inspiration—and as food for thought. Are people in your neighborhood and your workplace realizing savings from better engineering of buildings—and helping the planet in the process?

Problem—Speaking Different Business Languages

We know that if industry removes concentrated and structured matter from the ecological system faster than it can be replaced, and at the same time destroys the means of its creation, Earth's ecosystems and habitats, this introduces a fundamental problem into production. As Paul Hawken (1999) says, "The atmosphere does not distinguish whether CO_2 comes from U.S. oil or Chinese coal, nor do the record-breaking 240 mph winds recorded in Guam in 1997 lose force if you don't happen to believe in climate change." Globally, individuals and businesses must pay more attention to doing more with the resources we have, so we won't deplete our natural capital beyond the point of no return.

Most architects, engineers, and other designers are taught that design is the art of compromise. It means choosing the least unsatisfactory trade-offs between many desirable but incompatible goals. We need to revisit this time-worn design philosophy. Leading-edge designers and engineers are showing that when they take a wholistic approach to achieving design goals, they may not have to compromise. Energy-saving designs often cost no more. Where they do, though, engineers have typically been unable to convince corporate executives that an initial investment will pay big dividends in the future.

For example, energy-saving devices are typically chosen by engineers at a company's operating level, using a concept called "simple payback." The engineer figures out how many years of savings it will take to repay an investment in better efficiency—whether it's better insulation, windows, equipment, materials, layout—of any aspect of the facility. At the end of the payout period, the company will start earning clear profits from the energy-saving investment. Many firms are only concerned with what an asset costs initially. And about 80 percent of the U.S. firms that even bother to consider future efficiency savings use the simple payback method. They expect an extremely quick payback—less than two years on average—or they refuse to invest in the initially more-expensive installation.

A major part of this problem is that corporate executives think in terms of discounted-cash-flow measures of profitability. They focus on generating revenues and keeping profit margins up. Engineers think in terms of design costs and simple payback. These people just don't speak the same language.

Creative Solution—Translation Breakthrough

Geraldo, The finance officer of a Fortune 100 company mentioned to Hillary, the CEO, that their Detroit plant had an outstanding energy manager, Chris, who was saving the company $3.50 per square foot per year. Hillary said, "That's nice—it's a million-square-foot facility, so he must be adding about $3.5 million a year to our bottom line. . . . but I can't really get excited about energy cost—it's only a few percent of my cost of doing business."

Instead of letting this comment go by, Geraldo showed Hillary the arithmetic. If they achieved similar results in over 90 million square feet of company facilities they operated globally, they could boost their annual net earnings by 56 percent. Hillary listened with renewed interest.

Further, even using the high standard of 1.9 years for a simple payback of energy-saving investment, this is equal to a 71 percent real after-tax rate of return on their investment per year, or around six times the cost of additional capital. Hillary, like most CEOs, invested every day in ways to increase production and sales—ways that didn't return anywhere near 71 percent a year after taxes.

But it was Chris who was the real translator of engineering-speak into executive-speak. At a company-wide conference the previous week, Chris had approached Geraldo and said, "Man, do I have a deal for you! How would you like a risk-free return of 71 percent after tax! For that matter, how about looking at other energy-efficient investments that produce a 3-to-4-year payback. That's still a risk-free return of 27 percent after tax."

Geraldo posed this same question to Hillary. They began to realize that, like nearly all U.S. companies, they were not purchasing nearly enough energy efficiency. They asked Chris to change all that—after they promoted him to corporate energy officer.

Creative Techniques Using Rational Intelligence

CT 8.1 Move Beyond Rational

First, satisfy your rational mind by listing all the solutions or ideas that seem obvious. Now open up to ideas that are impractical, offbeat, irrelevant. Generate as many as you can. Go over them and see which ones might actually work, which could lead to more rational ideas, which could be modified to fit.

CT 8.2 Use Checklists

Develop your own checklist for examining situations for problems and opportunities. List all the techniques and reminders that are most effective for you in solving problems and capitalizing on opportunities. Depending on your job or assignment, you may need a checklist for accomplishing these tasks:

- Generating new product or promotional ideas
- Evaluating new ideas
- Conducting strategic audits that examine strategy
- Conducting management audits that examine overall management actions
- Conducting quality audits that examine quality compliance
- Conducting social audits that test for socially responsible activities
- Looking for product improvement opportunities

CT 8.3 List Complaints

Ask customers, employees, or other stakeholders to brainstorm a list of complaints. This can be done individually or in groups. Another approach is to list stumbling blocks, barriers, or other blocks to achieving their goals.

CT 8.4 Talk it Over

Verbalizing a situation and ideas for responding to it can 1) help you to become aware of ideas you didn't know you had and 2) get alternative ideas from other people. Suggest what you think the problem or opportunity is and get the other person's reaction. Each of you can offer ideas, debate them, criticize them, and defend them. This exploration can help you to be better understand the situation and respond to it.

CT 8.5 Play Devil's Advocate

Work with one or more partners. Take a position on what you think the problem or opportunity is. The other person(s) plays "devil's advocate" by pointing out what might be wrong with your position and/or suggesting other positions. Each person in turn takes a position while the other(s) plays devil's advocate. The process can help you to arrive at a better definition of the situation and ways to respond to it.

CT 8.6 Redefine the Problem or Opportunity

To help reach the best definition of the problem or opportunity, say the definition aloud, listening for something you haven't noticed before. How do you feel about this definition? Pretend you don't know what the problem is but you do know some of the variables involved. If you were one of the other key players, or a person working in another field or profession, how would you view the problem? How many different ways can you express the problem or opportunity? Try to define it in at least five different ways.

CT 8.7 Rewrite Your Goals

Identify some goals for this situation. Develop some criteria that any action plan must meet, ways you would evaluate action plans (for example, cost, durability, maintenance, image, etc.) Rewrite each goal in several different ways (For example, if your goal is to increase productivity, can you rewrite it to increase sales per employee, cut costs, be more efficient, or be more effective?) Rewrite each criteria. What insights do the rewrites suggest?

CT 8.8 Focus-In and Focus-Out

Focus-in on a problem or opportunity to discover its basic components—to get down to the nitty-gritty elements. Focus-out to discover more of its breadth, range, or scope—explore all the possibilities.

To focus-in on a situation, ask a "why" question and answer it as many ways as you can. Then ask "why" questions about your answers. Continue until you feel you've exhausted the possibilities.(*Why is this a problem? Because our sales are down; because our bonuses will be less; because some of us may lose our jobs. . . . Why are sales down? Because . . .*)

To focus-out on a situation, ask a "what" question and answer it in as many ways as you can. Then ask "what" questions about your answers. (*What is the real opportunity here? Getting more women customers to use our computer service; making our service user-friendly to the average woman; creating a company image that will grab potential women customers. . . . What kind of computer service are women looking for?*)

CT 8.9 Create a What-I-Know List

You have identified a problem or opportunity situation. That means you already know something about it, perhaps more than you realize you know. List everything of relevance that you know about it. Include your data, hopes, suspicions, evidence, people contacts.

CT 8.10 Go to School on Others' Experience

What are some similar problems that people have solved, or opportunities that people have capitalized on? What relevant information can you get about these successes? Where can you get it? From reports, articles, books, files, people? What can you learn from other people's experience in these similar situations?

CT 8.11 Set Time Targets

Do you work better when you have a time target, deadline, or some sort of time pressure to complete a task or project? Most people do, and research indicates that time pressure tends to stimulate right-brain activity (intuitive, sensory, associative).

CT 8.12 Develop an Idea File

The best ideas usually come when you're not focusing on the problem-opportunity at all. Write down all your ideas, no matter how small or trivial, before you forget them. Many little ideas can lead to a big one! Find a way to record your ideas and file them away—a method that works for you. Here are some ideas:

- Keep on hand post-it notepads, index cards, or other forms of paper

- Place them everywhere you work or engage in activities—by your bedside, in your wallet or pocket, in your notebook or briefcase, in your car—and use them to jot down your ideas.

- Collect these idea notes in a box, file folder, or other storage facility.

- Organize them by category; for example, keep several labeled folders or boxes.

- Enter them into computer files, where you can then play with them, cutting and pasting.

- Arrange and rearrange them in various patterns, making a collage on poster board, desktop, bulletin board, etc.

CT 8.13 Process Ideas

This technique can be especially helpful at the "choosing among alternatives" stage if you have many ideas to choose from. This may occur when you are working with a team. Put each idea on a post-it note, index card, or other media for displaying the idea and working with it. Process ideas in this way:

- *Combine* similar ideas

- *Exclude* anything not related to the goal (put these in a separate pile for possible future consideration)

- *Modify*, where appropriate, by rewriting

- *Defer* ideas that have merit but are not timely by putting into a separate pile to consider when the time is right.

- *Review* the ideas you've been processing, looking for new insights, ideas, suggestions.

- *Organize* similar ideas into batches of 7 or 8, if you have a surplus of ideas.

- *Label* each batch by topic or type of idea.

- *Rank* each idea within batches, based on its usefulness or importance to achieving the goal.

- *Reorganize* the ideas, placing the highest-ranked ones in one batch, the second-highest ranked ones in another batch, etc.

- *Evaluate* the results. What has this process suggested for choosing the best action plan?

CT 8.14 Use Scammperr Idea Processing

Scammperr is an acronym for the following kinds of idea processing. It's used primarily in the Generating Alternatives phase, but can also be used in other phases.

S ubstitute something

C ombine it with something else

A dapt something to it

M agnify or add to it

M odify it

P ut it to some other use

E liminate something

R earrange it

R everse it

Substitute

What can be substituted? Who else (could fulfill this need?)

What other procedure might work better?

Other material? Color? Approach? Change format?

Combine

Combine ideas? Purposes? Talents? What could be merged with this?

How about an assortment?

Adapt

What other idea can we incorporate? Can other processes be adapted?

Whom could we emulate? Put the product or service into a different context?

What ideas outside the field can we adapt? What else can be adapted?

Magnify

What can be made larger? What if we made it really enormous?

What can be added? What can be extended? Made longer? Higher? Overstated?

What extra features could we add? What can add more value?

Modify

How can this be altered for the better?

How can we change the nature or meaning (of any aspect of the situation)?

What other shape? New twist? How can we modify standard procedures? Attitudes?

Put to other uses

What else can we do with this? What else can be done with the waste? Other uses as is? Other uses if modified? Other extensions? Other markets? Other fields?

Eliminate

What can be streamlined? Omitted? Made smaller? What could be divided? Split up? Understated? What's not necessary?

Rearrange

Other corporate arrangement? Other payment plan? Pattern?

Can we change pace? Interchange components? Change layout? What are the negatives?

Reverse

Reverse it? Consider it backwards? Down instead of up?

Do the opposite? Reverse roles? Turn it around? Do the unexpected?

Case Studies—Applying the Creative Techniques

In working on these cases, you may use creative techniques from any of the chapters. However, the creative techniques described in this chapter may be especially appropriate. Keep these self-questions in mind.

1. What problems do I see?

2. How can I probe beneath the surface to get at root problems?

3. What opportunities (hidden or obvious) can I find to take initiative, cut costs, and/or make money?

4. What creative alternatives can I generate?

5. As a consultant, what should I recommend as the best viewpoints and actions?

6. To answer these questions, what creative techniques can I experiment with to respond to this case? After completing the case analysis, ask: Which creative techniques produce the best results?

Case 8.1 Come Fly With Me

Liu Wong is a supervisor at **Express, Inc**. His hard work has earned him a promotion to head of operations in the Livermore office.

Express is a national delivery service that prides itself on service and has been in business over ninety years. Liu's part of the operation provides package delivery service to the Tri-Valley region, part of a large metropolitan area on the West Coast. Tri-Valley was formerly farmland with a few villages, followed by suburban development. Recently it has also become a booming corridor of business activities and is experiencing growing pains. Freeways and towns built years ago are inadequate, as more automobiles and people fight for room. For example, on the major freeway carrying traffic from the central city through the Tri-Valley region, the outgoing traffic lanes resemble a packed parking lot during the Friday night commute. Towns that once were so carefully planned are now checkered with a hodgepodge of housing developments and strip malls.

Express's major business accounts in the Tri-Valley area have been accustomed to Express's responsiveness to their service issues. Many of their service agreements with Express specify an early morning delivery of packages coming to them, and a late afternoon pickup of their outgoing packages. However, as more companies relocate their warehouses in the Tri-Valley area, Express is having difficulty being as accommodating as it used to be.

Express recently began offering new types of services in order to compete. Their services now include international, next-day and second-day deliveries besides their regular ground service. These new service enhancements require that Express adopt new shipping practices. Airports are a major player in the transportation of premium packages for Express. The Express air sort facility is located 2,500 miles away, in Louisville, Kentucky. This means that flights from the West Coast must depart by 7:15 p.m. to ensure processing of packages for the following day. Liu must make sure the air packages his drivers pick up daily make it to the airport by 6:30 p.m. If his packages are late arriving at the airport, Express will incur additional charges by delaying a flight or having to find another flight.

Liu has set up a daily meet point near the freeway on-ramp for his 16 Livermore drivers to unload their air packages to the airport shuttle driver. The exchange of air packages takes between five and ten minutes, so ideally Express drivers should be at the meet point by 5:30 p.m. Liu knows that the latest his airport shuttle driver can leave Livermore is 5:45 p.m. in order to get the air packages there on time.

As drivers scramble from across town to make it to the meet point, customer complaints increase. No longer can their driver wait for that important last-minute package. Customers see Express as less service committed than they used to be and are looking at other options for their shipping needs.

- What problems or potential problems do you perceive?
- What potential or unrecognized opportunities?
- How would you address each problem or opportunity?
- Which CTs discussed in this chapter did you use in solving this case problem?
- Which CTs were most helpful and what ideas did they spark or inspire?

Case 8.2 Career Focus, Inc.

Career Focus, Inc. is a publishing firm that produces a weekly magazine with listings of available jobs in the area. Companies can run both classified-type job listings and larger advertisements that highlight their job offerings.

The magazine is sold locally at convenience stores, campus bookstores and in vending machine newsracks throughout Massachusetts. Career Focus has been operating for five years and shows great promise, but the firm has yet to generate consistent profits. The **founder, Tyrone Young,** is not sure how to stabilize and increase profit margins.

The company provides its magazine to a geographic territory about 200 miles long. Boston is the headquarters and operations run inland and westward to Springfield. Tyrone would like to expand further to the west, into Hartford, Connecticut, but he can't seem to get his salespeople to concentrate on that area.

The Sales Department consists of 20 part-timers. **Jennifer Schwartz, Sales Manager**, and **Ben Caine** are the only full-time salespersons.   Their focus is on-site visitations to sell advertising. Part-time salespeople concentrate primarily on selling job listings by telephone. Advertising sales are much lower than projected. When part-time salespeople have agreed to make on-site visits to sell advertising space, much of their activity has centered around locations close to their homes rather than the larger targeted sales areas.   Jennifer complains that she cannot concentrate on sales, telemarketing, training new salespeople, and promotion all at the same time.

The **Circulation Manager, Greg Chong**, is responsible for increasing circulation by increasing the number of outlets that carry the publication. **Luis Ruiz** is the full-time supervisor who oversees the drivers who distribute and pick up the publication.

Greg complains that his territory is too large, plus he has a number of responsibilities beyond overseeing circulation. He says there is enough stress in his job battling the major distributors who sell their own publications through local stores. The geographic area for circulation is as dispersed as the sales territory. Additionally, he maintains he cannot sell the publication to new vendors until the magazine has greater circulation. But circulation will not be boosted until customers get to know the product and spread the news to others by word of mouth.

Tyrone also has a wide range of responsibilities: training new salespeople, performing on-site visits, proofreading ads, answering the phones, and obtaining new vendors for distribution of the magazine.

- What problems or potential problems do you perceive?
- What potential or unrecognized opportunities?

- How would you address each problem or opportunity?
- Which CTs discussed in this chapter did you use in solving this case problem?
- Which CTs were most helpful and what ideas did they spark or inspire?

Case 8.3 Morrison Sportswear

Morrison Sportswear Company has been a major employer in Freeburg, a small Midwestern town, since the 1930s. With a permanent workforce of about 400 hourly employees, the company has survived the ups and downs of the economy without ever laying off an employee. This record has been a point of pride with Morrison and helps to explain an employee turnover rate of only 5 percent, the lowest of any employer in town, and one of the lowest in the clothing industry.

The corporate culture at Morrison also explains the low turnover rate. The company was started by James Morrison and has been run by the same family ever since. The pay, benefits, and working conditions have been good, so there's never been an effort by employees to unionize.

Five years ago, **Janus Industries**, based in Chicago, purchased Morrison from the Morrison family, but the change in ownership has made little difference in the day-to-day operations. **Glen Morrison, president** for the past 10 years, is still running the business with very little direction from Chicago. Glen has been assured that, as long as things go well, Chicago will stay out of the way.

Morrison produces sportswear in three distinct price ranges, which they call **Tank, Trend**, and **Rive**. Each line is in a separate department with its own assembly line and employees.

For the past two years, there has been a softening in sales of the Tank line. The turnaround that top management hoped for has begun to seem somewhat unlikely. The informal word comes down that the Chicago office is thinking about discontinuing the Tank line unless there is a significant increase in orders for this product line. Glen tells his top management team to treat this information as they would any other rumor and, if asked, to deny knowing about it.

Two more months of continued sales decline leads to the formal notification that the line will be discontinued. When this notice arrives in mid-March, it seems to ease some of the tension that the managers have been feeling. The management team meets to discuss the issue, and they realize that they've never before had to face this type of decision. The company has therefore never established a policy about how to handle the aftermath of discontinuing a line. Glen Morrison assures team members that their jobs are safe and that they can expect on-site transfers following the shutdown of Tank.

The management team agrees that it's important to proceed cautiously. Even though the Tank line will be terminated, the company will first fill all of its current orders for Tank merchandise. They estimate this will take about **five months**, and then about 90 employees, the entire Tank crew, will be laid off with little likelihood of being recalled.

All the managers agree that it's essential that the present Tank workforce be retained in order to avoid the expense of training new employees for such a short period of time. Because of differences in the various manufacturing processes, it won't be possible to transfer employees from the other departments to the Tank line without considerable training. The managers agree to keep the pending mass layoff under wraps in order to avoid triggering the departure of large numbers of employees before they complete the existing orders. Glen Morrison says, "Another factor is that business just might pick up, and Tank might not have to shut down after all."

It's common knowledge that sales of the Tank line have been sluggish, so some employees are concerned and ask questions. When line supervisors ask their managers such questions, the managers say, "You know as much as we do." Management rationalizes that there's no need to level with employees because so few jobs are available in the community for them to go to anyway.

In early May, a clothing manufacturing, Maxx, located in a town 20 miles from Freeburg, signs a long-term contract with a major discount chain and advertises to hire 40 workers who preferably have experience in the clothing industry. As soon as the news breaks, Glen Morrison calls a meeting of the management team and reassures them of their job security. He reminds them of the importance of not informing anyone of the upcoming layoff, which is **now 3 months away**. The plan, he says is to give the Tank employees **two months' notice** as required by law.

- What problems or potential problems do you perceive?
- What potential or unrecognized opportunities?
- How would you address each problem or opportunity?
- Which CTs discussed in this chapter did you use in solving this case problem?
- Which CTs were most helpful and what ideas did they spark or inspire?

References

De Beauport, Elaine. *The Three Faces of Mind*. Wheaton, IL: Quest Books, 1996.

Capra, Fritjof. *The Web of Life*. New York: Anchor Books, 1996.

Hawken, P., A. Lovins and L.H. Lovins. *Natural Capitalism: Creating the Next Industrial Revolution*. Boston: Little, Brown, 1999.

Langer, Ellen J. *Mindfulness*. Reading, MA: Addison-Wesley Pub Co Inc, 1989

Chapter 9
Creative Negotiation:
Working in Teams and Selling Your Creative Ideas

*Negotiation is the highest form of communication
used by the lowest number of people.* John F. Kennedy

People in today's workplace rarely bring creative ideas to fruition in isolation. In this era of work teams, collaboration, alliances, and cooperative enterprise, you must use your Creative Intelligence to collaborate, negotiate, and resolve conflict with many types of people and players in order to succeed. In this chapter you'll learn about 1) creative collaboration, 2) win-win negotiation, and 3) conflict resolution that turns clashes into creative input.

Creative Collaboration

"Next, please? " That's what the world is always saying in a creativity-driven market. Businesses must adopt a cultural and organizational framework of "Next, please!" or quite simply they go out of business. Create or die—the choices are that extreme. To succeed in today's innovative, fast-moving business world, you need to understand and use creative collaboration. You need to know how to recognize a creative collaboration, a collaborative corporation, a collaborative person, and a creative team. You need to know how to get a creative collaboration started.

What Is Creative Collaboration?

Creative collaboration involves people from varying backgrounds and viewpoints coming together to find shared goals, developing creative responses to opportunities, and finding solutions to problems.

Shared, understood goals

Creative collaboration involves framing goals and problems in ways that inspire people to collaborate—as opposed to doing their own thing and defending their own turf. It allows smart people with big egos to subordinate their egos while contributing to something significant and lasting. It creates a clearing that pulls people across different professional fields and allows them to create a common language.

New, shared understandings

Creative collaboration allows people to build shared understandings that lead to something new. The different perspectives and views in a collaboration are necessary for people to better understand each other and to light the spark of creativity.

An act of shared creation

Most people usually think and work along the lines of a single frame of reference. Creativity occurs when people are able to connect different frames of reference in ways that result in creating or discovering something new.

Many types of people and projects

Creative collaborations involve the creation of new value by doing something radically new or different—scientific breakthroughs, landmark legislation, new products. Successful collaborative groups are often made up of motley crews, of new combinations of diverse people.

Future fact?

Whenever anything of significance is being accomplished in the world, it's being accomplished by people collaborating across professional and cultural frontiers. The future belongs not just to stars, champions, or technical wizards who think and work in isolation, but to collaborative people who think and work together.

The Collaborative Corporation

Companies immersed in the high-tech global economy are more concerned with nurturing creative people, with a view toward creating resources that never existed before, than they are with cutting personnel and costs. Their focus is on engaging customers in a dialogue about their goals and problems. The main question is becoming: "What's missing in the way of innovative products and services?" Managers are asking, "What new patterns of relationship and interaction do we need to create to solve this complex customer problem?" They're following such role models as Bill Gates, Steve Jobs, and Jeff Bezos, who paid attention to what was missing, built it in collaboration with other firms, and delighted their customers.

Computer technology has enabled a new creative era. It expands the space for speculative thought through networks, groupware, and videoconferencing, which brings people an ever-widening array of ideas, opportunities, and challenges. It allows people to communicate instantly, and to freely feed the creative process. It brings together a wide diversity of people—and differing opinions are the raw material of the creative process. The power of creativity rises exponentially with the diversity and divergence of networked computer users.

Computers give you and your team members access to lots of information, which in turn allows you to engage in more creative conversations. You can't talk about what you don't know, but now you can find out by logging onto your computer. Your company can put online all kinds of information about business performance and project organization. Information technology, or infotech, is therefore one of the most important tools in the creativity toolkit.

Computer networks are nonlinear. They're wholistic, resembling the Web of Life, and through web connections they facilitate creativity. For example, they enable creative teams to have public conversations. They put people in touch with one another and create unexpected linkages across established organizational boundaries. They champion processes that, left to themselves, would go nowhere. They free us from concerns about how and where to get team members together. They provide speed, instantaneous transactions, and the ability to make transactions happen at all. A major type of computer linkage is groupware.

Groupware Environment—The Collaboratory

Groupware is software that connects team members' computers and allows them to brainstorm, argue, and collaborate online. People are easy to reach by groupware, which offers so much more than e-mail. Groupware takes teams a giant step closer to the brave new world of multimedia workgroup technology. It means they can set up their own private cyber-meeting, sometimes called a "collaboratory."

Using their personal computers, team members can communicate their own ideas, instantly see each other's ideas, comment on them, edit them, take off on them, and vote on them—among other things. For example, a product development team can be from diverse backgrounds and areas of expertise. Members can be located all over the world, all over the building, or all over the room. When they connect via collaborative groupware, the level of joint creativity can be very high. Such cyberspace meetings often consist of talking or brainstorming around a theme, bringing in organizational information and experiences, sharing unique knowledge that each member possesses, learning as a group, and making group decisions.

Collaborative People

Collaborative people usually take some sort of leadership role, regardless of their actual position within the company. They have a vision of a possibility they want to realize. They know collaborations don't just happen by chance but arise from the efforts of someone who is passionate about a possibility or opportunity. They're masters at building relationships and may have loud, exuberant conversations about what they want to create in the world, rather than staying silent or having muted, suppressed conversations.

They're gifted at "being with" people in rapt concentration, listening with a high quality of attention. They're often masters at organizing, bringing people with diverse opinions and backgrounds together for the purpose of identifying opportunities, solving problems, or creating value. They recognize where their own views, experiences, or skills are limited and have a basic attitude of learning and a beginner's mind.

They're often masters of cyberspace relationships, the new marriage of computers and communications technology. Cyberspace allows conversations to happen any time, anywhere, free of the limits of time, space. and personal status. Since anyone can talk with anyone else at any time anywhere, cyberspace becomes a meritocracy of talent. Collaborative conversations will come to full fruition in the form of full-blown, multimedia video and data conferencing services. These are just around the corner.

As a collaborative person, you may be a chief negotiator, a strategic broker of joint ventures, or the head of a cross-functional team made up of people who can each make a distinctive contribution to the effort. You'll form networks of communication, commitment, and support that are much more effective than the usual corporate structures.

Mental Blocks to Creative Collaboration

You can easily create a mental block to creative collaboration. For example, you can indulge in a typical American belief that you are either for something or against it—there's no middle ground. You can see taking sides as the only way to find the truth. When you hold this belief, you'll probably use war-like metaphors: fight the good fight, win that battle, rally the troops, kill the competitor, war on poverty, war on drugs, war on crime,

This tendency to see and think in black-and-white terms is seen by non-Americans as part of traditional American culture, so it's likely you may have taken this attitude from time to time. The difficulty dealing with ambiguity and shades of gray is a tendency of people with an "authoritarian personality." These traits are highly correlated with racism and other types of bigotry and prejudice, and they are the most studied aspect of human personality. They are tendencies you want to acknowledge and then expand beyond—because they dramatically limit your creativity.

We see the results played out in all types fundamentalism, with its polarized thinking: black-white, good-evil, right-wrong. When you think in these terms, you limit your options. You have difficulty seeing shades of differences and similarities, difficulty dealing with ambiguity and uncertainty, difficulty separating a person's actions and ideas from the person herself. You risk demonizing everyone who is on the "other side"—and coming across as a zealot or extremist. Fundamentalists tend to focus on what happens to "sinners": big doses of guilt, shame, punishment, and humiliation. All this creates a climate of fear—hardly conducive to creativity or creative collaboration

Collaborative Teams

Collaborative teams must have good communication processes, and to be creative they must ask and answer the right questions. The communications process is absolutely crucial for creative collaboration among team members. Here are some key components.

Keep the Process Open

Avoid reaching closure too soon. Creative work is exploratory and in the early stages, everyone should check their disbelief and cynicism at the door. Become the innocent child. Reserve skepticism and doubt until assessment time. Keep communication open and nonjudgmental even though you will of course need measurable results at some point.

Focus on What You Are "For"

Shift your way of thinking from "I'm against that" to "I'm for this." Ask yourself, "If I'm against that, then what am I for?" For example, if you don't like the idea of packaging the product in plastic, are you *for* packaging it in recyclable cardboard? Instead of rejecting an idea you think is problematic, you can say "That's an interesting idea. I agree we need to change our package. Let's just explore one other option." Think in terms of doubling and redoubling ideas. Don't judge, evaluate, or criticize at any point in the process. Such positive-speak inspires confidence and nurtures the climate of openness to ideas.

Use Beginner's Mind

Try to pose questions that return the discussion to the state of the beginner's mind. You ask a question, get an answer, then ask why. Do that five times and you will understand the essence of the situation. You will break through a superficial understanding to reveal the more basic issues.

Get to Know Each Team Member

Use all your intelligences to get to know a member. For example, ask exploratory questions to find out what's important in life to that person. Put yourself inside his or her head, encouraging feelings of empathy and compassion. This will give you a sense of the team member's personality and will help you to speak that person's language.

Make Creative Space

Creative, collaborative teams need the right environment to do their thing. The ideal play-space consists of several paradoxical elements. It needs to be both:

1. Bounded (by one problem-opportunity or project)—and open (to explore it freely)

2. Safe (for wild ideas)—and charged with risk (the company must innovate or die)

3. Individualistic ideas are welcomed—and group guidance is sought (for example, a team leader reflects back the group voice at key times).

4. Little, individual ideas and stories are treasured—and so are big ideas, broad in scope and depth, that put all the little ideas into a framework or context

5. Working alone is supported—and team and organizational resources support each member, allowing and helping each person to contribute

6. Silence is okay—and speaking up is welcomed

Ask Key Questions

The team must decide how to structure itself and how to function in order to generate a high level of creativity. Penetrating questions the creativity team should ask include:

Who is included? Should you include everybody, all employees?

Who will lead? Who will take responsibility for seeing that agendas are set and carried out? Who will define the task, establish milestones, call it quits? Will it be the team as a whole, a leader, or both? Sometimes one or the other?

Who is the disciplinarian? The great continuing challenge of managing creativity is handling the tension between discipline and the free play of intuition, insight, inspiration. The team must decide who will play the role of disciplinarian or "store minder." How will the tension between minding the store and free play lead to meaningful conversation?

What's the agenda? What's the venue? What kind of audience? What for? What's the purpose? The end result or goal? The product, purpose, service, or process that you're after? How will people define and evaluate the "product"? How will they draw protective lines around it? Determine its fate? Does the team decide or does the leader decide, or both?

Where? Where does all of the above take place? Under what conditions?

Rules for Success—Team Collaborations

Here are three rules for success in creative collaboration.

Rule 1: Create or find a project that makes a difference

Some ways of doing this:

- Find what you're passionate about and what you intuitively feel is an emerging opportunity
- Talk with customers and colleagues and others about the bothersome issues they face.
- Ask people in your network about what's going on and what they're into

Rule 2: Be a great collaborative team player and colleague

- Think of yourself first as an effective team person.
- As a colleague, offer to help others who have their hands full.
- Bring together a diverse team and start a deep dialogue on a customer's problem—to ground people from different disciplines in something real and to allow them to think and work together. Express your thinking as honestly as you can, being open to other takes on the topic. Think of this process as passing a ball of energy back and forth until a creative, shared interpretation emerges.

Rule 3: Be an expert in a distinct area that creates solid value

Let people know who you are and what knowledge and skills you can contribute. Ask yourself, "What do I know how to do that's distinctly different?" or "What real distinctive value can I bring to the table in this project?" Create your own marketing brochure, a vita, based on accomplishments, especially in groups and creative teams. Publicize what you can do to add value or team zest to your next project. Get on the talent list of 5 CEO's, on other people's "Who's Who," on their preferred e-mail lists to boost your chances of making a contribution.

Steps to Starting a Creative Collaboration

To get creative collaboration going, think in terms of having collaborative conversations. These may have five steps.

Step 1. Clarify the purpose of the collaborative conversation

Clarify the specific purpose of the conversation. Why are we here? For example:

- To declare new possibilities or opportunities
- To create a community of commitment that will go for a possibility
- To create a strategic plan
- To reach goals, solve problems, or resolve a dispute

You can move an impossibility to a possibility by making a declaration—a shared commitment to a collaborative goal.

Ask yourself, what role should I play in this phase, who do I need to be? For example, a deeply purposeful, clear, and focused person.

Think of purpose as a guiding light, a navigating beacon. Think of clarifying the purpose as focusing the conversation like a laser beam. Think of the purpose as a container that can hold whatever happens in the conversation. Clarify how you will "frame" the purpose.

Consider asking the group to reflect on these kinds of questions:

1. Is there a clear purpose for the conversation consistent with what matters to all of us?

2. Have we clarified a purpose for the conversation that is attainable?

3. Are the issues and problems we've defined solvable?

4. Will the way we've framed the goal or problem give us the results we want?

5. Will the conversation move the collaboration and learning along?

Step 2. Gather divergent views

See divergent views more as a source of strength than a source of conflict.

Ask yourself who you need to be during this phase; for example, someone who is warm, outgoing, gracious, who sees other people's truths as something to learn from, who doesn't have to win, and who can listen.

Think in terms of empowering people to come to the table and to speak up honestly and respectfully. Treat everyone as colleagues regardless of official status differences. Acknowledge any unresolved issues that are relevant to the conversation. Recognize and validate the different opinions and viewpoints. Give up the need to be in agreement. It's more important at this point to get the differences on the table than to agree.

Create an environment where chaotic communication is okay, but slow down the conversation when people are being left out. People have different rates of thinking, talking, and integrating info. Take breaks when some people need time to digest the info. Remember, in any creative project, there's a period of chaos and confusion before the breakthrough to clarity when things fall into place and make sense.

Step 3. Build shared understanding of divergent views

The purpose is to allow people to expand their views to include those of others and to get on the same wavelength. Here are some suggestions:

- Weed out false assumptions about each other and varying viewpoints.

- Inquire into each others' thinking, express emotions constructively, recognize other's defensive reactions, and work through them.

- Have a spirit of curiosity about how other people see their world, themselves, the situation they're in, what they want to achieve, and how.

- Set aside your position for the moment and begin to ask questions and listen in a deep way to build shared understanding.

- Look for new ways of seeing yourself and the others, for new awareness than can create new openings for possibility and action.

Ask yourself who you need to be in this phase; for example, someone who is curious and asks questions with a real sense of curiosity, someone who enjoys listening. Think in terms of being real, honest, and a learner, of open-minded and open-hearted listening. Balance your desire to persuade assertively with the need to question with curiosity. Establish a trading zone where you can exchange something of value without having to agree on everything or even understand each others' basic assumptions (see the discussions of tradeoffs in the negotiation section).

Learn the stories of others in the group. Listen to what they say—for what they mean and how they think. Discuss all the issues that are important to this creative collaboration, even if you thought some were off-limits for discussion.

When hostile energy from a group member comes your way, try verbal Aikido, stepping aside mentally and letting it just go by without hooking you emotionally. Then suggest that the two of you find a way to move forward together, perhaps by asking some well-meaning, constructive questions.

Step 4. Create new options by connecting different views

The purpose is to explore ways to creatively connect different views with an eye toward creating dramatically new, surprising, even delightful solutions. Creativity is more likely to occur when you have people from different frames of reference who think and work together on a shared goal. A pitfall: creating emotional tension when the views seem irreconcilable, leading to disillusionment with the whole process. The goal is creative tension that leads to a creative breakthrough and resolution. Key focus: avoiding the pitfall of emotional tension and collaborative breakdown.

Think in terms of creation itself rather than artistic creativity. Invent new options by expanding your view to include others. There are always more possibilities and options than people are aware of—open up to them, search for them. Expand your view to encompass opposing views that may look incompatible. Focus on what really matters, on areas of overlap. Forget for the moment areas that you can't resolve. Think "both . . . and" instead of "either . . . or."

Try putting the challenge or problem in one sentence, brainstorming multiple options, using metaphors to generate new ideas, using analogies to distinguish what's missing and to solve practical problems, immersing yourself in all the info and then giving it time to incubate.

Step 5. Start a conversation for action

Think of the creative process as a spiral, originating with new ideas that you can't quite express, that are then developed through metaphors and analogies, and that finally end in a sketch, prototype, or scale model. This becomes a shared work space that allows you to see if you have a shared understanding of what to create and how, as well as to test your idea through a prototype to see if it really works.

Ask yourself who you need to be in this phase; for example, a practical doer, someone whose obsessive-compulsive behavior in the nuts and bolts of the project may be responsible for the difference between successful action and just another idea—or a tinkerer with a desire to act by building something one chunk at a time.

Use language in a way that goes beyond predictions, descriptions, and explanations—to carve out a new possibility "between the lines," to ignite passion in people's hearts and fascination in their minds, to cause people to jump into action.

At this stage, if the group is a work team, the chain of command is replaced by a network of commitments, communication, and support. It's like passing a ball of energy back and forth until the collaborative project is brought to completion.

Think in terms of getting prototypes completed quickly rather than in terms of elaborate planning—in terms of creative frenzy rather than leisurely pace. You can alter your strategies and plans as you take action. Too much planning, analysis, and time douses the fires of creative passion.

Making bold promises has a powerful impact on transforming your possibility into reality. Here's what you need in order to make a bold promise work:

- A committed speaker—someone who makes a bold promise and follows through.
- A committed listener—someone who holds you accountable and encourages you to make bold promises that stretch your mind and skills
- Conditions of satisfaction—what will be delivered? Produced?
- A time frame

Creativity Showcase

Creative Collaboration Among Professionals

Some innovative solutions to current problems—for your information and inspiration—and as food for thought.   Could the following story have implications for professionals that you know?

Problems—Limited Ideas, Opportunities

Independent graphic artists and designers love the freedom to be themselves and to follow their own impulses. But there's a practical limit to the types of jobs an independent can take on. Most can handle only a few moderately-sized projects at one time. Cash flow can be erratic, with projects being won in a feast-or-famine pattern. And independents are somewhat isolated. Even if they have several assistants, they usually have no real peers available to consult or communicate with on a regular basis. Bottom line: they have great independence but limited opportunities and creative input.

Creative Solution: Partnering

Pentagram is a collaborative partnership of design professionals founded in London in 1962 by three designers. They now have offices in New York and San Francisco as well. With 17 partners, 160 employees, and annual revenues of $25 million, they are a mid-sized design firm. But they are at the top of the heap in power, clout, and prestige, and partners win awards with amazing regularity (Barker 1999).

Their client list includes United Airlines, Hewlett-Packard, Williams-Sonoma, Gymboree, New York's American Museum of Natural History, and London's Tate Gallery. Partnerships are notoriously problematic—the type of business setup most vulnerable to abuse and instability. So how has Pentagram lured highly successful independent designers to their fold and kept them there?

From the beginning the founding partners held to two key principles

1) Each partner runs his or her own design practice as a separate profit center within Pentagram. That means each one determines which work to take on, how much to charge, hires a design team, and decides how much to pay each team member, using Pentagram's general employer guidelines. As a result, partners retain their own design presence in the world, and a "Pentagram style" does not exist. The only requirement is that partners must remain profitable over time.

2) Partners are equal and get exactly the same salaries and bonuses each year. Making financial competition a non-issue encourages partners to share work with less-busy partners rather than hoarding it.

Recruiting new partners takes at least six months, and all partners get involved. The criteria are 1) doing high-quality work, 2) running one's own successful design firm, 3) being a responsible person, and 4) being the kind of person we'd want to hang out with.

What do the partners like most about creative collaboration at Pentagram?

- Collaboration enables you to do larger, more exciting projects.

- Professional image is enhanced. You're part of a well-known firm with an impressive office in a prestigious location. Image attracts more interesting, lucrative project offers.

- Larger projects mean you get to work with CEOs instead of their reports, which allows you to *think with* clients, not just execute for them. You may get to influence the entire company image—from stationery to buildings.

- The clout of your partners opens up new opportunities for you. Knowing you can consult with a partner who's an expert in an area you're new to allows you to take on new types of projects that expand your skills

- You get ideas from hanging out with partners—and you learn from them.

- With peers as partners, you get challenged and inspired.

- The shared income provides a safety net during "famine" times.

Win-Win Negotiation

Creative Intelligence involves many skills, among them creative negotiation strategies and techniques. Your creativity can be inspired and boosted by interactions with others, sometimes in work teams, others times in customer conferences, and in all types of business situations. You may need to sell your ideas in order to influence others to listen to you, to try a new product or service, and in many other types of situations. Win-win negotiation strategies include

- Get off to a good start
- Create tradeoffs and package deals
- Frame your offers attractively
- Keep the negotiation moving
- Negotiate around barriers and stalemates
- Know when and how to close a deal

Negotiation skills are also invaluable for resolving conflicts you may have with others or for leading conflict resolution among team members. You'll learn about this type of negotiation after you cover the negotiation basics.

Get Off to a Good Start

At the negotiation session, you want to get things off to a good start by preparing some good openers, building trust, sharing information, and asking questions to fill in your information gaps. You'll want to get all the issues on the table, frame options in ways that appeal to the other party, and focus on relevant information rather than just what's available or vivid. Most important, you'll want to think in terms of a win-win deal.

Technique 1: If You're Selling, Make Your Pitch

If the purpose of the negotiation is to first sell your idea, your first challenge may be setting up a meeting. You may have to ask yourself, "Who has the ear of the person(s) with the power to buy this idea and make it a reality?" In turn, you may need to formulate a strategy for finding the right go-between who will help you set up a meeting. Do your homework. Don't skimp on the research. You'll probably get only one opportunity to meet with the best person for supporting your idea, so make that meeting count.

Pitch the Paradox

Once you get a meeting lined up, you'll probably have very little time to make your pitch. If you're successful, negotiations about the terms of the deal come later. So make your pitch seductive. The heart of any pitch is the way you handle the paradox of having a hot new idea but one that's not so new it would be ahead of its time. In fact, pitching is really an exercise in paradox. You must show that you have something totally fresh, original, and new that's never been done before. Yet, you must prove that this type of thing has been wildly successful before. If you can find a way to create that paradox, you'll probably sell the idea.

To bridge the paradox, find a success story that has some commonality with your idea, yet doesn't overlap in a way that makes your idea seem familiar. *It's the Microsoft of telephone systems; just as Windows provided essential PC programs, my G-World provides necessary telecommunications links.* Notice you're speaking in the present tense. You're already experiencing G-World's success. Your idea is not in the same field as the computer software you're comparing it with, but the situations are similar. Both involve similar problems and opportunities calling for new ideas.

Anticipate Resistances

Put yourself inside the head of the persons you're selling. What will they be looking for? What kinds of criticisms and questions are they likely to ask? Test your pitch for gaps and contradictions by asking friends to play devil's advocate, looking for weak spots. What kinds of fears may they have? Two very common fears you must consider:

1. If I say yes to this idea and it fails, I'm in trouble.

2. If I say no to this idea and a competitor makes it a great success, I'm in trouble.

As you make you pitch, will your primary focus be proving your idea won't fail? Or will you focus on what a great success it is and imply that someone is going to be a great winner here?

Make It Hot

Once you've covered these bases, keep preparing by ask yourself these kinds of questions:

- *Is my idea pitchable?* Can I make it clear and deliciously tempting in one sentence? If not, you either don't have a pitchable idea, or you haven't refined it well enough.

- *Can I give my pitch in my sleep?* You must know your story inside and out. Tell it as many times in as many different ways as you need to until you have it down cold.

- *Do I exude passion?* If you aren't excited about your idea, it's highly unlikely that anyone else will be. Either re-think it or get in touch with your passion.

- *Can I see my idea as already in place and wildly successful?* Visualize successful completion over and over until it's in your bones. You must sound as if you've already experienced this reality and that it blew you away.

Once you can answer yes to all these questions, you're ready

Technique 2: If You're Negotiating, Prepare Good Openers

As you prepare good openers, keep in mind that win-win negotiation is a way of finding out each side's perceived needs and exploring ways of meeting those needs. It's a process of mutual education, an adventure in how to get to *yes*. It's *not* confession time, it's not a sparring match, and it's not an arm-twisting session.

Have several openings ready. Remember, *your first few sentences are usually throw-aways* because nobody remembers them. Therefore, make them merely a warm, agreeable hello. Focus on the sentences that follow for giving introductory information. Address the person with power, looking directly at this person. Use the key words that will appeal to that person's personality type. For example, use:

- *what* for an aggressive type: *This is what I propose to do for you*

- *how* for a detail person: *This is how I'm going to get it done.*

- *who* for a social type: *Here's who will benefit from this.*

- *why* for an analytical or nice-guy type: Here's *why* this needs to happen.

Focus first and foremost on the category that the person with power is most interested in, while touching on the other categories also. If you don't know the types you're dealing with, speak quickly to each category and watch for responses. One way to begin is to review the basics of why you're all here.

If it's a team decision, and the team is made up of varied types, you'll need to skillfully balance all categories, paying careful attention to responses. The aggressive member will probably try to run the process, but a detail or social person may have more actual decision making influence. In fact, the team's strategy may be to let one person play aggressor while the real decision maker sits back and watches.

Technique 3: Build Trust and Share Information

Often both sides end up with a better deal if you find some good tradeoffs. But you must build trust and share information in order to get there, which also builds ongoing relationships.

You and the other party may discuss a divide-the-plate rule before sharing information. One strategy is to set a rule for sharing any surplus benefit before exchanging confidential information. If you distrust each other, you could also agree to an independent review of all the financial assessments.

Speaking of distrust, you're aware that con artists exist, but how do you spot them when they show up for a negotiation? Ask yourself the follow questions:

- *Do I feel uncomfortable or do I doubt the other person?*

- *Is the deal too good to be true?*

- *Does the other person's behavior seem congruent, a fit, for their position?*

- *Does what they're saying fit with what I know about the situation?* If not, ask some questions you already know the answers to—and see if they give you correct information.

You need to be able to recognize con-artist tactics so you can devise an effective response. You also need to monitor your own actions to be sure you don't naively project a bit of a con-artist image. Some con-artist techniques to be wary of are:

- Repetition—saying the same things over and over in order to break down your resistance

- Good guy-bad guy routine. One person plays the good guy who starts off the negotiation and establishes a bond with you. Another person plays the bad guy who comes in and makes demands or refuses to concede. Then the good guy appeals to you to reach an agreement on the bad guy's terms.

- Righteous indignation intended to make you feel guilty for doubting their integrity
- Victim routine—acting nervous, fearful, sad, or dumb in order to catch you off guard, appeal to your protective side, play to your guilt and thus get their way
- Flattery, flirting, and other insincere seductive behavior
- Big Daddy or Big Mama—playing a nurturing role designed to lull you into a false sense of security, believing that your interests will be protected
- Verbal assaults intended to rattle you into agreeing

Break up these games by refusing to play your role. Don't play the rescuer or persecutor to the victim, the child to a parent type, or the victim to the aggressor or bad guy. Find a way to suggest that both parties deal with each other as adults in a straightforward manner. Consider whether you really want to reach an agreement with the people who are playing these win-lose games.

Remember, in win-win negotiation, both sides are seen as basically equal, even if one has some advantage. If *both* parties are committed to meeting the basic needs of both sides and there is mutual trust, you normally can work out an agreement.

Technique 4: Ask Questions to Fill Information Gaps

You know that the more information you have, the greater your negotiating power. So use the negotiation itself to fill in gaps in your information base. If the other person is not answering your questions in a useful way, consider giving away some information, which may break the information deadlock. When you give some information, the other party tends to return some information. You therefore stimulate the information sharing you need to create a mutually beneficial agreement. You may not want to specify your best alternative, but you could offer information concerning the relative importance of the issues to your side. Exchanging this kind of information can help you and the other party find side benefits, use them to make some tradeoffs, and end up with a deal. Here are some key questions to ask.

- Are the money resources there?
- Are the time resources there?
- Are qualified people online?
- How's the team spirit?
- Is technology up-to-date?

Create Tradeoffs and Package Deals

Most negotiations end in some sort of trade-off, where each side gives up something of lesser value to them in return for something of greater value. But if you think in terms of a *fixed plate of goodies*, where you either win or lose each goodie, you overlook strategies that could work to the advantage of both sides. For example, there may be many side-benefits that you could bring onto the bargaining table, and once they're there, you would have many possibilities for tradeoffs that could benefit both sides. But you won't bother to look for them because of your self-limiting belief in a fixed plate. Yet, some of these new pieces might benefit only their side, but would cost your side little or nothing—and now you'd have a chip to trade for something you want. You can see that beliefs in a *fixed-plate* and a *win-lose* strategy are self-limiting beliefs.

A related self-limiting belief is, *what's good for them must be bad for us.* Studies indicate that most people would reject a proposal presented by the other side and would accept the identical proposal if presented by someone from their own side. To move beyond such beliefs, be creative and pretend the proposal came from a neutral third party. Examine it first to see how it could benefit you, what advantages it offers. Then look to see what it might cost you, the disadvantages it would impose. Be open to giving up a goodie that's not very valuable to you in order to gain one that is.

Technique 1: Get All the Issues on the Table

If you focus on one issue or resource at a time, wrapping it up before going to the next issue, you're not discovering side benefits. Once you resolve an issue, it's rare that both sides want to go back and start over on it. Instead, try to get all the ideas on the table with the goal of generating alternative packages of issues. As you discuss the whole range of issues, you increase the chances of discovering new side benefits to put on the table. Most important, this approach increases the number of tradeoffs that are possible. While resolving one issue at a time seems rational, clean, and methodical, it's not the most effective approach.   A messy, even chaotic, approach is better suited to deal-making—and to deals that both sides will like to live with.

Technique 2: Look for Tradeoffs and Package Deals

Get as much information on the table as you can before making a proposal or responding to one. Locate all possible side benefits that could expand the plate of goodies and possible concessions that allow flexibility. These create more possibilities for tradeoffs.

Next, put together several package offers that are acceptable to you and present them all at the same time. By making multiple offers at the same time, you can collect valuable information about what's important to the other party. At the same time, you appear to be more flexible. For example, you can put together several job packages with varying combinations of job responsibilities and conditions, salary, benefits, and perks.

Technique 3: Explore Differences and Options

Learn to think of differences as opportunities rather than barriers. Typical areas of difference are expectations about what's likely to happen, risk preferences, time preferences, and cost-cutting possibilities. Look also at possibilities for adding more resources and finding new, creative options.

Expectation Differences

If the two parties have different expectations about what's likely to happen, maybe you can bet on your expectation and the other party can bet on theirs. For example, in a joint venture you think the greatest profit will be in the first year and the other party thinks it will be in the second year. You can agree to split the profit 80-20 the first year and 20-80 the second year. Such contingent contracts are bets that allow the parties to agree, even when they have different perceptions or opinions of the future. These differences can enhance the flexibility of the negotiation, increasing the chances of making a deal.

Risk Preference Differences

Rather than seeing one party's relative risk aversion as an obstacle to negotiation, you can use it as an opportunity to trade. One side gets a guarantee in return for increasing the expected value to the other. For example, *I'll guarantee you a 10 percent profit up to $10,000 if I can have 70 percent of any profit over $10,000.* Different risk-sharing strategies allow for trades that might not otherwise occur.

Time Preference Differences

When the other party feels strongly about some time issue, such as receiving earlier payment or delivery, it's an opportunity for a trade. Time preferences can include when to move, when to pay, when to receive shipment, when to ship, and any other matter of timing.

Cost-Cutting Possibilities

What would make it less costly for the other party to compromise on the primary issue? Cost-cutting calls for one party to get what it wants while the other has the costs associated with its concession reduced or eliminated. For example, you're willing to pay half the costs of shipping if the other party will use the shipping line you prefer, one that brings it to your door. The result is a high level of joint benefit, not because one party wins but because the other party suffers less. Cost-cutting means the party who makes the major concession receives something to meet the specific goals they gave up. It's similar to a tradeoff, but it focuses on reducing or eliminating costs for the party that makes a concession.

Sweetener Possibilities

If you have any added resources the other party wants, consider how you can add something to sweeten the deal. This can work, but only in areas where the parties' interests are not mutually exclusive. For example, I'll share a customer mailing list with you. It has some value to you and it will cost me little or nothing to provide it.

New Options

At a stalemate? Look for totally new options. Finding creative options often hinges on redefining the conflict for each side, identifying each side's underlying interests, and brainstorming for a wide variety of potential solutions.

Post-Settlement Options

After you reach an initial agreement, you can propose that you continue looking for a better one for both parties, but agree to be bound by this initial agreement, even if you don't find a better one. Agree that if you *do* find a better agreement, both of you will share the surplus benefits. This offers both of you a last chance to find the best deal with limited risk to either party.

Frame Your Offers Attractively

How you present the options that are available strongly affects the other side's willingness to make a deal. Frames include what the other person stands to gain, what they must give up, what you stand to gain, what you will give up, or what you'll both gain and give up. The what-you'll-gain focus is obviously very attractive, but the you-may-miss-out can also work. Framing can have a large impact on a side's willingness to take a risk, especially when they're uncertain about future events or outcomes. The base point the other side uses to evaluate an alternative as either a gain or a loss determines the positive or negative frame through which they view their options—and their later willingness to accept or reject those options—so you must play to the right base point.

Technique 1: Focus on Potential Gains

When you focus on what you can gain, the profits to be made, you're more likely to be concessionary about expenses or other side-benefits to the other person—and to make more deals—than when you focus on minimizing your expenses. It's true that minimizing expenses on average will result in a higher average profit per deal. On other hand, people who focus on the gains from making a deal tend to make more deals and their overall profitability is significantly greater.

For example, you and Joe sell computers. Joe focuses on minimizing his own expenses, so he refuses to pay for shipping, financing, or installation. He gets his full price and makes buyers pay all expenses, but he closes fewer deals than you. You focus on making some profit from a deal, so you're willing to absorb some of those expenses in order to get your price and make a deal. Your flexibility helps you close more deals than Joe, but on average you make less profit per deal than Joe. By the end of the year, you've made more money than Joe.

Understand Buyer and Seller Frames. Being a buyer or seller creates a natural frame. Sellers think about (frame) the transaction in terms of the dollars exchanged and see the process as gaining resources (dollars I get by selling). Buyers may frame the deal in terms of the loss of dollars (dollars I must give up). When you're the buyer (employer, for example), you want to frame your offer in terms of dollars the seller (applicant or employee) will get. When you're the seller (employee), you'll frame your offer in terms of what a great asset the buyer will get and the many great benefits he or she will gain.

Frame in Gain Terms. If you frame your proposal in terms of the other person's potential gain, you're more likely to induce them to assume a positive frame of reference—what they have to gain—and they're more likely to make concessions—in order to make a deal and thus take advantage of that gain. You can also emphasize the inherent risk in the negotiation situation for them—risks of waiting, of someone else getting the item, the terms being withdrawn and less attractive terms being left—and contrast that with the opportunity for a sure gain that you're offering.

For mediators, framing may be best used when meeting with each party separately. What you frame as positive for one is usually seen as negative by the other.

Technique 2: Frame in Terms of Movement from the Status Quo

The status quo is one of the most common base points. Most people evaluate their options in terms of whether they represent a gain or loss from where they stand now. It's surprisingly easy to modify what people include as part of their status quo.

Role of Attachment. Sellers often price items to include not only the market value but the value of the emotional attachment the seller has to the item. Simply owning something frequently increases the value people place upon an asset because they view giving it up as something of a loss. For example, you're interested in selling your expertise by doing some part-time free-lance work. But you do like the status quo of having evenings and weekends free from professional work. You may say, *If I can't average at least $100 an hour, I won't take a contract*. That becomes your (the seller's) base point. However, the buyers of your services have no emotional attachment to your time. Their base point is what they must pay for comparable services somewhere else.

Role of Risk. Suppose your bottom-line base point is $100, and someone offers you $90.

- The risk-averse choice is to accept an offered settlement.
- The risk-seeking choice is to wait for potential future concessions or better offers.

Obviously, which base point you choose determines whether you frame your decision as negative or positive. With a risk-averse frame, you think, *The $90 is close to the amount I thought I'd get and I have a contract nailed down; I'm happy*. With a risk-seeking frame, you think, *I took the $90, but I probably should have held out because someone could have come along who would be willing to give me $100 an hour*.

Role of Perspective. Putting things in perspective is an important part of framing—for example proposing a relatively small add-on *after* a large contract has been agreed upon. Suppose you're offering to complete a project for $900 (base price), one you think will take about 10 hours. After you agree on the $900 contract, you can frame a $50 add-on as a reimbursement of certain expenses. The $50 would loom large if you presented it earlier—or if you were making only $10 an hour, and the contract (base price) totaled $90. This is how base price affects people's perspective. Why do you suppose nearly half of new car buyers purchase extended warranties averaging $800, when they're mostly pure profit for the dealers? Only $130 on average goes to cover actual repairs, $110 goes to the auto manufacturer for administrative costs, and $560 is left for dealer profit. The reason is probably that the base price in the negotiation is the total price of the car, so the cost of the warranty seems small in comparison.

Technique 3: Play to the Belief in Fairness and Equity

How you frame a problem will affect how others judge the fairness of the solution. For example, employees will see a change in salary framed as a *wage cut* as unfair, but they may see a small wage increase that won't even cover inflation as more acceptable. That's because people think wages should go up, not down. They think of money as an arbitrary unit in dollar terms rather than in terms of money's real buying power—real dollars adjusted for inflation.

Try 50-50 Splits. Research indicates that people prefer equal over unequal outcomes, regardless of the reason or situation. People tend to view 50-50 splits as fair. Actually the fairness of a 50-50 split depends on the comparative fairness of each side's original offer. People who are aware of the appeal of the very term *50-50 split* realize that a variety of 50-50 splits using various original offers can be pulled out of a hat. For example, as seller you can set your asking price a little higher than normal, prompting a higher counter-offer by the buyer, and then agree to split the difference. People also use social comparison; for example, an employee compares her raise to the raise her male colleague got.

Be Generous to Set a Win-Win Tone. As a negotiator, your generosity and helpfulness tends to generate positive emotions from the other party. This makes people like you, feel more positive about human nature in general at the time, admire your problem-solving ability, and feel less aggressive and hostile. In some studies, when one negotiator gave the other a small gift, it induced a good mood. They were able to reach more creative and plate-expanding agreements, using tradeoffs, than negotiators who didn't give a small gift. The other party was less likely to use highly competitive or contentious tactics. Researchers also concluded that a positive mood can increase the need-based illusion of superiority.

Promote Positive Emotions. How do you avoid becoming angry and walking out, or having the other party do so? When you become angry, you tend to focus more on getting back at the other side than on creating a good deal for yourself. Studies show that even when you're in a positive relationship, you care far more about how your outcome *compares* with what the other side got than the actual *value* of what you got. But if the other side offers you several options to choose from, the comparisons become less important than simply getting the option with highest value to you.

Fairness and emotional considerations affect negotiations profoundly. You must understand the impact of these influences on your own judgments and decisions. You must anticipate the same influences on the other party's behavior. When you choose your negotiation strategies, keep in mind the real emotions and concerns for fairness that everyone has. Focus on thought trains that lead to expansive emotions—your own and the other person's.

To frame your proposals in ways that appeal to the other party, tune in to what *they might* be thinking and feeling. Negotiators who take into account the other party's perspective are most successful in negotiation simulations, according to research. They can better predict the other's behavior. This is important enough to highlight:

In a negotiation, if each side understands and can explain the viewpoint of the other, it increases the likelihood of reaching a negotiated solution.

Technique 4: Aim for a Win-Win Deal

Win-win negotiation is based on trust, a goodwill attitude, meeting the needs of both sides, and generating side-benefits that can lead to tradeoffs that mean a better deal for everyone concerned. A major goal is to build trust and enhance relationships. You can do this by focusing on understanding the other persons, remembering that you can't change anyone's mind but you might influence people to change their own minds. You also do it by separating the issues from the positions of people on each side. Focus on the issues and ways to resolve them that both sides can live with.

Keep the Negotiation Moving

After getting the negotiation session off to a good start, you want to keep it moving to closure. You need a crucial set of negotiation skills in order to move beyond stalemates, manage surprise moves, and overcome barriers that emerge during the meeting. You need to avoid typical pitfalls by getting adequate information, to negotiate around stalemates and barriers, to be cooperative but not a doormat, to know when to cut your losses and when and how to close a deal.

Technique 1: Ask Yourself Key Questions

Here are some self-questions that will help you avoid common mistakes that block negotiations and prevent successful closure.

1. Am I pursuing a negotiated course of action only to justify an earlier decision?
2. Am I assuming that what's good for me is bad for the other party, or vice versa?
3. Am I irrationally affected by an initial offer or base price?
4. Is there another frame that would put a different perspective on the negotiation?
5. Am I too affected by available information and ignoring other valid but less available information?
6. Have I fully thought about the decision of the other party?
7. Am I placing too much confidence in my own judgment?

Ask the same seven questions about the other party's behavior.

Technique 2: Avoid Typical Pitfalls by Getting Information

Pitfalls include conceding to demands when you should cut your losses, not predicting the results of winning (the winner's curse), focusing on the wrong information, and not getting adequate counsel and advice. You can minimize all these potential problems.

Know When to Cut Your Losses

Realize that the time and money you've already invested are sunk costs. You can't get them back and you should forget them when deciding what to do next. What you do next depends on the current situation and what you project for the future. Generate all the possible alternatives. Then evaluate your best estimate of the *future* costs and benefits of each alternative, forgetting past investments except for lessons you've learned from them.

Misdirected persistence occurs primarily due to misdirected ego. You commit yourself to getting something, the commitment biases your perception and judgment, causes you to make irrational decisions in order to manage what others think of you, which leads to an upward spiral of competition to get the thing you want.

Some corporate cultures see this as sticking with a bad decision—in the name of consistency. Top management should make it clear that sticking with a bad decision in order to protect personal image won't be tolerated.   People should be rewarded for actions and decisions that bring good results. They should know when to cut their losses. Outcome is more important than consistency.

Avoid the Winner's Curse

What will happen if you win and get the deal you want? Will it really be a good deal for you? In order to make a good deal, you need enough information to know what you're getting into and how the assets you're acquiring are likely to perform or work out.   If you cannot get adequate information, you can reduce your risks by assuming the information you're missing would be bad news that uncovers flaws in the asset. If you assume all is as it seems and pay accordingly, you win the asset but you must deal with what's commonly known as the winner's curse: you got what you wanted but it's not such a good deal.

Problem: Imbalance of Information. The key lesson of the winner's curse for negotiators is that one side, usually the seller, often has much better information than the other. Though everyone is familiar with the adage *buyer beware*, it's difficult to put this idea into practice when the other side knows more than you. Against a better informed party, usually the seller, your expected return from making a deal decreases dramatically.

Buyer Beware. In fact, when you're the buyer, especially when buying used goods, remember that the sellers have selectively chosen to sell these goods, and you have an information disadvantage. So, how can you avoid the winner's curse?

- Consider the seller's reputation—is it positive and reliable?

- Try to get warranties or guarantees that have a reliable track record.

- Ask yourself if you can rely on an ongoing relationship that the seller wants to maintain.

- Get advice from trusted experts.

- Reduce the amount you're willing to pay.

When you can't get adequate information to make a good decision about a deal, consider the odds of winning or losing, assume that what you don't know is bad news, reduce the price you're willing to pay accordingly, and walk away if the seller won't meet your upper price limit.

Focus on the Right Information

People tend to focus on the information that's up front in their minds, what's readily available to them, and what's most visible or memorable.   Unfortunately such information may be totally irrelevant to negotiating a good deal.

Readily-Available-Information Illusion.   Things or events you've experienced the most frequently are usually the easiest to remember. They're more readily available in your memory. However, the more vivid the event, the more likely you are to remember it, too. Something easy to recall seems more numerous than something more difficult to recall.   But such easy information may not be the most relevant information, so it can cause you to overestimate or underestimate the value of the other side's offer.

Vivid-Information Illusion. If you're normal, you tend to overestimate the probability of an unlikely event occurring if the memories you associate with the event are especially vivid and thus easier to recall. For example, if you actually see a house burn, you're more likely to believe that your house could burn than if you just read in the newspaper that a house burned.

Carry this idea into your negotiation. On the one hand, if you present information in colorful or emotionally vivid ways, you're more likely to influence the decisions of the other party—compared to making an equally informative presentation in a dull, matter-of-fact way. Both the amount of information and you way you present it can provide you with power and influence over the negotiation outcome. On the other hand, when you make your own negotiation decisions, identify and use truly relevant and reliable, not just available or vivid, information.

Get Good Counsel and Advice

You're in the process of becoming a skilled negotiator, but you can never know it all. What can you do to increase your chances of making a good deal?

- Remind yourself that you're most likely to be overconfident when your knowledge is limited—that's when you could use some expert advice.

- Ask yourself why your decision might be wrong, or not quite right, and write down the reasons—to help you see obvious problems in your judgment.

- Seek objective opinions about your position from a neutral party.

- Focus on how the other party probably views the situation and the rightness of their position as well as your own.

- Ask yourself whether you or others are operating from need-based illusions.

It's common for people to distort their perceptions of situations to make themselves feel more competent and secure, resulting in need-based illusions that motivate them. Such illusions make a situation seem more palatable, while influencing decision making and negotiation abilities. These illusions include the illusion of superiority, illusion of optimism, and illusion of control.

Illusion of superiority. You give yourself more responsibility for your own successes and take less responsibility for your own failures, but you hold other people responsible when they fail and don't give them credit when they succeed. Negotiators are especially likely to believe that they're more flexible, purposeful, competent, fair, honest, and cooperative than their opponents.

Illusion of optimism. You underestimate your chances of experiencing *bad* future events and overestimate the likelihood that you'll experience *good* future events.

Illusion of control You believe that you have more control over outcomes than you really do, even in such obviously random events as throwing dice.

Illusion that contradictory information is irrelevant. When you hold certain beliefs or expectations, you tend to ignore information that contradicts them. You don't seek to disprove an initial belief and are more likely to take at face value information you agree with and scrutinize more carefully information you don't agree with. A more useful role is to play devil's advocate. Realize that your initial strategy may not work and seek to disconfirm it by searching for new information. If you aren't open to disconfirming information, you'll have a harder time adapting when confronted by unexpected circumstances in a negotiation.

Negotiate Around Barriers and Stalemates

Constantly reassess the situation as the negotiation unfolds. If you're open and flexible, ready to modify your plan in ways that will help you make a good deal, you increase your chances of making that deal.

Technique 1: Recognize a Stalemate

How will you know when the negotiation stalls? Look for such signs as the following.

- The process is heading backwards.
- The other side switches negotiation styles.
- The other side becomes extreme or makes unreasonable demands.

What can you do? Your major options include calling for a brief break, scheduling another meeting, or ending the effort, although normally you don't want to be the part that calls it off.

Technique 2: Know How to Reassess

Your best bet is usually to call for a break to give you time to reassess, incorporate new information, and reformulate your strategy. Ask yourself such questions as:

- What's causing the blockage? What is the root problem here? Is it the apparent problem or an underlying one we haven't recognized? Is it a side problem? Is it something that happened earlier, such as a concession or statement made that someone now regrets or resents?

- What's happened so far? Review verbal and nonverbal messages and the sequence of events up to this point.

- Are there any critical messages, verbal or nonverbal, that you're failing to send?

- Are you pushing too hard, hanging on too tight to your bottom-line goals? Do you need to lighten up?

- Did you learn anything in the recent interaction that changes your assessment of the other party's price limit or interests, or the importance of issues?

- What's your updated assessment of the bargaining zone?

- Where should you now look for trades?

- Do you need to press for closure in order to move things forward?

- Do you need to improve your decision processes?

- What are the decision processes of the other party?

- Do you need to hold a caucus with your negotiation team to decide what to do next?

- Do you need to make some phone calls to get information or advice?

Technique 3: Try a Problem-Solving Mode

When you resume the negotiation, consider using a problem-solving mode and to identify problems that either side perceives. Is there a problem that could fatally block reaching an agreement? Why? Deal with that problem now, or determine whether dealing with other issues first could lead to a solution of that problem further down the road. Next, work on problems you feel you can solve. List issues in a workable sequence for resolving. This will give both sides a sense of forward movement.

Technique 4: Know When and How to Use Persuasion

Perhaps you see an approach to resolving the blockage, but you need to influence the other side that this is the best approach. Consider this sequence of persuasion:

- begin with an easy-to-resolve issue

- send the most attractive or acceptable message first

- present both sides of the issues

- be open and flexible about possible solutions

- repeat the benefits of reaching an agreement

Technique 5: Try Other Tactics

Consider these tactics for breaking a stalemate.

- Suggest brainstorming possible problems and solutions and ways to move forward.

- Ask several questions that you're sure will bring a *yes* response from the other side, shifting the process to a positive mode.

- Send up at least three or four trial balloons, what-ifs, never just one. The responses can give you clues about what the other side is thinking and feeling and can help lead to a solution. Ask them for suggestions and think creatively together.

- Present four alternative solutions to the problem, placing the alternative you prefer as third in the sequence. Aggressive persons tend to want to say *no*, and doing so a couple of times gives them satisfaction, but if they want to reach an agreement, they're likely to say *yes* the third time around.

- Make a concession or two, dramatizing them to stress their magnitude for you.

- Can you write up and sign what you've agreed to up this point and even act on this agreement, saving the remaining problems to resolve later?

Technique 6: Go Deeper to Identify Tough Barriers

If you're still blocked, consider what's going on in the following areas:

- What's the level of trust?

- Are both sides really listening?

- What are the needs of both sides at this point?

- Does one side seem to be winning and the other side losing?

- What new alternatives might meet the needs of both sides?

What if both sides conclude that an agreement is not possible at this time? Now's the time to be philosophical and to avoid showing anger, bitterness, or other contracting emotions. Remember that you may be able to work together at a future date. See if you can get the other side to say why they can't agree or negotiate further. What do each of you want to say about the negotiation process? By discussing the problem, each side may learn something, so at least mutual education will result from the time and effort spent.

Technique 7: Handle Surprise Moves

What if the other side makes a surprise move? Surprises may range from learning new information about the history of the current situation to where you'll meet or what time you'll start or finish. See if you can turn the surprise into an opportunity. This requires quick thinking on your feet and looking for options. Remain polite and cooperative. Becoming angry or irritable is likely to block your ability to later turn the change to your advantage.

Technique 8: Know How to Deal with Frustration

What if the other persons become frustrated, bored, or tired? Clues that this is occurring include interrupting often, drumming fingers on the table, kicking the floor, studying the wallpaper or pictures, darting eye movements, and packing up their papers. When this occurs, shift what you're doing and try this:

- Summarize what's been agreed upon.

- Repeat the concessions you've already made.

- Ask them to be more specific about what they want.

- Offer new concessions or favors.

- Ask for a brief break or suggest continuing the meeting on another day.

Tune into the other persons' need for pacing the negotiation and be considerate. Always keep in mind the timing and try to intuit when the time is right to push for closure and agreement. It usually pays to avoid unnecessary conflict by cooperating as long as the other side does.

- *As a general rule, don't be the first to walk away.*

Know When and How to Close a Deal

All your efforts will come to naught unless you know when and how to close a deal. You must recognize when it is time to move toward closure. You must understand how to finalize the terms of the deal so that all are clear about the agreement. Finally, you must follow up to be sure the agreement is carried out properly if you want to build a credible reputation and ongoing business relationship.

Technique 1: Recognize When It's Time to Close

Your goal is to make a good deal or to reach a resolution of some kind. How do you know when you're nearing that goal? Ask such questions as:

- *Are both sides coming to an understanding?*
- *Can I see what we both need in order to do business together?*
- *Are we starting to work out an agreement that will settle some conflict between us?*

Intuition and timing are crucial to recognizing when it's time to go for an agreement and close the negotiation.

Technique 2: Finalize the Terms

When both sides say they're in agreement, refer to your notes to finalize the terms of the agreement. Your notes should show the concessions, compromises, and other points that have been agreed to during the negotiation process. As part of the agreement, is it necessary to designate how future disagreements will be handled? If so, do you need to discuss this now?

If the deal calls for a written agreement, consider having both parties sign a contract or a preliminary document, perhaps a draft you've brought with you. You may add key information or mark out or change certain clauses. Even a handwritten agreement done on the spot is usually legal. The purpose is to nail down the major points of agreement in writing while they're fresh in everyone's mind. If appropriate, a final version of the document can be signed later.

Technique 3: Follow Up to Build Trust

Remember to follow up. In order to continue building trust and laying the foundation for further business or good relationships, follow through on your part of the agreement.

- Do everything you agreed to do.
- If you have problems following through, contact the other side and work through the problems.
- Be available when they need you.
- Maintain a positive relationship by such actions as mentioning the benefits of the agreement and touching base even when you don't need to discuss the agreement.

Conflict Resolution: Creative Clashes

Diverse perceptions, viewpoints, and ideas are essential to spark creative ideas. When ideas clash, the results can be highly creative. But the members or their leader must apply some negotiating skills in order to moderate conflict and make it a win-win situation.

You can use many of the negotiating skills and procedures we've just discussed. As a leader, you'll find many opportunities to resolve conflicts among employees, groups, and perhaps even organizations. Without the right skills and expertise, conflicts are a headache, even a nightmare. With them, conflicts become opportunities to create, innovate, contribute, and lead.

Techniques include thinking in terms of win-win outcomes, letting both sides air their views, helping people find the root cause of the conflict problem, identifying the resolution strategies of the parties, creating proposals for solution, and reaching a resolution that all can live with.

Technique 1: Manage Conflict as a Learning Process

If you're the leader of your group, you have the greatest influence on how conflict is handled. If you watchful for signs of differences of opinion and see that they are considered and respected, you'll teach your people by your actions that conflict can be constructive. Use such approaches as including everyone, sharing information, and building others' self-esteem. Tune into how people are feeling, draw people out in order for all to understand what's happening, listen between the lines, support honest expression, verbalize what you sense is going on, and help people connect and find common ground.

Get in touch with any bottled-up feelings of resentment, frustration, and other stressful feelings, which can poison relationships and work environments. Conflict offers all parties an opportunity to learn about what's really going on with the other side, as well as numerous other learning opportunities. Conflict may also add force, energy, and more intense interest in the idea or situation in question. When conflict is handled constructively, opposing opinions and ideas are discussed openly. This airing of ideas can lead to creative, innovative approaches—and conflict build-up is prevented.

When you view conflict as a natural and healthy aspect of group effort, the people you lead or influence are more likely to be open about their opinions and ideas. Conflicts among your people will surface, and it will be possible to discuss problem situations at a stage when candid discussion is most helpful in defining the source of problems and in developing alternate solutions before resentments fester and positions harden. As a leader, therefore, your key to avoiding *ongoing* conflict lies in accepting *initial* conflict among workers and airing it as openly as possible. Any time an employee is harboring stressful feelings about an issue or event, it's worth exploring and resolving that conflict.

Technique 2: Set the Stage for a Win-Win Outcome

Before you set up a meeting to negotiate a conflict resolution, think about how you'll provide a supportive atmosphere for airing differences and reaching solutions. How will you set the stage so the parties will have the best chance of finding a win-win resolution? Consider timing, ground rules, evaluative criteria for proposals, process, and positive tone.

Be sure the time is right

Establish that the parties to the conflict are ready to sit down and try to resolve it. Until they are, everyone will be wasting time.

Establish some ground rules

Make sure that each side has equal time to present its views. Take steps to see that the most powerful or aggressive people don't dominate the situation unfairly. Insist on no interruptions while each side is presenting its view. If the other side refuses to respect the basics of common courtesy, the situation will probably only worsen. Consider suggesting an end to this meeting with rescheduling to occur only when the rules of courtesy are agreed upon.

Aim for the rule of consensus

If the conflict involves groups, they must set a ground rule about how each group will decide on proposals and resolutions. Majority rule is the most common ground rule for making group decisions, but consensus rule is increasingly used. In consensus rule, all group members must agree to a decision. The stance most often taken is that all members need not be enthusiastic about the decision, but they must feel that they can live with it and agree to cooperate in implementing it. Whatever decision rules the group chooses can affect both the complexity of the interaction and the divvying up of outcomes.

Know Why Consensus Groups Make More Agreements

People in a group tend to have varying motives for the outcome of the conflict, so most groups are mixed-motive groups. In a purely competitive group, majority rule is the most efficient and may be the best way to avoid an impasse. In a mixed-motive group, however, majority rule is not so effective. It doesn't reveal how strongly people feel about their preferences, so members don't have much chance to learn the values others place on the issues. People may not say *why* they're voting one way or another, how they feel about a particular issue, or the relative importance they place on the outcome. Without getting this information out into the open, it's much harder to find side-benefits to trade off and to find expanded-plate agreements that are based on differing preferences.

Studies have found that mixed-motive groups, negotiating under a consensus rule, reach more valuable outcomes. To reach a unanimous agreement, each party has to make tradeoffs that lead to an expanded-plate outcome. Group members must learn other members' preferences and find ways to expand the plate of resources to accommodate them. It's time-consuming, but it forces group members to consider creative alternatives to increase the plate and satisfy the interests of all group members.

Understand How Consensus Works

Consensus rule has three phases.

1. Considering the proposal for decision
2. Stating and resolving members' concerns about the proposal
3. Resorting to alternative options if consensus can't be reached.

When a proposal to be decided upon is presented, members ask questions and state legitimate concerns. The presenter clarifies and responds to the concerns. The leader then calls for consensus, asking if there's any objection to the decision. If there's none, consensus is reached.

If there are one or more concerns that members can't live with, then the entire group addresses these concerns and tries to resolve them. Sometimes the proposal is changed; sometimes the member who objects agrees to stand aside, meaning he or she will live with the decision and support it. If not, then the group may need to reevaluate its purpose and values as well as individual motives in an effort to resolve the concern. As a last resort, the group may try one of these alternatives.

- Postpone the decision.

- Withdraw the proposal.

- Ask for a nonbinding show of hands to gain a sense of support for the proposal.

- Send the proposal to a subgroup.

- Ask concerned members to retreat together until they work out their differences.

- Create team building where underlying problems come to light.

Finally, if all else fails, the group can decide that a two-thirds majority vote, a 90 percent majority vote, or some other agreed-upon figure will approximate consensus.

Go for a High-Quality Agreement

To evaluate the quality of a group-negotiated agreement in a mixed-motive situation, you can use the following criteria. Ask, in reaching this agreement, did the group:

- Expand its focus to include all important negotiation issues in the discussion?

- Discuss priorities and preferences among issues?

- Focus its efforts on problem solving?

- Consider unique and innovative solutions?

- Consider trading off issues of high-priority interest?

Recognize the Problem of Coalitions

The major difference between two-person and group negotiations is the potential for two or more persons within a group to form an informal coalition in order to pool their resources and have a greater influence on outcomes. Coalitions, or factions, involve fewer people than the entire group and are therefore easier to manage. They reduce coordination problems, the interests and goals of members are more consistent, and motivating them to act is easier. This gives the coalition an edge over the other group members. Members in a powerful coalition can get what they want using majority rule. However, people often focus on the interests of their particular coalition, or their personal interests, rather than what's best for the group.

Research indicates that when group members have equal power, the group achieves more expanded-plate agreements and uses resources more effectively than groups where coalitions are formed and power is distributed unevenly. In groups already suffering from power imbalances, group members are much more likely to form coalitions to take advantage of that imbalance. The bottom line is, you need to recognize that coalitions are inherently unstable, and they often lead to agreements that are not in the best interests of the organization.

Establish an atmosphere that supports openness

Allow for expression of feelings without attack. Accept the feelings that are expressed. Encourage open communication. Be noncritical and nonevaluative. Focus on the problem or situation itself and avoid making people wrong. Focus on the pronouns *we, us, our*, terms that include both sides and imply a partnership in resolving the issue.

Propose a Three-Step Negotiation Process

Cooperative or competitive groups typically function best when operating under agendas that keep them focused on finding the most effective decision in an orderly and efficient manner. In mixed-motive negotiation, however, groups using an issue-by-issue agenda usually reach less expansive agreements than groups that use a process for getting all issues on the table first.   If the group can consider all the issues as part of the plate that's on the table, they can recognize the possibilities for expanding the plate.   Mixed-motive groups should use agendas that structure the following three-step process.

1.   Identify and prioritize all the issues and benefits

2.   Reveal group members' individual needs and wants for the outcome

3.   Suggest creative approaches to solving the problems—generate package deals

Focus on benefits from resolving the conflict

Prepare a list of benefits to be gained by cooperation and losses to be suffered by ongoing conflict.   Each side must understand that more is to be gained by resolving the conflict than by continuing it.

Technique 3: Air Opposing Views

Begin the negotiation meeting by setting the tone through your opening remarks, which are optimistic, nonjudgmental, and designed to generate expansive emotions.   Present a brief summary overview of the meeting's purpose.   Get agreement on ground rules, and the process for reaching agreement.   Consider getting agreement on criteria for evaluating any proposed resolution—unless that would become a conflict in itself.

Each side states their views

Listen carefully with the purpose of finding a clue to possible solutions—and for identifying each side's resolution strategy.   Here are suggestions for all parties.

* Describe the others' actions and why you think this behavior is a problem.

* Share your perceptions and feelings; avoid judging and blaming.

* See the conflict as a mutual problem to be resolved in a win-win way; avoid viewing it as a win-lose battle.

* Share your needs, feelings, and goals and avoid taking rigid positions.

* Listen in order to learn more about the other sides' needs, interests, and feelings; show how your proposals address these.

* Put yourself in the others' shoes.

* Focus on making accurate assessments of the others' feelings and motives.

* Focus on similarities of goals, needs, wants, methods.

* Clearly communicate that you understand the needs, goals and desires of the others.

* Ask question to clarify any aspects you don't understand, with the goal of thoroughly understanding the views of the other side.

* Take a step-by-step approach to discovering all the issues in the conflict and any resources that can be divided, but aim to get them all on the table before you start bargaining for who will do what and who will get what.

* After both sides have presented their views, each side might want to summarize what they've heard but others may have missed.   Start building up the *we* toward *our common purpose and goal*.

Clarify, Summarize, Give Feedback

As the leader of the negotiation, listen, clarify, summarize, and give feedback. Encourage and support people on both sides. Try to find mutual feeling and common ground. Look for opportunities to reduce tensions. Your goal should be to strengthen the personal relationships between the parties or at least to avoid their deterioration. Remember, the person who listens has more control. Make your listening goal: *I need to hear what they're really concerned about.* Take notes regarding what you specifically agree or disagree with.

Stay interested, calm, and rational. Don't let angry emotions rob you of self-control. Stay on top of things. Always consider the purpose of what you say: does it support the negotiation?

Technique 4: Isolate the Cause of the Problem

Once conflicting opinions and ideas have been adequately discussed, your function is to guide the parties to a satisfactory resolution of the conflict. To do so, you must be aware of the immediate or superficial *reasons* for the conflict, and often you must dig deeper to the root causes underlying the problem actions. Look at four main areas: faulty communication, resentment of another's past behavior, conflicting goals, and conflicting choice of solution.

Faulty communication

The conflict may be more imagined than real because it resulted from faulty communication. First look for signs of faulty perception, misunderstanding, or oversensitivity. The best way to reduce imagined conflicts is to encourage frequent discussion of problems.

Resentment of past behavior

Constructive discussion of a problem may be jeopardized because one of the parties is harboring resentment of another member's past behavior. See whether such resentment can be brought into the open. Try to get the person who resents the behavior to state the objection and describe the behavior specifically. Frequently the first objections brought up do not get at the heart of the problem. Conflicts based on unvoiced resentment need to be explored in an atmosphere in which feelings are respected so that true feelings can come to the surface.

Conflicting goals

Problems that arise because of conflicting goals are often the most difficult to resolve. Try to get both sides to pinpoint the specific goals they have for the outcome of the situation. Then see whether they can agree on some common goals, such as increased productivity or even the survival of the company.

Conflicting ways to achieve goals

Sometimes everyone agrees on the major goal to be achieved in a situation, but they can't agree on the best way to achieve that goal. When this happens, be sure everyone thoroughly discusses and understands the conflicting approaches. If conflict persists, search for alternate courses of action that incorporate the best aspects of the conflicting solutions.

Technique 5: Identify the Resolution Strategy of Each Party

It's important to know how each party to the conflict is trying to resolve the problem. An awareness of strategies for conflict resolution can help you make sure that individuals' concerns or feelings are not squelched, ignored, or avoided. It can also help you equalize power in the situation. Here are five basic strategies for resolving conflict.

- *Competitive*—a win-lose approach in which each side attempts to dominate the other and to win sympathy for their concerns at the expense of the other.

- *Avoidant*—a head-in-the-sand approach characterized by an indifference to the concerns of other parties and to the conflict itself. Behaviors include withdrawal, isolation, evasion, flight, and apathy.

- *Accommodating*—a nonassertive approach characterized by appeasement. One side gives up taking care of their own concerns in order to make peace by giving in to the other's concerns.

- *Give-and-take*—a compromise approach that seeks to find a solution somewhere in-between the desires of all parties, giving each party moderate but incomplete satisfaction.

- *Collaborative*—a cooperative approach in which all parties try to integrate their concerns so that all are fully satisfied.

If both sides use a collaborative strategy, your job as leader is much easier. You goal is to show the benefits to both sides of a collaborative approach. You want to promote a negotiation that's fair and a resolution that both sides will carry out in good spirits. You must therefore see that the side with a competitive strategy doesn't unfairly dominate the side with an accommodating strategy. You must build trust with the avoidant side and find ways to bring their hidden issues onto the negotiating table. Once you identify the underlying negotiation strategy of each party, you're in a better position to move toward integrating their concerns and proposals and creating options for solution.

Technique 6: Integrate Proposals and Create Options

Through open discussion, you've been moving toward a shared understanding of the conflict. As you can begin to integrate each others' viewpoints, you can start creating various options for resolving the conflict. Consider the following suggestions:

- *Establish Criteria*. If you haven't already established the criteria that any proposal must meet, consider doing that now.

- *Look for common goals*. Remember that incompatible positions and proposals don't necessarily mean that basic goals and interests are in conflict.

- *Meet people's needs*. Keep in mind that when a resolution meets the needs of both parties, both are then committed to making the resolution work.

- *Find payoffs for all*. Remember, in ongoing relationships there is rarely a *fixed-plate*, in which the more one side gets, the less the other gets. Instead, reaching a satisfactory resolution has unforeseeable future payoffs for both sides.

- *Brainstorm alternatives*. Welcome brainstorming, and creating as many alternatives as possible, before evaluating them.

- *Be creative*. At least consider each alternate proposal and look for creative new combinations of options. Avoid thinking in terms of *either my plan or their plan*.

- *Look for partial agreements*. Identify those issues or parts of proposals that both sides agree to.

- *Rearrange, combine*. Consider bundling ideas together and proposing package deals, perhaps with a settlement of one issue being linked to a settlement of another.

- *Facilitate tradeoffs*. Explore differences as a way to create tradeoffs.

You already understand how exploring the differences in what people need and want can generate side-benefits that expand the plate of goodies on the negotiation table, which in turn leads to tradeoffs. You know that differences can boost your chances of making a good deal. When you're working with groups of people, or with two or more organizations, the same principle applies, but the negotiation is usually more complex.

Technique 7: Reach a Resolution and Learn

The last step in the conflict resolution process is to not only reach a resolution but to consider what all parties have learned from this process.

Reach a Resolution

Now is the time to seriously consider all proposals—and to keep repackaging or restructuring them until you find one that both sides can live with. If you've been able to get agreement on the criteria for evaluating proposals, now is the time to measure how well each proposal meets mutual needs and reconciles opposing interests. Determine what each party sees as a possible solution and whether there *can* be a solution that will satisfy all parties. Explore possible alternatives that the parties have not considered. Help the sides find the solution that meets these general criteria.

- It's best for the organization
- It's best for *all* parties
- It provides the best foundation for future harmony and cooperation

Your role is to guide people in selecting the solution that best meets these criteria and any other specific criteria they've set, and to negotiate differences in reaching an agreement that all can live with.

The agreement should indicate that the conflict will end, describe how people will behave differently in the future, describe what will happen if people fail to abide by the agreement, and set future dates to discuss the resolution to see how well it's working. If resources, such as money or equipment, are involved, the agreement should state how they'll be divided or used. Be sure the resolution can be implemented and sustained by both sides. When the agreement is done, suggest some sort of celebration that establishes new, positive bonds.

Learn From the Process

Help both sides recognize how learning to manage conflict together creates cooperative bonds. Make the conflict a learning process by getting both sides together to review what they've learned about the relationship and their approach to conflict. They can give each other tactful feedback. Ask people to address such self-questions as:

- *What ideas and actions were dysfunctional?*
- *What ideas and actions were effective?*
- *How have my negotiation skills improved?*
- *How have my sensitivities deepened?*
- *How could I have improved the process?*

Acknowledge the courage, patience, and fortitude it takes to admit that a conflict is occurring, to deal with it in depth, and to work through it together to resolution.

Case Studies—Applying the Creative Techniques

In working on these cases, you may use creative techniques from any of the chapters. However, the creative techniques described in this chapter may be especially appropriate. Keep these self-questions in mind.

1. What problems do I see?

2. How can I probe beneath the surface to get at root problems?

3. What opportunities (hidden or obvious) can I find to take initiative, cut costs, and/or make money?

4. What creative alternatives can I generate?

5. As a consultant, what should I recommend as the best viewpoints and actions?

6. To answer these questions, what creative techniques can I experiment with to respond to this case? After completing the case analysis, ask: Which creative techniques produce the best results?

Case 9.1   Erica Negotiates to Buy a Business

Erica is ready to make a career change. She has been working as a sales rep for Wilhaven Wholesale Spice and Preservative Co. for ten years. She currently sells about $1.5 million of product per year, and her annual income, including salary, commission, and perks is about $75,000.

Erica believes she has the expertise and customer loyalty to start her own wholesale business selling additives to food processing companies and large food preparation outlets. She has an opportunity to buy Norris Suppliers, a smaller firm that competes with Wilhaven. Norris financial statements indicate they have $100,000 in assets and last year had $3 million in gross sales with a net profit of $150,000.

Erica is interested in buying this business because it's a going concern, so it would free her from the hassles of starting a business from scratch. She makes an appointment to negotiate the terms of possibly buying Norris Suppliers.

- What are the potential advantages and disadvantages of buying this business?

- What goals should Erica set for the outcome of the negotiation?

- What key points should she keep in mind for the negotiation?

- Which CTs discussed in previous chapters did you use in solving this case problem?

- Which CTs were most helpful and what ideas did they spark or inspire?

Case 9.2 Conflict Resolution for Andy and Barbara

You are team leader at a Cost-Less Pharmacy, one in a chain of pharmacies. Andy and Barbara have a recurring scheduling conflict. Barbara requested schedule changes four times during the past month. Each time she asked to come in later than scheduled, which means Andy must work until she gets there, which is inconvenient for him.

Barbara is a university student who attends classes on Tuesday and Thursday from 8 a.m. to 12:30 p.m. You agreed when she came to work at Cost-Less that her schedule could be somewhat flexible to allow her to meet course requirements at the university. This past month has been hectic because it's the end of the semester and she must complete various team projects and study for finals with her study group. Her group generally meets for two or three hours after lunch on Tuesday or

Thursday, meeting from 1:30 to 3:30 or 4:30. So she can't get to work until 4 or 5 p.m. She's willing to come in earlier the next morning because she doesn't have classes on those days.

Andy is the father of two children, ages 9 and 11. He normally works from 7 a.m. to 3 p.m., but he was told when he was hired that he could not get a guaranteed schedule, although management policy is to be flexible in helping staff arrange workable schedules. Andy usually needs to leave by 3:00 in order to take the children to their various activities. He's been willing to change his schedule a little for Barbara, but he's getting frustrated. He worries about how these schedule changes will affect the commitments he's made to his children and their friends and instructors.

As team leader, you decide a conflict resolution session is in order.

- What should you do to prepare for the session?
- What should you set as a goal for the outcome of the conflict resolution?
- What are some key points to keep in mind as you conduct the session?
- Which CTs discussed in previous chapters did you use in solving this case problem?
- Which CTs were most helpful and what ideas did they spark or inspire?

Case 9.3 High-Tech Culture Clash

Delcore, Inc. is a large, global corporation that designs and manufactures analog and mixed signal semiconductor products. The company has a worldwide staff of over 10,500 employees. Last year its total sales were $2.5 billion.

Delcore's primary mission is to develop technologies for the growing array of Internet access devices. Its large Research and Development department has been focusing mainly on developing analog and mixed signal technologies. Delcore is moving forward with plans to combine these underlying technologies with memory and microprocessor technology on a single chip. Wilcox executives view his integrated chip as their wave of the future, an innovation that will create a new niche in the market and assure the success of their company, at least for the near future.

Delcore CEO Joy Rosen recently discovered that **Winger Technologies** is further along with certain aspects of this integrated chip than Delcore is. She made a strategic move to acquire a majority of Winger's stock in order to gain access to their technological breakthroughs.

Winger CEO Robin Bowen considers himself a human resources expert first and foremost. During the negotiation for the sale of his stock, he said the only way would sell was if he could come on board as Delcore's VP of Human Resources. Joy resisted but the two finally agreed to a compromise that allowed Robin to be Director of Human Resources for the new Winger Division of Delcore.

Delcore paid this personnel price plus a premium for the stock, but Joy and her executive team consider it a sound investment, in line with the Delcore's mission and strategies. Most important, Winger's technology will help Delcore get their new integrated chip to market more quickly.

Winger was much smaller than Delcore, with a staff of about 500 employees. The company's past success was built on microprocessor technology. They have been focused on overtaking **Horizon Inc.**, which is their major competitor in the microprocessor market and the current Market Monster. Now, one year after the acquisition, Winger still operates much like a separate corporation within Delcore. Though the staffs of the research, administration, marketing, and sales departments are formally consolidated, they don't act like it much of the time.

Gray Manning, the Delcore VP of Human Resources, says, "We tell the Winger people, 'We're not out to kill Horizon,' and they don't listen . . . so we say it again . . . louder." Robin and the Winger employees have tried to bring the Delcore people around to their way of thinking about the importance of overtaking Horizon, but the Delcore people aren't interested.

Gray comes into Joy's office one day to talk about the situation. "You know we bought Winger for its technological know-how, which is harbored in the minds of the people, but many of them are leaving the company for positions in microchip startups dedicated to the 'Kill Horizon' mission. Many who remain grumble about what they perceive to be repressive conditions. Obviously, this means the overall morale among Winger employees is dropping. In fact, their progress on the integrated chip is almost at a standstill. And that's affecting the Delcore R&D people—I think their motivation has been dampened by all this. My network tells me that rumors fly around the employee's lounge. Will Winger people give in to Delcore? Or will the Delcore people give in to Winger?"

- What are the root problems you see operating in this situation?
- What opportunities are the Delcore and Winger people overlooking?
- How would you address each problem or unmet opportunity?
- Which CTs discussed in this chapter did you use in solving this case problem?
- Which CTs were most helpful and what ideas did they spark or inspire?

References

Barker, Emily, "Partners With an Edge," *Inc.*, September 1999, 59-64.

Bazerman, M.H. and M.A. Neale. *Negotiating Rationally*. New York: Macmillan, Inc., 1992.

Brandenburger, Adam M. and Barry J. Nalebuff. *Co-opetition*. New York: Doubleday, 1996

Fisher, Roger, and William Ury. *Getting to Yes: Negotiating Agreement Without Giving In*. New York: Penguin Books, 1993.

Hargrove, Robert. *Mastering the Art of Creative Collaboration*. New York: McGraw Hill, 1998.

Kao, John. Jamming: *The Art and Discipline of Business Creativity*. New York: HarperCollins, 1996

Saint, S. and J. Lawson. *Rules for Reaching Consensus*. San Diego, CA: Pfeiffer, 1994.

Schapiro, Nicole. *Negotiating for Your Life*. New York: Henry Holt, 1993.

Sellers, Patricia, "Women, Sex and Power," *Fortune*, August 5, 1996.

Tjosvold, Dean, *Learning to Manage Conflict*, New York: Lexington Books, 1993.

Ury, William. *Getting to Negotiate a Raise*. New York: Bantam, 1991.

Chapter 10
Creative Futures
Paradigms and Scenarios

Coming events cast their shadows beforehand. Goethe

Future scenarios are vehicles for an imaginative leap into the future. Writing them can help you, and your team, generate a range of new ideas for people in the organization to think about. When creative teams involve a wide diversity of people in the scenario-writing process, they create an idea-friendly environment for divergent thinking. Future scenario writing forces an organization to envision an "official" future. It stimulates individual and collective creativity and makes everyone consider the paradigms that currently surround them, paradigm shifts that are either on the horizon or in process, and some alternatives for facing the challenges and opportunities that paradigm shifts always bring. Recognizing paradigms and writing future scenarios are powerful creative skills in the current workplace environment—skills that enable you and your organization to survive and thrive in the chaos of rapid change.

Myths & Realities

Future scenarios are stories about change in the future. Many myths surround our cultural ideas about change, about stories, and about the future.

Myth 1. No news is good news.

Wishful thinking says that no news means things will stay as they are. This idea really cloaks a resistance to change. A related myth is "If it ain't broke, don't fix it." Reality is that you and your organization can't afford to wait until you learn that something is "broke." If you want to consciously create your life, don't wait passively for news to come—good or bad. You must continually obsolete and reinvent yourself, your firm, your products, processes, and services—before your competitors do. Actively go out and get the news. That way you're likely to be able to create your own good news—for you and your firm.

Myth 2. Stories and storytelling are only for children.

Stories are the stuff of myth and legend. They're a crucial element of all cultures—from the global networked culture, to national and regional cultures, to corporate cultures. Storytelling is a hot skill in today's workplace. You'll learn to spin stories from the most captivating, enchanting, magnetic aspects of yourself, or your firm, or your products—in order to sell them to the right people. You'll learn to weave together the most significant trends and predictions for the future into a few scenarios—stories that will motivate you and your organization to prepare for the challenges and opportunities the future holds in store.

Myth 3. You can't know the future.

Life would be ever-so-boring if you knew for sure all that the future holds in store for you. On the other hand, you can gather a real treasure trove of information about current trends and how they might play out. You can tap your intuition, your superconscious, and your other intelligences to get a sense of "what next?" And you can mentally rehearse and prepare yourself for a variety of eventualities, so that regardless of the twists and turns of fate, you're ready to make the most of it

Paradigm Shifts

The entire planet is tied together in a single electronic market moving at the speed of light,

Walter Wriston, former Citicorp chairman.

Since future scenarios are based on ways that current trends are likely to affect the future, you must recognize the paradigm patterns your organization is bounded by. Then you'll be in a position to identify paradigm shifts that are in the making and predict future shifts that might occur. You'll need this information to predict the problem-opportunities your organization is likely to face and to offer some creative suggestions for preparing and responding to these events.

Learn to Recognize Paradigm Shifts

A paradigm is a mental model of how something works. To be considered a paradigm, according to Joel Barker [1993], the model must include three factors:

1) a set of rules that

2) establishes or defines the boundaries of the model and

3) tells you how to behave inside the boundaries in order to succeed.

The people who adopt a particular paradigm will measure the success of any idea or activity by its ability to solve problems within the paradigm.

You can think of a culture, society, worldview, organization, or business as a forest of paradigms. Each paradigm is a tree in the forest. For example, a business will have management paradigms, sales paradigms, human resource paradigms, recruitment paradigms. We're defining a paradigm as a mental model, but it is also seen by various people as a set of beliefs or principles, a theory, a method, a protocol, standards, routines, assumptions, conventions, patterns, habits, common sense, consensus reality, conventional wisdom, a mindset, a frame of reference, traditions, customs, prejudices, ideology, rituals. The forest of paradigms we find in a business, a culture, or a worldview are interdependent, so you never change just one paradigm. When you change one, it affects all the others, so they too must shift to some degree—from very slightly to dramatically.

Paradigm Shifts

A paradigm shift is a change from the current model to a new model, with a new set of rules and boundaries. It's a new game that requires different behavior in order to succeed. For example, when women started moving into power positions 20 or 30 years ago, this was a major paradigm shift that has affected business, marriage, family, child-rearing, education, courtship, and perhaps most of the trees in our cultural forest. The mental model of what it means to be a good wife, mother, husband, father all began to shift. People are still trying to figure out all the new rules and boundaries.

To identify where paradigm shifts are likely to occur, notice where people are trying to change the rules, because that's the earliest sign of significant change possibilities. When the rules change, the whole world can change.

Paradigm Phases

When do the rules change—when do new paradigms appear? Usually when someone figures out how to solve one or more major problems that cannot be solved using the rules and boundaries of the old paradigm. In effect, someone figures out how to do something better, something important that really needs to be done better, and enough people jump on the bandwagon to make a shift occur. Often it's when someone solves a problem in a new, strange way—not using the old rules. Such explorers often think this new way could be a new model for solving a wide range of similar problems. Let's look at typical phases of a paradigm shift, as shown in Figure 10.1, along with their relationship to the complexity-chaos process

Figure 10.1 Paradigm Shifts:
Technological Change, Economic Change, Cultural Change

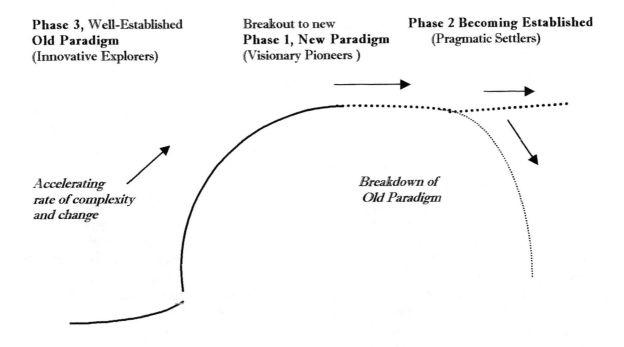

Phase 3, Well-Established
Old Paradigm
(Innovative Explorers)

Breakout to new
Phase 1, New Paradigm
(Visionary Pioneers)

Phase 2 Becoming Established
(Pragmatic Settlers)

*Accelerating
rate of complexity
and change*

*Breakdown of
Old Paradigm*

Well-Established Phase 3 of an Old Paradigm

- The well-established paradigm has unsolved problems or limitations, and so eventually begins to seem less effective.

- Innovative Explorers work on solutions to problems, look for breakthrough innovations.

- People in the field who are affected begin to lose trust in the old rules.

- Turbulence and a sense of crisis grow as trust is reduced.

Beginning Phase 1 of a New Paradigm

This is the breakthrough period when a new mental model is first proposed and tried out.

- Turbulence and crisis increase even more as paradigm conflict becomes obvious.

- People in the field become very upset and demand clear solutions.

- People begin to believe that one of the proposed new paradigms can solve a small set of significant problems that the old paradigm cannot.

- *Innovative Explorers*, step forward to propose a solution—a new paradigm. It may be a radically new way of doing things, or it may be an old idea whose time has come.

- *Visionary Pioneers* take the lead to accept the new paradigm, based on their intuition that it will work.

During the Beginning Phase 1, the new paradigm is usually in competition with other paradigms that are also being developed to solve the problem. The paradigm that can survive to the Becoming-Established Phase 2 will almost always win—even if other paradigms would be better in the long run. For example, many people say Apple had a better computer operating system, but Microsoft found ways to make its operating system the one chosen by most computer users—so its system and related software became the New Paradigm.

Becoming-Established Phase 2 of a New Paradigm

This is the phase when Innovative Explorers, Visionary Pioneers, and Pragmatic Settlers who are entrepreneurial types can make great profits.

- As support and funding for this new paradigm grow, acceptance of it increases.

- Turbulence and crisis decrease as this new paradigm starts solving the problems and as people in the field realize that this is a new, more successful, way to deal with the world.

You and your organization will have significant competitive advantage if you can anticipate paradigm shifts, obviously. Then you can become a *Visionary Pioneer* in adopting a new paradigm that allows you to lead people out of the old paradigm.

Meanwhile, what's happening with those competing paradigms that have been battling to get established as the new paradigm? Suppose these paradigm explorers face artificial barriers—such as government regulation, a distorted marketplace, or big companies that crush competition. Then their competing paradigms may not have much of a chance until the accepted New Paradigm has become established and has moved into the Well-Established Phase 3. However, it's most likely that their competing paradigm—or a new competing paradigm—will appear and be accepted late in this Becoming-Established Phase 2. That's because there will be enough unsolved problems at this stage to trigger the search for new solutions. The need is felt.

Paradigm Players

Who are the players that drive or thrive in one phase of a paradigm shift and resist or get squeezed out in another phase?. Here are some key questions you can metaphorically ask about each player in order to understand who's who.

1. *Are you an Innovative Explorer?* Are you one of those leaders who will start to develop a new way of solving the problems—in Beginning Phase 1? Or are you dealing with problems that are subtle, sophisticated, expensive, and intensive—in Well-Established Phase 3—moving toward a new Phase 1?

2. *Are you a Visionary Pioneer?* Are you one of those leaders or entrepreneurs who's willing to take a chance on a new paradigm that's being developed by an Innovative Explorer—early in Becoming-Established Phase 2?

3. *Are you a Pragmatic Settler?* Are you one of those managers who focuses on solving problems with efficiency and effectiveness—later in Phase 2?

4. *Are you a Conservative Resister?* Are you one of those people who resists any major change that might move people out of the well-established paradigm, the one you're so comfortable with?

Let's look at these four types of paradigm players: Innovative Explorers, Visionary Pioneers, Pragmatic Settlers, and Conservative Resisters.

Innovative Explorers

Explorers start with the unsolved problems in Well-Established Phase 3 and see that they must be solved outside the current paradigm, which moves them into Phase 1 of a new paradigm. They stir up the thinking of the prevailing-paradigm community.

Where is the Innovative Explorer likely to come from? Usually it's an outsider, someone who really doesn't understand the prevailing paradigm in all its subtleties—or at all. It may be a someone who's new to the field and isn't stuck in its accepted beliefs. It may be a loner who's been working at the fringes of the field and knows it but isn't boxed in by its rules. It may be a tinkerer who gets in there himself to work on a problem that's in the way.

Visionary Pioneers

Pioneers buy into Innovative Explorers' thinking. They bring in the needed brainpower, muscle power, time, effort, money, or other resources, to create the critical mass that drives the new paradigm toward the Becoming Established Phase 2. Both Innovative Explorers and Visionary Pioneers follow their intuition, their heart, their feelings and take the risk of backing a new paradigm. Pioneers, however, are the ones most likely to reap huge financial rewards from being the first to invest heavily in the Becoming –Established Phase 2 of the new technology, method, process, product, or service.

Pragmatic Settlers

Settlers enter later in the Becoming-Established Phase 2 and so take much smaller risks. They also tend to profit from the new paradigm but far less so than the Visionary Pioneers who got to market first.

Conservative Resisters

Resisters cling to the Well-Established status quo because it worked for them and they're not willing to take the risks and make the changes necessary for success in the new paradigm. When a paradigm shifts, everyone functioning within it goes back to zero. Your expertise in solving the old problems with the old rules is not worth much except for the basic skills you can transfer, such as basic problem-solving, decision-making, people skills etc. For example, directive managers, who tell employees what to do and when to do it, find themselves irrelevant when workers are reorganized into self-managing teams. When you ask someone to change their paradigm, you're asking them to give up their investment in the status quo and the rewards it provides them. Conservative Resisters are usually the corporate insiders who have much to lose from major change. On the other hand, corporate outsiders have nothing invested and everything to gain.

These players are important forces that can block or enhance your organization's successful response to paradigm shifts.

Personal Impact of Paradigm Shifts

You can relate the paradigm shift process to complexity theory and chaos theory by focusing on the acceleration of change in today's workplace and society and how that acceleration builds to the point of breakdown of the old and breakout into the new.

Acceleration

Not only is technological change accelerating, so is every aspect of life. We all feel the acceleration of the pace of modern life. We have too much to do, there is more information coming at us, and it is more complicated and dense than ever. We don't have much time to spend on any one thing. We must move fast to keep up or we'll be left behind. We'll fail. Traditional boundaries are collapsing as we move into new situations at a faster and faster pace. Every area of human activity seems to be escalating at an exponential rate. Maybe you spend every free moment you can grab just cocooning to get ready for tomorrow's onslaught. The speed of the workplace, marketplace, and digital world has become the speed of your body-mind.

Breakdown

You reach a critical point where you can't go any faster. Your beliefs, attitudes, thinking, feeling, decisions, and choices will no longer handle the increasing tension. You may begin to question the beliefs and habits—those that you accepted without thinking much about them. You may begin to challenge everything you see, have doubts, be cynical. Even though you try harder to succeed, your efforts are no longer effective. You feel you must disconnect from the constant buzz in order to retain your sanity. You're right. In the breakdown phase, it pays to march to a different drummer.

You need fresh eyes and new thinking in order to decide where to go next. You must redefine who you are and what your skills, products, or services are. Things must dissolve, break down, destruct. Leadership becomes the ability to break down existing forms and to provoke others to do the same. Breakdown is a time of cleaning out, changing priorities, and giving up control.

Chaos

During the chaotic phase, no one knows for sure what they're doing or what's going on. Old forms have broken down but new ones are not yet in place. It's a time with few if any rules, when identity begins to come apart. The old knowledge seems useless. Boundaries are moving, form is missing, and power relationships are shifting. You need to find the center within, to keep your head even when people around you are losing theirs. Get in touch with your purpose in life (tap your motivational intelligence) in this sea of chaos.

The external boundaries and rules are gone, so each person's individual values and motivations are all that's left. In a world without form, images are the only way to think, for imagination is how the new forms will emerge.

Breakthrough

Breakdown and chaos release huge flows of energy from the previously stable system. This energy seeks out a new level of order and stability, and at this moment it becomes a "dissipative structure," in the words of Ilya Prygione, the biologist. At this critical moment there is a qualitative break from the past and an entirely new world of possibilities opens up. The study of how new order arises from chaos is called complexity theory or chaos theory. You can gain the ability to entirely rewrite your perceptions of what lies ahead. Instead of dwelling on solutions, focus on discerning new paradigms, shifts in *how* you look at a problem.

How can you grow most effectively in these new, fast-moving, turbulent systems? What new patterns can you develop in response to new cultural and business demands? You need:

- new perceptual skills

- new emotional paths

- new relationship skills

The most powerful element of building future scenarios is that it opens doors for you to begin tuning into your own personal sense of what lies ahead. You must be able to see unfolding patterns before they occur and as they occur. You must recognize what's happening in that subtle zone where what you already know is dissolving into something you haven't yet imagined. This is the threshold, the edge, the door to the future.

You must learn to think, sense, know, feel, and act in entirely new patterns. You must boost your intelligences—all of them. You don't have to do this overnight or in quantum leaps. Even tiny shifts in the right direction can change the path you take—and many tiny shifts eventually add up to a dramatically different way of functioning. The part of you that's getting smarter is the part that's beginning to focus in on what's really important: your personal strengths and your most passionate, heartfelt desires.

Thriving in the Network Economy

The network economy itself is a major paradigm shift. We're now involved in a major process of expanding and enhancing the relationships and communications between all persons and all things. Wealth in this economy comes directly from innovation, not by perfecting what we already have, but by imperfectly creating something we don't have.

- If you want to encourage creativity, provide people with plenty of chances to network.

- Taming this creativity means moving beyond what you already know, undoing what you have perfected.

- Within this networked economy, the cycle of "find the new, nurture it, destroy the old" happens faster and more intensely than ever before.

Once networks have invaded every space in our lives, an entirely new paradigm will take hold. In the meantime, futurist Kevin Kelly [1997] offers some rules of thumb for success in the networked economy.

Many Little Connections = Smart Power

Rapid paradigm shifts are changing the old rules about wealth. Soon all manufactured products will contain embedded chips of some sort. Farm moisture sensors send data to weather satellites, which beam down these collected images. Store cash registers emit streams of information. Hospital monitors beep out numbers. Implants in farm animals beep away, letting the farmer know the location of each grazing animal.

As we implant "a billion specks of our thought" into everything, we're also connecting them to each other by infrared, radio, and other wireless webs, much larger and more complex than the wired web. These chips don't need to be artificially intelligent. They work on the "dumb power" of a few bits or nodes linked together. When you network dumb nodes into a smart web, you get dumb power. It's what the Internet did with relatively dumb personal computers. It created an amazing intelligence called the World Wide Web. Dumb parts, properly connected, yield smart results. We're not waiting for artificial intelligence to make intelligent systems. We're doing it with the dumb power of omnipresent computing devices and connections. We're in the process of connecting all to all.

- How do you make a better product? Let the parts talk to each other.

- How do you improve manufacturing? Let the materials speak to the machines.

- How do you make traffic safer? Let the vehicles talk among themselves and pick their own traffic patterns.

The More Users in a Network, the More Value

As the number of nodes in a network increases arithmetically, the value of the network increases exponentially. Adding a few more members to a network can dramatically increase its value for all the members.

In the past, the more scarce an item, the more valuable it tended to be. And if it became plentiful, it was devalued. But in a network economy, plenty can create value—the more copies of the product, the better. For example, when only a handful of people owned televisions, there wasn't much of a television industry, such as TV broadcasting, TV advertising, and TV manufacturing. The price of TVs had to come down to where a mass of people could buy them. Then advertisers had an audience to influence, stations could sell commercials, etc. A critical mass of people must have access to such devices before related industries become prosperous—whether it's personal computers with modems, teleconferencing capability, or fax machines. If few people have e-mail programs, who can you e-mail? What good is your program?

What's valuable is the scattered relationships—linked by access to the device—that become involved in a network of relationships. The relationships spiral upward in value as the users increase in number.

Universal Standards Sell Products

Successful devices rely on universal standards, interchangeability. The more common a device is, the more it pays to stick to a standard, such as a Windows operating system, or AAA batteries. For example, who wants a portable cassette or CD player that you can never find the right batteries for? As for PCs, in the early days, before Windows, if you needed to send a file of information to someone, you were often out of luck. That person's software was not likely to be able to read your file.

Success is Exponential

Exponential expansion is often explained by the water lily example. Water lilies take many days to cover a small portion of a pond, but they grow exponentially, at an ever-faster rate. Once they've covered that small portion, their growth quickly covers half the pond. At that point, on the next day they cover it all. So it is with networks. Fax machines took 20 years to reach a critical mass of users. So did Microsoft's computer programs, Fedex's delivery system, and the Internet itself. As membership in a network increases, the value of each member, and the network itself, explodes exponentially, bringing in yet more members. This virtual circle expands until all potential members have joined.

Certain forces feed on each other to boost a company's influence on a network into powerful standards, such as the Windows environment, almost "overnight." But these same forces can also work in reverse to obsolete the standards overnight. When there's a paradigm shift to a new model with a new standard, breakdown of the old is rapid.

Timing is Everything

Networks grow slowly at first. If they're able to navigate through the challenges to success, they come to a point where the momentum is so great that they become a run-away success. By the time this point is reached, its too late for late-comers to take full advantage of the run-away growth. Entrepreneurs must pay attention before this point, before the momentum builds.

In the Network Economy, it's the idea that counts. A company may get in with relatively low fixed costs and small marginal costs and still be able to achieve rapid distribution of their service or product. Smaller initial efforts can lead to run-away dominance. The period before the runaway growth begins is the "threshold of significance," the beginning of Phase 2 Becoming Established. Recognizing the threshold makes all the difference. In the past, an innovation's momentum indicated significance. Now, significance precedes momentum, so your organization must get in earlier, either by creating a new paradigm, Phase 1, or becoming involved very early in Becoming-Established Phase 2.

Paradigm Shifts—Coming Fast and Faster

Paradigm shifts happen ever-more frequently. This means you and your organization have a shorter time frame for riding out a new model and latching onto the next one. The initial boundaries and rules that give a network its power quickly become rigid standards and rules. They unleash the power of increasing returns for everyone who has a piece of the pie, but those who own or control the standard may receive huge rewards. For example, Microsoft's competitors in the Network Economy have tolerated Microsoft's billions because so many competitors have made their collective billions on the advantages of Microsoft's standards, which yield ever-increasing returns.

But which new paradigm should you and your organization latch onto? Which new idea is likely to become a new paradigm? That's the jackpot question. One thing we know: closed systems don't work in the Network Economy. So look for a paradigm that has many dimensions open to member input and member creativity. The more ways that members can contribute creatively, the more likely the new model is to produce increasing returns. These can feed the network, and the system will feed on itself and prosper. For example, most software companies introduce a new program first as a free beta version and let the public work out the bugs.

Paradox: The Best Keeps Getting Cheaper

The best products get cheaper every year. This paradox is a major engine of the Network Economy. Computers can be used to create the next improved version of computers. By compounding learning in this way, we get more out of less materials. Compounding chip power touches everything—including such products as cars, clothes, and food. Computer chips enabled just-in-time production systems and other practices that lower the prices of all sorts of products.

Telecommunications is about to experience the process of getting cheaper each year. For example, experts believe that for the next 25 years, the total bandwidth of communication systems will triple every 12 months and the price per bit transmitted will become almost free.

All items that can be copied, tangible and intangible, become cheaper as they improve. While vehicles will not be free, the cost per mile will become almost free. While this is heaven for consumers, it's hell for companies. Any competitor who comes along and offers better quality will snag the customers for almost-free products and services. The only way to make more profit is to expand what the product or service used to be.

Companies and entrepreneurs must continually create new goods and services to replace their almost-free goods and services that were previously profitable. This is easier to do in a Network Economy because of the cross-fertilization of ideas, the linking of relationships, the many alliances, and the rapid addition of new members to the web. Each new product or service that consumers use can create the opportunity and desire for two more. For example, as TVs, computers, VCRs, and digital cameras come down in price, households want one for every member—as well as related accessories, such as software, tapes, and batteries. Also, as the best gets cheaper, it opens a space around it for something new that people will pay for.

Free Stuff Can Create Great Value

Amazon was the first to sell its products, books, on a nonprofit basis in order to bring millions of customers to its website. Why? Now the website has great value to advertisers for one thing. Now Amazon "owns" a customer base, which offers an array of money-making opportunities. Its book sales may never generate a profit. So what?

Almost-free computers? Computer makers have deals with internet service providers (ISPs) to give huge rebates on computer purchases to people who agree to use the ISP for a year. If you're America Online (AOL) or Microsoft Network, you want to "own" a customer base for the same reasons as Amazon.

Many companies give away software—to get users to purchase related items or to later pay for upgrades. Since a flood of copies increases the value of all the copies, once a product's worth and usefulness is established, the company can sell related service or upgrades. How are companies to survive?

1. Think of "free" as a design goal for pricing. There is a drive toward the free. A very small flat rate may have the same effects as free.

2. When one product is free, this usually positions other products or services to be valuable.

3. Structure your business as if you think what you're creating is free, in anticipation of where its price will go.

Okay, what *is* scarce in this world of abundantly free and cheap products and service? Human attention. Giving your product away gets you that attention, that mindshare that can lead to market share. For example, web indexes were given away early on. They helped people focus on a few Websites out of thousands and drew attention to those sites. Webmasters then aided the indexer's efforts, and indexes were soon everywhere, enabling other related Web services, and boosting stock values for the indexers.

The big question: What do you see that's free now that may later lead to profits? Entrepreneurs are looking at Web digesters, guides, cataloguers, FAQs, remote live cameras, Web splashes, and numerous bots. Each of these may some day have profitable companies built around them.

Take Care of Your Web

In the Network Economy, a company's main focus moves from maximizing the firm's value to maximizing the value of the whole infrastructure. For example, successful game companies devote as much energy to promoting their web of users and hardware makers as they do to their product. Unless their web thrives, they die. For example, customers who want to try a new game must be able to find the hardware, the device needed to play it, as well as the game software.

Take care of your web and your web will take care of you. The best way for a company to raise its own abundance is to raise the system's abundance.

Standards make a network more powerful. Their rules create a pathway that speeds up innovation and evolution. Organizations must give top priority to setting common standards in order to manage the choice among myriad possibilities. Companies positioned at the gateway to a standard will make the biggest profits. And as that company prospers, so do those in its web. "The net is a possibility factory, churning out novel opportunities by the diskful" [Kelly 1997]. Standards are merely an attempt to harness the overwhelming number of competing possibilities so customers can actually use some of them.

Networks have no clear center and no clear outer boundaries. The vital distinction between "us" and "them" that you find in an organization becomes less meaningful in a Network Economy. If you're on the network, you're inside, and your loyalty tends to move away from organizations and toward the network. In this way a network is like a country, but nets and countries are also different in the following ways:

- No space or time boundaries exist on the net

- Relations are tighter, more intense, more persistent, and more intimate in many ways

- You find many overlapping networks, with many overlapping loyalties.

Understand the High-Tech Life Cycle

High-tech companies live with the most frequent paradigm shifts of any industry. Most people in these companies must like living on the edge because few seem to understand just when and how these changes are likely to occur. High-tech consultant Geoffrey A. Moore (1995) has worked at high levels of the industry long enough to recognize a pattern in the shifts. This pattern is determined by what he calls the High-Tech Adoption Life Cycle, which consists of four phases:

1. Early Market—when a breakthrough technology first emerges

2. Niche Market—when the technology is made workable for a few select clients

3. Whirlwind of Demand—when an entire industry arises around the technology

4. The Mall—when the general public adopts a "plug-and-play" version of the technology

Your management team can use this pattern to identify which phase your product is in and what role your company is able to play. It is crucial that key people agree on this.

Early Market—Phase I

A breakthrough technology, developed by an Innovative Explorer, emerges and arouses the interests of a Visionary Pioneer.

Target Audience: Innovative Techies

Definition—Early Market Phase

Your company is an Innovative Explorer that develops a brand new category of product offering. This is a breakthrough technology that replaces a whole class of infrastructure. Innovative Techies must accept it because they influence the Visionary Pioneers who have the financial decision-making clout to adopt it.

Competition—Early Market

Competition is among alternative breakthrough possibilities. Visionary Pioneers want the dramatic competitive advantage they can gain by adopting a new paradigm. Your competition is other companies with their own new paradigms, which are competing for the Pioneer's attention. How you win: your idea has the ability to break through the problems that are blocking progress and your company is flexible enough to adapt your idea to the Pioneer's needs.

Role of Strategic Partners – Early Market

A new paradigm of open architecture and inter-vendor cooperation has emerged, introduced by Apple in the Apple II, and then broadly disseminated by the PC division of IBM and by Sun Microsystems. These companies recruited partners to fill the open slots inside their computer cases. this means whole products can get to market much faster because multiple companies compete to provide each part. Work on all the parts can go forward in parallel.

In open systems solutions, everything is assumed to plug and play. In reality, nothing really does in the beginning. The whole product is a barely complete core product that's surrounded by the custom services needed to make any particular application work. Visionary buyers take a product that may be about 80 percent complete and use it as the foundation for creating an application breakthrough. They must rely heavily on the service of systems integrators who pull the whole project together.

The initial question to ask about forming partnerships: Are we partnering on a single revenue opportunity for a potential revenue stream—or to capture market leadership? Market leadership is the only strategic reason to partner—because it focuses on the whole product that you must offer in order to win top position in a target market

Power Hierarchy—Early Market

Power lies with the technology provider who attracts visionary buyer—and the systems integrator needed to make the technology work.

Organizational Leadership—Early Market

From the beginning the company needs a cross-functional team to see it through the various phases. In the first phase the key leader needs product marketing.

Niche Market—Across the Gap to Phase II

Now you customize your product or service for a buyer and then expand to similar buyers to create a niche market.

Target audience: Visionary Pioneers

Visionary Pioneers are intuitive, independent risk-takers who are motivated to search out future opportunities and capitalize on them.

Definition—Niche Market Phase

Your company provides a usable product/service to a particular market niche—to the point that you have a satisfied customer. Your market is not yet defined by a particular product, but by your customers' application of your new technology. It's still the customers' market, not yours—they are your sponsors and your protectors and you'll need that protective umbrella for a while. But this is your start in the mainstream market. Each niche requires its own whole product to be fully complete before it can adopt the new paradigm.

Short-Term Goal

To find the Visionary Pioneers with the most compelling needs to buy your new technology— then develop your technology into a whole product for this particular niche.

Long-Term Goal

To emerge as the Market Monster when you get to the Whirlwind of Demand phase. Look for that moment when it becomes more effective for the marketplace to organize itself away from niche markets and rally instead around the emerging product category of the Demand Phase. Now's when you must simplify, simplify, simplify your product to make it suitable for general-purpose use and easier and less costly to acquire and maintain.   Remember, the Niche Phase is just a phase—necessary but not one you want to get stuck in.

Key strategies—Niche Market

- Meet customer needs—that's your top priority now
- Focus on the economic buyer and end user in client organizations
- Emphasize to buyers that return on investment is the reason to buy—money gained by solving a current problem or removing a current barrier
- Differentiate your whole product for a single application
- Partner with a company that can serve as a distribution channel that adds value to the whole product—to ensure that your customized solution is delivered to the end user in usable form
- Base your prices on the value your product/service provides to clients
- Avoid competition to gain niche market share
- Position your products within vertical market segments   (all the phases of delivering a product or service to an end user, within a particular niche market)
- Give up an R&D-based product-centered approach and adopt a customer-based application-centered approach.   Vertical marketing requires becoming an adjunct to another industry's market—and giving up being the center of attention.

Competition—Niche Market

How you win: Being the first to provide a differentiated whole product that solves a particular problem or allows a specific breakthrough. You must provide a whole product and you must be first in order to win in this phase.

Role of Strategic Partners – Niche Market

To cross the Gap and become accepted by Pragmatist Settlers, the company must develop a whole product, at first for a specific niche of customers. Now every part of the product must be part of the package, and no part needs to be created from scratch by a technician. To accomplish this as rapidly as possible, the lead company must recruit partners who will commit to completing one or more specified parts of the whole product. Here the network of informal partnerships is born.

The responsibility of the market leader is to make a market for the other partners. If the partnership really is strategic, giving the business away to the right strategic partner is the lowest cost, highest return investment in market development.

Power Hierarchy—Niche Market

Power centralizes in the leader of the niche market attack, the company that has seen the market opportunity where nobody else did.

Organizational Leadership—Niche Market

Marketing and finance people are key to making it across the high-tech adoption gap and gaining a toehold niche. In the Niche phase vertical market managers, partner managers, and market-focused sales teams take over. Now the company needs a hands-on leader who spends more time with the customers and the troops than reviewing reports or winning points with top management—someone with these traits and skills:

- a team leader, very focused and disciplined in the approach to reaching goals
- charismatic and personable with colleagues and customers

- strongly committed to the end goal but with great flexibility about how to attain it

Danger Signs—Niche Market

Never go after a niche where the current expenditures on your category of product are larger than your current annual revenue. "Pick on somebody your own size" is the rule. To succeed in the Niche Market phase, you must win at least 40 percent of its new business over a year to 18-month period. Then word of mouth starts spreading the message that you're the Market Monster. That means your share of the next years' sales should go well beyond 50 percent. Pragmatic Settlers want to buy what other Settlers have bought.

How big a target niche can you handle? To answer that question, look at your goal for the coming year, how much you hope to ship. Say, it's $10 million. At best you might get 60 percent of your revenue from your target niche, meaning $6 million from that niche. Remember, you must win at least 40 percent of this business, so 100 percent of that niche should be $15 million. That's the maximum amount this niche can spend next year if you are to end up being its dominant supplier. If you know it will be greater, you can't handle it. If you try, you'll create demand you can't fulfill, which in turn creates a market for some other competitor.

Leveraging Your Toehold—Niche Market

Next you must leverage that toehold in order to sell to a related niche market, adapting your new technology to that particular arena. Moving from one niche to another, you work toward building a critical mass of niches. If you succeed, then your product becomes interesting to the Pragmatist Settlers in the larger marketplace.

Strategy: Sell to the end-user community, the economic buyer, the line manager in the end-user organization. Frame the buying issues in terms that economic buyers can understand and buy into.

- Show how your product can solve some previously unsolvable problem that's costing them money.

- Show them how this problem is part of the current IT infrastructure's paradigm for supporting their end users.

- Show that you can solve this problem because your new paradigm redesigns the end users' work flow to eliminate the problem's root cause.

- Show that you've studied and understand their particular application requirements, so you not only have the necessary core product but the whole product they need.

Methodically work through all the elements of this whole product, showing your understanding of their business. This overcomes the resistance of Pragmatist Settlers in the organization and brings them over to your side. You become a true partner to your customer. You can charge any price that the Visionary Explorer sees is worth the investment.

Which niche do you target next? Generally, take a vertical approach. Say your technology is accepted for some specific tasks in the human resources function in a bank. If your technology can be applied to other departments within that same company, target those. If not, then target human resources departments in other banks. Then expand to human resources functions in another financial sector, such as investment companies. Expand from one related niche to another.

Taking a vertical approach during the Niche phase will achieve your goal of building a critical mass of support for becoming the Market Monster. Taking a horizontal approach will defeat it. Going horizontal into the mass market is tempting because that's where the big money is, but a premature entrance into the mainstream will permanently cripple your company and discredit the technology.

Role of Niche Markets

Niche markets do the following:

1. They simplify the whole-product challenge in the early stages of the technology. You can earn Visionary Explorer customers immediately instead of having to wait for another round of development.

2. They're inherently profitable because you are replacing an inefficient problem situation.

3. They help you become self-funding, which gives you more control over the timing of your entry into the Whirlwind of Demand phase.

4. They represent territories of loyal customers that you can capture and who will sponsor your architecture in the "standards war" that will take place during the Demand phase.

5. They can be leveraged so that victory in one segment overflows into victories in adjacent segments. If the overflow is powerful enough, it can trigger the Demand phase

Breaking Through Paradigm Barriers—Niche Market

Two types of paradigm shift can shape the High-Tech Life Cycle: paradigm shock and "killer apps" Each presents barriers that your company must overcome.

Paradigm shock may be experienced by end users or by the infrastructure that supports them— as a form of technological shock or as cultural/psychological shock.

For example, the electric car affects automobile owners as end users. The infrastructure that supports auto owners includes gas stations, mechanics, corporations that employ owners. All must learn new ideas, make new investments, and adopt new behaviors. Their resistance can put a brake on adoption of new technology.

Your company must single out the issues of a specific niche segment and reduce paradigm shock by implementing a limited niche-specific solution that provides application breakthroughs. Later the company can support all the variations of a general solution set.

In the case of electric automobiles, the new hybrid electric-gas cars run 55 miles on a gallon of gasoline, which provides users an immediate operational savings and eases the transition from gas to electric infrastructure.

Killer Apps are application breakthroughs, new and practical ways to use the new technology. Killer Apps allow end-user roles to dramatically change and improve, resulting in dramatic returns on investment or savings for the company that installs the technology. These lucrative breakthroughs accelerate the adoption of the new technology, and so the term "killer app."

For example, in phone services, paradigm shock for the Baby Bells included such new technologies as fax, conferencing, call forwarding, and caller ID but these did not provide significant application breakthroughs for end users. On the other hand Voice Response Units did provide a Killer App breakthrough by allowing companies to replace human telephone customer service personnel with automated telephone answering services. This provided huge payroll cost savings.

Getting Ready for the Whirlwind of Demand Phase

Price point is a key indicator of Whirlwind readiness. For example, when your product gets under $1,500, it gets you into the small office market, where getting under $1,000 enables a Whirlwind. Getting under $700 gets you into the home market, where getting under $300 enables a Whirlwind.

A Whirlwind needs the whole product as a plug-and-play commodity. As long as even one significant part requires scarce expertise in order to integrate it into the end user's situation, the market will have difficulty getting into the Whirlwind phase.

One big signal for a Whirlwind is the emergence of a Killer App. Such a breakthrough will supply the universal infrastructure that appeals to a mass market, and can become a commodity.

Whirlwind of Demand—Phase II

This is the big-payoff phase, when an entire industry arises around your technology.

Target Audience: Pragmatist Settlers

Pragmatist Settlers tend to be analytical conformists who like to stick with their neighbors and are motivated to solve current problems. They consult with other Settlers trying to get a sense of when it's time to shift to a new technology. They want to see a clear market leader that's able to establish a vision—and the architectures and standards that will make the technology work in the mainstream market.

Definition—Whirlwind of Demand

During this phase the Pragmatist Settlers move together as a community. They apply these three principles

1. When it's time to move, let's all move together.
2. When we pick the vendor to lead us to the new paradigm, let's all pick the same one.
3. Once the move starts, the sooner we get it over with, the better.

A new order, a hierarchy, is created in this phase. One company will emerge with at least 50 percent of the business—the Market Monster. This company will rake in about two-thirds of the profits during the life of this technology. Two or three companies will capture most of the remaining market and profits—the Big Munsters. Any number of smaller companies will emerge around the margins—the Little Munsters. It's only during this phase that all-out battles for market share make sense. All high-tech fortunes are based on winning this battle.

The Whirlwind occurs when the general marketplace for your type of product shifts its allegiance from the old architecture to the new. Now it's time to take your R&D investment and, with modest additional work, secure entirely new niches, which gives you a very profitable situation.

Mass-market adoption occurs. The demand for the new far outstrips the supply. The company that becomes the Market Monster is the one that can sell, sell, sell—capturing customers for the lifetime of the technology—and deliver, delivery, deliver a "whole product" that's feasible and usable. It is in this phase that huge revenues and profits are won and the company may become one of the Fortune 500.

If you become the Market Monster, you'll create a market for many Munsters. Every customer who buys your platform becomes a potential Mall Phase customer for the additional bells and whistles that Munster companies will create around your infrastructure. Munsters add value and enrich the whole-product. Customers are able to do more with the technology, which drives more sales, which in turn attracts still more Munsters who create more bells and whistles. The result is an ever-expanding whole-product family.

Becoming the Market Monster gives you many advantages: You can charge more money for your product, even with a bug or two in it. You ship the highest volumes, so you enjoy the lowest cost per unit. When you charge the highest price and achieve the lowest cost, your profit margins soar. You enjoy lower cost of sales because Settlers want to buy your products—so selling them is easy. In addition, Little Munsters will often pay you to let them create products that fit in with yours. Your product not only benefits generally from their supportive products, but your company immediately benefits, bottom line.

Key Strategies—Whirlwind of Demand

1. Beat out the competition at all costs and establish a common standard for your infrastructure.

2. Focus on the infrastructure buyer within client organizations, ignoring economic buyers and end users

3. Ignore return on investment as a reason buyers should buy

4. Price competitively to maximize market share.

5. Focus on developing a reliable infrastructure and rapidly getting it installed

6. Commoditize your whole product for general purpose use in horizontal, global markets

7. Position your products horizontally as global infrastructure

8. Distribute through low-cost, high-volume channels for maximum market exposure

9. Attack competition to gain mass market share. In this phase, it's a zero-sum game, so every new customer you win is one that your competitors lose—for the life of the technology.

10. Just ship! Don't segment the market. Don't customize the product. Don't commit to any special projects. Just ship.

11. Do anything you can to streamline the creation, distribution, installation, and adoption of your whole product—avoid friction and distraction.

12. Focus on supply chains and quality in order to avoid getting returned product

13. Focus on your own organizational needs to sell and ship, not on individual customer needs.

Competition—Whirlwind of Demand

How you handle competition in this phase depends on your status in the marketplace.

As Market Monster. Focus on the distribution channel. At the high end, it's a competition for good sales reps and at the low end for the most shelf space. When competing against Little Munsters, reset the standard, temporarily making their offerings obsolete, as Intel has done with its new chips. Big Munsters may come up with new innovations, and you must meet their challenge as soon as possible with your own versions.

As Little Munster. Your reference competitor is the Monster's product but your real competition comes from other Little Munsters. Your role is to fulfill overflow demand, to provide what's needed around the margins. Your strategy should therefore be: Take the money and run. Cash out the business every day. You have nothing to gain here except the sale itself. Invest in nothing; defend nothing. The only way you can ever become a Monster is through providing a differentiated whole product to a niche segment, thus becoming a Big Munster and then taking that product to a Whirlwind phase.

As Big Munster. You have a major investment in your own technology. You are competing first and foremost for distribution of your product, simply to get access to the pent-up customer demand. You can focus and innovate within a local segment, staking out turf that's not yet committed to the Monster. You should adopt a Niche approach during the Whirlwind phase. By carving out a niche or two, there may be a place for you when the Whirlwind is over.

In the meantime, remember that Pragmatist Settlers may want to support you as a safe alternative to the Monster, in case they need it. On the other hand, they don't want to upset the Monster's authority to set de facto standards. It's the market, not the Monster, that prevents you from overtaking the Monster and becoming the leader. This has to do with the current alignment of massive amounts of wealth and powerful interest groups that are already committed to the Monster's standards. You can be aggressive but only go so far. You must keep your products current with the market's evolving standards. You can't fight the Monster on its own turf. Your question: What's the value of market share to me?

Role of Strategic Partners—Whirlwind of Demand

Once the product enters the Whirlwind phase, the pressure is to drive costs down and reliability up, so the whole product must become increasingly plug-and-play. For example, the personal computer must come with all key software programs already installed, ready to plug in and go to work. This means the Market Monster must eliminate the very partnerships that brought the product to Whirlwind readiness.

Power Hierarchy

Power is centralized here in the Market Monster company and its Big Munster partners. If it's a major technology, the market may select a Monster for each component. They are elected as the solution set within which every part is guaranteed to be compatible with every other part. The PC market is certainly major, allowing several Market Monsters. For PC operating systems market, it's Microsoft, and Big Munsters are IBM and Apple. In PC microprocessors, the Market Monster is Intel, in hard drives it's Seagate, in DRAM memory, it's Toshiba. For corporate client/servers, the Market Monster is Oracle and Big Munsters are H-P and SAP. For corporate work stations, it's Sun Microsystems.

Organizational Leadership—Whirlwind of Demand

During the Whirlwind, the line functions of manufacturing, purchasing, and quality control become crucial, as does human resources—all to provide the operational excellence that's needed to win. The original cross-functional team should become a product marketing council to ensure communication flow and problem resolution among the various line functions during the Demand phase

The company needs a leader who can function above the fray, see the forest without getting caught in the trees, use fire prevention instead of fire fighting, a leader who is unflappable and disciplined, with a process-driven management style. The leader needs expertise in making systems work, both external and internal systems. External systems must help customers mesh the old and new paradigms to create a workable infrastructure that performs effectively. Many new hires are coming on board so key internal systems include H.R. Orientation, getting people off to a good start. On the financial side, cash flow management is critical.

How to Become the Market Monster

Timing and luck are crucial but there are some things you can do to improve your chances. For example, the two greatest whirlwinds of the 1980s each went through two rounds.

Midrange computers—computers at a power level between mainframes and personal computers went through the Whirlwind first . Demand developed around DEC's minicomputer architecture, subsequently replaced by Hewlett Packard's Unix architecture with Oracle's software providing the driving energy in both rounds.

Personal computers—smaller computers went through an even greater Whirlwind. IBM provided the large-scale infrastructure and Lotus the software in the first round. Microsoft's Windows software and Intel's chips won the second round with no Monster hardware vendor. Big Munsters were Dell and Compaq.

Lessons that Oracle taught the industry about winning the Demand Phase include attack the competition ruthlessly, expand your distribution channel as fast as possible, and ignore the customer.

Lessons that H-P taught include just ship, drive to the next lower price point, and extend distribution channels. If you fail to supply any channel with your product, you leave that flank unprotected. Finding the next lower price point gives your company the first crack at a whole new customer base that wants to enter the market once prices get down to their level. Whirlwind markets will be served—it's not a question of if but of who will do it.

Lessons Microsoft and Intel taught include design partners in, institutionalize the whole product as the market leader, then commoditize the whole product by designing out your partners. This is an essential part of the commoditization, fusing together as a whole what the market has endorsed as the standard set of component parts.

The market's goal: serve as many customers as possible by reducing cost and eliminating distribution friction. The fewer the component parts and suppliers, the lower the price can be. Market forces will make this process occur. The only question is how you align your strategy with it. The market not only expects the Monster to dominate, it requires it. It's the Monster's job to beat out the competition so that one clear standard emerges.

Rules if You're Winning the Whirlwind

Don't try to control the whirlwind; you can't. Serve the tornado by driving down prices and profit margins per unit.

Don't introduce breakthrough innovations during the Whirlwind. Stay the course with your old product architecture, coming out with upgrades instead of brand new technology. Continuous innovation favors market leaders, while discontinuous innovation favors market challengers.

Design service out, not in. Make the product as "plug-and-play" as possible, with minimal need for service from vendors, retailers, or service organizations.

Betting on Who'll be Market Monster

How do savvy investors, Pragmatic Settlers, potential partners, and similar bystanders respond at the beginning of a Whirlwind battle for dominance? They place their bets on all likely winners. Then one by one they shift them away from each apparent loser toward the emerging winner. As soon as one competitor lags, they kill it immediately and reinvest that resource in the ones that are still gaining.

The Mall—Phase 4

The final phase of the high-tech life cycle we might call The Mall Phase because that's when products hit the malls and many other retail outlets frequented by the general public.

Target Audience: Conservatives, Resisters, and Holdouts

Definition—Mall Phase

Growth comes primarily from serving your own installed customer base and not from attacking the base of other companies. For most customers, it's too disruptive to switch vendors. Now you must shift your strategy away from a focus on beating out the competition and go back to putting the customer first.

Key Strategies—Mall Phase

1. Sell to end users—focusing on their experience of the product, meeting their individual needs
2. Differentiate the commoditized whole product with Add-On features targeted at specific niches
3. Distribute through the same channels but focus on merchandising to advertise the Add-On marketing messages.
4. Celebrate the Add-On offers to gain margins above the low-cost clone

5. Compete against your own low-cost offering to gain margin share

6. Position yourself in niche markets that reflect individual preferences of end users.

Competition—Mall Phase

Strategies for dealing with the competition in the Mall Phase varies, depending on what role you're playing.

As Market Monster. You can take a two-pronged attack. Attack the product-as-commodity market with a low-end offering. Attack the premium market with a series of Add-On niche offerings. Continue to innovate enough to keep the Little Munsters scrambling. If you shift the standards a little, you give customers an easy-to-absorb add-on while making the Little Munsters reengineer their clone products in order to keep up.

As Big Munster. Focus on marketing into Add-On niches where you can retain the customer, or on R&D investment, hoping to create a new paradigm shift.

As Little Munster. You provide the clone product. You can establish the rules by setting the lower price point in the market, which becomes the reference price for the Monster and Big Munsters. You compete by reducing overhead to an absolute minimum.

Role of Strategic Partners—Mall Phase

This beat-out the competition strategy of the Whirlwind Phase continues into the Mall Phase—until Add-On marketing is needed to differentiate the now-low-margin commodity. At this point you'll again find limited opportunities to develop partner relationships.

Power Hierarchy

Power shifts to the distribution channel. In the PC industry it shifts to such superstores as Comp USA.

Organizational Leadership—Mall Phase

Traditional management models become feasible, with key roles being product marketing, marketing communications, and product management. The company needs a leader who is people-oriented and focused on customer satisfaction and staff development.

Where's Your Company in the H-T Life Cycle?

In order to succeed your company must know where it fits in this High-Tech Life Cycle and what role it can play. Just as important, all the key people must agree on this.

First, decide what *type* of product yours is. Only then can you identify which phase of the life cycle it's in. Deciding on a clear category is a must. If you identify your product as both A and B, you have nothing marketable. Stores have to know what department to sell it in, and everyone must know which products to compare it with so they can decide if the price is fair. Once you identify the type, you must determine whether this product category is in the Early Market, Niche Market, Whirlwind of Demand, or Mall phase—in order to know what strategies to adopt. Then you must market-position the category of product as a whole—not your particular product.

Boost Your Creative Intelligence

As you work with paradigm shifts and market phases, you'll integrate all your intelligences, and this work will give a big boost to your Creative Intelligence. You'll need that Creative Intelligence to play with future scenarios. And, if you have some ideas about how to take a leadership role in the midst of these technological paradigm shifts, you'll be do a better job at predicting them. You'll write powerful stories that prepare you and your organization for most of the likely eventualities.

Let's look at how you can use your paradigm savvy to boost leadership success, to identify the opportunities and threats that a paradigm shift may bring, and to stay a step ahead of shifting paradigms. You'll need to understand the forces of the net economy with its dot.com businesses. You and others in your organization must use a net-oriented leadership style to integrate people into teams and networks, harness innovation in now-time, and focus on lifelong learning and knowledge, being sure to include people from diverse groups.

Booster 1. Use Paradigm Savvy

Recognizing paradigms helps you know when it's time to focus on management skills, entrepreneurial skills, and leadership skills.

Manage Better

You manage within a paradigm by applying the mission, the strategies, tactics, and techniques, the goals, the systems, the procedures, the guiding principles—what we're loosely calling the rules. A manager's job is paradigm enhancement—taking the rules and making them better. This is what most executives and managers in most corporations spend about 90 percent of their work time doing.

Lead Better

You lead when you take the risk of leaving one paradigm while it's still successful and going to a new unproved paradigm. You use your intuitive judgment, assess the risk, and if you decide it's time to shift paradigms, you convey your vision of the new paradigm to employees. You inspire them to follow that vision and bring it about. That's what good leaders and entrepreneurs do with the other 10 percent of their work time. Because of the increasingly rapid rate of paradigm shifts, you need to be good at that as well as paradigm enhancement in order to succeed in today's marketplace and workplace.

The old leadership style was to create a vision and sell it down to others, using a brilliant, take-charge, rally-the-troops approach. This style won't work any more. The new enterprise sees the leader as a collective, networked, virtual workforce with power flowing from a jointly created and shared vision. Leadership is preferably not embodied in one person but in a collective body. Vision is achieved and transmitted collectively.

Infotech creates within an organization whole networks of human intelligence and new knowledge power as people work to transform both the enterprise and themselves. It's collective leadership. Net-oriented leadership begins in teams through the collective action of people working to create a new vision or solve problems. Of course there must still be a CEO. If the CEO encourages Net-oriented leadership, the networked teams can take the leap into the transformation process and keep obsoleting, then recreating, themselves.

Leadership can and will be achieved virtually on computer networks—more and more. Human intelligence can be networked, and this network has far greater capacity for pervasive vision and collective action than does the lone leader at the top. As people online share their verbal ideas and their facial expressions, body language, designs, notes, drawings, tools—the potential for collective thinking and action expands across the company and beyond.

Personal use of the technology creates leaders. The big driver for change is the growing personal use of technology by everyone. To be an effective manager these days, you must use a Net-oriented computer. As you do, your horizons will broaden and your curiosity will soar. You'll become aware of the issues, problems, and challenges facing you, your team, and your organization.

There's a chicken-egg relationship between being informed and participating in the world. According to John Seely Brown, participant at the 1993 Aspen Institute on Telecommunications Policy, you can't really be informed unless you participate—and you can't really meaningfully participate unless you're informed. It's engagement through being, and information technology is the essential tool. If you want to, you can be a leader in the transformation.

Map the Future

To take the lead, you must break free from the past, from the old technology legacy. How? With your team, create a model of the future and of how your business must look in order to succeed in that future. Map that to the technology you now have. Do a gap analysis between where you are and where you need to go. Build a set of migration scenarios and plans for getting there—so your team can invest their time and energy in moving toward the new business model. Increasingly the tools you need for doing this will be available on the Net and won't have to be constructed internally by your company.

Become a Change Master

These rapidly changing paradigms call for change masters who can take the lead in transforming the organization. Transformation doesn't mean just adapting here and there—it means becoming a whole new organization—over and over again as times change. This new kind of leader is one who:

- Has the curiosity and confidence to lead people into new paradigms
- Can balance the need for business growth and profit with the needs of employees, customers, and society for privacy, fairness, and a share in the wealth they create
- Has the vision to think socially, the courage to act, and the strength to lead their people over and around barriers

Reward Paradigm Shift Behavior

If leaders are not willing to seriously listen to employees' ideas on how to do something better, they're sending the message that people must stay within the prevailing paradigm. The only way you can convince your employees to break the rules is to show your willingness to support that kind of behavior. Invite people to step outside the boundaries and find new ways to solve old problems. The more actively you search for new paradigms yourself—and talk about that search—the more likely your team members are to search with you and for you. Two basic things can happen when you step outside the boundaries of your current paradigm:

- You find ways to apply the prevailing paradigm rules in a new, uncharted area—you do what your company knows how to do but you do it in a new arena.
- You find a new domain that will require a new paradigm to solve the problems in it.

In the first instance, you use the old paradigm but move out the boundaries. For example, you find a new type of customer with problems that can be solved with your current paradigm—moving out your customer boundary line. In the second instance, you attack problems that cannot be solved with your current paradigm. Perhaps your current customers have such problems. They're open to allowing your company to solve them but you must find a new paradigm in order to do so.

Allow and reward cross-talk between people from different departments or divisions—people functioning within different paradigms. They need to understand one another's problems. People will begin making connections in their minds about how to use some rule or tool in their own paradigm to help their peer in another division solve a problem. They'll begin connecting what a colleague has explained about a rule or tool with a possible solution to their own problem.

Listen to all the crazy ideas—in order to create an idea pool. Listen for connections as your mind mulls over the pool. Keep and open mind and be constantly alert for the possibility of connecting two or four or more ideas.

Make Creative Play-Space

Encourage people to find innovative new solutions to problems by reducing the risks they face when they propose new boundaries, rules, and paradigms. For example, create an Innovation Committee that periodically holds Explore New Ideas Sessions in which people can offer their ideas. If the committee believes the ideas might work, they and the proposer carry the idea to top management. If not, the idea might go anonymously into an idea pool where periodically ideas are reviewed for possible connections and combinations. The committee rules must be: never make a person or idea wrong, never ridicule, and always value and appreciate the proposers' effort. The idea is to build trust, create a safe play space for creativity, and reduce the risk of being wrong.

Booster 2. Identify Paradigm Shift Opportunities and Barriers

How can you identify problems that need a new paradigm in your field? Ask yourself, What are the problems all my peers want to solve and don't have the slightest idea of how to do it? Write them down. Then ask yourself, Which phase am I functioning in? Who's likely to support and resist my change ideas? You must understand the phases and forces, how major shifts differ from continual improvement, and how paradigm blindness affects most people.

Paradigm Shifts Versus Continual Improvement

North American business usually takes the lead in exploring and discovering new paradigms, breaking out of an old Phase 3 into a new Phase 1. But Japanese business has often taken the lead in pioneering, getting in early in Phase 2 and staying the course—whether it's computer chips or VCRs. Continuous improvement is a paradigm discovered in the U.S. but perfected in Japan. The goal of continuous improvement is to find a way, every day, to get just one-tenth of one percent improvement in what you make or do. Over a work year of 240 working days that's a 24 percent improvement.

If you use continuous improvement from the beginning of Becoming-Established Phase 2, you solve more of the problems of the paradigm quicker. This can give you an enormous competitive advantage over anyone who gets into the new paradigm after you. For example, the Sony Walkman added auto reverse, then bass and treble, special smaller headphones, shock resistance, water resistance, electronic radio tuning, smaller size, rechargeable batteries, still smaller size, Dolby, alarm clock.

Paradigm pioneers who practice continuous improvement never give an even break to the settlers who come later in Becoming-Established Phase 2. The Visionary Pioneers can always be a step ahead to make their product more irresistible to the buying public. And every day a Pragmatic Settler delays getting into the market, the less of the market is left for them and the more it costs to enter and compete with the trailblazers. For Visionary Pioneers, it's first-in – big risk, but also first-in = big potential advantage.

Paradigm Blindness

A survey of large U.S. high-tech companies found that 97 percent of competitive failures resulted from not paying attention to market signals or failure to act on known vital information [Fuld 1999]. What you perceive is dramatically determined by your paradigm—after all, that's the mental model you see through and work from. What may be perfectly visible and obvious to the people with one paradigm may be quite literally invisible to people with a different paradigm. In other words, it's possible that you will not be able to see data that's right before your eyes if it doesn't fit into your paradigm. In fact, all the senses have paradigm filters, so you can listen but not hear, touch not but feel, and sniff but not smell. You see best what you're supposed to see or expect to see. You see poorly, if at all, that data that does not fit into your paradigm.

Most of us have heard the story of seventeenth century European explorers who anchored their sailing ships in New World ports and rowed in to meet the natives. When the explorers pointed out their ship to the natives, they couldn't see the vessel—huge by their standards—sitting far out in the bay. This was because it's simply not within their experience or mindset. They couldn't pick it out from the haze, the waves, the clouds, the rest of the environment. A similar phenomenon occurs when as a student you first go to biology lab and try to see the tiny organisms you've been assigned to identify. A lab assistant has to help you identify boundaries and recognize key visual aspects of the organism before you can change your mental focus and piece it out.

Paradigms define what's important and what's not, and you ignore or eliminate input that doesn't fit—or you alter it to fit your expectations. You can also create needed data that doesn't exist and totally believe that it's real. To see the future more clearly, put aside the certainties of your paradigms and begin to examine the fringes and see if you can find the people who are changing the rules and boundaries.

Booster 3. Stay a Step Ahead of Shifting Paradigms

You, and the leaders of the organization, can identify the possibility of a paradigm shift in your field by asking yourself:

- What really needs to be done but is impossible to do, but if it could be done, it would fundamentally change my field?

- What problem really needs to be solved, but no one has been able to solve it—and if they did, it would fundamentally change the field?

Ask the questions often, of everyone. Listen to the answers. It will keep you in touch with that strange space on the other side of your boundaries where you could be put back to zero. Your best job insurance is to know what your prevailing paradigm is and how it might change. You can't stop the process but you can learn to solve the problems the paradigm addresses. If you can spot the signs of change early, know what the changes are, you can take part in the paradigm shift, even become a trailblazer. This will help guarantee that you're a part of it.

Booster 4. Understand Net Business

The Net provides a way for all the computers in the world to communicate with each other. Global networks of distributed intelligence are allowing us to share information, to connect and to communicate as a global community—changing the way we do business and changing what it takes to succeed in business. This obviously leads to finding better solutions to our problems—more quickly than ever—and to moving on to those unsolved problems whose solutions call for new paradigms. Three sectors are converging to create a new net-oriented economy:

- the computing sector of hardware and software

- the communications sector of television, radio, and telephone

- the content sector of publishing and entertainment

These sectors are converging to provide us with interactive multimedia. Instead of the one-way communication mode provided by broadcasts, newspapers, and books, we're moving into interactive communication in which we send as well as receive. Instead of one or two mediums—text, audio, video—we're moving toward combining all three—and for virtual reality we've added a fourth medium, kinesthetics.

Productivity is growing the fastest in the computing sector, but jobs are growing fastest in the publishing-entertainment sector. The profits are moving to content because that's where value is created for customers. The computers, software, and transmission lines are becoming utilities, commodities. In most cases new employment growth is not occurring in large companies but in startups and smaller companies. The information highway is the engine of new employment and most jobs are not low-skilled service jobs but high-value, high-paying jobs.

The new media are transforming the way scientific research is done, the way education is delivered, the artistic process, virtually all productive activity in our society. They're changing organizations as we know them and the way we do business, work, play, live, and think.

Knowledge knows no boundaries—it's not limited to a region or country. Knowledge is becoming the key resource, so we've moved to a world economy. Vital for success now are ad hoc alliances, strategic partnering, and information technology. Collaboration is going beyond the old boundaries of two companies to groups of companies that link together for a common purpose. The entire planet is linked together and any linked business can readily do business with any of the other linked parties. Technology has enabled globalism, and in turn globalization is driving the expansion of technology.

Link Together Teams, Suppliers, Customers

The new organization is a network of cross-functional teams that often reach out to customers, suppliers, and others. The next major wave of change is probably the ability of your organization to integrate its internal information services with various external information services via the Net. For example the widespread use of Electronic Data Interchange (EDI) is becoming fully realized through the simplified and readily available services on the Net. EDI links computer systems between suppliers and their customers for purchase orders, invoices, billing, and record keeping—allowing both buyer and seller to dramatically reduce the time and expense of handling an order. It's the beginning of a tidal wave of electronic commerce that will shift the pulse of business to real time and change the way companies relate and do business.

The firm as we once knew it is breaking up. Effective persons, working in high-performance team structures become integrated organization networks of clients and servers that reach out to customers, suppliers, others. They move onto the public Net, changing the way products and services are developed, sold, and distributed. This means new paradigms for making money.

Anticipate Paradigm Shifts

Competitors can emerge from unexpected places. The Internet and the Web are wild cards that can affect everything. For example, the sales and delivery systems for many types of products and services may rely more and more on Web Pages. Competitors will be new start-ups, who create their own Web Pages, or established computer firms, such as Microsoft and Intel. For example, Microsoft made moves to take over the banking industry, trying to use personal computers, accounting software, and home banking as the main banking vehicle.

Companies that survive and thrive must be on the leading edge of introducing technologically advanced products—because the first to offer such products can lock up lucrative markets. What's most important is getting in at the right time—timing is crucial. If a competitor gets the technological edge, it can be difficult to impossible to stay in the game. On the other hand, executive teams must be very careful about spending huge amounts on a particular technology unless they're very clear about what it will accomplish for them. Technology moves so quickly that a company's expertise could become obsolete by the time it's been acquired. One executive said, "You could be cornering the buggy whip market—if you bet on the wrong technology."

Buy and Sell Through E-Commerce

Global e-commerce functions through business exchanges of merchandise providers that list goods they want to buy or sell on a website's electronic bulletin board. They can negotiate anonymously. If they make a deal, the system helps them initiate credit checks, arrange financing, and get legal and customs paperwork completed by local companies. Thousands of industrial equipment manufacturers might list their products and services in the website's large electronic catalog, for a fee. Their goal is to also process orders for that equipment and transfer payments for it—in exchange for a small service fee on each transaction, paid to the catalog company. Here's the process:

- Customers browse an electronic catalog, click on items they want to purchase, and the computer sends the orders directly to the merchant's computer.

- Merchant's computer checks the customers' credit and determines that the goods wanted are available.

- Merchant's warehouse and shipping departments are notified and the goods are readied for shipping.

- Merchant's accounting department bills the customers electronically.

- The customers pay the bills electronically.

The time this takes depends primarily on the delivery system—the time it takes to get the merchandise from the warehouse to the customer. Total time could be only 24 hours. Other e-commerce arrangements are springing up almost daily.

How does your organization buy supplies? Is it the most cost-effective process available? Since the 1970s manufacturing giants, such as General Motors, have used electronic data interchange (EDI) to order parts automatically from suppliers. Yet in 1996 most business-to-business sales were still done with paper forms. A paper order costs on average $150, whether it's for $10 or $10,000. E-commerce has cut the cost to about $25. Most companies reduced the number of suppliers so they could negotiate volume-discount purchases with a few favored suppliers.

The business staff of a large university discovered that the school was doing business with about 20,000 vendors of office and laboratory supplies each year. About 87 percent of the orders were for less than $500. They developed in-house computer expertise and a high-speed intranet as the basis for a new purchasing system. Now staff people can order paperclips or petri dishes by clicking through a Web-based catalog, which makes sure nobody spends more than their authorized limit. Payments are made with purchasing cards from Visa. Those 20,000 vendors were reduced to two main suppliers—one for office supplies, and one for laboratory supplies. They deliver most items within a day or two right to the user's desk.

Upgrade Go-Between Services to Survive and Thrive

All sorts of specialty markets for selling products and services are popping up on the Web. Such e-commerce is powerful and is spreading in patches and spurts. Even though it isn't spreading consistently across the entire retail sector yet, we know that in the long run buyers will use the markets that are most convenient and economical for them. Most experts think that markets will increasingly be e-markets. Most buying and selling will eventually take place in virtual marketplaces that allow buyers and sellers to meet electronically and trade in goods and services without the aid, or cost, of traditional brokers and agents.

Travelers can make their own plane and hotel bookings on the Internet. Food producers can accept customer orders on the Internet and deliver food to their homes without wholesalers or even supermarkets. Artists, such as musicians, painters, actors, and writers—and their producers—can sell their artistic productions on the Net with little or no need for agents, recording and publishing companies, retail outlets, or broadcasters. Clothes, bicycles, cars can be custom made to meet people's individual measurements and needs and shipped from the manufacturer to the user. Employees can access information and make decisions formerly provided by middle managers.

What does all this mean for the go-betweens of the world? How does it affect agents, wholesalers, distributors, retailers, brokers, and other persons functioning between suppliers and users—as well as middle managers? Obviously, they must provide additional value if they're to survive in the net economy. These people in the middle of the value chain must do more than just pass along the product or process. They must have the valuable contacts, the hard-to-get information, the inspirational or innovative ideas—something essential for the deal, or something that makes it so much better that it's worth extra money. If they can't add some value, they're not needed and won't survive. The innovative ones who find new niches, ways to become indispensable, will thrive.

Change the Focus from Mass to Individual

Mass media is breaking down into millions of channels, potentially one for every person who interacts on the Internet. For example, custom jeans, offered through a company's website and made by computerized manufacturing processes, turn what was formerly "mass production" into production runs of one pair. Similarly, as marketers identify specific customer groups or persons to receive the firm's sales information, what was formerly "mass marketing" becomes segmented or individualized marketing,.

The net organization, therefore, is based on the individual customer as the smallest unit, a business unit of one. These customers are served by motivated, self-learning, entrepreneurial workers who use Internet tools to collaborate to give the customer the right product or service. These employees apply their knowledge and creativity in order to create value, and they often cluster in teams. The new computerized info-structure greatly enhances their capacity to develop new relationships. The company provides the base structure for their activity, and it looks more like a web than a pyramid.

Booster 5. Integrate People into Teams and Networks

The Net-oriented organization is a vast web of relationships from all levels and all business functions. The boundaries inside and outside are ever-changing and penetrable—suppliers and customers come in and out at times, for example. Small companies can band together to act like large ones, achieving large-company massive buying power and access to money and other resources. Larger companies are breaking down into smaller clusters so they can achieve the advantages typical of small companies—agility, autonomy, and flexibility. They can retain the resources of the large parent corporation without being burdened by its old deadening bureaucracies. Integrating people into teams that network with others has become a way to create wealth.

The Virtual Corporation

In virtual corporations much of the work, the meetings, and communication take place on computer screens, fax machines, car phones, voice mail, and video conferences. Work teams may include company specialists, independent contractors, suppliers, customers, and investors. They may be scattered around the globe, change from month to month, and never meet face to face. Or they may be self-managing teams that meet every day. They may work together to develop the plans, set the standards, identify and solve the problems, make the decisions, and provide the products and services. In any case, the degree of success or failure depends heavily on people's relationships with one another.

The Net-oriented enterprise is becoming a far-reaching extension of the virtual corporation because it will access external business partners and constantly reconfigure its business relationships, perhaps with a dramatic increase in outsourcing. It will act like the Internet—participative and synergistic. The overall economy will act the same way. Already walls are coming down between manufacturers, suppliers, customers, and even competitors. We're seeing Net-oriented business, government, learning, and health care, as well as other segments. The major utility of the twenty-first century is the information infrastructure—the broad-band highway of fiber optics.

Customers as Team Members

Including customers in the creation and implementation process is becoming commonplace. Television viewers or Internet users, for example, can become producers of the product or service they get. For example, they can highlight the top 10 topics they're interested in and specify the preferred news sources, talk shows, and graphic styles they want in their custom news report. Consumers become co-producers when they create and send messages to colleagues, contribute to bulletin board discussion groups, select the movie ending they want to see from several alternative endings, walk through virtual homes, or test drive virtual cars.

With the new computer capabilities, organizations can do more than just consume information and technology. They can produce infotech. For example, automobile manufacturers can do more than just assemble cars. They can produce on the net the infomercials, driver navigational tools, and other services that customers want.

Booster 6. Harness Innovation—in Now Time

The net economy is an innovation-based economy. Leading-edge companies know they must make their own products obsolete before someone else does. As soon as they develop a great product, the next goal is to develop a better one that will make the current one obsolete. Most large U.S. companies introduce more than one new product a day. In 1995 Sony introduced 5000 new products. Microsoft executive Kim Drew says, "No matter how good your product, you're only 18 months away from failure." Products come and go more rapidly all the time. The average time to create and manufacture a new product has dropped from 2500-person days per product to three hours. About 90 percent of Millers' beer revenues come from beers that didn't exist 24 months ago.

Companies must also obsolete their own businesses—creating a new type of business with new relationships before a competitor does. Toyota's motto is to "reinvent our company proactively in order to ride the wave of change."

Do it now and then immediately work on doing it better. This motto is a key driver and variable in the economic activity and business success of the net organization. In the past, such inventions as cameras and copy machines provided revenues for decades. Today consumer electronic products have a typical product life of two months. Just-in-time applies to everything from when goods are received from suppliers to when products are shipped to customers.

Human imagination is the main source of value in this high-tech world. The company's major challenge is to create a climate in which innovation is valued, encouraged, and rewarded. Most growth is coming from small- and medium-sized businesses.

With the fast pace of change and complexity of markets, customers often don't know what what's possible and what to ask for. Business leaders must innovate beyond what their customers can imagine. They must understand the needs of their customers. They must thoroughly understand what's possible with the emerging technologies—then provide products and services that surprise and delight customers. To accomplish this in your organization, its leaders must establish a climate where risk-taking is rewarded, human imagination can fly free, and creativity can blossom.

Booster 7. Focus on Knowledge and Lifelong Learning

The key to an organization's success in the net economy lies in the knowledge and creative genius of the product strategists, developers, and marketers. What counts is a company's ability to attract, retain, and continually grow the capabilities of knowledge workers and provide the environment for innovation and creativity. Lifelong organizational learning becomes the only sustainable competitive advantage a company can create.

If a picture is worth a thousand words, the right multimedia document accessed at the right time is worth a thousand pictures. E-mail and groupware are just the beginnings of a whole new way of human collaboration. Product planners and designers are working as one collaborative team that may be scattered in various locations—home, hotel room, office—around the world.

The costs of information and coordination are dropping. More than ever we're able to create wealth by adding knowledge to each product at every step. Theoretically, all a person needs in order to succeed in today's economy are a good brain, a telephone, a modem, and a personal computer. But in practice most knowledge workers also need motivation and trustful team relationships to be effective. Knowledge workers are the owners of this new means of production, and they're better positioned than any work group in history to share in the wealth.

Effective leaders must understand what makes today's knowledge workers tick and how to keep them motivated in the Net-oriented firm. To begin with, businesses must provide more and more of the learning—relying less on traditional schools for two reasons.

1. Working and learning are becoming the same activity for most people.

2. Knowledge is such an important part of products.

Products and services designed to help people learn are badly needed, and there are huge and growing opportunities for those who can deliver them. Self-paced interactive learning delivered through computer disks is just one of the new learning technologies that's meeting employees' needs for continual learning. Courses offered through the Internet are another.

On the other hand, individual employees also must take responsibility for lifelong learning. The entrepreneurial process creates the environment where people can take the initiative and it provides the structure necessary for people to do so. Leaders are responsible for building organizations where people can continually expand their capacities to understand complexity, clarify vision, and improve their shared mental models—organizations where people can take responsibility for their own learning.

Booster 8. Aim for Diversity

High tech offers enormous opportunities and advantages. But what about the disadvantages? They include possible invasion of privacy over the Net, security problems, and confidentiality issues. We're in the process of solving most of these problems.

The more difficult problem is the growing socioeconomic gap. Compare the types of people who own computers by ethnicity and age, according to Don Tapscott (1996):

• Asian Americans 36 percent

• European Americans (Caucasians) 29 percent

• Latino Americans 12 percent

- African Americans 9.5 percent

- People over 55 and under 25—the least likely age categories to own computers, the older group because many don't use computers, the younger group because many can't afford them or use their parents'

Those who don't have the educational basics—the ability to continually expand their knowledge base to keep up with the net economy—will fall further and further behind. The gap between the *haves* and *have-nots* is already widening. We must find a way to provide the education that allows these people to join the Net-oriented enterprise. You can use your influence to support such education and training.

Future Scenarios

Business leaders who are successful have no option but to visualize the future, various scenarios that might play out. This helps them to anticipate paradigm shifts and ways to not only survive them but to profit from them. If you want to be a business leader, you must learn to predict how these various possibilities might affect your firm. You must imagine what new opportunities might arise that would offer chances for meeting customer needs or desires, for dreaming up products or services that would intrigue or delight customers. You must foresee how new situations might threaten your services or products, your company's very existence. You must be constantly coming up with new products and services that make your current ones obsolete. You must help your firm reinvent itself on a regular basis—before a competitor makes reinvention a necessity, and before it's too late! Now you'll have a powerful tool for all this—your skill at creating future scenarios.

What Are Future Scenarios?

Scenarios are stories. Ideally, you will create three stories of the future for your firm—one that is quite optimistic, one that is quite pessimistic, and one that lies somewhere between. You—like all humans—have an innate ability to build scenarios and to foresee the future. You have a drive to tell yourself all kinds of stories about the future—everything from returning something you bought to finding a marriage partner. You can and do simulate the past and future in your mind all the time. You mentally practice ways of handling things and deciding which way is best. In your dreams each night, you spin entire scenes that may be rehearsals of possible futures.

You'll improve your ability to create future scenarios with training and practice. Intuition is a very important factor. Also, encourage your imagination, your love of the new and different, and your sense of the absurd—as well as your sense of realism.

Scenarios are not about predicting the future, but about perceiving possible and probable futures while living in the present moment. Scenarios deal with the world of facts and the world of perceptions. They explore for facts but they aim at perceptions inside the heads of decision makers. Their purpose is to gather and transform information of strategic significance into fresh perceptions. When it works, it's a creative experience that leads to an emotional "Aha" and allows people to see strategic insights they were previously unable to see.

Important questions about the future are usually complex and imprecise, so the language of story and myth helps us to grasp the answers. Stories are about meaning, helping to explain why things could happen in a certain way.

- They give order and meaning to events, helping us to understand future possibilities.

- They open us up to multiple perspectives. They allow us to show how different characters view certain events and find various meanings in those events.

- They help us to cope with complexity.

- Scenarios are stories that give meaning to events.

Inventing characters may or may not be helpful. What is necessary is to imagine attitudes of key players who will affect future events. They're often large groups of people in the form of organizations. Their attitudes are in fact myths, histories with meaning that are widely shared. Myths are consensus reality, the way things are as people in a particular culture or organization believe them to be. They're paradigms people refer to when they try to understand their world and its behavior. Myths are the patterns that people have in common—patterns of belief, perception, behavior. They're not necessarily fictitious.

In writing scenarios, we spin myths, old and new, that will be important in the future. These mythic scenarios help us come to grips with forces and feelings that otherwise seem vague and elusive. Myths help us describe the forces and feelings, envision them, bring them to life—in a way that helps us make use of them. Story-telling in the form of myths can reveal something about what we feel, hope, expect, or fear for the future (Schwartz 1991).

What Is the Scenario-Writing Process?

The process you'll use in developing future scenarios has seven steps.

Step 1. Ask, what are the key decisions I need to make?

Step 2. Use three points of view—optimistic, pessimistic, and status quo

Step 3. Gather the information about trends

Step 4. Identify driving forces, knowns, and unknowns

Step 5. Compose three plots, stories, scenarios

Step 6. Rehearse the future, living through each scenario as if it were unfolding

Step 7. Review the scenarios a year later—as a learning process.

Step 1: Discover the Decisions You Need to Make

Begin by looking inward, examining the mindsets you personally use, either consciously or unconsciously, to make judgments about the future. Do inner research, gathering information from within yourself. If you're writing future scenarios for an organization, ask and get good answers to these questions. What is the organization's current mission and goals? How do our company leaders feel about prospects for the future? What are their mindsets and how might their viewpoints affect the organization's future? Isolate the key decisions that need to be made now in order to be ready for the future.

Step 2: Develop Three Viewpoints

View the decision from 3 points of view: optimistic, pessimistic, status quo

- Let the optimist within temporarily to set aside the rose-colored glasses and look at the possible traps on the path to success.

- Let the pessimist within temporarily put on rose-colored glasses and look for unexpected breakthroughs and triumphs that might occur.

- Let the status quo mentality prepare itself to recognize change when it does occur and not just assume that it's insignificant.

Refine the focus. You'll constantly move between narrow questions related to specific situations (Should this new product target people in their 20s?) and broad ones, related to the world at large (What if the inflation exceeds 5 percent?).

Step 3. Find and Gather Information about Trends

Scenarios work when the story resonates in some ways with what people already know, and then leads them from that resonance to a new way of perceiving the world. So you must sample evidence from the work and build it into the story. Look for those facts and perceptions that challenge your assumptions—look for evidence that undermines them.

Be flexible in your perspective. Focus on questions that matter to you, but also keep your awareness open for the unexpected. Learn to pick out a key piece of vital information from the mass of data you encounter. Keep your radar screen on, so when something unusual shows up, you notice it. Put yourself in other characters' shoes:

"If I were a Chinese business woman, what would I . . ."

"If I were chair of the Federal Reserve, how would I . . ."

Then look for the information you'd want if you were that character. Concentrate on educating yourself about how key players would view various events. From that perspective, pass information through your mind so it affects your outlook. Tune your attention in different ways. Focus more on how people will perceive information than on the information itself.

Research current topics that affect business decisions. Look for current trends likely to affect the future most significantly. Some typical topics that affect most business decisions are shown here.

Technology and science

These segments literally shape the future and taken together are the most important drivers of future events. For example, virtual reality.

Perception-shaping events

Look for signs that public perception is changing in certain areas. For example, environmental pollution.

TV images

Mass media images both reflect people's beliefs and help shape them. The snapshot images are shared by billions of people around the globe. They give a glimpse of the public agenda. Watch the first reactions of the society as a whole. Does an event touch a responsive chord. When the response is particularly deep and wide, a more profound paradigm shift can occur—a deep change in belief systems. When this occurs, the people just can't seem to get enough of the images and the talk, and the broadcasters respond by focusing incessantly on the topic. An early example was the Gulf War. Later examples include the deaths of John F. Kennedy, Jr. and Princess Diana, the trials of O.J. Simpson, William Kennedy Smith, and Lorena Bobbitt, and the Monica Lewinsky scandal.

Music

Trends in music can show you how people are feeling and the form that freedom is likely to take in the future. Rap music is mainly about anger and rage and can tell us about the growing divisiveness among U.S. subcultures. World Music includes music from Egypt, Ethiopia, Morocco, Iran, Turkey, India, and other equatorial countries. Its a trend that reflects serenity, enthusiasm, and mutual respect among these countries. It may mean that a remarkable transformation is taking place. Historic, indigenous cultures could become elements in a new type of global culture that's not dependent on Western values, but is available to the world through Western technology, It suggests a growing unity

Fringes

Pay attention to what's going on at the fringes of society because new knowledge develops here. As you investigate the fringes, you begin to develop a sense about which people are mapmakers and which are crackpots.

Remarkable people

Look for people who may be creating a paradigm shift, diverse people from various cultures and backgrounds. Travel can help you recognize remarkable people. Look for people whose thinking is unorthodox. Find people who challenge your preconceptions. Read challenging books and articles. Contact the authors. Personal relationships are the source of facts and of judgment. Don't evaluate people by how often they're right, but by how often they push you to look at something in a new way. Get to know people that you disagree with but can talk agreeably with. Let their remarks set you to thinking along new paths.

Sources of surprise

Read outside your immediate specialty. Become enchanted with other fields of information. Read book reviews. Browse the internet. Each month go to a local bookstore to browse the bookshelves and to scan several magazines. Skim books and articles. Look for surprises, viewpoints that are new to you. Nonfiction is usually the most useful.

Immersion in the New

Immerse yourself in new, challenging environments. Travel is the best way to force yourself to adopt a new viewpoint. If you can't do it physically, do it mentally by reading about other cultures, watching films, spending time with people from other countries.

The Internet

It's the best way to reach many people and to find experts in any field.

Step 4. Identify Driving Forces, Knowns, Unknowns

The building blocks you need for scenarios are the current trends and the ways they're likely to change the future scene. Envision the newspaper headlines of tomorrow that describe various alternative futures or scenarios in which your company must operate. Then look at three types of trends that will be your story-writing building blocks: 1) driving forces, 2) things that are known, and 3) things that are unknown.

Driving Forces

Every organization is driven by some key forces. Some are internal, such as company mission and goals and the company workforce. Others are external, such as government regulations that affect the company. Many of these outside factors are not intuitively obvious because you're not aware of them. You must examine the driving forces in order to build upon your initial ideas about the future. Without this step, you can't really think through a scenario.

Among the many forces within the company and outside it, you must determine which ones are really significant. Then find any hidden forces that underlie them. Trust your instincts. You'll be interested in the factors that affect the decision you need to make. You'll quickly see that some driving forces are critical to the current decision, and others don't have much impact. Use team work. Diverse teams are best. Driving forces often seem obvious to one person and hidden to another. Do your work individually first. Then brainstorm together.

Look at trends in all the following segments. Determine which trends are driving forces that affect your organization and your scenario decision.

Society

Look at baby booms, baby busts cultural beliefs, what's hot, what's not.

Technology

Look at telecommunications, virtual reality, biogenetics.

The technology explosion means that education levels are going up rapidly worldwide as people realize their financial survival depends on it. World-changing innovations will occur more rapidly than ever. Which are on the horizon? What's in the research pipeline? Tech change alone may be strong enough to provide prosperity in spite of other global problems. Look at biotech and biomedicine. Also research nano-technologies, such as molecular engineering and new industrial materials fabricated from the atomic or molecular level. Project how that will affect infrastructures.

Economy

Look at regional, national, global, ups and downs, global competitiveness, new markets

The global information economy will create new forms of organization. The computer, financial, entertainment, and communication industries are leading this transition. Key economic relationships are being transformed. The speed of global transactions is generating speculative wealth even faster than it's generating new products and services. The new definition of wealth is the exchange of information, not possession of material resources. World paper financial transactions are already more than 10 times larger than physical trade transactions.

Regional currencies will become more common, leading to an eventual world currency or exchange unit. The global economy is being dominated more by market dynamics and multinational interests than by old political structures. Events to watch: evolution of telecommunication standards and regulation of international securities trading.

Environment

Focus on global warming, pollution, cleanup.

The amount of energy people consume is a powerful driving force in political matters, technology, and global ecology. Two forces are holding back energy consumption: the under-estimation of damage being done to the environment, as well as the bottom-line benefits to be gained from energy efficiency.

Population is a critical driving force. For example, if every Chinese citizen had just one motor scooter, the world's oil demand would increase dramatically and prices would increase. The rapid growth of population in economically developing countries will push up energy demand, but it's not clear how energy-intensive the economic growth in those countries will be. New and unproven energy options, such as large-scale solar power may play a crucial role. So may small-scale electric generators, using fuel cells or gas-fired turbines. It could mean the end of the electric grid that underlies industrial civilization. It could mean that business would experience no fundamental long-term constraint from lack of available energy.

Political-governmental-legal developments

Review these at the local, national, and global levels of specific countries. Focus on whether the trend is toward more or less democracy, probabilities of war, human rights, and government regulations that stem from change in other segments

Global pragmatism, for example, is transcending politics. "Whatever works" is becoming more important than left versus right or capitalism versus socialism. This mood is so pronounced that experts can't imagine a plausible scenario that would contradict it, unless local cultural conflicts come to play a much larger role on the world stage, for example conflicts in the Soviet Union, Middle East, or South Asia. The downside of global pragmatism is a loss of certain belief structures and a widening gap in society between rich and poor.

The Knowns

Look for what you already know that's relevant to this scenario.

Remember, data is raw, unconnected pieces of knowledge—bits and pieces from here and there, such as employee complaints, inflation rates, number of products. Data is pooled into information so you can make some connections. Then it's analyzed further into intelligence that allows you to make decisions. Intelligence is analyzed information. Research indicates that the best source of competitive information in a high-tech company is its sales force, following by internal management sources and the Internet [Fuld 1999].

Here are some typical "knowns."

Slow-changing phenomena, such as the growth of populations, the development of resources, the building of infrastructure.

Constrained situations, such as limited money, space, personnel, technology.

Things in the pipeline, such as how large a generation of children will be in 5 years.

Inevitable collisions, such as growing population of urban drivers and lack of new roadway systems, leading to gridlock.

The Unknowns

Look for what you don't know that may be critical to this scenario. Seek out the critical unknowns in order to prepare for them. Find them by questioning your assumptions about predetermined elements. What might cause a change in the population, such as greater number of immigrants than anticipated.

Uncover the predetermined elements and the critical uncertainties. These often overlap with each other and with driving forces. Analyze each one for different purposes, in different ways. Weave together these conceptual building blocks in order to deepen your understanding of the world and the elements of your scenario. Clarify your understanding of the dynamics and patterns of the situation.

Step 5. Write Three Scenarios

Now you begin to write the scenarios. Remember story telling is an art. Focus on how you perceive elements in various situations. If you have trouble distinguishing driving forces from predetermined elements from uncertainties, think of a story important to your own life. Create an image of the elements in that story. Scenarios often fall into 3 groups:

1. more of the same, but better
2. worse than now
3. different from now, and better

A common trap in choosing three scenarios is the temptation to make one represent the high road, one the low road, and one the average of the two. Try to make that first path a bit off the wall, to avoid a business-as-usual path. See the examples of brief scenarios at the end of this chapter.

Picking a Plot

Three main plots that show up are winners and losers, challenge and response, and evolution.

Winners and losers plots

Most plots start with a motive that drives the characters. The winners and losers plot starts with the viewpoint that the world is basically limited, that resources are scarce, and that if one side gets richer, the other must get poorer. The zero-sum game shows up often in politics and in mature industries. Conflict is inevitable, but often the sides compromise in a balance of power. This typically leads to a gradual buildup of tension, suspicion, and uneasy alliances. Winners and losers plots lead to secret alliances. People with this view may rely on conspiracy theories. In the past, this logic has led to war.

Challenge and response plots

In adventure stories, an individual faces one unexpected test after another. Each time, as a result, the tested person emerges different from the way she or he was before. Overcoming the test is important because of its effect on the heroine's or hero's character. The challenge even gives life meaning. Each difficulty is an opportunity to learn.

Evolution plots

Evolutionary changes involve slow change in one direction—usually either growth or decline. They're hard to spot if you're not attuned to them, because they take place so slowly. Once spotted, though, they're easy to manage because they don't suddenly leap out at you. The most common evolutionary plot today is technology. New innovations sprout from earlier technologies, gradually ripening, and then bursting upon the world. Technological growth involves the development of new niches. It's also evolutionary because new tools fit within an existing system. A designer must think about the web of systems that would support the new product or service. Economic control tends to move to the places where technology evolves the fastest.

Other Plots

Other plots are revolution, cycles, infinite possibility, Lone Ranger, and my generation plots.

Revolution plots. This refers to a sudden dramatic change, usually unpredictable in nature, a discontinuity. Ask, Where are the big discontinuities likely to be?

Cycle plots. Economic matters often occur in cycles. In building your plot, bring in your knowledge of economic theory. For example, if the Federal Reserve increases the money supply, then interest rates normally go down, then people borrow and spend more, so inflation occurs, which in turn causes to Fed to restrict the money supply. The timing of cycles is important, and unpredictable unless you look for clues.

Infinite possibility plots. This starts with a public perception that the world will expand and improve, infinitely. This may mean institutions pour money into research, people spend instead of saving for the future, excess is evident in many forms.

Lone Ranger plots. This plot focuses on the individual against a system. It says that the ordering principles of politics, business, and technology cannot reach the basic individual at the soul level. When two or more Lone Rangers butt heads, it creates a nasty winners-losers conflict.

My Generation plots Scenarios should always include the influence that the culture has on people's values, especially the culture of large generations of people.

Composing Your Plots

To compose your plots, begin by describing how the driving forces might plausibly behave, based on how those forces have behaved in the past. They might behave in many different ways. Explore some of the alternatives, based on the plots, or combination of plots, that are most worth considering. To find plausible plots, use the uncertainties that seem most important. Eventually, sketch out the plausible plots in a way that helps you foresee a good strategy for dealing with three eventualities.

Interaction of Plots

You'll rarely consider your plots alone. You'll look at the ways the different plots might handle the same forces.

The Straight-Line Myth

Don't expect events to travel in a straight line, either toward disaster or toward perfection. When things get worse, people often expect them to get much worse, until they're disastrous. But there is also a reaction to any action. People will resist, look for solutions, and otherwise try to prevent disaster. When things get better, many people want to get on the bandwagon and claim their share of the rewards, which can impede a straight line to more wealth for all.

Working with a Team

Developing future scenarios is a huge undertaking in many companies. They naturally involve the efforts of many persons working in a team situation. When this is the case, members usually do some research on their own, after some meetings to establish the decision and other factors. Eventually the team comes together to create the future scenarios. Whether you're working in a team or on your own, at this point, you need to develop ideas that respond to these kinds of questions:

- What are the driving forces?
- What is inevitable?
- What do we think is uncertain?
- How about this or that scenario?

Get to a point where ideas are churning. Then break off. Go home and sleep on it. People will inevitably come up with new ideas.

Writing the Scenarios

The main elements of all stories are:

1. Setting - idea
2. Characters
3. Plot

Usually several plot lines will intersect. Look at converging forces and try to understand how and why they might intersect. Then extend that image into coherent pictures of alternative futures.

- Review typical driving forces. Ask, are there any others?
- Review the typical plots. Ask, are there any others?

Finding the Characters

The *characters* tend to be either driving forces or institutions, such as nations, companies, or regional bodies. In institutions, business leaders reflect wider forces within the institution itself, forces that choose them and influence them. Your task is to define the forces inside and outside the company and analyze which plots they fit.

Looking at the Knowns

Examine the relevant known factors. Tease out 5 or 6 variations that fit this situation. Eventually, narrow and combine these into three fully detailed descriptions of what might happen.

Naming the Scenarios

The name of a scenario carries much symbolic weight. A good scenario name becomes a critically important form of shorthand when planners and managers meet in groups. One powerful name for a status-quo scenario is The Official Future. It stands for the set of implicit assumptions behind many institutional policies: that things will work out all right once the proper people get into power and can put their policies into effect. Most official futures turn out to be mere propaganda, but everyone in an organization subscribes to them almost unconsciously. Your first task is to discover the organization's version of the Official Future. Then you'll usually want to present it as one of a group of scenarios so people can see it for exactly how likely or unlikely it is.

A powerful title for your dark scenario is Our Worst Nightmare. This gives people a chance to determine what they would do if their worst nightmare occurred. Often there are options people haven't considered because their fear paralyzes them. A scenario forces them to consider it anyway. Ask, "What's the worst that could reasonably happen?"

The optimistic scenario gives you a chance to pick a name that will inspire and motivate people. You can do better than "Rosy Future," can't you?

Writing the Alternate Scenarios

The trick in constructing plots is deciding where, in the story, to start the diverging alternative futures. Develop one that frightens management enough to think in new ways, but not so much that they want to close the business. What plots might make them do something different and constructive? Here is a set of three stories that you could use.

Future Scenario #1 - A Rosy World. This is a story, told in the present tense, about what the world is like five years from now, assuming things go very well. It has a plot, characters, and the other elements discussed in this chapter. Tell how these developments may affect the company, what opportunities these developments present, and how the company might respond most effectively.

Future Scenario #2 - The Status Quo. This story has all the elements of #1 except that it assumes no dramatic changes within the coming five years, although of course there will be some changes and future trends give a good idea of what they will be. This scenario is about more-or-less predictable change with no big surprises. Again, tell how these developments may affect the company, what opportunities these developments present, and how the company might respond most effectively.

Future Scenario #3 - A Dark World. This story also has all the elements of #1, except that it assumes things will not go so well. While not necessarily a disastrous, worse-case scenario, it should paint a clear picture of a world where many things have gone bad. It should certainly alert the company's leaders as to possible downsides and major problems that could occur. Again, tell how these developments may affect the company, what opportunities these developments might present, and how the company might respond most effectively.

Keeping Them Simple

Scenarios must be simple, dramatic, and bold—to cut through the complexity and aim directly at the heart of the decision. Often the core of the decision is simple: Should we invest in this product or service or not? The role of scenarios is to arrange the factors so that they throw light on the decision rather than make it even murkier. To do this, start by questioning your belief in the inevitability of more of the same.

Step 6. Rehearse the Future

Individually and as a team, run through each scenario of simulated events as if you were already living them. In this way you can train yourself to recognize which drama is unfolding when it actually begins to happen. That helps you avoid unpleasant surprises and to know how to act. The performance of a scenario will take you again to your original question, What key decisions need to be made now in order to be ready for the future. But now you approach that question differently: "Should I do 1, 2, or 3 in order to be ready for the future?"

Keep an Open Mind

Take several different viewpoints. For example, play the part of customers who have been beamed back from some future date. Through such playful scenarios you get out of the mindset that your future will be decided by technology – and into the idea that your goals and vision will be the driving force of what technology will actually be created. Think in terms of the problem to be solved and the strategy to be used—not just the technology issues.

You may have an irresistible desire to choose one scenario over the other. The point of scenario planning is to help you suspend your disbelief in certain of the futures—to allow you to think that any of them might take place. Then you can prepare for what you don't think is going to happen. That's why you should avoid single scenarios and predictions. If you present several possible futures, you and your audience can consider plots that they would not otherwise accept.

Dramatize Possible Events

First, try role playing each scenario yourself. Then rehearse with your team. Finally, get company leaders to play out parts of the scenarios. If you, and they, literally rehearse each possible future, you'll better understand the implications of each one. Role playing each scenario will usually show exactly why the official future that people assume will happen is unlikely.

Above all, when you present your scenarios to the others, you must spark their interest. Set a goal to immerse people in the future through listening to dramatic stories, watching or engaging in scenario simulations (role playing or acting out dramatic experiences). Ask yourself, What imaginative interpersonal processes can I devise that will challenge people's preconceived ideas, engage new ideas, and draw them out?

For example, ask people to storyboard a television ad for the point in time of the future scenario. This can push their thinking into a different dimension. It gives them a process, a structure that can spark their imaginations.

As you prepare your presentation, ask, How can I make it real—in a multi-sensory, emotionally engaging way? People must become emotionally engaged before they will make a commitment to change.

Step 7: Learn from the Process

Good scenarios help you and all the organization's leaders understand what events mean and how you, and the organization, should respond to them. Practice makes perfect. As you learn how well your predictions of the future work out, you can become more adept at creating future scenarios.

Look for Early Detection Signals

Use specific events as warning signs to help you decide which scenario is coming to pass. For example, the diversity scenarios. What events would signal which scenario was occurring and what decisions should a particular business make in response to that?

After the Fact: Review and Learn

The most powerful aspect of creating scenarios may be their learning value. Always go back to old scenarios from time to time. Ask, What did I not see? Or What led me to really see that surprise that nobody else thought about? The important issue is not whether you got the future right but whether people changed their behavior because they saw the future differently—and was their changed behavior in the right direction? All good decisions include a consideration of the bigger picture. Our fates are interconnected. Scenarios helps us perceive the nature of these interconnections.

For greater career success, train yourself to look for plots. We miss the clues leading up to events because we deny them and we lack the tools for finding them. Openness is the first key, and a good scenario plot is the tool.

Future Scenario Examples

Here are two sets of very brief scenarios, one set from the viewpoint of managing diversity and another set from a general global viewpoint. These are skeletal outlines upon which you would add information relevant to your company. Then you would develop the forces, characters, and story that would indicate how each scenario would affect your firm.

Scenario Set 1: From a Managing Diversity Viewpoint

Worst Nightmare

During a recession, many in the dominant group became very restless and fearful. They elected government officials dedicated to ending affirmative action. In addition, attitudes of many dominants was to protect their own rights and privileges. As a result, the gap between the dominant group and minorities, between rich and poor, has widened dramatically. This was intensified by the increasing size and power of global megacorporations. In the United States they tend to hire only highly educated, high-tech-savvy employees.

Tension is high, riots are an increasingly regular problem, and the crime rate has skyrocketed. The well-off pay dearly for their lifestyle. Most live in gated communities and must pay fleets of private police to provide safety and security.

Breakthrough Abundance

The main thrust has been toward moving beyond tolerance of diversity to valuing it and creating organizational cultures that include and welcome people from all the demographic groups. Economic success and abundance has been stimulated by the remarkable diversity of African American, Asian American, Latino American, European American, and other subcultures coming together at all levels of the workplace and in the global marketplace to achieve new business success. Creative collaboration leads to an explosion of innovative breakthroughs, making worklife and home life easier and more pleasurable.

Official Future

In the United States, a melting-pot society in which everyone adapts to the upper middle class European American norm and lives the way affluent whites have been living for the past few decades. A steady pace of high-tech innovation has produced a fairly stable economy. Gradual improvement in education and job training have helped those in lower socioeconomic brackets move up and improve their lifestyle somewhat.

Scenario Set 2: From a General Global Viewpoint

Here are the brief summaries of three scenarios written by the Global Scenario Group. These are three stories of how the world might evolve in the coming century.

Free-Marketers' World

Free-Marketers see a positive future based on evolving technology and a strong economy. They cite the vigorous and dynamic economies of Western nations and some Asian nations. Their approach is deeply rooted in traditional economics, and they cite statistics that predict a world that's greatly improved and on a rapid upward-growth path. They want us to rely on innovation, investment, and individual freedom. This will bring a bright future for everyone, a level of material abundance that has strong appeal to nearly all the world's peoples. They're also optimistic about the environment. They believe that markets will normally send strong, appropriate price signals that will trigger timely responses to environmental damage. We will be able to either repair the damage or create technological breakthroughs in efficiency and productivity that will solve the ecological problems.

They predict that current free-market patterns will continue. Economic and human progress occur almost automatically or with modest economic reforms, driven by the liberating power of free markets and human initiative. There will be evolution, expansion, and globalization but without major surprises or changes in direction. Economic reform and technological innovation fuel rapid economic growth. Developing regions are integrated into the global economy, creating a powerful global market and bringing modern techniques and products to virtually all countries. The result is widespread prosperity, peace, and stability.

This is the vision held by many corporate leaders and economic theorists. They cite the failure of communism (and by implication socialism) in the USSR to justify this view. It's reflected on the editorial pages of the *Wall Street Journal* and the *Economist*. This is the basis for your plot, characters, and story that tell how this market world is likely to affect the firm.

Socialists' World

Various types of socialism are alive today. Socialists see the chaotic and terrible economic conditions that followed the rise of runaway capitalism in Russia during the 1990s. They say the economy of Russia now benefits a minority at the expense of a majority that has become disadvantaged, both materially and socially. They cite the fact that there is a growing gap between the rich and the poor, globally, and they see more poverty and suffering in the future under global capitalism. They view one aspect of human capital, labor, as the principal source of global wealth. They believe the capitalist exploitation of labor is the basis of injustice, impoverishment, and ignorance.

Their vision is a pessimistic view involving historical transitions in the fundamental organizing principles of society. They see the dark side of global capitalism. Unconstrained markets and business greed create social and environmental problems that threaten human progress and diminish its promise. Enclaves of the wealthy prosper and coexist with the poor masses in their widening misery and growing desperation. Large segments of humanity are left out of the prosperity that markets bring. This vision dooms hundreds of millions of human beings to lives that are nasty, brutish, and short. It therefore brings about rising conflict, violence, and instability. These failures eventually destroy the resources and the social framework on which markets and economic growth depend. Economic stagnation spreads as more resources are diverted just to maintain security and stability. Economic fragmentation spreads, and conflict dominates and/or the social order breaks down as market-led growth fails to redress social wrongs and to prevent environmental disasters.

They predict an explosion of ethnic and racial conflict and wars in the United States, as well as similar conflicts in many other parts of the world.

Environmentalists' World

Ecosystems form the world of environmentalists, so they focus on depletion of natural resources, damage to ecosystems, pollution of the environment, and population growth as an environmental threat. They worry about Earth's carrying capacity and ask, How large can the economy grow before it outstrips its host, Mother Earth? Their policies are based on how many and how much, the number of people, and the amount of impact each person can have upon the environment before irreversible damage is done. They are interested in free-market mechanisms and the related "externalities" of doing business (depletion, pollution, etc.). Most of these costs are presently ignored by the corporations that pollute and deplete resources, but society is paying and will pay in the future. They want these "externalities" to be fully integrated into producer costs and consumer prices so that markets become "mindful" of environmental costs.

Environmentalists point to the 1998 State of the World report by the Worldwatch Institute: as the population explodes, "forests are shrinking, water tables are falling, soils are eroding, wetlands are disappearing, fisheries are collapsing, rangelands are deteriorating, rivers are running dry, temperatures are rising, coral reefs are dying, and plant and animal species are disappearing." The libertarian Cato Institute disagreed with the report, citing increased life expectancy, decreasing child mortality, and improved nutritional intake as proof that standards of living improve as population grows. Paul Hawken (1999) responds that both sets of data are correct, but we are living on borrowed time and the "ability to accelerate a car that is low on gasoline does not prove the tank is full."

Centrists' World

Centrists agree with the views of all the other groups, but not all of them and not entirely. They are optimistic about people, and they believe that process will win the day, that people who tell others what is right lead society astray. They reject the future projected by the other three groups as too extreme. They prefer a middle way of integration, reform, respect, and reliance. They reject ideologies, regardless of whether they are based on economic systems, social systems, or ecosystems. Concerning economic systems, they say the level playing field never existed because of market imperfections, lobbying by big business and special interest groups, government subsidies to those groups, and the concentration of capital in the hands of a few. About social systems, they say solutions will naturally arise from place and culture rather than from socialist or capitalist ideology. On ecosystems, they argue that while some problems are global, solutions must be local. Solutions can emerge only when local people are empowered and honored. Good leaders make followers feel as if they succeeded by themselves.

Many centrists take an optimistic view. They envision fundamental social and political changes that lead to enlightened policies and voluntary actions that direct market forces and supplement them. Values and cultural norms may change for the better. In this vision of society, the human condition is transformed to offer a better life, not just a wealthier one, and those benefits are extended to all of humanity. Power is more widely shared and new social coalitions work from the grass roots up to shape what institutions and governments do. The needs of people and their environment prevail over business interests. Although markets become effective tools for economic progress, they do not serve as a substitute for deliberate social choices by the people at large. Economic competition exists, but it doesn't outweigh the larger needs of the world's people for cooperation and solidarity and for the fulfillment of basic human needs. This vision asserts the possibility of fundamental change for the better—in politics, in social institutions, and in the environment.

Samples of Current Trends and Predictions
Idea Starters for Scenario Research

As you write your future scenarios, you'll consult many resources for ideas. This section is a teaser to get you started. First, glimpse the future through the eyes of Cultural Creatives. Then consider an immediate major paradigm shift beyond the personal computer, and imagine how new technology is changing consumer. Finally, look further into the future to the decades of the New Millennium.

The Cultural Creatives' Future World

You know that about 20 percent of the U.S. population have been identified as Cultural Creatives who are quite future-oriented and tend to have an influence greater than their numbers would suggest. Cultural Creatives prefer a future that will benefit the masses of people in the world versus most benefits going to the few—wealthy stockholders and business executives of multinational corporations. Here are some specifics of that future.

Worldview—toward Web of Life principles versus survival of the fittest and competitive principles. This view sees the world as:

- self-organizing
- conserving and sharing
- localized and adapted to place
- diverse and creative

Economy—mindful markets versus free-trade multinational-corporation-driven capitalism, micro-lending of very small loans to start very small businesses (Grameen bank type), which lifts people out of poverty

Money—more use of community money to encourage local trade versus national currencies and submission to huge global influences

Business—new types of business ownership, such as employee ownership, co-ops, and government or nonprofit trusts—versus decisions based upon pressures from stock market demands

Society—civic capital, social capital, social product versus business capital only

Energy use—a switch to solar, which is sustainable versus current polluting, depleting sources.

Environment—putting more land into "commons" for all people, saving the waters, lands, skies, and air for the use of all humans and future generations.

Medical system—toward one-on-one caring (Patch Adams type) versus assembly-line treatment

Major Paradigm Shift: Beyond the PC

The Internet is feeding an explosion of innovation in handheld computers, mini-laptops, Web phones, Web fax machines, palm-size scanners, digital cameras and TVs, and Web browsers for the kitchen countertop that double as TV and CD players.

Not only do Intel and Microsoft know that their product upgrades will be obsolete soon after emerging, they know that the future of their companies no longer depends solely on the personal computer. Bill Gates believes that more non-PC devices than PCs will be attached to the Internet within the first decade of the New Millennium. Microsoft is already creating software for easy-to-use products, such as set-top TV boxes, electronic organizers, and car navigation systems.

New Linking Devices.

In this coming paradigm shift, digital smarts won't be limited to PCs, minicomputers, or mainframes. A vast array of devices aimed at nearly every aspect of our daily lives will involve computing. Think "many simplified, specialized appliances" instead of one multi-use personal computer. The PC is so general purpose that most people use only 5 percent of its capabilities, Instead of putting more and more features into computers, companies will design new devices to perform only a few specific functions. These information appliances, such as the handheld Palm computers and WebTV, will be simple and convenient. Winning in the digital appliance business will depend on identifying consumer needs—when, where, and how they need a computer function—and satisfying them with products that are simple and easy to use.

About 95 percent of the people who used the Net in 2000 did it through their PCs, but by 2002 only about 64 percent are predicted to do it by PC. Instead we'll use small appliances such as TV set-top boxes, Web phones, and palm-size computers. About 48 percent of U.S. homes now have a PC, but experts predict that number will top out at 60 percent, with new appliances taking their place. For the first time, PCs will have serious competition from other appliances.

Quantum computers

Computer science has melded with subatomic physics, to create computers based on quantum particles—such as atomic nuclei, photons, and electrons—instead of silicon chips. Quantum computers use qubits of information, each equivalent to a traditional digital bit. Bits are either on or off, one or zero, but qubits can be both on and off at the same time.

Conventional computers step through calculations one at a time. But the effect between quantum particles, known as "spooky entanglement," lets quantum computers perform all calculations simultaneously, as though in parallel. These two features allow quantum computers to perform massive computations in a fraction of a second. They're expected to be invaluable at creating uncrackable security codes, as well as cracking other codes; at storing and retrieving information in huge, unstructured databases; and simulating complex quantum phenomena.

A 7-qubit computer was in the experimental stage in 2001. Some experts predicted that a 15-qubit computer—equivalent to the 2001 desktop PC—would be built by 2002, and a 30-qubit machine more powerful than the most powerful supercomputer of 2001 would be built by 2004.

The Changing Consumer

New technology and business practices are creating new consumers with new buying habits, according to futurist Shirley Roberts [1998] Let's look first at nine traits of the new consumer

1. Far less homogeneous (no such thing as a typical family, for example).

2. Independent thinkers, seeking self-reliance and control over their lives.

3. More educated and sophisticated, with greater access to comparative pricing

4. Want a higher quality of life, such as more personal-discretion time.

5. Extremely demanding of quality, service, selection, information, safety, speed, etc.

6. Optimistic but well grounded in reality

7. Seekers of new experiences and innovation

8. Pursuers of wellness and environmentalism

9. Aging but more active than previous generations

Here are some trends in emerging consumer behavior. We must watch for them and predict where they're likely to lead us.

Economy: The gap will widen between winners and losers. Standardized work will decline. Female influence will increase

Technology: Digital networks will mean fewer go-betweens, more direct transactions from producer to end user. Product life cycles will shorten. Technologies will converge.

Retailing: Lines of competition will continue to blur between types of retailers

Globalization: Expansion of trade will open up new markets

Environment: Environmentalism will become a way of life. Environmental abuse will remain a serious problem

Demographics: Ethnic and regional diversity will grow. Lifestyles will be less influenced by age

Consumer psyche: People will seek spirituality and human reconnection

Wellness: The incidence of disease will increase. Alternative medicines will become more popular

New Millennium Predictions

There will be far greater transformations in the first two decades of the 21st century than in the entire 20th century, according to futurist Ray Kurzweil [1999], and change will accelerate throughout the first century. Here are some specific predictions:

First Decade: Wireless World

Cables are disappearing, as wireless technology takes over. Developing countries are already skipping the phase of connections by telephone and electrical wires. They're going directly to satellite-based wireless for telephone and computer connections. Most routine business transactions will take place between a human and a virtual personality—just as it's difficult to find a human being at the end of a business telephone call now. We'll have telephones that can translate languages. Workers will react to technology that puts them out of work.

Second Decade: Digital Pervasiveness, Nanotechnology

Ordinary desktop computing devices will be equal to the ability of the human brain for certain rational functions. Most computers will be embedded in other objects and therefore invisible. Eyeglasses and contact lenses will contain access to 3-D virtual reality displays.

Nano-engineered machines will begin to be applied to create raw materials "from scratch" at the molecular level. Most learning will happen through software-based, simulated teachers. Automated driving systems will be embedded in most major roads.

Third Decade: Brain Implants, End of Poverty.

Ordinary desktop computing will have the capacity of 1,000 human brains for certain rational functions. Brain implants will allow high-bandwidth connections to the human brain. These implants will enhance a person's visual and auditory perception, cognition, interpretation, memory, and reasoning ability.

Poverty will be essentially ended because nearly all humans will have their basic life needs met.

End of First Century: Eternal Life?

Human thinking will be merged with the world of machine intelligence. For intelligent beings, "life expectancy" is no longer a meaningful term.

Case Studies—Applying the Creative Techniques

The following case is designed to give you material for writing future scenarios. While this makes it somewhat different from the cases you've analyzed in previous chapters—it's much longer, for one thing—you'll still want to consider the usual self-questions.

1. What problems do I see?

2. How can I probe beneath the surface to get at root problems?

3. What opportunities (hidden or obvious) can I find to take initiative, cut costs, and/or make money?

4. What creative alternatives can I generate?

5. As a consultant, what should I recommend as the best viewpoints and actions?

6. To answer these questions, what creative techniques can I experiment with to respond to this case? After completing the future scenarios, ask: Which creative techniques produced the best results?

Case 10.1 Maxland Retail Chains

Maxland Corporation owns more than 1,100 retail stores in the United States, making it one of the largest American general merchandise retailers. It owns and operates three separate chain stores, each chain focusing on a different target market.

1. **Moregoods** is a large discount chain that competes with such stores as WalMart and K-Mart throughout the United States. It accounts for more than 70% of Maxland's profits

2. **Meyers** is a chain of midrange department stores that competes with such stores as Penney's and Montgomery Ward. It offers a wide range of family apparel, both private label and well-known brand names. It also offers many home products, such as bedding and bath products. The store locations are focused on the West Coast. Meyers carries many brand names, such as Levi's, Bugle Boy, Nike, Union Bay, and Lee. Its customers are primarily working mothers, age 25 to 49. Almost all the stores are located in malls or at least in busy, neighborhood-shopping areas. Each store is designed the same, with no differentiation in floor layout, and offers the same clothing lines and styles, whether the location is in San Francisco, Fresno, or Las Vegas.

3. **Mayfield** is a chain of upscale department stores located primarily in the Midwest. It competes with such stores as Macy's and Bloomingdale's.

The market researchers at Maxland Corporation report that Americans are spending less time and money shopping in retail stores. Sales in U.S. retail stores, which had shown an average gain of about 4% a year in the 1970s and 1980s, decreased an average of 2% a year in the 1990s. Not only have customer tastes changed, the way they shop has changed. Warehouse-type discount stores, catalog sales, and internet retail websites have all had an impact on traditional retail stores. To intensify the problem, even while overall sales were slipping, retail space was still expanding.

Maxland's profit and market share have been steadily declining, especially in the Meyers mid-range stores and somewhat less in the higher-range Mayfield stores. Therefore, Maxland CEO **James Maxxam** has scheduled a meeting for next month with the division heads of each chain to discuss strategic plans for the upcoming year. A major agenda item will be the lagging sales of Meyers retail stores. Meyers was a superstar in the 1970s and 1980s, but lately it's badly slipping.

Jan Duarte, Meyers president, has called her own meeting with her Meyers executive team to examine the sales problem. They need to come up with a plan that focuses on strategies to increase market share. They'll present it to CEO James Maxxam and his executive team at the meeting next month. Because Meyers is a midrange department store, it cannot compete with the high volume, discount operation of Moregoods. Jan Duarte has heard rumors that the board of directors is considering splitting up the divisions, perhaps to sell the less successful chain(s) and focus on Moregoods, which accounts for most of the revenues and profits.

- How do paradigm shifts and high-tech life cycles enter into this picture? What phase is Maxland in and how does that affect the strategies its executives should adopt?

- What opportunities or threats are present for Meyers retail—and for the overall Maxland operation—and how should management respond?

- If you were Meyers President, Jan Duarte, what would you focus on?

- If you were the Maxland CEO, James Maxaam, how would you view the future of the three chains and Maxland as a whole—and what would you propose to do?

Case 10.2 Justice Technology

Dave Gomez, cofounder and CEO of Justice Technology, is having lunch with **Josh Foreman**, a veteran telecommunications executive. Dave mentions that his long-distance phone company, Justice Technology, has a "hot cut" planned for tomorrow. That means Justice's customers' phone traffic will be rerouted from one electronic hub to a new one over a period of a few minutes, even while customers continue to make calls.

Josh bursts into laughter, saying, "I've never heard anyone use the phrase "hot cut" so calmly." Dave responds, "Really? Why not?" Dave's a trim, energetic man who comes across as something between a Mel Gibson and a Richard Simmons. Josh peers at Dave strangely. "Don't you know how many phone companies have gone out of business because of hot cuts that ended up taking *days*?" Actually Dave doesn't know about such disasters. In fact, he knows almost nothing about hot cuts, even though he's just bet his company's future on one. Dave believes that spunk is one of the keys to his success. "We don't know enough to know what it is we aren't supposed to be able to do. We just go ahead and do it."

Justice not only refuses to play by the rules—it won't even commit to a particular game. Dave, only 33, has staffed his company with people in his own image: young, brash, and a little off-the-wall. They like playing with fire. They know they can get burned, for example, by unexpected changes in regulations, technological miscues, or a sudden urge on the part of big competitors to swat them aside. They can also get very rich because taking the risks they do can result in a log of growth. Since Justice incorporated five years ago, their revenues have zoomed to $55 million. They've parlayed success in a tiny niche market to virtual domination of certain segments of the global phone business. Most people who call other countries these days have done business with Justice, though they didn't know it.

Dave says now, "In some ways we're starting to look like a real phone company. In the near future, if our current plans work out, you may be using Justice to call next door as well as overseas."

Dave's Background

Dave earned a degree in economics from the Wharton School and a masters in psychology from UCLA. He wanted to work in Argentina for a change of pace and went to work as a management trainee in the American Express Rio office. Dave quickly zeroed in on phone costs. Argentina had a state-run phone company that levied huge charges for international calls, like most countries outside the U.S. Amex Argentina was therefore running up a monthly phone bill of $25,000. Dave stumbled onto an article that described a new type of U.S.-based phone service called "callback" service.

How Callback Works

You're based in a country other than the U.S. and you want to call another country. You start by dialing a number in the U.S. that's connected to a callback-service-operated "switch," which is a computerized version of the old-fashioned switchboards that telephone operators used to sit in front of, manually plugging one phone line into another to make a connection. You hang up while the phone is still ringing. Even though the switch hasn't answered the phone, it recognizes your phone number as that of a customer and calls you back. Your phone rings. You pick it up and the switch connects you to a U.S. dial tone—which means you're now paying a low U.S. phone rate. Now you can dial your international party, and the switch will connect the call. (The industry calls this "terminating" the call.) When you're through, you owe the local exorbitantly priced phone company nothing because your initial call to the U.S. was never terminated. You owe the callback service the cost of the switch's call from the U.S. to you and the cost of your call from the U.S. to your party in whatever country you called. The cost of these two U.S.-originated calls combined is typically 50 percent to 75 percent less than it would cost to call your party directly. This is the simple part of the business.

How Justice Was Born

Dave was very excited by this discovery and presented the idea of callback to his bosses at Amex. They had no interest in possibly irritating Argentina's only phone company, which was at least semi-reliable. Dave, with his manager's approval, took a moonlighting job for the callback-service provider. Dave's job was to pitch the service to business people at social gatherings. He landed a few customers over the next month or so.

Dave needed to return to the U.S. for a month. Just before he left, he met **Rick Lane,** a 22-year-old liberal arts graduate of Brown University who was bumming around Argentina looking for a job. Dave set Rick up in his apartment and showed him how to sell the callback service. When Dave returned from the U.S., Rick reported that he had signed up more than 20 corporate customers, including some large banks. Each one had paid from $250 t o $700 as an up-front connection charge and was paying a $250 monthly fee for one line—in addition to the per-call charges, which average $2,000 per customer per month. Suddenly Dave was running a real company. Good-bye, American Express.

Rick continued to sell the service all over the place, using this simple pitch: The service will hack off roughly two-thirds of your international phone bill. And here are sample bills from other multinationals to prove it. As the business grew, Dave and Rick discovered a Basic Principle.

Lesson 1: Pay attention to the peculiarities of doing business in a foreign culture.

For example, as impressive as the savings detailed call by call on the bills were, some customers were horrified that the calls were detailed at all, which not standard practice in Argentina. Dave learned that many Argentine business people keep Swiss bank accounts that they'd just as soon not advertise to the government via phone bills that list calls to Switzerland. Others expressed concern about their wives' discovering multiple calls to certain numbers. One secretive company wasn't pleased to see its bills detailing the fact that 90 percent of its calls went to Iran and Nicaragua, tow countries that had little in common other than that they were of great interest to the American intelligence community. Dave laughs, "We could have made a lot of money charging people to *not* have call detail on their bills.

Money was pouring in from customers such as UPS, British Airways, and the Danish embassy, but Dave was getting to keep only 25 percent of the line charge. The rest was going to the callback provider—Dave was merely acting as an agent.

His wheels were turning, though. Why not start his own service and outsource the actual phone switching? Dave went back to the U.S. and visited every callback provider he could find, pumping each for more and more information. Worldcom turned out to be the outfit that offered the best service at the lowest cost. Dave made a case with the president as to why Worldcom should handle his switching business for a mere 50 percent of gross profits. The finals agreement has Worldcom keeping 60 percent of gross profits.

Now Dave and Rick can bring new customers into their own full-fledged callback company and the begin gradually converting all their old customers to Worldcom. Within a year monthly revenues were passing the $200,000 mark. They have plenty of competition from other callback services but the market is still wide open and no one can undercut them on price, thanks to the deal Dave got from Worldcom.

Lesson 2: Being the lowest-cost provider covers a lot of sins.

Disaster Strikes

Then one day the service simply stops working. When a customer got the U.S. dial tone and started dialing, the line went dead. And this happened to every customer, every time they tried to dial. Finally, David and Rick realized that the state-run telephone company had programmed its switches to listen for the sound of touch-tone dialing on calls that had come into the country. When the tones were detected, the switch automatically disconnect the call. The phone company had a more-or-less legal right since callback was technically illegal in Argentina at the time, as it was in many other countries. The law wasn't really prosecutable because the service's operations were in the U.S.

Rick to the Rescue. Rick was excited by the challenge. He contacted an engineer and told him he wanted a device to attach to customer's phone to intercept the number being dialed and send it out to the U.S. switch not as touch-tones but as computer data. The device worked perfectly, and Rick and Dave were back in business.

Disaster 2. Next. the Argentine phone company realized that all of Dave's customers' calls went to the same U.S. area code and "exchange"—the first three digits of the seven-digit phone number. So the phone company simply blocked all calls from Argentina to that exchange. Dave reflected later, "What did they care if they occasionally blocked off a call to that exchange that wasn't even to our switch?"

Dave to the Rescue. Dave thought of a scheme to make them care. He called Pacific Bell and bought all the phone numbers that had a certain area code and three-digit exchange and then distributed those new numbers to his customers. The phone company quickly moved to block all calls to the new exchange—but removed the blocking the next day,. The exchange was the same one used by the Argentine consulate in L.A.

Dave and Rick were having a ball winning these games. What could be more fun?

Lesson 3: There's no problem in the phone business that can't be solved with technology and a little flair.

A Worldwide Marketing Campaign

If Dave and Rick were doing so well in Argentina, why couldn't they clean up in other countries? Dave decided to head back to the U.S. to set up the company as a multinational business. He rented an office, hired a marketing manager, **Matt Judson,** *and* called Rick with a major question: How should they modify their renegade, freewheeling style to suit the buttoned-down telecommunications industry? Their conclusion: they wouldn't. They would modify the industry to suit their style.

Meanwhile Matt launches a worldwide marketing campaign with a budget of zero dollars. All the company's profits are being invested in building its infrastructures, including its tracking and billings systems and its network capacity. Matt, working on commission, doesn't see any cash for more than a year. He scours the U.S. Department of Commerce database of foreign companies for multinationals that have anything to do with phone systems and sends them each a letter soliciting them as customers and, more important, as agents for that country. Matt says, "We need people on the ground who speak the language and understand the customs. Matt gets 50 responses from the 500 letters he sends out. He used every trick he knew to give contacts the impression that Justice was a huge company. Ten of the 50 respondents eventually became agents for Justice. Dave offers the agents a commission averaging 10 percent of net revenues they collect. In effect agents are the bill collectors. If a customer skips out on its bills, half the loss is charged against the agent's commissions. Some agents complain, saying "you're the one checking the credit histories." Dave replies, "Yes, but you're the one looking them in the eye. You should be able to make a judgement about their reliability."

Thriving on Challenge and Risk

Almost all Justice's growth is bootstrapped. Dave puts in $80,000 of his own money over time and occasionally makes short-term loans to the company. His father lends the company $100,000, which is paid back with interest within a year.

But every time the company is sailing, Dave succumbs to the need to take on a new business opportunity that Justice appears incapable of handling, putting the company in danger again. For example, early on a large South American insurance agency wanted 100,000 prepaid international phone cards ready to give away as a promotion in three months. Dave said "sure, no problem." Never mind that Worldcom doesn't do prepaid phone cards, Dave thought, I'll find a way. He did.

Later, customers are asking for international fax and paging service. Dave says, "Sign them up. We'll figure out how. And they do.

> *Lesson 4: It's better to scramble to deliver a product you've already sold than to struggle to sell a product you've spent money preparing to deliver.*

"I don't feel comfortable unless I'm bringing us out on a limb of a limb of a limb. We'd have to turn the company upside down to make it happen, but that's when things get fun. It's what we all thrive on here."

Next, Worldcom is acquired and the new owners give Justice six weeks' notice of their intention to pull the plug on the switch that served as the physical hub of Justice's entire business. No way was there enough time to find another phone company that would provide as good a deal and then to get set up on its switch. No problem, said Dave. Justice will get its own switch and program and operate it itself. It would become a full-fledged phone company. Dave later says, "Luckily, we didn't know that doing this on such short notice was totally impossible." Three months later, the hot cut—the one that so amused and astonished his lunch mate Josh—somehow went off without a hitch.

Now that they're a full fledged phone company Matt searches out new opportunities, alerts Dave, who usually authorizes him to go for it. Matt gets the orders, and Rick always finds a way to deliver. Many of the opportunities are still in callback, especially in countries where government regulation is still oppressive, such as most African and South American nations, and many Asian ones. Dave wants no niche left unfilled. Matt discovers, for example, that European cell-phone users are naturals for callback services, because in most European countries you're not charged for airtime when you receive a call, only when you place one. Also, Dave is very interested in developing a phone-via-Internet service—and in going after, of all things, conventional local phone business.

Still, deregulation of the phone business is beginning to sweep the world, causing price drops in those countries, eroding callback's advantage. So Justice is coming into the direct-dial business. It now owns local switches in several countries and has even bought small local phone companies in the Netherlands and Argentine, allowing many of their customer to dial straight through without callback.

Termination accounts for 70 percent of Justice's cost, so Dave is constantly negotiating with every international phone service provider he can find to try for lower costs. Cheap termination is the name of the game; it's what allows Justice to undercut competitors and protect its gross margins, which average around 40 percent. Dave promises long-term, exclusive deals if they'll shave their lower prices for him. Dave's staff spends two years and close to $2 million to build a complex computer program called Pipeline, which tracks the cost of every second of every call so that he can find and stamps out any inefficiencies hiding in the traffic. The program tells salespeople minute to minute how low they can cut their prices and still keep a profit.

Next, it occurs to Dave that he can make money off other phone companies' envy of his cheap termination. He can sell it to them. Instead of buying termination cheaply just for use by Justice's customers, he can buy everything he can get his hands on at a great price and resell the extra capacity to other phone companies, wholesale. Within a few months this part of the business accounts for 60 percent of company revenues.

With this kind of revenue, Dave begins to wonder about his financial system: accounts payable kept in paper form in an employee's desk drawer, no lines of bank credit; routine loans from Dave to the company; no plans for raising capital.

Counter-Culture

Justice gradually builds a multicultural staff, and now the company has 115 employees in a remodeled warehouse that looks like a colorful, ultramodern version of the company's old warehouse. This is typical of the way Dave and Rick work to maintain a counter-cultural culture—believing that this translates into outrageous performance. The company benefits are an example: free dog care and subsidies for anyone who bicycles or skateboards to work. Pranks are legendary. Most important, the company tries to hire people who groove on the offbeat challenge and then puts them straight to the test. On Matt Judson's first day at work, he was met at the door by a highly agitated employee. "Thank God you're here," she said. "You've got a really important decision to make. Follow me."

Dave says of his management style, "I don't tell people what to do. I just want things to get done. As long as people can explain why they did what they did, I'm okay. I just want to make sure they're thinking. People who can't function with the lack of structure leave within a few weeks."

Justice Technology has hired you as a consultant. Your assignment: Do three future scenarios for the global situation 5 years from now. In each scenario indicate how Justice Technology would fare. Specifically indicate to Justice executives:

- What are potential problems for Justice within each of the three scenarios?
- What creative solutions do you recommend for each problem?
- What are the likely opportunities for Justice within each scenario?
- What creative actions or strategies do you recommend to generate opportunities within each scenario—or to take advantage of those likely to present themselves?
- Which CTs discussed in previous chapters did you use in solving this case problem?
- Which CTs were most helpful and what ideas did they spark or inspire?

Self-Awareness Activities

SAO 10.1 What Paradigms Define Your Success?

Purpose: To develop skill in recognizing paradigms and paradigm shifts.

Identifying a paradigm:

1. In your area of expertise, the area you work in, what needs to be done differently but can't be done differently and if it were, it would fundamentally change the way people play the game and do their work?

2. What problem in your area or field needs to be solved but hasn't been and if it were, it would fundamentally change the game?

3. How would you describe the paradigm(s) you uncovered in your answer to Questions 1 and 2? Use the following questions as guidelines.

- What are the rules of the game?

- What are the boundaries or limits of the game?

- What are the success behaviors they define?

Seeing beyond a paradigm:

4. What can you do to enhance the current paradigm?

Any ideas for solving a problem or doing something so differently that it would create new rules and boundaries?

SAO 10.2 Your Future Self

Purpose: To make real the concept of your Future Self.

Instructions: After you read through the steps, kick back, relax, close your eyes and visualize your Self five years ago, noticing what comes up. Then visualize your Future Self, allowing the questions to guide you.

Step 1. Examine Your Past Self

Think back to your Self five years ago and browse through these questions.

- What were you like?

- Whom were you closest to—which friends and family members? What were those relationships like?

- Whom did you avoid or have conflicts with? What were those relationships like?

- What were your major interests? Concerns? Goals? Expectations?

- How were your beliefs and attitudes different from those you hold today?

- What do you remember about your thinking and feeling patterns? How have they changed?

- What were your activities back then? How have they changed?

Some of these questions will pull up more vivid memories than others. Focus on the strong images and feelings that come up when you ask yourself these questions. The purpose is to get a sense of your Self five years ago. At that point in time you had Future Selves and one of them was the Self you are today. Back then, did you ever have an inkling of the Future Self you have since become—that you are today?

You *were* a Possible Future Self, one of many possibilities that existed back then and have always existed. As time went by you became a Probable Future Self, one of a few. Now you are that one Self that evolved out of all the possible selves and, later, probable selves.

Step 2. Imagine Your Future Self

Have some fun imagining your Future Self, who you might be five years from now. Relax, close your eyes, and invite your Intuition to come in to play. Imagine that you're meeting your Future Self in person. Ask the same types of questions you asked in Step 1.

- What's your Future Self like?

- Whom is your Future Self closest to—which friends and family members? What are those relationships like?

- Are there people your Future Self avoids or has conflicts with? What are those relationships like?

- What are your Future Self's major interests? Concerns? Goals? Expectations?

- How are your Future Self's beliefs and attitudes different from yours?

- How would your describe your Future Self's thinking and feeling patterns? How are they different from yours?

- What activities is your Future Self involved in? How are they different from yours?

Step 3. Write.

Write about the key aspects of these experiences with your past self and future self.

SAO 10.3 Personal Future Scenario

Purpose: To create a future scenario of your life 5 years from now.

Based on your experience with your Future Self in SAO 10.2, write three Future Scenarios of your personal life five years from now. Include all the important aspects, such as personality traits, worldview, beliefs and attitudes, patterns of thinking and feeling, major life activities, relationships, career.

Which scenario do you choose to create?

References

Barker, Joel A. *Paradigms: The Business of Discovering the Future*. New York: HarperCollins, 1993.

Christensen Clayton M. *The Innovator's Dilemma* Cambridge: Harvard Business School Press, 1997.

Fahey, Liam, Ed., *Learning from the Future: Competitive Foresight Scenarios,* John Wiley & Sons, 1997.

Fuld, Leonard, The Futures Group, www.fuld.com. See Intelligence Index for 400 links that hyperlink based on industry classification or application. Research reported in "The Intelligentsia," *Business 2.0* July 1999, 135-136.

Kelly, Kevin, "New Rules for the New Economy," *Wired*, September 1997, 140-190.

Kurzweil, Ray. *The Age of Spiritual Machines*. New York: Viking, 1999.

Moore, Geoffrey A. *Inside the Tornado: Marketing Strategies from Silicon Valley's Cutting Edge*. New York: HarperCollins, 1995.

Naisbett, John, and Patricia Aburdene. *Megatrends 2000: Ten New Directions for the 1990's*. New York: William Morrow and Company, 1990.

Popcorn, Faith. *Clicking*. New York: HarperCollins, 1996.

Roberts, Shirley. *Harness the Future: The 9 Keys to Emerging Consumer Behavior*. New York:: John Wiley & Sons, 1998.

Schwartz, Peter. *The Art of the Long View*. New York: Doubleday 1991

Tapscott, Don and Art Caston. *Paradigm Shift*. New York: McGraw-Hill, 1993.

Tapscott, Don. *Digital Economy*. New York: McGraw-Hill, 1996.

Resources:

The Futurist, a monthly magazine of forecasts, trends, and ideas about the future. World Future Society, Bethesda MD. www.wfs.org.

Institute for the Future www.iftf.org;

International Forum on Globalization www.ifg.org;

Positive Futures Network www.futurenet.org;

Trend Letter, a twice monthly newsletter published by Global Network, 1101 30th Street NW, Washington, DC.